QUALITATIVE METHODOLOGY

Respect the nature of the empirical world and organize a methodological stance to reflect that respect.

Herbert Blumer, *Symbolic Interactionism: Perspective and Method*

QUALITATIVE METHODOLOGY: FIRSTHAND INVOLVEMENT WITH THE SOCIAL WORLD

Edited by

WILLIAM J. FILSTEAD

Associate Director of Research and Education
Alcoholism Rehabilitation Center
Lutheran General Hospital, Park Ridge, Illinois

MARKHAM PUBLISHING COMPANY / CHICAGO

MARKHAM SOCIOLOGY SERIES

Robert W. Hodge, Editor

ADAMS, *The American Family: A Sociological Interpretation*

ADAMS, *Kinship in an Urban Setting*

APPELBAUM, *Theories of Social Change*

FARLEY, *Growth of the Black Population: A Study of Demographic Trends*

FILSTEAD, ed., *Qualitative Methodology: Firsthand Involvement with the Social World*

LAUMANN, SIEGEL and HODGE, eds., *The Logic of Social Hierarchies*

ZEITLIN, ed., *American Society, Inc.: Studies of the Social Structure and Political Economy of the United States*

To my Mother and Father

PREFACE

This book has two purposes: first, to examine the many facets of a methodological approach to reality I have chosen to call qualitative methodology, and secondly, to provoke those who measure everything and understand nothing.

Qualitative methodology, although as old as sociology itself, holds a position of minor importance as a methodological approach to social reality. The historical reasons for this low social prestige and the numerous problems associated with utilizing this methodological perspective form the core material for this reader.

If one reads the material quite closely (and at times between the lines) he will become aware of my second purpose—that of provoking those who measure everything and understand nothing. It is not my intention to reify the already reified dichotomy of quantitative versus qualitative methodology. All I am urging is that the sociologist use a method that is appropriate to his particular area of investigation. I am questioning the value of highly complex measuring devices that become ends in themselves rather than intermediary tools used to increase the amount of sociological understanding. It is inexcusable to force the research problem into an *a priori* scheme of technical paraphernalia rather than observing it in the context of the empirical world being investigated.

My hope is that this book might contribute to a "clearing of the air" surrounding the critical questions and implications of quantitative versus qualitative methodology. If the book does nothing more than familiarize its readers with the issues involved in this dichotomy, it will have accomplished an important task.

Although this work is directed primarily at issues and problems encountered by sociologists using qualitative methodology in their research, the ramifications of these ideas are broad enough to be useful to any social or behavioral scientist interested in investigating social phenomena by using the tools and techniques of qualitative methodology.

I wish to acknowledge my indebtedness to Professors Herbert Blumer and Irwin Deutscher who, through their writings, provided me with the initial insight for this work; and to thank them and B. K. Tan for their invaluable comments and suggestions on earlier drafts of the manuscript. My thanks also go to Robert W. Hodge for his critical analysis of the manuscript at various stages of preparation. I, however, assumé sole responsibility for the final form of the material. I would also like to express my thanks to the numerous authors and journals for permitting their material to appear in this reader. Finally, I want to thank my wife, Diane, whose understanding, encouragement, and patience were priceless assets.

CONTENTS

CHAPTER 1

Introduction

Since its humble beginning, the discipline of sociology has made remarkable progress. Sociology has had a long, hard struggle gaining respectability in the house of science, yet that stage of development has passed. No longer need we debate whether or not we are a science; the question now is the degree to which we are scientific. With the recognition of sociology as a behavioral science secured, attempts are being made to increase its understanding of the empirical social world through a refinement of the discipline's theoretical, methodological, and conceptual schemes of explanation.

An increasing number of sociologists[1] and other behavioral scientists[2] have serious doubts concerning the direction of present-day sociology in particular, and of the behavioral sciences in general. Specifically, these doubts concern the theoretical, methodological, and conceptual schemes of the behavioral sciences; the behavioral sciences' interpretation of the empirical social world; and, of greatest importance, the behavioral sciences' interpretations of reality and the manner in which the individual relates to it. These doubts are by no means new. What is new is the increasing validity of these doubts as they relate to the present direction of the behavioral sciences. In order to discuss the above points in detail, I shall limit my discussion to sociology in particular. However, it is my opinion that the following discussion is applicable to all of the behavioral sciences.

Paradoxically, the sociologist—who studies the complexities of society in its many facets, and who attempts to interpret, explain, predict, and understand human behavior—rarely comes in contact with that which he is trying to understand. Irving Horowitz,[3] Marshall Clinard,[4] and others[5] have made the point that the sociologist is greatly removed from the subject matter of his discipline. If the ultimate goal of sociology, the understanding of human behavior, is based upon the sociologist's ability to discover the complexities of human behavior, then this understanding should decrease as a result of current theoretical, methodological, and conceptual tendencies that widen the gap between the sociologist and the empirical social world that contains the ultimate test of his understanding.[6]

The overwhelming bulk of what passes today as methodology is made up of such preoccupations as the following: The devising and use of sophisticated research techniques, usually of an advanced statistical character, the construction of logical and mathematical models, all too frequently guided by the criterion of elegance, the elaboration of formal schemes of imported schemes such as input-output analysis, system analysis and stochastic analysis, studious conformity to the canons of research design; and the promotion of particular procedures, such as survey research, as *the* method of scientific study.[7]

We are gaining technical specialties with little thought as to their usefulness in terms of assaying the reality of the empirical social world. This increasing trend toward quantification has led to a lessened understanding of the empirical social world. The artificial conception of reality that is fostered in present-day theoretical, methodological, and conceptual schemes results in the paucity of explanatory schemes of human behavior. In order to increase their understanding of human behavior, sociologists must become, not more detached from, but more involved with the phenomena of the empirical social world. I want to make it clear that theory per se is not the villain; the villain is deductive theory, with its labyrinth of various logical, mathematical, and technical paraphernalia. What I am suggesting is the need for more *inductive* "grounded theory" à la Glaser and Strauss.

SOCIOLOGY OF KNOWLEDGE: THE POPULARITY OF THE NATURAL SCIENCE MODEL

At this point several crucial questions present themselves: (1) What factor(s) led to the present concern over the current direction of sociology? (2) How can firsthand involvement with data be accomplished? (3) How will this involvement close the gap between the empirical social world and the theoretical, methodological, and conceptual schemes purporting to explain it?

At the risk of over-simplification, it can be said that the single most important factor that has led to the mounting dissatisfaction with the present direction of sociology is the sociologist's obsession with *The Scientific Method.* The tremendous determination to make sociology as scientific as the natural sciences has led to the present state of concern over the direction of sociology.

Irwin Deutscher has stated the dilemma quite succinctly.

In attempting to assume the stance of a physical science, we have necessarily assumed its epistemology, its assumptions about the nature of knowledge and the appropriate means of knowing, including the rules of scientific evidence. . . . One of the consequences of using the natural science model was to break down human behavior in a way that was not only artificial but which did not jibe with the manner in which the behavior was observed.[8]

It was the faith in the use of the natural science model to accelerate the respectability and sophistication of sociology that led, in the late 1920's and early 1930's, to the development of neo-positivism. Men like Thurstone and Bogardus were laying the foundation for the basic techniques of scaling procedures; Lundberg, Ogburn, and Chapin were developing the theoretical, methodological, and conceptual schemes of neo-positivism, all of which contributed to the goal of improving the status of sociology as a science.

There never appeared to be any doubt as to whether or not the natural science model was a valid analytical model for sociology. After what other model could the discipline pattern itself in order to gain needed respectability? During this period sociology was attempting to sever its ties with the image of the do-gooders and social problem-solvers and to benefit from the respect for the natural sciences. This attempt was based on nothing more than the desire for increased social prestige.

As a direct result of the decision by sociologists in the late 1920's and early 1930's to adopt the natural science model as *the* paradigm for sociological investigation, the shift from armchair theorizing to empirical research began. But it began with the understanding that the natural science model was the only suitable approach for sociological investigation of reality. This predisposition to believe that sociology had inherited enough theory from our sociological forefathers was another factor in the trend toward research and the increased awareness of methodological problems. Although more collaboration between theory and research was sorely needed in order to establish a firm foundation for the developing discipline, the adoption of the natural science model for sociological investigation created an exaggerated concern with problems relating to the reliability (but not necessarily the validity) of the data collected.

The following quotations from Deutscher describe a condition that still exists.

It does, nevertheless, appear that the adoption of the scientific model in the social sciences has resulted in an uncommon concern for methodological problems centering on issues of reliability and to a concomitant neglect of the problem of validity. . . . We concentrate on consistency without much concern with what it is we are being consistent about or whether we are consistently right or wrong. As a consequence we may have been learning a great deal about how to pursue an incorrect course with a maximum of precision. . . . It is not my intent to disparage the importance of reliability per se; it is the obsession with it to which I refer.[9]

The import of this natural science approach to the subject matter of sociology is that sociologists have tended to bend, re-shape, and distort the empirical social world to fit the model they use to investigate it. Wherever possible, social reality is ignored. Most sociologists seem to have forgotten that reality exists only in the empirical world and not in the methods sociologists use to measure it. I can find no methodological or epistemological justification that would support the natural science model as being the best model for presentation of the empirical social world.

To force all of the empirical world to fit a scheme that has been devised for a given segment of that world is philosophical doctrinizing and does not represent the approach of a genuine empirical science.[10]

There are other reasons for adhering to the natural science model: ego fulfillment; the achievement of scientific respectability; the quest for social status on a par with that of the natural scientists; and grantsmanship, which, although it is not necessarily helpful in ascertaining the validity of the data, does enhance both those who collect data in the appropriate fashion and the discipline that fosters adherence to those appropriate methods of data collection.[11]

However, not all sociologists adhere to this dogmatic natural scientistic position in sociology. There is a tradition in sociology which does not emphasize adherence to the natural science approach in the study of human behavior. The tradition of *verstehen* or understanding,[12] or what I refer to as qualitative methodology, has had its greatest influence in formulating the position that recognizes the importance of both an inner and an outer perspective of human behavior.

The latter assumes that the study of man's behavior or conduct is adequate to produce knowledge about social life. The inner perspective assumes that understanding can only be achieved by actively participating in the life of the observed and gaining insight by means of introspection.[13]

The inner perspective places emphasis on man's ability to know himself and, hence, to know and understand others through "sympathetic introspection" and "imaginative reconstruction" of "definitions of the situation," thereby emphasizing one of the basic underlying assumptions of human behavior: that man, being a symbol manipulator, is only "understandable" through the perception and understanding of those symbols that are being manipulated. Through Meadian social-psychology, sociologists can role take the part of those under investigation, thereby understanding the meaning of human behavior.

This method of understanding enables sociologists to perceive and interpret human behavior at a greater depth than the outer perspective would allow. Objects "can be known purely from the outside, while mental and social processes can be known only from the inside," as well as through the shared meanings and interpretations we give to the objects. "Hence, insight may be regarded as the core of social knowledge. It is arrived at by being on the inside of the phenomena to be observed. . . . It is participation in an activity that generates interest, purpose, point of view, value, meaning, and intelligibility, as well as bias."[14]

This in no way suggests that the researcher lacks the ability to be scientific while collecting the data. On the contrary, it merely specifies that it is crucial for validity—and, consequently, for reliability—to try to picture the empirical social world as it actually exists to those under investigation, rather than as the researcher imagines it to be.

Sociologists who subscribe to the qualitative methodological approach, contrary to those who subscribe to the natural science model of explanation, do not assume that knowledge and the ability to understand behavior increase directly with the distance from the subjects under investigation; qualitative methodologists adhere to an indirect relationship. To facilitate understanding of the subject matter, the researcher must be aware of the tremendous qualitative differences between objective "knowledge about" and intersubjective "acquaintance with" the data of reality.[15]

... with respect to things human, it is not disinterest that makes knowledge possible but the opposite; without the factor of *interest* in the primary sense of concern or care, there can be no recognition of the subject matter in its distinctive human character—and hence no real awareness of its situation and no understanding of its behavior.[16]

To acknowledge the unique prerogative of the behavioral scientist to understand that which he studies—to combine both the inner and outer perspectives of knowing—in no way detracts from the scientific nature of the behavioral sciences. This dual perspective is of great utility in trying to assess the possible forms of behavior. This ability should be utilized, not relegated to a second-class, inferior status. Then, and only then, will the behavioral scientist's interpretations of the empirical social world be both valid and reliable.

Because of the increased concern with the problems of methodological sophistication—the problem of reliability in particular—sociologists began to equate tests of reliability with confirmation of validity. Apparently, substantiation of a technique's reliability *ipso facto* stamped it a valid assessment of the empirical social world. By defining reliability and validity synonymously to refer to the consistency with which researchers could replicate other empirical investigations, sociologists operationally defined away the concern for validity.

NEW DIRECTIONS: INTERSUBJECTIVITY AND TRANSOBJECTIVITY

What remains to be considered is how qualitative methodology as an approach can be implemented, and how it can close the gap between the empirical social world and the researcher's interpretations of it.

Most sociologists do not deny the immense heuristic value of qualitative data; to do so would indicate poor professional judgment. However, very few recognize qualitative methodology as a legitimate source of either data collection or theory construction. It would not be an exaggeration to state that qualitative methodology has very little social prestige among most sociologists.

The tendency to adhere to Lazarsfeld-Stouffer's position that qualitative research is exploratory in function—is prefatory to quantitative research—has led to the increasing de-emphasis of qualitative methodological techniques and the increasing emphasis on quantitative research in the advancement of social theory. The recent awareness of the applicability of qualitative methodological techniques to theory construction,[17] the development of what might be referred to as a sect of qualitative methodologists,[18] and the use of this methodology in the areas of deviance[19] and the sociology of medicine[20] by sociologists who are genuinely concerned with understanding human behavior, point to a growing interest in closing the gap between present theoretical, methodological, and conceptual elements and the interpretation of the empirical social world. To narrow this gap, sociologists have to devise a methodology that will enable them to take into account the inner perspective as well as the outer perspective of the subjects under investigation. This is what qualitative methodology does.

Qualitative methodology refers to those research strategies, such as participant observation, in-depth interviewing, total participation in the activity being investigated, field work, etc., which allow the researcher to obtain first-hand knowledge about the empirical social world in question. Qualitative methodology allows the researcher to "get close to the data," thereby developing the analytical, conceptual, and categorical components of explanation from the data itself—rather than from the preconceived, rigidly structured, and highly quantified techniques that pigeonhole the empirical social world into the operational definitions that the researcher has constructed.

The direct examination of the empirical social world embodies a comprehensive analytical, descriptive, and in-depth analysis of the data. The fabricated models of human behavior employing the lock-step research design of data collection, which are pervasive and deeply entrenched among sociologists, prevent such in-depth analysis. Validity becomes a serious problem in scientific research when *a priori* assumptions and artificial schemes of explanation are imposed upon social reality. When qualitative methodological procedures are employed, the problem of validity is considerably lessened and concern over the reliability of the data is increased. This simply highlights the fact that sociology's present intellectual, technical, and methodological sophistication has not addressed itself to this problem of ascertaining the reliability of qualitative methodological procedures. We are in need of an all-out effort in the direction of substantiating the reliability of the various qualitative methodological procedures.

The prevailing disposition and practice is to allow the theory, the model, the concept, the technique, and the scientific protocol to coerce the research and thus to bend the resulting analytical depictions of the empirical world to suit their form.[21]

Qualitative methodology is an approach that is constructed in such a fashion as to yield verifiable knowledge about the empirical social world. In order to predict behavior, sociologists have to understand the complex processes that precipitate human interaction. To understand these complex processes, sociologists must obtain information relevant to the various attitudinal, situational, and environmental factors that compose the real world for those under investigation. Failure to obtain such information subjects the sociologist's data to a challenge of credibility.

It is no simple task to acquire this wealth of knowledge; whether it can ever be completely acquired is problematic; but, the more intersubjective personal knowledge sociologists have at their disposal, the more accurate will be their interpretations and predictions of human behavior. The researcher has "to get to know well the persons involved and to see and hear what they do and say"[22] if he hopes to come close to understanding human behavior. The tendency in sociology to dehumanize the subject matter by reducing everything to an inventory-like describability has to be re-thought. The knowledge needed to understand human behavior is embedded in the complex network of social interaction. To assume what it is without attempting to tap it; to refuse to tap it on the grounds of scientific objectivity; or to define this knowledge with constricting operational definitions, is to do a grave injustice to the character and nature of the empirical social world that sociologists seek to know and understand.

To try and catch the interpretative process by remaining aloof as a so-called "objective" observer and refusing to take the role of the acting unit is to risk the worst kind of subjectivism—the objective observer is likely to fill in the process of interpretation with his own surmises in place of catching the process as it occurs in the experience of the acting unit which uses it.[23]

In short, qualitative methodology advocates an approach to examining the empirical social world which requires the researcher to interpret the real world from the perspective of the subjects of his investigation. The canons of *The Scientific Method* are not enough; sociologists need inter-subjective[24] and transobjective[25] understanding of their data.

Increasing societal pressures on the behavioral sciences to become involved in addressing themselves to the needs of society may force the practitioners of the various disciplines to establish, maintain, and develop theoretical, methodological, and conceptual schemes that will enable them to maintain closer ties with social reality. If the inner and outer perspectives can be fruitfully combined (and I believe they can), then the progress in the behavioral sciences will be greatly accelerated toward the long sought-after respectability of a legitimate approach to the empirical social world.

All of the preceding discussion can be condensed into a succinct but provocative challenge to all behavioral scientists. "Respect the nature of the empirical world and organize a methodological stance to reflect that respect."[26]

I would like to make one final point. In writing this introduction I had considered the possibility of taking a neutral position on the issue of subjective understanding as an essential criterion for the validation of data and as a crucial component of the research process. I decided instead to take a position advocating qualitative methodology as a legitimate approach to both theory construction and the research process because it has been shortchanged in the history of sociology. The assets of qualitative methodology in sociology need to be stressed and the shortcomings of quantitative methodology need to be exposed in their boldest relief, because the majority of sociologists are oblivious to the assets of the former, and euphoric about the techniques of the latter. Herbert Blumer has stated: "This opposition needs to be stressed in the hope of releasing social scientists from unwitting captivity to a format of inquiry that is taken for granted as the naturally proper way in which to conduct scientific study. . . .[27]

The epistemological questions raised by qualitative methodology present real dilemmas to the sociologist who conceives of his field solely in terms of the natural science model. Quantification is a very useful approach to reality; however, there are other approaches to the empirical social world. Qualitative methodology represents an equally important and valid approach to reality. Until sociologists realize the interrelationship and interdependence of both quantitative and qualitative methodology, they will remain incapable of truly understanding the complexities of human behavior.

NOTES

[1] The following is a partial list of sociologists concerned with the present direction of the field:

Herbert Blumer, *Symbolic Interactionism* (Englewood Cliffs, N.J.: Prentice-Hall, 1969); Irwin Deutscher, "Words and Deeds: Social Science and Social Policy," *Social Problems*, 13: 233-254 (1966); Marshall B. Clinard, "The Sociologist's Quest for Respectability," *The Sociological Quarterly*, 7: 399-412 (1966); Severyn Bruyn, *The Human Perspective* (Englewood Cliffs, N.J.: Prentice-Hall, 1966); Howard S. Becker, "Whose Side Are We On?" *Social Problems*, 14: 239-249 (1967); Alvin Gouldner, "Anti-Minotaur: The Myth of Value Free Sociology," *Social Problems*, 9: 199-213 (1961); Irving L. Horowitz, "Social Science Objectivity and Value Neutrality: Historical Problems and Projections," *Diogene*, 39: 16-44 (1962).

[2] Joseph Tussman, *Obligation and the Body Politic* (New York: Oxford University Press, 1960) is concerned about the external perspective of the theorists of political behavior and their subsequent neglect of the internal perspective of the subjects under investigation. Floyd W. Matson, *The Broken Image* (Garden City, N.Y.: Anchor Books, 1966), is concerned "that the historic reliance of the social sciences upon root metaphors and routine methods appropriated from classical mechanics has eclipsed the ancestral liberal vision of 'the whole man, man in person' (to use Lewis Mumford's phrase)—and has given us instead a radically broken self image." pp. v-vi.

[3] Irving L. Horowitz, "Anthropology for Sociologists," *Social Problems*, 2: 201-206 (1965).

[4] Marshall Clinard, "The Sociologist and Social Change in Underdeveloped Countries," *Social Problems*, 10: 207-219 (1963); Clinard, "The Sociologist's Quest for Respectability," *The Sociological Quarterly*, 7: 399-412 (1966).

[5] Herbert Blumer, *Symbolic Interactionism*, pp. 21-47; Severyn Bruyn, "The New Empiricists: The Participant Observer and Phenomenologist," *Sociology and Social Research*, 31: 317-322 (1967); Irwin Deutscher, "Looking Backward: Case Studies on the Progress of Methodology in Sociological Research," *The American Sociologist*, 4: 34-42 (1969); James K. Skipper, et al., "The Sacredness of .05: A Note Concerning the Uses of Statistical Levels of Significance in Social Science," *The American Sociologist*, 2: 16-18 (1967).

[6] Future work in this area will concentrate on examining the interrelation of the following theoretical, methodological, and conceptual relationship. Rather than trying to develop a definitive list to support my position, allow me to cite examples of what I refer to:

Theoretically: To some social scientists, theory is the rigorous logico-deductive model. It involves a set of postulates from which testable hypotheses or propositions can be derived. Check: Hans L. Zetterberg, *On Theory and Verification in Sociology* (3rd ed.; Totowa, N.J.: Bedminster Press, 1965); George C. Homans, "Contemporary Theory in Sociology," in Robert E. Faris, ed., *Handbook of Modern Sociology* (Chicago: Rand McNally, 1964), Chap. 25; Clarence Schrag, "Elements of Theoretical Analysis in Sociology," in Llewellyn Gross, ed., *Sociological Theory: Inquiries and Paradigms* (New York: Harper and Row, 1967), pp. 220-253; Karl R. Popper, *The Logic of Scientific Discovery* (New York: Wiley, Science Edition, 1961); Carl Hempels, *Aspects of Scientific Explanation* (New York: Free Press, 1965); William R. Cattons, Jr., *From Animistic to Naturalistic Sociology* (New York: McGraw-Hill, 1966).

Methodologically: James C. Lingoes, "IBM-7090 Program for Guttman-Lingoes Multidimensional Scalogram Analysis I," *Behavioral Science*, 11: 76-78 (1966); Stanley Lieberson and Arnold Silverman, "The Precipitants and Underlying Conditions of Race Riots," *American Sociological Review*, 30: 887-898 (1965); Edward Laumann and Louis Guttman, "The Relative Associational Contiguity of Occupations in an Urban Setting," *American Sociological Review*, 31: 169-178 (1966); Edward Laumann, "The Social Structure of Religious and Ethnoreligious Groups in a Metropolitan Community," *American Sociological Review*, 34: 182-197 (1969); H. M. Blalock, Jr., "On Graduate Methodological Training," *The American Sociologist*, 4: 5-6 (1969); Elbridge Sibley, *The Education of Sociologists in the United States* (New York: Russell Sage Foundation, 1963). In reading Sibley's book, one becomes well aware of the trend in the graduate training of sociologists to emphasize and value the mathematical and statistical research methods rather than to value and emphasize the importance of firsthand experience with the data.

Conceptually: Herbert Blumer, "The Problem of the Concept in Social Psychology," *American Journal of Sociology*, 49: 707-719 (1949); Blumer, "What Is Wrong with Social Theory," *American Sociological Review*, 19: 3-10 (1954); A. Etzioni, "Mathematics for Sociologists," *American Sociological Review*, 30: 943-945 (1965).

[7] Herbert Blumer, *Symbolic Interactionism*, pp. 26-27.

[8] Irwin Deutscher, "Words and Deeds," p. 241.

[9] Ibid.

[10] Blumer, *Symbolic Interactionism,* p. 23.

[11] Marshall Clinard discusses these and other factors that lend support to the natural science approach in sociology. Marshall Clinard, "The Sociologist's Quest for Respectability." For a succinct statement concerning the reasons for adopting the natural science model in sociology check: Irwin Deutscher, "Looking Backward," p. 34.

[12] For a discussion of the philosophical and sociological aspects of this approach, check the following: Max Weber, *Theory of Social and Economic Organization,* trans. Talcott Parsons (New York: Oxford Press, 1947), Chap. I; Edward A. Shils and Henry A. Finch, eds., *Objectivity in the Social Sciences* (Glencoe, Ill.: Free Press, 1949); Emory Bogardus, *The Development of Social Thought* (New York: Longmans, Green, 1940); Chap. 31 entitled "Weber and Social Understanding"; G. H. Mead, *Mind, Self, and Society* (Chicago: University of Chicago Press, 1934); W. I. Thomas and Florian Znaniecki, *The Polish Peasant in Europe and America,* 5 vols. (Chicago: University of Chicago Press, 1918-1920). The writing of Dilthey had a pervasive effect on the philosophical orientation of existentialism and phenomenology, as well as on the orientation of European social science. Martin Buber, *Between Man and Man* (Boston: Beacon Press, 1955).

[13] Severyn Bruyn, "The Methodology of Participant Observation," *Human Organization,* 21: 224-235 (1962).

[14] Louis Wirth, Preface to Karl Mannheim's *Ideology and Utopia* (New York: Harcourt, Brace, 1949), p. xxii. Wirth vigorously supported this position of qualitative methodology when he stated "that in the realm of the social, the observer is part of the observed and hence has a personal stake in the subject of the investigation," p. xxiv.

[15] Check Matson's excellent discussion of this problem, Matson, *The Broken Image,* especially Chap. 7, "The Human Image." Also note the discussion of this distinction in Alfred Schutz, *Collected Papers, Volume 1 and Volume 2: The Problem of Social Reality,* ed. by Maurice Natanson (The Hague: Martinus Nykoff, 1967); E. Paul Welch, *The Philosophy of Edmund Husserl* (New York: Columbia University Press, 1941); William James, *Pragmatism* (New York: Washington Square, 1907).

[16] Matson, *The Broken Image,* pp. 242-243.

[17] Blumer, *Symbolic Interactionism;* Bruyn, *The Human Perspective;* Barney Glaser and Anselm Strauss, *The Discovery of Grounded Theory* (Chicago: Aldine, 1967); Glaser and Strauss, "The Discovery of Substantive Theory: A Basic Strategy Underlying Qualitative Research," *American Behavioral Scientist,* 8: 5-12 (1965).

[18] Harold Garfinkel, *Ethnomethodology* (Englewood Cliffs, N.J.: Prentice-Hall, 1967); David Sudnow, *Passing On* (Englewood Cliffs, N.J.: Prentice-Hall, 1967).

[19] Donald W. Ball, "An Abortion Clinic Ethnography," *Social Problems,* 14: 293-302 (1967); Howard S. Becker, *Outsiders: Studies in the Sociology of Deviance* (New York: Free Press, 1963); Sherri Cavan, *Liquor License: An Ethnography of Bar Behavior* (Chicago: Aldine, 1966); Ned Polsky, *Hustlers, Beats, and Others* (Chicago: Aldine, 1967).

[20]Barney Glaser and Anselm Strauss, *Awareness of Dying* (Chicago: Aldine, 1965); Glaser and Strauss, *Time for Dying* (Chicago: Aldine, 1968); Howard S. Becker, et al., *Boys in White* (Chicago: University of Chicago Press, 1961); Fred Davis, *Passage Through Crisis* (Indianapolis, Ind.: Bobbs-Merrill, 1962); Julius Roth, *Timetables* (Indianapolis, Ind.: Bobbs-Merrill, 1963).

[21]Blumer, *Symbolic Interactionism*, p. 34.

[22]E. E. Evans-Pritchard, *Witchcraft, Oracles and Magic Among the Azande* (New York: Oxford University Press, 1937), p. 511.

[23]Herbert Blumer, "Society as Symbolic Interactionism," in Arnold Rose, ed., *Human Behavior and Social Processes* (Boston: Houghton, Mifflin, 1962), p. 188.

[24]For an excellent analysis of Husserl's phenomenology, see Welch, *The Philosophy of Edmund Husserl;* Schutz, *Collected Papers Volume 1 and Volume 2.*

[25]Edward Tiryakian, "Existential Phenomenology and the Sociological Tradition," *American Sociological Review,* 30: 674–688 (1965); Tiryakian, *Sociologism and Existentialism* (Englewood Cliffs, N.J.: Prentice-Hall, 1962).

[26]Blumer, *Symbolic Interactionism,* p. 60.

[27]Ibid., p. 47.

PART ONE

Concern with the Present Direction of Sociology

CHAPTER 2

Whose Side Are We On?

Howard S. Becker

To have values or not to have values: the question is always with us. When sociologists undertake to study problems that have relevance to the world we live in, they find themselves caught in a crossfire. Some urge them not to take sides, to be neutral and do research that is technically correct and value free. Others tell them their work is shallow and useless if it does not express a deep commitment to a value position.

This dilemma, which seems so painful to so many, actually does not exist, for one of its horns is imaginary. For it to exist, one would have to assume, as some apparently do, that it is indeed possible to do research that is uncontaminated by personal and political sympathies. I propose to argue that it is not possible and, therefore, that the question is not whether we should take sides, since we inevitably will, but rather whose side we are on.

I will begin by considering the problem of taking sides as it arises in the study of deviance. An inspection of this case will soon reveal to us features that appear in sociological research of all kinds. In the greatest variety of subject matter areas and in work done by all the different methods at our disposal, we cannot avoid taking sides, for reasons firmly based in social structure.

We may sometimes feel that studies of deviance exhibit too great a sympathy with the people studied, a sympathy reflected in the research carried out. This feeling, I suspect, is entertained off and on both by those of us who do such research and by those of us who, our work lying in other areas, only read the results. Will the research, we wonder, be distorted by that sympathy? Will it be of use in the construction of scientific theory or in the application of scientific knowledge to the practical problems of society? Or will the bias introduced by taking sides spoil it for those uses?

We seldom make the feeling explicit. Instead, it appears as a lingering worry for sociological readers, who would like to be sure they can trust what

This chapter was originally published by the Society for the Study of Social Problems, in *Social Problems,* 14: 239–47, and was prepared as the presidential address delivered at the annual meeting of the Society for the Study of Social Problems, in Miami Beach in August 1966.

they read, and a troublesome area of self-doubt for those who do the research, who would like to be sure that whatever sympathies they feel are not professionally unseemly and will not, in any case, seriously flaw their work. That the worry affects both readers and researchers indicates that it lies deeper than the superficial differences that divide sociological schools of thought, and that its roots must be sought in characteristics of society that affect us all, whatever our methodological or theoretical persuasion.

If the feeling were made explicit, it would take the form of an accusation that the sympathies of the researcher have biased his work and distorted his findings. Before exploring its structural roots, let us consider what the manifest meaning of the charge might be.

It might mean that we have acquired some sympathy with the group we study sufficient to deter us from publishing those of our results which might prove damaging to them. One can imagine a liberal sociologist who set out to disprove some of the common stereotypes held about a minority group. To his dismay, his investigation reveals that some of the stereotypes are unfortunately true. In the interests of justice and liberalism, he might well be tempted, and might even succumb to the temptation, to suppress those findings, publishing with scientific candor the other results which confirmed his beliefs.

But this seems not really to be the heart of the charge, because sociologists who study deviance do not typically hide things about the people they study. They are mostly willing to grant that there is something going on that put the deviants in the position they are in, even if they are not willing to grant that it is what the people they studied were originally accused of.

A more likely meaning of the charge, I think, is this. In the course of our work and for who knows what private reasons, we fall into deep sympathy with the people we are studying, so that while the rest of the society views them as unfit in one or another respect for the deference ordinarily accorded a fellow citizen, we believe that they are at least as good as anyone else, more sinned against than sinning. Because of this, we do not give a balanced picture. We focus too much on questions whose answers show that the supposed deviant is morally in the right and the ordinary citizen morally in the wrong. We neglect to ask those questions whose answers would show that the deviant, after all, has done something pretty rotten and, indeed, pretty much deserves what he gets. In consequence, our overall assessment of the problem being studied is one-sided. What we produce is a whitewash of the deviant and a condemnation, if only by implication, of those respectable citizens who, we think, have made the deviant what he is.

It is to this version that I devote the rest of my remarks. I will look first, however, not at the truth or falsity of the charge, but rather at the circumstances in which it is typically made and felt. The sociology of knowledge cautions us to distinguish between the truth of a statement and an assessment of the circumstances under which that statement is made; though we trace an argument to its source in the interests of the person who made it, we have still not proved it false. Recognizing the point and promising to address it eventually, I shall turn to the typical situations in which the accusation of bias arises.

When do we accuse ourselves and our fellow sociologists of bias? I think an inspection of representative instances would show that the accusation arises, in one important class of cases, when the research gives credence, in any serious way, to the perspective of the subordinate group in some hierarchical relationship. In the case of deviance, the hierarchical relationship is a moral one. The superordinate parties in the relationship are those who represent the forces of approved and official morality; the subordinate parties are those who, it is alleged, have violated that morality.

Though deviance is a typical case, it is by no means the only one. Similar situations, and similar feelings that our work is biased, occur in the study of schools, hospitals, asylums and prisons, in the study of physical as well as mental illness, in the study of both "normal" and delinquent youth. In these situations, the superordinate parties are usually the official and professional authorities in charge of some important institution, while the subordinates are those who make use of the services of that institution. Thus, the police are the superordinates, drug addicts are the subordinates; professors and administrators, principals and teachers, are the superordinates, while students and pupils are the subordinates; physicians are the superordinates, their patients the subordinates.

All of these cases represent one of the typical situations in which researchers accuse themselves and are accused of bias. It is a situation in which, while conflict and tension exist in the hierarchy, the conflict has not become openly political. The conflicting segments or ranks are not organized for conflict; no one attempts to alter the shape of the hierarchy. While subordinates may complain about the treatment they receive from those above them, they do not propose to move to a position of equality with them, or to reverse positions in the hierarchy. Thus, no one proposes that addicts should make and enforce laws for policemen, that patients should prescribe for doctors, or that adolescents should give orders to adults. We can call this the *apolitical* case.

In the second case, the accusation of bias is made in a situation that is frankly political. The parties to the hierarchical relationship engage in organized conflict, attempting either to maintain or change existing relations of power and authority. Whereas in the first case subordinates are typically unorganized and thus have, as we shall see, little to fear from a researcher, subordinate parties in a political situation may have much to lose. When the situation is political, the researcher may accuse himself or be accused of bias by someone else when he gives credence to the perspective of either party to the political conflict. I leave the political for later and turn now to the problem of bias in apolitical situations.[1]

We provoke the suspicion that we are biased in favor of the subordinate parties in an apolitical arrangement when we tell the story from their point of view. We may, for instance, investigate their complaints, even though they are subordinates, about the way things are run just as though one ought to give their complaints as much credence as the statements of responsible officials. We provoke the charge when we assume, for the purposes of our research, that subordinates have as much right to be heard as superordinates, that they are as likely to be telling the truth as they see it as superordinates, that what they say about the institution has a right to be investigated and have its truth or falsity established, even though responsible officials assure us that it is unnecessary because the charges are false.

We can use the notion of a *hierarchy of credibility* to understand this phenomenon. In any system of ranked groups, participants take it as given that members of the highest group have the right to define the way things really are. In any organization, no matter what the rest of the organization chart shows, the arrows indicating the flow of information point up, thus demonstrating (at least formally) that those at the top have access to a more complete picture of what is going on than anyone else. Members of lower groups will have incomplete information, and their view of reality will be partial and distorted in consequence. Therefore, from the point of view of a well socialized participant in the system, any tale told by those at the top intrinsically deserves to be regarded as the most credible account obtainable of the organizations' workings. And since, as Sumner pointed out, matters of rank and status are contained in the mores,[2] this belief has a moral quality. We are, if we are proper members of the group, morally bound to accept the definition imposed on reality by a superordinate group in preference to the definitions espoused by subordinates. (By analogy, the same argument holds for the social classes of a community.) Thus, credibility and the right to be heard are differentially distributed through the ranks of the system.

As sociologists, we provoke the charge of bias, in ourselves and others, by refusing to give credence and deference to an established status order, in which knowledge of truth and the right to be heard are not equally distributed. "Everyone knows" that responsible professionals know more about things than laymen, that police are more respectable and their words ought to be taken more seriously than those of the deviants and criminals with whom they deal. By refusing to accept the hierarchy of credibility, we express disrespect for the entire established order.

We compound our sin and further provoke charges of bias by not giving immediate attention and "equal time" to the apologies and explanations of official authority. If, for instance, we are concerned with studying the way of life inmates in a mental hospital build up for themselves, we will naturally be concerned with the constraints and conditions created by the actions of the administrators and physicians who run the hospital. But, unless we also make the administrators and physicians the object of our study (a possibility I will consider later), we will not inquire into why those conditions and constraints are present. We will not give responsible officials a chance to explain themselves and give their reasons for acting as they do, a chance to show why the complaints of inmates are not justified.

It is odd that, when we perceive bias, we usually see it in these circumstances. It is odd because it is easily ascertained that a great many more studies are biased in the direction of the interests of responsible officials than the other way around. We may accuse an occasional student of medical sociology of having given too much emphasis to the complaints of patients. But is it not obvious that most medical sociologists look at things from the point of view of the doctors? A few sociologists may be sufficiently biased in favor of youth to grant credibility to their account of how the adult world treats them. But why do we not accuse other sociologists who study youth of being biased in favor of adults? Most research on youth, after all, is clearly designed to find out why youth are so troublesome for adults, rather than asking the equally interesting sociological question: "Why do adults make so much trouble for youth?" Similarly, we accuse those who take the complaints of mental patients seriously of bias; what about those sociologists who only take seriously the complaints of physicians, families and others about mental patients?

Why this disproportion in the direction of accusations of bias? Why do we more often accuse those who are on the side of subordinates than those who are on the side of superordinates? Because, when we make the former accusation, we have, like the well socialized members of our society most of us are, accepted the hierarchy of credibility and taken over the accusation made by responsible officials.

The reason responsible officials make the accusation so frequently is precisely because they are responsible. They have been entrusted with the care and operation of one or another of our important institutions: schools, hospitals, law enforcement, or whatever. They are the ones who, by virtue of their official position and the authority that goes with it, are in a position to "do something" when things are not what they should be and, similarly, are the ones who will be held to account if they fail to "do something" or if what they do is, for whatever reason, inadequate.

Because they are responsible in this way, officials usually have to lie. That is a gross way of putting it, but not inaccurate. Officials must lie because things are seldom as they ought to be. For a great variety of reasons, well-known to sociologists, institutions are refractory. They do not perform as society would like them to. Hospitals do not cure people; prisons do not rehabilitate prisoners; schools do not educate students. Since they are supposed to, officials develop ways both of denying the failure of the institution to perform as it should and explaining those failures which cannot be hidden. An account of an institution's operation from the point of view of subordinates therefore casts doubt on the official line and may possibly expose it as a lie.[3]

For reasons that are a mirror image of those of officials, subordinates in an apolitical hierarchical relationship have no reason to complain of the bias of sociological research oriented toward the interests of superordinates. Subordinates typically are not organized in such a fashion as to be responsible for the overall operation of an institution. What happens in a school is credited or debited to the faculty and administrators; they can be identified and held to account. Even though the failure of a school may be the fault of the pupils, they are not so organized that any one of them is responsible for any failure but his own. If he does well, while others all around him flounder, cheat and steal, that is none of his affair, despite the attempt of honor codes to make it so. As long as the sociological report on his school says that every student there but one is a liar and a cheat, all the students will feel complacent, knowing they are the one exception. More likely, they will never hear of the report at all or, if they do, will reason that they will be gone before long, so what difference does it make? The lack of organization among subordinate members of an institutionalized relationship means that, having no responsibility for the group's welfare, they likewise have no complaints if someone maligns it. The sociologist who favors officialdom will be spared the accusation of bias.

And thus we see why we accuse ourselves of bias only when we take the side of the subordinate. It is because, in a situation that is not openly political, with the major issues defined as arguable, we join responsible officials and the man in the street in an unthinking acceptance of the hierarchy of credibility. We assume with them that the man at the top knows best. We do not realize that there are sides to be taken and that we are taking one of them.

The same reasoning allows us to understand why the researcher has the same worry about the effect of his sympathies on his work as his uninvolved colleague. The hierarchy of credibility is a feature of society whose existence we cannot deny, even if we disagree with its injunction to believe the man at the top. When we acquire sufficient sympathy with subordinates to see things from their perspective, we know that we are flying in the face of what "everyone knows." The knowledge gives us pause and causes us to share, however briefly, the doubt of our colleagues.

When a situation has been defined politically, the second type of case I want to discuss, matters are quite different. Subordinates have some degree of organization and, with that, spokesmen, their equivalent of responsible officials. Spokesmen, while they cannot actually be held responsible for what members of their group do, make assertions on their behalf and are held responsible for the truth of those assertions. The group engages in political activity designed to change existing hierarchical relationships and the credibility of its spokesmen directly affects its political fortunes. Credibility is not the only influence, but the group can ill-afford having the definition of reality proposed by its spokesmen discredited, for the immediate consequence will be some loss of political power.

Superordinate groups have their spokesmen too, and they are confronted with the same problem: to make statements about reality that are politically effective without being easily discredited. The political fortunes of the superordinate group—its ability to hold the status changes demanded by lower groups to a minimum—do not depend as much on credibility, for the group has other kinds of power available as well.

When we do research in a political situation we are in double jeopardy, for the spokesmen of both involved groups will be sensitive to the implications of our work. Since they propose openly conflicting definitions of reality, our statement of our problem is in itself likely to call into question and make problematic, at least for the purposes of our research, one or the other definition. And our results will do the same.

The hierarchy of credibility operates in a different way in the political situation than it does in the apolitical one. In the political situation, it is precisely one of the things at issue. Since the political struggle calls into question the legitimacy of the existing rank system, it necessarily calls into question at the same time the legitimacy of the associated judgments of credibility. Judgments of who has a right to define the nature of reality that are taken for granted in an apolitical situation become matters of argument.

Oddly enough, we are, I think, less likely to accuse ourselves and one another of bias in a political than in an apolitical situation, for at least two reasons. First, because the hierarchy of credibility has been openly called into question, we are aware that there are at least two sides to the story and so do not think it unseemly to investigate the situation from one or another of the contending points of view. We know, for instance, that we must grasp the perspectives of both the resident of Watts and of the Los Angeles policeman if we are to understand what went on in that outbreak.

Second, it is no secret that most sociologists are politically liberal to one degree or another. Our political preferences dictate the side we will be on and, since those preferences are shared by most of our colleagues, few are ready to throw the first stone or are even aware that stone-throwing is a possibility. We usually take the side of the underdog; we are for Negroes and against Fascists. We do not think anyone biased who does research designed to prove that the former are not as bad as people think or that the latter are worse. In fact, in these circumstances we are quite willing to regard the question of bias as a matter to be dealt with by the use of technical safeguards.

We are thus apt to take sides with equal innocence and lack of thought, though for different reasons, in both apolitical and political situations. In the first, we adopt the commonsense view which awards unquestioned credibility to the responsible official. (This is not to deny that a few of us, because something in our experience has alerted them to the possibility, may question the conventional hierarchy of credibility in the special area of our expertise.) In the second case, we take our politics so for granted that it supplants convention in dictating whose side we will be on. (I do not deny, either, that some few sociologists may deviate politically from their liberal colleagues, either to the right or the left, and thus be more liable to question that convention.)

In any event, even if our colleagues do not accuse us of bias in research in a political situation, the interested parties will. Whether they are foreign politicians who object to studies of how the stability of their government may be maintained in the interest of the United States (as in the *Camelot* affair)[4] or domestic civil rights leaders who object to an analysis of race problems that centers on the alleged deficiencies of the Negro family (as in the reception given to the Moynihan Report),[5] interested parties are quick to make accusations of bias and distortion. They base the accusation not on failures of technique or method, but on conceptual defects. They accuse the sociologist not of getting false data but of not getting all the data relevant to the problem. They accuse him, in other words, of seeing things from the perspective of only one party to the conflict. But the accusation is likely to be made by interested parties and not by sociologists themselves.

What I have said so far is all sociology of knowledge, suggesting by whom, in what situations and for what reasons sociologists will be accused of bias and distortion. I have not yet addressed the question of the truth of the accusations, of whether our findings are distorted by our sympathy for those we study. I have implied a partial answer, namely, that there is no position from which sociological research can be done that is not biased in one or another way.

We must always look at the matter from someone's point of view. The scientist who proposes to understand society must, as Mead long ago pointed out, get into the situation enough to have a perspective on it. And it is likely that his perspective will be greatly affected by whatever positions are taken by any or all of the other participants in that varied situation. Even if his participation is limited to reading in the field, he will necessarily read the arguments of partisans of one or another side to a relationship and will thus be affected, at least, by having suggested to him what the relevant arguments and issues are. A student of medical sociology may decide that he will take neither the perspective of the patient nor the perspective of the physician, but he will necessarily take a perspective that impinges on the many questions that arise between physicians and patients; no matter what perspective he takes, his work either will take into account the attitude of subordinates, or it will not.

If he fails to consider the questions they raise, he will be working on the side of the officials. If he does raise those questions seriously and does find, as he may, that there is some merit in them, he will then expose himself to the outrage of the officials and of all those sociologists who award them the top spot in the hierarchy of credibility. Almost all the topics that sociologists study, at least those that have some relation to the real world around us, are seen by society as morality plays and we shall find ourselves, willy-nilly, taking part in those plays on one side or the other.

There is another possibility. We may, in some cases, take the point of view of some third party not directly implicated in the hierarchy we are investigating. Thus, a Marxist might feel that it is not worth distinguishing between Democrats and Republicans, or between big business and big labor, in each case both groups being equally inimical to the interests of the workers. This would indeed make us neutral with respect to the two groups at hand, but would only mean that we had enlarged the scope of the political conflict to include a party not ordinarily brought in whose view the sociologist was taking.

We can never avoid taking sides. So we are left with the question of whether taking sides means that some distortion is introduced into our work so great as to make it useless. Or, less drastically, whether some distortion is introduced that must be taken into account before the results of our work can be used. I do not refer here to feeling that the picture given by the research is not "balanced," the indignation aroused by having a conventionally discredited definition of reality given priority or equality with what "everyone knows," for it is clear that we cannot avoid that. That is the problem of officials, spokesmen and interested parties, not ours. Our problem is to make sure that, whatever point of view we take, our research meets the standards of good scientific work, that our unavoidable sympathies do not render our results invalid.

We might distort our findings, because of our sympathy with one of the parties in the relationship we are studying, by misusing the tools and techniques of our discipline. We might introduce loaded questions into a questionnaire, or act in some way in a field situation such that people would be constrained to tell us only the kind of thing we are already in sympathy with. All of our research techniques are hedged about with precautionary measures designed to guard against these errors. Similarly, though more abstractly, every one of our theories presumably contains a set of directives which exhaustively covers the field we are to study, specifying all the things we are to look at and take into account in our research. By using our theories and techniques impartially, we ought to be able to study all the things that need to be studied in such a way as to get all the facts we require, even though some of the questions that will be raised and some of the facts that will be produced run counter to our biases.

But the question may be precisely this. Given all our techniques of theoretical and technical control, how can we be sure that we will apply them impartially and across the board as they need to be applied? Our textbooks in methodology are no help here. They tell us how to guard against error, but they do not tell us how to make sure that we will use all the safeguards available to us. We can, for a start, try to avoid sentimentality. We are sentimental when we refuse, for whatever reason, to investigate some matter that should properly be regarded as problematic. We are sentimental, especially, when our reason is that we would prefer not to know what is going on, if to know would be to violate some sympathy whose existence we may not even be aware of. Whatever side we are on, we must use our techniques impartially enough that a belief to which we are especially sympathetic could be proved untrue. We must always inspect our work carefully enough to know whether our techniques and theories are open enough to allow that possibility.

Let us consider, finally, what might seem a simple solution to the problems posed. If the difficulty is that we gain sympathy with underdogs by studying them, is it not also true that the superordinates in a hierarchical relationship usually have their own superordinates with whom they must contend? Is it not true that we might study those superordinates or subordinates, presenting their point of view on their relations with their superiors and thus gaining a deeper sympathy with them and avoiding the bias of one-sided identification with those below them? This is appealing, but deceptively so. For it only means that we will get into the same trouble with a new set of officials.

It is true, for instance, that the administrators of a prison are not free to do as they wish, not free to be responsive of the desires of inmates, for instance. If one talks to such an official, he will commonly tell us, in private, that of course the subordinates in the relationship have some right on their side, but that they fail to understand that his desire to do better is frustrated by his superiors or by the regulations they have established. Thus, if a prison administrator is angered because we take the complaints of his inmates seriously, we may feel that we can get around that and get a more balanced picture by interviewing him and his associates. If we do, we may then write a report which *his* superiors will respond to with cries of "bias." They, in their turn, will say that we have not presented a balanced picture, because we have not looked at *their* side of it. And we may worry that what they say is true.

The point is obvious. By pursuing this seemingly simple solution, we arrive at a problem of infinite regress. For everyone has someone standing above him who prevents him from doing things just as he likes. If we question the superiors of the prison administrator, a state department of corrections or prisons, they will complain of the governor and the legislature. And if we go to the governor and the legislature, they will complain of lobbyists, party machines, the public and the newspapers. There is no end to it and we can never have a "balanced picture" until we have studied all of society simultaneously. I do not propose to hold my breath until that happy day.

We can, I think, satisfy the demands of our science by always making clear the limits of what we have studied, marking the boundaries beyond which our findings cannot be safely applied. Not just the conventional disclaimer, in which we warn that we have only studied a prison in New York or California and the findings may not hold in the other forty-nine states—which is not a useful procedure anyway, since the findings may very well hold if the conditions are the same elsewhere. I refer to a more sociological disclaimer in which we say, for instance, that we have studied the prison through the eyes of the inmates and not through the eyes of the guards or other involved parties. We warn people, thus, that our study tells us only how things look from that vantage point—what kinds of objects guards are in the prisoners' world—and does not attempt to explain why guards do what they do or to absolve the guards of what may seem, from the prisoners' side, morally unacceptable behavior. This will not protect us from accusations of bias, however, for the guards will still be outraged by the unbalanced picture. If we implicitly accept the conventional hierarchy of credibility, we will feel the sting in that accusation.

It is something of a solution to say that over the years each "one-sided" study will provoke further studies that gradually enlarge our grasp of all the relevant facets of an institution's operation. But that is a long-term solution, and not much help to the individual researcher who has to contend with the anger of officials who feel he has done them wrong, the criticism of those of his colleagues who think he is presenting a one-sided view, and his own worries.

What do we do in the meantime? I suppose the answers are more or less obvious. We take sides as our personal and political commitments dictate, use our theoretical and technical resources to avoid the distortions that might introduce into our work, limit our conclusions carefully, recognize the hierarchy of credibility for what it is, and field as best we can the accusations and doubts that will surely be our fate.

NOTES

[1] No situation is necessarily political or apolitical. An apolitical situation can be transformed into a political one by the open rebellion of subordinate ranks, and a political situation can subside into one in which an accommodation has been reached and a new hierarchy been accepted by the participants. The categories, while analytically useful, do not represent a fixed division existing in real life.

[2] William Graham Sumner, "Status in the Folkways," *Folkways* (New York: New American Library, 1960), pp. 72-73.

[3] I have stated a portion of this argument more briefly in "Problems of Publication of Field Studies," in Arthur Vidich, Joseph Bensman, and Maurice Stein (eds.), *Reflections on Community Studies* (New York: John Wiley and Sons, 1964), pp. 267-284.

[4] See Irving Louis Horowitz, "The Life and Death of Project Camelot," *Transaction,* 3 (Nov./Dec., 1965), pp. 3-7, 44-47.

[5] See Lee Rainwater and William L. Yancey, "Black Families and the White House," *Transaction,* 3 (July/August, 1966), pp. 6-11, 48-53.

CHAPTER 3

Words and Deeds: Social Science and Social Policy

Irwin Deutscher

The Society for the Study of Social Problems was established by and continues to attract sociologists with a dual commitment. We seek, on the one
hand, to achieve a better understanding of the problems society creates for
some of the people within it and, on the other, more effective application of
socially relevant knowledge to the solution of those problems. Ultimately
most of us are concerned with finding ways to alter this world in such a
manner that more people may find it a better place in which to live. Our
orientation leads us to search for effective alterations of the society rather
than effective adjustments of individuals to the society. We tend, therefore, to
shun efforts to improve treatment of individuals who reflect symptomatically
the malfunctionings of the society—whether they be defined as sick, deviant,
pathological, nonconformists, outsiders, or whatever. Since our focus is upon
the society rather than the individual, whatever changes we have to recommend, whatever advice and criticism we have to offer, must be directed
toward those who make or influence policy in our society. I will conclude this
address with some comments on our increasing responsibility in the arena of
public policy, but I will start elsewhere.

My point of departure is the basic research, the evaluative studies, and
the demonstration projects which are the "scientific" materials from which
social scientists generally derive their recommendations to policy makers. Our
scientific conclusions, for the most part, are based on analyses of verbal
responses to questions put by an interviewer. Those responses may be written
or oral and the questions may range from forced choice to open ended, but
the fact remains that what we obtain from such methods are statements of
attitude, opinion, norms, values, anticipation, or recall. The policy maker is
interested in none of these things; as a man of action, he is interested in overt

This chapter was originally published by the Society for the Study of
Social Problems in *Social Problems,* 13: 233-54, and was prepared as the
presidential address delivered at the annual meeting of the Society for the
Study of Social Problems, August 28, 1965. The author acknowledges the
assistance of Blanche Geer, Warren C. Haggstrom, and Alphonse Sallett.

behavior. Although we rarely study such behavior, we do insist that the object of our discipline is to understand and even to predict it. Therefore, to oblige the policy maker, as well as ourselves, the assumption must be made that verbal responses reflect behavioral tendencies.

In his definitive volume on interviewing, Hyman makes this assumption explicit: "If one could wait around indefinitely," he writes, "the natural environment would ultimately liberate behavior relevant to a given inference. However, practical limitations preclude such lengthy procedures. As Vernon puts it: 'Words are actions in miniature. Hence by the use of questions and answers we can obtain information about a vast number of actions in a short space of time, the actual observation and measurement of which would be impracticable.'"[1] This inferential jump from verbal behavior to overt behavior appears to be tenuous under some conditions.

Acting out a relationship is not necessarily the same as talking about a relationship. We have known this for a long time and we have known why for a long time, but we proceed as if we did not know. With the advantage of hindsight, I intend to suggest that we began to make incorrect choices in the early 1930's, and once having begun, managed easily to build error upon error. Although we have frequently proceeded with rigor and precision, we have, nevertheless, been on an erratic course. In retrospect, we may well have had a thirty-year moratorium in social science.

Symbolizing the period during which we had the choice to make is a classic experiment designed by Richard LaPiere and reported in 1934 under the simple title, "Attitude vs. Actions."[2] Since this address has the reactionary intent of picking up where LaPiere left off, I will review some of the events leading to his experiment and refresh you on its details.

THE LAPIERE EXPERIMENT

Richard LaPiere's quest for answers to a haunting methodological problem can be traced through a trilogy of his papers, the last of which is "Attitudes vs. Actions." If such quests can be thought of as being initiated at a specific point in time, LaPiere's probably began while he was attending a seminar with Malinowski at the London School in 1927.[3] During the course of that seminar, the term "verbalization" was employed to indicate a distinction between what informants may say and what may be the actual custom of the primitive society. LaPiere was formulating a comparative survey of race prejudice in France and England.[4] Interested in the concept of "verbalization," he attempted to check his questionnaire findings against actual practices. This he accomplished by questioning hotel proprietors about their policy. The results left LaPiere satisfied at the time that he had found a fair concordance between verbal responses and nonverbal responses and, consequently, that his survey results were sufficiently valid.

Upon his return to the United States, LaPiere undertook a study of an Armenian community,[5] as a result of which he writes, "I began again to doubt the certain value of verbal evidence."[6]

Perhaps as a result of this doubt, LaPiere reconsidered the evidence from his French study and realized that "at that time I overlooked the fact that what I was obtaining from the hotel proprietors was still a 'verbalized' reaction to a symbolic situation."[7] He had not compared verbal and nonverbal behavior. What he had done was to compare attitudes with self-reports of behavior. His concern resulted in the carefully designed and controlled experiment which consumed two years in the field and over ten-thousand miles of driving and culminated in the publication of "Attitudes vs. Actions."

Traveling with a Chinese couple, twice across country and up and down the West Coast, the investigator recorded the treatment they received in hotels, auto camps, tourist homes, and restaurants.[8] *Of the 251 establishments approached in this manner, one auto camp refused to accommodate them.* Here then was an estimate of Caucasian-Oriental intergroup *behavior.*

Allowing a time-lapse of six months after being served by an establishment, a questionnaire was sent to each. Half of them were asked only, "Would you accept members of the Chinese race as guests in your establishment?" The other half were asked additional questions about other ethnic groups. *Only one "yes" response was received*—this from a lady who reminisced about the nice Chinese couple she had put up six months earlier.[9] Here then was an estimate of Caucasian *"attitudes"* toward Orientals.

Most important is the juxtapositioning of these two estimates. We have then, in 1934, strong empirical evidence, not only that there may be no relationship between what people say and what they do, but that under some conditions there may be a high inverse relationship between the two.

LaPiere's conclusions are primarily theoretical and methodological. With scientific caution he restricts *empirical* conclusions to the empirical data and warns against careless generalization. He reminds us that the conventional questionnaire is a valuable tool for identifying such phenomena as political or religious *beliefs.*[10] But, he continues, "if we would know the extent to which [his belief] restrains his behavior, it is to his behavior that we must look, not to his questionnaire response:

... Sitting at my desk in California I can predict with a high degree of certainty what an "average" businessman in an average Mid-Western city will reply to the question, Would you engage in sexual intercourse with a prostitute in a Paris brothel? Yet no one, least of all the man himself, can predict what he would actually do should he by some misfortune find himself face-to-face with the situation in question.[11]

In LaPiere's work we find a line of continuity leading toward new theoretical insights into human behavior, new methods for attaining knowledge, and new kinds of evidence which could be used with confidence by policy makers bent on reducing some of the problems of the contemporary world. But that line of continuity has hardly extended beyond the publication of "Attitudes vs. Actions" in March, 1934. Some of the occasional and discontinuous efforts to proceed along this path are mentioned in the pages which follow. For the most part social science proceeded in other directions.

LaPiere contends that no one has ever challenged his argument that what men say and what they do are not always in concordance. "On the other hand," he writes, "it seems to have had no effect at all on the sociological faith in the value of data gathered via opinion, attitude, and other kinds of questionnaires. The 'Attitude vs. Action' paper was," he continues, "cited for years by almost everyone who wrote on attitudes or opinions as a sort of caution not to take their data too seriously; whereupon each author promptly ignored the caution and proceeded to assume that his data was indicative of what people would actually do in real-life circumstances."[12]

LaPiere was certainly not alone; there were other voices crying in the wilderness. In the late thirties some of the best young minds in American sociology were clearly concerned with the problem. Reading a paper at the 1938 meetings of the American Sociological Society, Robert K. Merton was critical of his own recently-acquired survey data on attitudes toward Negroes. He wondered if it wasn't possible that Northerners treat Negroes less favorably than they talk about them and that Southerners talk about Negroes less favorably than they treat them. He asks, "May we assume the amount and direction of spread between opinion and action to be relatively constant for members of different groups? To my knowledge," Merton continues, "no systematic research on this problem has been carried out."[13]

At about the same time, C. Wright Mills argued, "Perhaps the central methodological problem of the social sciences springs from recognition that often there is a disparity between lingual and social-motor types of behavior." Mills suggested that we need to know "*how much* and *in what direction* disparities between talk and action will probably go."[14]

Herbert Blumer has been the most consistent spokesman for the point of view suggested by LaPiere's data. For the past 35 years in at least a half-dozen articles, Blumer has argued the logic of this position, in terms of theory,[15] in terms of method,[16] and in terms of substantive fields such as Industrial Relations[17] and Public Opinion Polling.[18] In his presidential address to the American Sociological Society in 1956, Blumer suggests that, not only do we know nothing about behavior or the relation between attitudes and behavior, but that we don't know much about attitudes either: "The thousands of 'variable' studies of attitudes, for instance, have not contributed to our knowledge of the abstract nature of an attitude; in a similar way the studies of 'social cohesion,' 'social integration,' 'authority,' or 'group morale' have done nothing so far as I can detect, to clarify or augment generic knowledge of these categories."[19] Yet, in the closing lines of his address, after

35 years of persistence, Blumer acknowledges defeat with the wistful hope that people at least know what they are doing. He concludes, "In view, however, of the current tendency of variable analysis to become the norm and model for sociological analysis, I believe it important to recognize its shortcomings and its limitations."[20]

Why have both the empirical evidence and the theoretical rationale been ignored? There is adequate reason to suspect that behavior toward words about social or cultural objects (i.e., responses to questions) may not provide an adequate basis for imputing behavior toward the objects themselves (i.e., responses to the people or situations to which the words refer). Three decades ago LaPiere's explanation was couched in terms of economy and reliability: "The questionnaire," he observed, "is cheap, easy, and mechanical. The study of human behavior is time consuming, intellectually fatiguing, and depends for its success upon the ability of the investigator. The former method gives quantitative results, the latter mainly qualitative. Quantitative measurements are quantitatively accurate; qualitative evaluations are always subject to the errors of human judgment. Yet," he concludes, "it would seem far more worthwhile to make a shrewd guess regarding that which is essential than to accurately measure that which is likely to prove quite irrelevant."[21]

Others, like Mills, have assumed a more cynical explanation. Turning to the sources of research finance, he suggests that: "Many foundation administrators like to give money for projects that are thought to be safe from political or public attack, that are large-scale, hence easier 'to administer' than more numerous handicraft projects, and that are scientific with a capital S, which often only means made 'safe' by trivialization. Accordingly," Mills concludes, "the big money tends to encourage the large-scale bureaucratic style of research into small-scale problems as carried on by The Scientists."[22]

These explanations have persisted and most of them remain as valid today as they were in the past, but I suspect that they reflect a deeper and perhaps more basic problem. It is possible that the apparent anomoly of acknowledging the correctness of one position while pursuing another can best be explained in terms of the sociology of knowledge.

EPISTEMOLOGY AND RESEARCH METHODS

It has been suggested that the sociology of knowledge "is devoted to digging up the social roots of knowledge, to searching out the ways in which knowledge and thought are affected by the environing social structure."[23] We may indeed have some roots to dig in our attempt to understand the directions taken by American sociology during the last three or four decades. The perceptions of knowledge—notions of the proper or appropriate ways of knowing—which were fashionable during the late twenties and early thirties, when sociology had its choices to make, surely impinged upon those choices.

Men like LaPiere and Blumer and, later, Mills were arguing from a basically anti-positivistic position at a time when a century or more of cumulative positivistic science was resulting in a massive payoff in our knowledge and control of physical forces. And sociology had its alternatives. L. L. Thurstone was giving birth to what was to become modern scaling. Emery Bogardus was translating some of these ideas into sociological scales of contemporary relevance. And the intellectual brilliance of men like George Lundberg and Stuart Chapin was creating the theoretical and methodological rationale for the new "science." Incisive critiques of the new sociology and the logic of its quantitative methods were plentiful,[24] but if we listen to Richard LaPiere's recollections of the temper of the times it becomes apparent that logic may not have been the deciding factor:

... What you may not know, or at least not fully appreciate, is that well into the 1930's the status of sociology and hence of sociologists was abominable, both within and outside the academic community. The public image of the sociologist was of a blue-nosed reformer, ever ready to pronounce moral judgments, and against all pleasurable forms of social conduct. In the universities, sociology was generally thought of as an uneasy mixture of social philosophy and social work. . . . Through the 1920's the department at Chicago was the real center of sociology in the United States [but] . . . the men who were to shape sociology during the 1930's were, for the most part, products of one or two-men departments (e.g., Columbia) of low status within their universities; they were, therefore, to a considerable degree self-trained and without a doctrinaire viewpoint, and they were exceedingly conscious of the low esteem in which sociology was held. Such men, and I was one among them, were determined to prove—at least to themselves—that sociology is a science, that sociologists are not moralists, and that sociology deserves recognition and support comparable to that being given psychology and economics. It was, I think, to this end that toward the end of the 20's, scientific sociology came to be identified with quantitative methods . . . and by the mid-thirties American sociologists were split into two antagonistic camps—the moralists . . . and the scientists. . . . Now as to my own uncertain part in all this. I was one of the Young Turks, and I shared with Lundberg, Bain, Stouffer, etc., the distaste for sociology as it had been and the hurt of its lowly status. But unlike the majority of the rebels, I did not share their belief that the cure for bad sociology was quantification [although] I did set off in that direction. . . .

LaPiere sees the history of American sociology between the two world wars as an effort, not to build knowledge, but to achieve respectability and acceptability. In terms of this goal we have been successful. "For it has in considerable measure been sociological reliance on quantitative methods that has won for sociology the repute and financial support that it now enjoys. That in gaining fame, sociology may have become a pseudo-science is another, and quite different, matter. Now that sociology is well-established, it may be possible for a new generation of Young Turks to evaluate the means through which sociology has won respectability."[25]

With the security of respectability perhaps now we can afford to take a more critical look at alternatives which were neglected at other times for reasons which are no longer cogent. Perhaps now we can begin again to achieve some understanding of the tenuous relationships between men's thoughts and their actions. One strategic point of departure for such a re-evaluation is an examination of some of the consequences of the choices we have made. In attempting to assume the stance of physical science, we have necessarily assumed its epistemology—its assumptions about the nature of knowledge and the appropriate means of knowing, including the rules of scientific evidence. The requirement of clean empirical demonstration of the effects of isolated factors or variables, in a manner which can be replicated, led us to create, by definition, such factors or variables. We knew that human behavior was rarely if ever directly influenced or explained by an isolated variable; we knew that it was impossible to assume that any set of such variables was additive (with or without weighting); we knew that the complex mathematics of the interaction among any set of variables, much less their interaction with external variables, was incomprehensible to us. In effect, although we knew they did not exist, we defined them into being.

But it was not enough just to create sets of variables. They had to be stripped of what little meaning they had in order that they might be operational, i.e., that they have their measurement built into their definition. One consequence, then, was to break down human behavior in a way that was not only artificial but which did not jibe with the manner in which that behavior was observed.

Having laid these foundations and because the accretion of knowledge is a cumulative affair, we began to construct layer upon layer. For example, in three decades we "advanced" from Bogardus to Guttman.[26] Merton suggests that the cumulative nature of science requires a high degree of consensus among scientists and leads, therefore, to an inevitable enchantment with problems of reliability.[27] Merton is wrong in his equation of scientific method with maximum concern for problems of reliability: *all* knowledge, whether scientific or not, is cumulative and all men who think or write stand on the shoulders of those who have thought or have written before. It does, nevertheless, appear that the adoption of the scientific model in the social sciences has resulted in an uncommon concern for methodological problems centering on issues of reliability and to the concomitant neglect of problems of validity.

We have been absorbed in measuring the amounts of error which results from inconsistency among interviewers or inconsistency among items on our instruments. We concentrate on consistency without much concern with what it is we are being consistent about or whether we are consistently right or wrong. As a consequence we may have been learning a great deal about how to pursue an incorrect course with a maximum of precision.

It is not my intent to disparage the importance of reliability *per se*; it is the obsession with it to which I refer.[28] Certainly zero reliability must result in zero validity. But the relationship is not linear, since infinite perfection of reliability (zero error) may also be associated with zero validity. Whether or not one wishes to emulate the scientist and whatever methods may be applied to the quest for knowledge, we must make estimates of, allowances for, and attempts to reduce the extent to which our methods distort our findings.

This is precisely why C. Wright Mills identifies the "disparities between talk and action" as "the central *methodological* problem of the social sciences."[29] Mills' plea for systematic investigations into the differences between words and deeds is based on the need for the "methodologist to build into his methods standard margins of error"—to learn how to appropriately discount variously located sources of data. Just as Mills is concerned about reliability in the historical method, Hyman has documented the need for estimates of reliability in social anthropological and clinical psychiatric observations. He reminds us, for example, that the village of Tepoztlan as described by Lewis is quite different from the same village as it was described earlier by Robert Redfield.[30] Hyman cites Kluckhohn's lament that "the limited extent to which ethnologists have been articulate about their field techniques is astonishing to scholars in other disciplines."[31]

One of the few positive consequences of our decades of "scientific" orientation is the incorporation into the sociological mentality of a self-consciousness about methods—regardless of what methods are employed. As a result, those few sociologists who bring ethnological field techniques to bear on their problems are constrained to contemplate methodological issues and to publish methodological observations. I have in mind, specifically, the continuing series of articles by Howard S. Becker and Blanche Geer.[32] Regardless of the importance of reliability, there remains a danger that in our obsession with it, the goals—the purposes for which we seek knowledge—and the phenomena about which we seek knowledge, may become obscured.

One of the more regretful consequences of our neglect of the relationship between words and deeds has been the development of a technology which is inappropriate to the understanding of human behavior, and conversely, the almost complete absence of a technology which can facilitate our learning about the conditions under which people in various categories do or do not "put their monies where their mouths are." We still do not know much about the relationship between what people say and what they do—attitudes and behavior, sentiments and acts, verbalizations and interactions, words and deeds. *We know so little that I can't even find an adequate vocabulary to make the distinction!*[33]

Under what conditions will people behave as they talk? Under what conditions is there no relationship? And under what conditions do they say one thing and behave exactly the opposite? In spite of the fact that all of these combinations have been empirically observed and reported, few efforts have been made to order such observations.[34] Furthermore, and perhaps of even greater importance, we do not know under what conditions a change in attitude anticipates a change in behavior or under what conditions a change in behavior anticipates a change in attitude. Again, both phenomena have been empirically observed and recorded.

It is important that my comments not be misunderstood as a plea for the simple study of simple behavioral items. This would be a duplication of the same kinds of mistakes we have made in the simple study of simple attitudinal items. Overt action can be understood and interpreted only within the context of its meaning to the actors, just as verbal reports can be understood and interpreted only within the context of their meaning to the re-spondents. And in large part, the context of each is the other. But the fact remains that one of the methodological consequences of our recent history is that we have not developed a technology for observing, ordering, analyzing, and interpreting *overt behavior*—especially as it relates to attitudes, norms, opinions, and values.

The development of a new technology could take any of a number of directions. Ideally, we should seek to refine the model provided by LaPiere, whereby we obtain information from the same population on verbal behavior and interaction behavior under natural social conditions. Surely, the kind of cleverness which creates situational apparati for the psychological laboratory could also create refined situational designs for research under conditions which have meaning for the actors. The theoretical and methodological rationalization of participant-observer field techniques, begun by Becker and Geer, is a promising alternative. There may be as yet untapped possibilities in contrived laboratory experiments—if we can learn how to contrive them in such a way that their results are not denuded of any general meaning by the artificial specificity of the situations. If someday reliable and valid projective instruments are developed, we may have made a significant technological step forward. There is considerable developmental work under way at present on instruments which facilitate self-reporting of overt behavior and allow comparisons to be made between attitudes and behavior on the same people, although still on a verbal level.[35]

There was a time earlier in this century when we had a choice to make, a choice on the one hand of undertaking neat, orderly studies of measurable phenomena. This alternative carried with it all of the gratifications of conforming to the prestigious methods of pursuing knowledge then in vogue, of having access to considerable sums of monies through the granting procedures of large foundations and governmental agencies, of a comfortable sense of satisfaction derived from dealing rigorously and precisely with small isolated problems which were cleanly defined, of moving for 30 years down one track in an increasingly rigorous, refined, and reliable manner, while simultaneously disposing of the problems of validity by the semantic trickery of operational definitions. On the other hand, we could have tackled the messy world as we knew it to exist, a world where the same people will make different utterances under different conditions and will behave differently in different situations and will say one thing while doing another. We could have tackled a world where control of relevant variables was impossible not only because we didn't know what they were but because we didn't know how they interacted with each other. We could have accepted the conclusion of almost every variant of contemporary philosophy of science, that the notion of cause and effect (and therefore of stimulus and response or of independent and dependent variables) is untenable. We eschewed this formidable challenge. This was the hard way. We chose the easy way.

Yet the easy way provides one set of results and the hard way provides another. The easy way for LaPiere in 1934 would have been to conduct as rigorous as possible a survey of attitudes of hotel and restaurant managers toward Orientals. But this leads to a set of conclusions which are the opposite of what he finds when he does it the hard way, i.e., traveling thousands of miles in order to confront those managers with Orientals.[36] One of our graduate students, after reviewing some of the literature on the relationship between attitudes and overt behavior,[37] concluded that laboratory experimental studies such as those by Scott,[38] Janis and King,[39] and DeFleur and Westie[40] tend to show a positive correlation between attitude and behavior, while observational field studies such as those by LaPiere, Kutner and Yarrow,[41] and Saenger and Gilbert,[42] tend to show no such correlation. Although there are important exceptions to this rule,[43] it serves as a reminder that our choice of methods may not be unrelated to our conclusions.

EMPIRICAL EVIDENCE AND THEORETICAL SUPPORT

Why do I fuss so, largely on the basis of a primitive field study on a Chinese couple done over thirty years ago and the stubborn polemics of a Herbert Blumer?[44] Frankly, that would be sufficient to cause me considerable concern! But there is other empirical evidence as well as a variety of theoretical support for the argument that more attention needs to be directed toward the relationship between what men say and what they do.[45]

There is reason to believe that this problem transcends *American* attitudes toward *Chinese tourists thirty years ago*. There is evidence that interracial attitudes and behavior are not identical *in Brazil*,[46] that sentiments about *Negroes* in northern American communities to not coincide with behavior toward Negroes in those communities,[47] that interracial attitudes and behavior between customers and department *store clerks* are inconsistent,[48] and that divergences between interracial attitudes and behaviors persist *in 1965* as they did in 1934.[49]

Perhaps of even greater importance are the bits of empirical evidence that *this discrepancy between what people say and what they do is not limited to the area of racial or ethnic relations:* it has been observed that trade union members talk one game and play another,[50] that there is no relationship between college students' attitudes toward cheating and their actual cheating behavior,[51] that urban teachers' descriptions of classroom behavior are sometimes unrelated to the way teachers behave in the classroom,[52] that what rural Missourians say about their health behavior has little connection with their actual health practices,[53] and that the moral and ethical beliefs of students do not conform to their behavior.[54]

It has also been reported that Kansans who vote for prohibition. maintain and use well-equipped bars in their homes,[55] that small-time steel wholesalers mouth patriotism while undercutting the national economy in wartime,[56] that employers' attitudes toward hiring the handicapped are not reflected in their hiring practices,[57] and that the behavior of mothers toward their children is unrelated to their attitudes toward them.[58] If it were possible to observe bedroom behavior, I wonder what would be the relationship between Kinsey's survey results and such observations? I don't know, nor does anyone else, but a contemporary novelist has a confused fictional respondent muse about a sex survey, "But what do they expect of me? Do they want to know how I feel or how I act?"[59]

Students of aging suspect that what older people have to say about retirement has little relationship to their life during that stage of the life cycle.[60] A pair of industrial psychologists, interested in assessing the current state of knowledge regarding the relationship between employee attitudes and employee performance, covered all of the literature in that area through 1954.[61] Treating various classes of studies separately, they find in every category "minimal or no relationship between employee attitudes and performance."

It would be a serious selective distortion of the existing evidence to suggest that all of it indicates an incongruence between what people say and what they do. Consumers sometimes do change their buying habits in ways that they say they will,[62] people frequently do vote as they tell pollsters they will, urban relocation populations may accurately predict to interviewers the type of housing they will obtain,[63] local party politicians do in fact employ the campaign tactics which they believe to be most effective,[64] and youngsters will provide survey researchers with reports of their own contact or lack of contact with the police which are borne out by police records.[65]

The empirical evidence can best be summarized as reflecting wide variation in the relationships between attitudes and behaviors. As a result of their review of all of the studies on employee attitudes and performance, Brayfield and Crockett observe, "The scarcity of relationships, either positive or negative, demonstrated to date even among the best designed of the available studies leads us to question whether or not methodological changes alone would lead to a substantial increase in the magnitude of the obtained relationships."[66] Having arrived at the point where they are able to question the assumption that a relationship must obtain between what people say and what they do, these authors can now question whether or not the failure to observe such a relationship is necessarily a consequence of the inefficiency of the measuring instruments. This is an important breakthrough, since it permits them, and us, to look at alternative explanations—especially at conceptual considerations.

A cursory review of the conceptual frameworks within which most of us work suggests that *no matter what one's theoretical orientation may be, he has no reason to expect to find congruence between attitudes and actions and every reason to expect to find discrepancies between them.* The popular varieties of balance theory in current social science, such as functionalism in sociology and anthropology and cognitive dissonance in psychology, posit a drive or strain toward consistency. This image of man and society must carry with it the assumption that at any given point in time a condition of imbalance or dissonance or inconsistency obtains.

The psychoanalytic concepts of the unconscious and the subconscious assume that people cannot themselves know how they might behave under specified conditions and such mechanisms as repression suggest that they may not be able to tell an interviewer how they have behaved in the past. Such dissimilar sociological ancestors as Charles H. Cooley and Emile Durkheim built their conceptions of man in society around the assumption that human nature is such that it requires the constraints of society. Under such conditions there is an inherent conflict between man's private self and his social self and the area of role theory is developed to help us understand some of the mechanisms by which man is constrained to act as he "ought."

On the gross societal level, such concepts as social disorganization and cultural lag suggest that people can be caught up in discrepant little worlds which make conflicting demands upon them. The immigrant to a new world has been described as assuming new forms of behavior while clinging to older attitudes and beliefs. In the developing countries of Africa, the idea of cultural lag leads us to expect that the rapid acceptance of new behaviors may outrun, at least for a while, the rejection of old norms. Or perhaps behavioral changes may not be able to keep pace with the rapid acceptance of new norms. Either way, the outcome must be inconsistent attitudes and behaviors!

When we consider the behavior of individuals in groups smaller than societies, we frequently think in such terms as situational contingencies, the definition of the situation, public and private behavior, or reference-group theory—all of which relate what one does or what one says to the immediate context, both as it exists objectively and as it exists in the mind of the actor. Do we not expect attitudes and behaviors to vary as the definition of the situation is altered or as different reference groups are brought to bear?

The symbolic interactionists have traditionally exhibited the greatest sensitivity to this problem in sociology. Among others, both Blumer and LaPiere have insisted that we act, either verbally or overtly, in response to the symbolic meaning the confronting object has for us in the given situation. A question put to me by an interviewer concerning how I feel about Armenian women forces me to respond to the words and to the interviewer; standing fact-to-face with a real flesh and blood Armenian woman, I find myself constrained to act toward a very different set of symbols. Is there any reason to assume that my behavior should be the same in these two radically different symbolic situations? Arnold Rose has developed a vigorous symbolic interactionist argument regarding the theoretical independence of attitudes and behaviors.[67]

One conceptual framework which we tend to neglect lies in the undeveloped field of sociolinguistics. Although it may be many other things, sociolinguistics should also deal with an analysis of the meanings of verbal communications.[68] It provides an untapped potential for understanding the relation between what people say and what they do. What differences in meaning can be conveyed by different people with the same words? The eloquent teen-age Negro prostitute, Kitten, can find herself involved in a $100 misunderstanding only because she thinks she is listening to someone who speaks the same language.[69] The truth of the matter is that, unfortunately, she and her Babbitt-like college sophomore protagonist employ the same vocabulary to speak different languages. Might this not also occur occasionally between interviewer and interviewee? What is the relationship between language and thought and between language and action? Should we assume that a response of "yah," "da," "si," "oui," or "yes" all really mean exactly the same thing in response to the same question? Or may there not be different kinds of affirmative connotations in different languages? And, of course, can we assume that the question itself means the same thing simply because it translates accurately?

We have a great deal to learn from comparative linguistics if we can bring ourselves to view language from the perspective of the symbolic interactionist—as social and cultural symbolism—rather than from the perspective of those psycholinguists who reduce language to mathematical symbols and thus effectively denude it of its socio-cultural context. I would suggest that it is impossible to translate any word in any language to any word in any other language. Words are fragments of linguistic configurations; they mean nothing in isolation from the configuration. The basic linguistic problems of cross-cultural and cross-class survey research have hardly been recognized, much less dealt with.

Let me suggest that, as an intellectual exercise, you take whatever other conceptual frameworks you may be partial to or comfortable with and determine whether or not they permit you to assume that you can expect people to act in accordance with their words. Meanwhile, I will return to Brayfield and Crockett, who helped me earlier with the transition from method to theory: "Foremost among [the] implications," of their review of research, "is the conclusion that it is time to question the strategic and ethical merits of selling to industrial concerns an assumed relationship between employee attitudes and employee performance."[70] It is but a slight extension of this conclusion to question the strategic and ethical merits of selling anything to anyone or to any establishment based on the dubious assumption that what people say is related directly to what they do.

SOCIAL RESEARCH AND SOCIAL POLICY

If I appear to have belabored some obvious points, it is because it is necessary to build as strong a backdrop as possible to the implications of all of this for the role of social science research in policy recommendations. Research aimed at demonstration and evaluation tends to make precisely the assumption which I have been challenging: the notion that what people *say* is a predictor of what they will *do*.

Thus far, I have tried to restrict my attention to the relatively simple question of the relations between attitudes and behaviors—simple as compared to the issues raised when we turn to the relationship between attitudinal and behavioral *changes*. If we are to be relevant to social policy, then we must consider this more complex question. Can we assume that if we are attempting to alter behavior through a training program, an educational campaign, or some sort of information intervention, a measured change in attitude in the "right" direction results in a change in behavior?

Leon Festinger, encountering a statement in an unpublished manuscript, reports that he was "slightly skeptical about the assertion that there is a dearth of studies relating attitude or opinion change to behavior."[71] Although no examples occurred to him, he was certain that there must be many such studies. "After prolonged search," he writes, "with the help of many others, I succeeded in locating only three relevant studies, one of which is of dubious relevance and one of which required reanalysis of data. The absence of research and of theoretical thinking, about the effect of attitude change on subsequent behavior is," Festinger concludes, "indeed astonishing."[72]

The three relevant studies all involve study and control populations and pre- and post-tests of attitude. Some form of persuasive communication was injected into the study groups and either self-reports or behavioral observations are obtained. The studies deal with attitudes of mothers of infants toward the age at which toilet training should begin; the training of industrial foremen in human relations; and attitudes of high school students toward proper dental care.[73] *In all three cases the process of persuasive communication resulted in a significant change of attitude in the desired direction. In all three cases there is no evidence of a change in behavior in the desired direction.* To the contrary, Festinger concedes that he has not "grappled with the perplexing question raised by the persistent hint of a slightly inverse relationship," and he confesses his inability to explain the possibility of such a reversal.[74]

It seems to me that we have sufficient grounds to reject any evaluation of an action program which employs attitudinal change as a criterion of "success," except in the unlikely event that the goal of the program is solely to change attitudes without concern for subsequent behavioral changes. And even under these conditions, the validity of our attitudinal measurements can be seriously challenged. For example, Ehrlich and Rinehart recently reported the results of their analysis of a stereotype measuring instrument which has been used in identical or slightly modified form in dozens of studies since 1933. They observe that the results achieved in these studies have all been roughly consistent and then proceed to demonstrate that these reliable results are of doubtful validity.[75] In effect, we have achieved over thirty years' worth of cumulative, consistent, and misleading information about prejudice.

If we do not know enough about the behavioral consequences of attitude change to make policy recommendations with confidence in their validity, what do we know about the attitudinal consequences of behavioral change? There is some evidence in the American Soldier studies that the integration of army units may lead to more favorable attitudes toward Negroes on the part of the integrated white soldiers.[76] Integrated public housing projects are reported to increase friendly contacts between races and to reduce stereotyping and prejudice among the white occupants.[77] In Yarrow's report of a controlled experiment in a children's camp, the experimental (desegregated) cabins did produce a significant reduction in prejudice as measured by pre- and post-sociometric interviews.[78] But another study in an integrated camp concludes that four weeks of intimate contact on the part of the children produced no change in attitude.[79] Similarly, Bettelheim and Janowitz found in their study of veterans that intimate contact with members of the minority group does not seem to disintegrate prejudices.[80]

These bits of evidence concerning the attitudinal consequences of behavioral change are all limited to the specific case of coercively integrated residential enclaves, i.e., army units, public housing projects, and children's camps. Although it has been reported that interracial occupational contacts may also result in changed attitudes, the evidence is limited.[81] The invasion-succession process which occurs when people are not coerced in their residential arrangements suggests that, by and large, they prefer flight (avoidance) to attitudinal change. Furthermore, there is some evidence that even when attitudinal changes appear to have occurred in one area, such as the work situation or the housing situation, they are not necessarily generalized to other interactional areas.[82]

Aside from the case of interracial attitudes and behaviors, there are an infinite number of situations where attitudinal consequences of behavioral change can be studied. In a country such as Britain where employers are coerced by law under certain conditions to employ handicapped workers, do their attitudes toward such workers change? If a group of Jaycees can be induced to undertake work with delinquent boys, does the experience alter their attitude toward such boys? Does a relatively indifferent adolescent drafted and shipped to Viet Nam consequently develop hostile attitudes toward the Viet Cong?

There can, of course, be no simple "yes" or "no" answer to such simple questions. To polarize attention upon two variables labeled "attitude" and "behavior" and to operationally define them so that we can measure their relationship is to continue down the same track. It is what goes on in between—the process—toward which we must direct our attention. We need to ask what intervenes between the change in behavior and the change in attitude.[83] Such questions need to be reformulated and qualified so that we ask "under what conditions do what kinds of people change their attitudes as a consequence of induced behavior?" We need to recognize that change probably occurs in both directions—from thought to act and from act to thought —sometimes separately, sometimes simultaneously, and sometimes sequentially.

Taking such a balanced position, Bettelheim and Janowitz reject on theoretical grounds "the view that social practice must invariably precede attitude or personality changes." They argue, "It is a serious oversimplification to assume that changes in overt behavior necessarily bring about desired changes toward increased tolerance," and that "attitude changes often anticipate overt political and social behavior. Thus," they conclude, "it becomes necessary to assess the policy implications of our research on both the levels of social and personal controls."[84]

It would seem that, in spite of our facile use of such concepts as socialization, internationalization, re-enforcement—all of which imply attitudinal development as a consequence of behavioral experience—we cannot blandly suggest to the policy maker that if he changes behavior, a change in attitude will follow. Nor can we lead him to assume that if he can alter attitudes, he need only wait patiently for the appropriate behavior to develop.

In view of the arguments and evidence reviewed, I should allude to the possibility that changes in policy are not necessarily related to subsequent changes in behavior. It follows that the process of influencing policy makers may at times have negligible impact on the resolution of social problems.[85] Nevertheless, I am concerned with the consequences of doling out to policy makers wrong advice, based on bad research and justified in the name of science. How many good programs are halted and bad ones continued because of "scientific" evaluations? There are increasing demands being made upon social science. There are expectations that we can be helpful—and we ought to be. We do not know the current extent of our influence or its future limits. No doubt it will increase. It may be that as consultants or advisors or sources of information we are used by policy makers only when our knowledge is expedient to bolster positions they have already arrived at for other reasons. But the fact remains that we are used.

You are all aware of the psychological, sociological, and anthropological documentation of the Supreme Court's historic decisions on segregated education in 1954. You know of the intimate involvement of sociologists as architects of President Kennedy's Committee on Juvenile Delinquency and Youth Crime. You must realize the multiple influences of social scientists on President Johnson's "War on Poverty." And our role in local school systems, urban renewal and relocation programs, social agency programs, hospitals, and prisons is probably more pervasive than anyone—including ourselves—realizes.

There are new terms in the language we use to describe ourselves and we ought to be self-conscious about their implications. To what new phenomenon are we referring when we invent the phrase "behavioral science"—and why? What are the implications of beginning to refer to selected disciplines as the "policy sciences?" Why is a new magazine launched in 1965 which is described as concerning itself with "problems of public policy especially," on the grounds "that the social sciences (particularly economics, politics and sociology) have become inextricably linked to issues of public policy...?"[86]

The myth of a value-free social science was exploded with finality by a recent past president of this society.[87] To make such a pretext reflects either hypocrisy or self-delusion. As social scientists, we have responsibility for encouraging and working for social change. The theme of these meetings is based in part upon that assumption and upon the consequent requirement we place upon ourselves to ask, "change for what and why?" The sacred political documents of the United States refer repeatedly to certain kinds of equality and freedoms from constraints in our kind of democracy. There is a discrepancy between the words which most of us honor and the deeds which we all observe. I have no reluctance—in fact, feel an obligation—to bring about a maximum congruence between the word and the deed.

I think that, in large part, this is what the so-called current social revolution in the United States (and probably elsewhere) is all about. It is not a revolution in the sense of seeking to replace existing political and social values with new ones; it is the opposite—a conservative movement which demands that we live by old values. It is rebellion, if at all, only against an hypocrisy which claims that there are no inequitable social, political, educational, or economic barriers in our kind of democracy, while in fact there are. It is rebelling against an hypocrisy which claims that universities are establishments where highest values are placed upon teaching and learning, while in fact they are not.

Actually, it makes no difference whether we view the nature of man through the dark lenses of a Hume or a Hobbes—"beastly," with each warring against all others—or through the rose colored glasses of a Locke or Rousseau —as essentially "good" but corrupted by society. It makes no difference since either way man is constrained to behave in ways which are contrary to his supposed nature; either way, the dialect between man's private self and his social self must create occasional and sometimes radical inconsistencies between what he says and what he does; either way, inconsistency between attitudes and behavior may be assumed.

The dilemma of words and deeds is not peculiarly American, as Gunnar Myrdal would have it, nor is it peculiar to the race question. It is a universal condition of human nature. If our inability to recognize and contend with this condition between World War I and World War II was largely a consequence of the scientific temper of the times, perhaps one day it will be written that in the temper of the new times between World War II and World War III, sociology did flourish and come of age.

NOTES

[1] Herbert Hyman et al., Interviewing in Social Research (Chicago: University of Chicago Press, 1954), pp. 17-18. The quotation is from P. E. Vernon, The Assessment of Psychological Qualities by Verbal Methods, Medical Research Council, Industrial Health Research Board, Report No. 83 (London: H. M. Stationery, 1938).

[2] Richard T. LaPiere, "Attitudes vs. Actions," Social Forces, 13 (March, 1934), 230-237.

[3] In addition to the three Social Forces articles (1928, 1934, 1936), I was fortunate to receive a lengthy communication from Professor LaPiere in which he reminisces about some of his early research experiences and about the general state of American sociology in the twenties and thirties. Many of my observations in this section are derived from that communication (dated October 23, 1964).

[4] Richard T. LaPiere, "Race Prejudice: France and England," Social Forces, 7 (September, 1928), 102-111.

[5] Richard T. LaPiere, "Type-Rationalizations of Group Antipathy," Social Forces, 15 (December, 1936), 232-237.

[6] Personal communication.

[7] LaPiere, "Attitudes vs. Actions," op. cit., p. 231.

[8] LaPiere employed a variety of methodological precautions; for example, in order to control for abnormal behavior or self-consciousness on the part of the Chinese couple, he did not inform them about the experiment in which they were participating. He made it a practice to hang back so that the Chinese undertook all negotiations. He also recorded such things as the condition of his and his subjects' clothing in relation to the quality of the establishment.

[9] With "persistence," responses were obtained from 128 establishments. Ninety-two per cent of the hotels and 91 per cent of the restaurants responded with an out-and-out "no." The rest were either uncertain or stated that it depended upon the circumstances. In order to control for the effect of the previous experience he had created, the investigator sent the same questionnaires to hotels and restaurants in the same areas but at which he and his subjects had not stopped. The distribution of responses from this control sample was the same.

[10] LaPiere, "Attitudes vs. Actions," *op. cit.*, p. 235.

[11] *Ibid.*, pp. 235-236.

[12] Personal communication.

[13] Robert K. Merton, "Fact and Factitiousness in Ethnic Opinionnaires," *American Sociological Review*, 5 (February, 1940), 21-22.

[14] C. Wright Mills, "Methodological Consequences of the Sociology of Knowledge," *American Journal of Sociology*, 46 (November, 1940), 316-330. Reprinted in Irving L. Horowitz (ed.), *Power, Politics and People: The Collected Essays of C. Wright Mills* (New York: Ballantine Books, 1963), p. 467.

[15] Herbert Blumer, "What Is Wrong with Social Theory," *American Sociological Review*, 19 (February, 1954), 3-10; "The Problem of the Concept in Social Psychology," *American Journal of Sociology*, 45 (May, 1940), 707-719; "Science without Concepts," *American Journal of Sociology*, 36 (May, 1931), 515-533.

[16] Herbert Blumer, "Sociological Analysis and the Variable," *American Sociological Review*, 21 (December, 1956), 683.

[17] Herbert Blumer, "Sociological Theory in Industrial Relations," *American Sociological Review*, 12 (February, 1947), 271-277.

[18] Herbert Blumer, "Public Opinion and Public Opinion Polling," *American Sociological Review*, 13 (March, 1948), 542-549.

[19] Blumer, "Sociological Analysis and the Variable," *op. cit.*, p. 684.

[20] *Ibid.*, p. 690.

[21] LaPiere, "Attitudes vs. Actions," *op. cit.*, p. 237.

[22] C. Wright Mills, "IBM Plus Reality Plus Humanism = Sociology," *Saturday Review*, May 1, 1954, reprinted in Horowitz (ed.), *Power, Politics and People, op. cit.*, p. 570. I have reason to believe that "the big money" may be more tolerant now than it was when Mills was writing. My suspicion is based in part on the fact that I have received fellowships independently from the National Science Foundation and the National Institute of Mental Health to pursue the questions raised in this paper over the next two years.

[23] Robert K. Merton, *Social Theory and Social Structure* (rev. ed.; Glencoe, Ill.: The Free Press, 1957), p. 440.

[24] *Cf.* Merton, "Fact and Factitiousness in Ethnic Opinionnaires," *op. cit.* Among the sources cited by Merton (pp. 15-16n.) are Morris Cohen and Ernest Nagel, *An Introduction to Logic and Scientific Method* (New York, 1934), Chap. 15; H. M. Johnson, "Pseudo-Mathematics in the Mental and Social Sciences," *American Journal of Psychology*, 48 (1936), 342-351; Clifford Kirkpatrick, "Assumptions and Methods in Attitude Measurements," *American Sociological Review*, 1 (1936), 75-88.

[25] Personal communication from LaPiere. That this defensiveness persisted well into the 1940's is evidenced in the "Discussion" of Blumer's "Public Opinion and Public Opinion Polling" in which he challenges the empirical relevance of sampling procedures. Newcomb completely misses the

point and with a comparison to "our older-brother sciences" bemoans the fact that "Blumer's stand is one which delays scientific progress" (p. 551). Woodward, the second discussant, gets the point and even makes a number of positive suggestions for implementing it. But his ultimate reaction is one of self-conscious dismay at the image of sociology Blumer may be projecting both within academia and among pollsters. Woodward concludes that "this is too bad" (p. 554).

26Louis Guttman, "A Structural Theory for Intergroup Beliefs and Action," *American Sociological Review,* 24 (June, 1959), 318-328.

27Merton, *Social Theory and Social Structure, op. cit.,* p. 448.

28My references to reliability here and on the following pages have to do with inter-rater, inter-item, interviewer, informant, or observer reliability. The notion of test-retest or any other "reliability" measure involving a time sequence is antithetical to social science since it must make the incorrect assumption that human thought and behavior is static and, therefore, that any change in response is a reflection of either instrument error or deception. In fact, such recorded changes are more likely to reflect shifts in attitude or behavior on the part of the respondent.

29Mills, "Methodological Consequences of the Sociology of Knowledge," in Horowitz, *op. cit.,* p. 467 (italics added).

30Hyman et al., *Interviewing in Social Research, op. cit.,* pp. 4-5.

31Clyde Kluckhohn, "The Personal Document in Anthropological Science," in *Social Science Research Council Bulletin,* No. 53 (New York: SSRC, 1945). Cited by Hyman, *op. cit.,* pp. 5-6.

32See, for example, Howard S. Becker and Blanche Geer, "Participant Observation and Interviewing: A Comparison," *Human Organization,* 16 (Fall, 1957), 28-32; Howard S. Becker, "Problems of Inference and Proof in Participant Observation," *American Sociological Review,* 23 (December, 1958), 652-660; Howard S. Becker and Blanche Geer, "Participant Observation: The Analysis of Qualitative Field Data," in R. N. Adams and J. L. Preiss (eds.), *Human Organization Research* (Homewood, Ill.: The Dorsey Press, 1960); Blanche Geer, "First Days in the Field," in P. E. Hammond (ed.), *Sociologists at Work* (New York: Basic Books, 1964), pp. 322-344.

33Since what people write, say, or do, can all be viewed as different kinds of "behavior," it is possible to engage in the spurious operation of eliminating the distinctions by subsuming everything under this single rubric. I doubt that this is an adequate solution to the problems posed in this paper. It is possible that the conceptual problem can be broached by viewing verbal behavior and overt behavior as different segments of a single act in process. Apparent inconsistencies can then be conceptualized as resulting from errors in interpretation on the part of the actor or from re-interpretation of the meaning of the act during the interval between the moment of verbal expression and the moment of overt behavior. This formulation also sensitizes the investigator to the possibility that the apparent inconsistency is a result of the actor's perception of the verbalization and the overt behavior as segments of two different acts, i.e., regardless of the investigator's intent, the word and the deed may be perceived by the actor as relating to different objects. This conceptual framework, and the behavioral theory which it forms, is spelled out in Herbert Blumer, "Sociological Implications of the Thought of George Herbert Mead," *American Journal of Sociology,* 71 (1966).

34Examples of some very different attempts to make sense out of apparent inconsistencies between attitudes and behaviors include: A. J. Diekema, "Some Postulates Concerning the Relationship Between Attitudes and Behavior," paper read at the Annual Meeting of the Ohio Valley Sociological Society, May, 1965 (mimeo.); Louis Guttman, "A Structural Theory for Intergroup Beliefs and Action," *American Sociological Review,* 24 (June, 1959), 318-328; Ulf Himmelstrand, "Verbal Attitudes and Behavior: A Paradigm for the Study of Message Transmission and Transformation," *Public Opinion Quarterly,* 24 (1960), 224-250; Kiyoshi Ikeda, "Discriminatory Actions and Intergroup Attitudes: A Re-examination," ca. 1962 (ditto). Identifying the problem of apparent inconsistencies as one of the more im-. portant ones confronting social psychology, the Society for the Psychological Study of Social Issues devoted a full issue of the *Journal of Social Issues* to consideration of that problem as it relates to intergroup relations (Vol. 5, No. 3, 1949). Although the intent of the editors was to encourage thinking and research, as far as I can determine their results were slim. See, for example J. H. Mann, "The Relationship between Cognitive, Affective, and Behavioral Aspects of Racial Prejudice," *Journal of Social Psychology,* 49 (1959), 223-228.

[35]Robert H. Hardt and George E. Bodine, *Development of Self-Report Instruments in Delinquency Research* (Syracuse, N.Y.: Syracuse University Youth Development Center, 1964). Novel methodological innovations do lie buried in the literature. Kohn and Williams, for example, have suggested a method of deliberately introducing new factors in to natural situations for observational purposes. See Melvin Kohn and Robin Williams, "Situational Patterning in Intergroup Relations," *American Sociological Review,* 21 (April, 1956), 164-174. Occasionally a social psychologist devises a laboratory experiment of such diabolical cleverness that the situation must surely appear real to his subjects. See, for example, Stanley Milgram, "Group Pressure and Action Against A Person," *Journal of Abnormal and Social Psychology,* 69 (August, 1964), 137-143. One group of psychologists has evolved a design which enables them to exploit the subject's definition of a dummy experimental situation in order to distract him from the actual experiment which appears as a natural event unrelated to the experiment. See, for example, Philip Himelstein and James C. Moore, "Racial Attitudes and the Action of Negro- and White-Background Figures as Factors in Petition-Signing," *The Journal of Social Psychology,* 61 (December, 1963), 267-272.

[36]Cook and Sellitz have examined the different results which may be obtained by employing different methods of assessing attitudes—including both self-reports and behavioral observations. Stuart W. Cook and Claire Sellitz, "A Multiple Indicator Approach to Attitude Measurement," *Psychological Bulletin,* 62 (July, 1964), 36-58.

[37]David J. Hanson, "Notes on a Bibliography on Attitudes and Behavior," 1965 (unpublished).

[38]W. A. Scott, "Attitude Change Through Reward of Verbal Behavior," *Journal of Abnormal and Social Psychology,* 55 (1957), 72-75; "Attitude Change by Response Reinforcement: Replication and Extension," *Sociometry,* 22 (1959), 328-335.

[39]B. T. King and I. L. Janis, "Comparison of the Effectiveness of Improvised Versus Non-improvised Role-Playing in Producing Opinion Changes," *Human Relations,* 9 (1956), 177-186.

[40]Melvin L. DeFleur and Frank R. Westie, "Verbal Attitudes and Overt

Acts: An Experiment in the Salience of Attitudes," *American Sociological Review*, 23 (December, 1958), 667-673.

[41]B. Kutner, C. Wilkins, and P. B. Yarrow, "Verbal Attitudes and Overt Behavior Involving Racial Prejudice," *Journal of Abnormal and Social Psychology*, 47 (1952), 649-652.

[42]Gerhart Saenger and Emily Gilbert, "Customer Reactions to the Integration of Negro Sales Personnel," *International Journal of Opinion and Attitude Research*, 4 (Spring, 1950), 57-76.

[43]For example, a controlled laboratory study showing no relationship between attitude and behavior is reported in Michael Zunich, "Relationship Between Maternal Behavior and Attitudes Toward Children," *Journal of Genetic Psychology* (March, 1962), pp. 155-165. On the other hand, behavior under natural conditions which has been observed to conform to expressed attitudes is reported in Irwin Deutscher and Laurence Cagle, "Housing Aspirations of Low Income Fatherless Families" (Syracuse, N.Y.: Syracuse University Youth Development Center, 1964, mimeo).

[44]Blumer may be a prophet with honor. In a review of a public opinion textbook published in 1964, Angus Campbell recollects Blumer's comments of two decades earlier with a touch of nostalgia and no little remorse: "It is curious that Blumer's hopes for the functional analysis of public opinion have been so little realized. The ability to conduct effective research on the problems he would have selected seems to elude us. The direction research has actually taken has been heavily influenced by the methods available." See Angus Campbell's review of Lane and Sears, *American Sociological Review*, 30 (August, 1965), 633. Cf. note 25 in this article.

[45]The following series of references is selected from a bibliography of some 200 items I have found to be related to the central theme of this paper. See Irwin Deutscher, "Bibliography on the Relation Between Sentiments and Acts" (Syracuse, N.Y.: Syracuse University Youth Development Center, Jan., 1966, mimeo). Available in limited quantity on request.

[46]R. Bastide and P. L. van den Berghe, "Stereotypes, Norms, and Interracial Behavior in Sao Paulo, Brazil," *American Sociological Review*, 22 (December, 1957), 689-694.

[47]Wilbur B. Brookover and John B. Holland, "An Inquiry into the Meaning of Minority Group Attitude Expressions," *American Sociological Review*, 17 (April, 1952), 196-202.

[48]Saenger and Gilbert, "Customer Reactions to the Integration of Negro Sales Personnel," *op. cit.*

[49]Lawrence S. Linn, "Verbal Attitude and Overt Behavior: A Study of Racial Discrimination," *Social Forces*, 43 (March, 1965), 353-364.

[50]Lois Dean, "Interaction, Reported and Observed: The Case of One Local Union," *Human Organization*, 17 (Fall, 1958), 36.

[51]Linton C. Freeman and Turkoz Ataov, "Invalidity of Indirect and Direct Measures Toward Cheating," *Journal of Personality*, 28 (December, 1960), 443-447.

[52]Jules Henry, "Spontaneity, Initiative, and Creativity in Suburban Classrooms," *American Journal of Orthopsychiatry*, 29 (1959), 266-279. Reprinted in George D. Spindler (ed.), *Education and Culture: Anthropological Approaches* (New York: Holt, Rinehart and Winston, 1963), pp. 215-233. See esp. p. 228.

[53]Edward Hassinger and Robert L. McNamara, "Stated Opinion and

Actual Practice in Health Behavior in a Rural Area," *The Midwest Sociologist* (May, 1957), pp. 93-97.

[54]Snell Putney and Russell Middleton, "Ethical Relativism and Anomia," *American Journal of Sociology,* 67 (January, 1962), 430-438. "Religion, Normative Standards, and Behavior," *Sociometry,* 25 (1962), 141-152.

[55]Charles K. Warriner, "The Nature and Functions of Official Morality," *American Journal of Sociology,* 64 (September, 1958), 165-168.

[56]Louis Kriesberg, "National Security and Conduct in the Steel Gray Market," *Social Forces,* 34 (March, 1956), 268-277.

[57]Vera Meyers Schletzer *et al., "*Attitudinal Barriers to Employment," *Minnesota Studies in Vocational Rehabilitation: XI,* Industrial Relations Center, Bulletin No. 32 (University of Minnesota, Minneapolis, 1961).

[58]Michael Zunich, "Relationship Between Maternal Behavior and Attitudes Toward Children," *op. cit.*

[59]Irving Wallace, *The Chapman Report* (New York: Signet Books, 1961), pp. 106-107.

[60]Leonard Z. Breen, "Retirement: Norms, Behavior, and Functional Aspects of Normative Behavior," in R. H. Williams, C. Tibbitts, and W. Donahue (eds.), *Processes of Aging,* Vol. 2 (New York: Atherton Press, 1963); William E. Henry and Elaine Cumming, *Growing Old: The Process of Disengagement* (New York: Basic Books, 1961). See esp. section dealing with normative responses.

[61]A. Brayfield and D. M. Crockett, "Employee Attitudes and Employee Performance," *Psychological Bulletin,* 52 (September, 1955), 396-428.

[62]Harold H. Martin, "Why She Really Goes to Market," *Saturday Evening Post,* September 28, 1963, pp. 40-43.

[63]Deutscher and Cagle, "Housing Aspirations of Low Income Fatherless Families" *op cit.*

[64]Richard T. Frost, "Stability and Change in Local Party Politics," *Public Opinion Quarterly,* 25 (Summer, 1961), 221-235.

[65]Dramatic evidence of this is provided in Robert H. Hardt, "Juvenile Suspects and Violations: A Comparative Study of Correlates of Two Delinquency Measures," unpublished doctoral dissertation (Syracuse University, 1965), Table 8, p. 73ff. See also Maynard L. Erickson and Lamar T. Empey, "Court Records, Undetected Delinquency and Decision Making," *Journal of Criminal Law, Criminology and Police Science,* 54 (December, 1963), 456-469; Harwin L. Voss, "Ethnic Differentials in Delinquency in Honolulu," *Journal of Criminal Law, Criminology and Police Science,* 54 (September, 1963), 322-327; Hardt and Bodine, *Development of Self-Report Instruments in Delinquency Research, op. cit.,* pp. 19-25.

[66]Brayfield and Crockett, "Employee Attitudes and Employee Performance," *op. cit.,* p. 415.

[67]Arnold M. Rose, "Intergroup Relations vs. Prejudice: Pertinent Theory for the Study of Social Change," *Social Problems,* 4 (October, 1956). For a symbolic interactionist approach to explaining inconsistencies, see note 33 in this paper.

[68]For a reflection of the current primitive state of sociolinguistics see Charles A. Ferguson, "Directions in Sociolinguistics: Report on an Interdisciplinary Seminar," *Social ·Science Research Council Items,* 19 (March, 1965), 1-4. The participants of the seminar described in that report appear to have skirted the central core of the relevance of linguistics to sociology and

social psychology and concentrated instead on several marginal areas of mutual interest.

69Robert Gover, *The One-Hundred Dollar Misunderstanding* (New York: Ballantine Books, 1963).

70Brayfield and Crockett, "Employee Attitudes and Employee Performance," *op. cit.*, p. 421.

71Leon Festinger, "Behavioral Support for Opinion Change," *Public Opinion Quarterly*, 28 (Fall, 1964), 405.

72*Ibid.* For reasons which are unclear to me, Festinger insists that he is "not raising the question of whether or not attitudes are found to relate to relevant behavior." He accepts the conclusion that they are related and cites DeFleur and Westie to document the fact. See DeFleur and Westie, "Verbal Attitudes and Overt Acts: An Experiment in the Salience of Attitudes," *op. cit.*

73The first of these, data from which Festinger reanalyzed, is N. Maccoby *et al.*, *"Critical Periods" In Seeking and Accepting Information* (Paris-Stanford Studies in Communication; Stanford, Calif.: Institute for Communication Research, 1962). The other two are E. Fleishmann *et al.*, *Leadership and Supervision in Industry: An Evaluation of a Supervisory Training Program* (Columbus: Ohio State University, Bureau of Educational Research, 1955), and I. Janis and S. Feshback, "Effects of Fear-arousing Communications," *Journal of Abnormal and Social Psychology*, 48 (1953), 78-92.

74Leon Festinger, "Behavioral Support for Opinion Change," *op. cit.*, p. 416.

75Howard J. Ehrlich and James W. Rinehart, "A Brief Report on the Methodology of Stereotype Research," *Social Forces*, 43 (May, 1965).

76Samuel A. Stouffer *et al.*, *The American Soldier; Adjustment During Army Life*, Studies in Social Psychology in World War II, Vol. 1 (Princeton, N.J.: Princeton University Press, 1949), p. 594ff. For a more detailed analysis of these data see "Opinions about Negro Infantry Platoons in White Companies of Seven Divisions," in Guy E Swanson *et al.*, *Readings in Social Psychology*, (New York: Holt, 1952), pp. 502-506.

77Morton Deutsch and May Evans Collins, "Interracial Housing," in William Petersen (ed.), *American Social Patterns* (New York: Doubleday Anchor Books, 1956), esp. pp. 19-46. See also Daniel M. Wilner, Rosabelle P. Walkley, and Stuart W. Cook, "Residential Proximity and Inter-group Relations in Public Housing Projects," *Journal of Social Issues*, Vol. 8, No. 1 (1952), 45-69.

78Marian Radke Yarrow, "Interpersonal Dynamics in a Desegregation Process," Special Issue, *Journal of Social Issues*, Vol. 14, No. 1 (1958).

79Paul H. Mussen, "Some Personality and Social Factors Related to Changes in Children's Attitudes Toward Negroes," *Journal of Abnormal and Social Psychology*, 45 (July, 1950), 423-441.

80Bruno Bettleheim and Morris Janowitz, *Social Change and Prejudice Including Dynamics of Prejudice* (New York: The Free Press of Glencoe, 1964).

81See, for example, Barbara K. MacKenzie, "The Importance of Contact in Determining Attitudes Toward Negroes," *Journal of Abnormal and Social Psychology*, 43 (October, 1948), 417-441.

82Joseph Lohman and Dietrick C. Reitzes, "Deliberately Organized Groups and Racial Behavior," *American Sociological Review*, 19 (June, 1954),

342-348; Arnold Rose, "Inconsistencies in Attitudes Toward Negro Housing," *Social Problems,* 8 (Spring, 1961), 286-292; R. D. Minard, "Race Relationships in the Pocahontas Coal Field," *Journal of Social Issues,* 9(1952), 29-44.

[83]Kelman properly phrases the abstract question in his theoretical analysis which leads to a consideration of the variables which intervene between an action and a possible change in attitude: "What are the conditions under which the induction of action does lead to attitude change, and what are some of the mechanisms and processes that account for the phenomenon when it does occur?" See Herbert Kelman, "The Induction of Action and Attitude Change," *Proceedings of the XIV International Congress of Applied Psychology* (Copenhagen: Munksgaard, 1961), p. 82.

[84]Bettelheim and Janowitz, *Social Change and Prejudice Including Dynamics of Prejudice, op. cit.,* pp. 79-80.

[85]For an example of low level subversion of high level policy with the tacit approval of middle level management, see my chapter, "The Bureaucratic Gatekeeper in Public Housing," in Irwin Deutscher (ed.), *Among the People: Encounters with the Urban Poor,* (New York: Basic Books, 1966).

[86]Undated memorandum from Daniel Bell and Irving Kristol to members of the American Economic, American Political Science and American Sociological Associations announcing the quarterly magazine, *The Public Interest.*

[87]Alvin Gouldner, "Anti-Minotaur: The Myth of a Value-Free Sociology," *Social Problems,* 9 (Winter, 1962). No myth is ever exploded with absolute finality. There remain occasional protests that sociology is or should be a value-free science, *viz.,* Ernest Van den Haag, "On Mobilization for Youth," *American Sociological Review,* 30 (August, 1965), 587-588.

CHAPTER 4

What Is Wrong with Social Theory?

Herbert Blumer

My concern is limited to that form of social theory which stands or presumes to stand as a part of empirical science.[1]

The aim of theory in empirical science is to develop analytical schemes of the empirical world with which the given science is concerned. This is done by conceiving the world abstractly, that is, in terms of classes of objects and of relations between such classes. Theoretical schemes are essentially proposals as to the nature of such classes and of their relations where this nature is problematic or unknown. Such proposals become guides to investigation to see whether they or their implications are true. Thus, theory exercises compelling influence on research—setting problems, staking out objects leading inquiry into asserted relations. In turn, findings of fact test theories, and in suggesting new problems, invite the formulation of new proposals. Theory, inquiry and empirical fact are interwoven in a texture of operation with theory guiding inquiry, inquiry seeking and isolating facts, and facts affecting theory. The fruitfulness of their interplay is the means by which an empirical science develops.

Compared with this brief sketch of theory in empirical science, social theory in general shows grave shortcomings. Its divorcement from the empirical world is glaring. To a preponderant extent it is compartmentalized into a world of its own, inside of which it feeds on itself. We usually localize it in separate courses and separate fields. For the most part it has its own literature. Its lifeline is primarily exegesis—a critical examination of prior theoretical schemes, the compounding of portions of them into new arrangements, the translation of old ideas into a new vocabulary, and the occasional addition of a new notion as a result of reflection on other theories. It is remarkably susceptible to the importation of schemes from outside its own empirical field, as in the case of the organic analogy, the evolutionary doctrine, physicalism, the instinct doctrine, behaviorism, psychoanalysis, and the doctrine of the conditioned reflex. Further, when applied to the empirical

This chapter was originally published by the American Sociological Association in *American Sociological Review,* 19: 3-10, and was read at the annual meeting of the American Sociological Society, August 1953.

world social theory is primarily an interpretation which orders the world into its mold, not a studious cultivation of empirical facts to see if the theory fits. In terms of both origin and use social theory seems in general not to be geared into its empirical world.

Next, social theory is conspicuously defective in its guidance of research inquiry. It is rarely couched in such form as to facilitate or allow directed investigation to see whether it or its implications are true. Thus, it is gravely restricted in setting research problems, in suggesting kinds of empirical data to be sought, and in connecting these data to one another. Its divorcement from research is as great as its divorcement from its empirical world.

Finally, it benefits little from the vast and ever growing accumulation of "facts" that come from empirical observation and research inquiry. While this may be due to an intrinsic uselessness of such facts for theoretic purposes, it also may be due to deficiency in theory.

These three lines of deficiency in social theory suggest that all that is needed is to correct improper preoccupations and bad working practices in theorizing. We hear repeatedly recommendations and injunctions to this effect. Get social theorists to reduce drastically their preoccupation with the literature of social theory and instead get in touch with the empirical social world. Let them renounce their practice of taking in each other's washing and instead work with empirical data. Let them develop their own conceptual capital through the cultivation of their own empirical field instead of importing spurious currency from alien realms. Get them to abandon the practice of merely interpreting things to fit their theories and instead test their theories. Above all, get them to cast their theory into forms which are testable. Have them orient their theory to the vast bodies of accumulated research findings and develop theory in the light of such findings.

These are nice injunctions to which all of us would subscribe. They do have a limited order of merit. But they neither isolate the problem of what is basically wrong with social theory nor do they provide means of correcting the difficulties. The problem continues to remain in the wake of studies made with due respect to the injunctions. There have been and there are many able and conscientious people in our field, alone, who have sought and are seeking to develop social theory through careful, sometimes meticulous preoccupation with empirical data—Robert E. Park, W. I. Thomas, Florian Znaniecki, Edwin Sutherland, Stuart Dodd, E. W. Burgess, Samuel Stouffer, Paul Lazarsfeld, Robert Merton, Louis Wirth, Robin Williams, Robert Bales and dozens of others who equally merit mention. All of these people are empirically minded. All have sought in their respective ways to guide research by theory and to assess their theoretical propositions in the light of empirical data. Practically all of them are familiar with the textbook canons of empirical research. We cannot correctly accuse such people of indifference to the empirical world, or of procedural naivete, or of professional incompetence. Yet their theories and their work are held suspect and found wanting, some theories by some, other theories by others. Indeed, the criticisms and counter-criticisms directed to their respective work are severe and box the compass. It is obvious that we have to probe deeper than the level of the above injunctions.

In my judgment the appropriate line of probing is with regard to the concept. Theory is of value in empirical science only to the extent to which it connects fruitfully with the empirical world. Concepts are the means, and the only means of establishing such connection, for it is the concept that points to the empirical instances about which a theoretical proposal is made. If the concept is clear as to what it refers, then sure identification of the empirical instances may be made. With their identification, they can be studied carefully, used to test theoretical proposals and exploited for suggestions as to new proposals. Thus, with clear concepts theoretical statements can be brought into close and self-correcting relations with the empirical world. Contrariwise, vague concepts deter the identification of appropriate empirical instances, and obscure the detection of what is relevant in the empirical instances that are chosen. Thus, they block connection between theory and its empirical world and prevent their effective interplay.

A recognition of the crucial position of concepts in theory in empirical science does not mean that other matters are of no importance. Obviously, the significance of intellectual abilities in theorizing, such as originality and disciplined imagination, requires no highlighting. Similarly, techniques of study are of clear importance. Also, bodies of fact are necessary. Yet, profound and brilliant thought, an arsenal of the most precise and ingenious instruments, and an extensive array of facts are meaningless in empirical science without the empirical relevance, guidance and analytical order that can come only through concepts. Since in empirical science everything depends on how fruitfully and faithfully thinking intertwines with the empirical world of study, and since concepts are the gateway to the world, the effective functioning of concepts is a matter of decisive importance.

Now, it should be evident that concepts in social theory are distressingly vague. Representative terms like mores, social institutions, attitudes, social class, value, cultural norm, personality, reference group, social process, social system, urbanization, accommodation, differential discrimination and social control do not discriminate cleanly their empirical instances. At best they allow only rough identification, and in what is so roughly identified they do not permit a determination of what is covered by the concept and what is not. Definitions which are provided to such terms are usually no clearer than the concepts which they seek to define. Careful scrutinizing of our concepts forces one to recognize that they rest on vague sense and not on precise specification of attributes. We see this in our common experience in explaining concepts to our students or outsiders. Formal definitions are of little use. Instead, if we are good teachers we seek to give the sense of the concept by the use of a few apt illustrations. This initial sense, in time, becomes entrenched through the sheer experience of sharing in a common universe of discourse. Our concepts come to be taken for granted on the basis of such a sense. It is such a sense and not precise specifications that guides us in our discipline in transactions with our empirical world.

This ambiguous nature of concepts is the basic deficiency in social theory. It hinders us in coming to close grips with our empirical world, for we are not sure what to grip. Our uncertainty as to what we are referring obstructs us from asking pertinent questions and setting relevant problems for research. The vague sense dulls our perception and thus vitiates directed empirical observation. It subjects our reflection on possible relations between concepts to wide bands of error. It encourages our theorizing to revolve in a separate world of its own with only a tenuous connection with the empirical world. It limits severely the clarification and growth that concepts may derive from the findings of research. It leads to the undisciplined theorizing that is bad theorizing.

If the crucial deficiency of social theory, and for that matter of our discipline, is the ambiguous nature of our concepts, why not proceed to make our concepts clear and definite? This is the nub of the problem. The question is how to do this. The possible lines of answer can be reduced a lot by recognizing that a great deal of endeavor, otherwise conscientious and zealous, does not touch the problem. The clarification of concepts is not achieved by introducing a new vocabulary of terms or substituting new terms—the task is not one of lexicography. It is not achieved by extensive reflection on theories to show their logical weaknesses and pitfalls. It is not accomplished by forming or importing new theories. It is not achieved by inventing new technical instruments or by improving the reliability of old techniques—such instruments and techniques are neutral to the concepts on behalf of which they may be used. The clarification of concepts does not come from piling up mountains of research findings. As just one illustration I would point to the hundreds of studies of attitudes and the thousands of items they have yielded; these thousands of items of finding have not contributed one iota of clarification to the concept of attitudes. By the same token, the mere extension of research in scope and direction does not offer in itself assurance of leading to clarification of concepts. These various lines of endeavor, as the results themselves seem abundantly to testify, do not meet the problem of the ambiguous concept.

The most serious attempts to grapple with this problem in our field take the form of developing fixed and specific procedures designed to isolate a stable and definitive empirical content, with this content constituting the definition or the reference of the concept. The better known of these attempts are the formation of operational definitions, the experimental construction of concepts, factoral analysis, the formation of deductive mathematical systems and, although slightly different, the construction of reliable quantitative indexes. Although these attempts vary as to the kind of specific procedure that is used, they are alike in that the procedure is designed to yield through repeated performances a stable and definitive finding. A definition of intelligence as being the intelligence quotient is a convenient illustration of what is common to these approaches. The intelligence quotient is a stable and discriminating finding that can be checked through a repetition of clearly specified procedures. Ignoring questions as to the differential merit and the differential level of penetration between these approaches, it would seem that in yielding a specific and discriminating content they are the answer to the problem of the ambiguous concept in social theory. Many hold that resolute employment of one or the other of these methods will yield definitive concepts with the consequence that theory can be applied decisively to the empirical world and tested effectively in research inquiry.

So far, the suitability of these precision endeavors to solving the problem of the ambiguous concept remains in the realm of claim and promise. They encounter three pronounced difficulties in striving to produce genuine concepts related to our empirical world.

First, insofar as the definitive empirical content that is isolated is regarded as constituting by itself the concept (as in the statement that, "X is the intelligence quotient") it is lacking in theoretic possibilities and cannot be regarded as yielding a genuine concept. It does not have the abstract character of a class with specifiable attributes. What is "intelligence quotient" as a class and what are its properties? While one can say that "intelligence quotient" is a class made up of a series of specific intelligence quotients, can one or does one point out common features of this series—features which, of course, would characterize the class? Until the specific instances of empirical content isolated by a given procedure are brought together in a class with common distinguishing features of content, no concept with theoretic character is formed. One cannot make proposals about the class or relate it to other abstractions.

Second, insofar as the definitive empirical content that is isolated is regarded as qualifying something beyond itself (as in the statement that, "Intelligence is the intelligence quotient" wherein intelligence would now be conceived as including a variety of common sense references such as ability to solve business problems, plan campaigns, invent, exercise diplomatic ingenuity, etc.), the concept constituted by this is something which is beyond the definitive empirical content. But since this "something beyond" is not dealt with by the procedure yielding the definitive empirical content, the concept remains in the ambiguous position that originally set the problem. In other words, the concept continues to be constituted by general sense or understanding and not by specification.

Third, a pertinent question has to be faced as to the relation of the definitive empirical content that is isolated, to the empirical world that is the concern of the discipline. One has to have the possibilities of establishing the place and role of the specific content in the empirical world in order for the empirical content to enter into theory about the world. A specific procedure may yield a stable finding, sometimes necessarily so by the internal mechanics of the procedure. Unless this finding is shown to have a relevant place in the empirical world under study, it has no value for theory. The showing of such relevancy is a critical difficulty confronting efforts to establish definitive concepts by isolating stable empirical contents through precise procedures. Incidentally, the establishment of such relevancy is not accomplished by making correlations. While classes of objects or items covered by concepts may be correlated, the mere establishment of correlations between items does not form concepts or, in other words, does not give an item as an instance of a class, a place or a function. Further, the relevance of an isolated empirical content to the empirical world is not established merely by using the concept to label given occurrences in that empirical world. This is a semantic pit into which scores of workers fall, particularly those working with operational definitions of concepts or with experimental construction of concepts. For example, a careful study of "morale" made in a restricted experiment may yield a stable finding; however, the mere fact that we customarily label many instances in our empirical world with the term, "morale," gives no assurance, whatsoever, that such an experimental construct of "morale" fits them. Such a relation has to be established and not presumed.

Perhaps these three difficulties I have mentioned may be successfully solved so that genuine definitive concepts of theoretic use can be formed out of the type of efforts I have been considering. There still remains what I am forced to recognize as the most important question of all, namely whether definitive concepts are suited to the study of our empirical social world. To pose such a question at this point seems to move in a reverse direction, to contradict all that I have said above about the logical need for definitive concepts to overcome the basic source of deficiency in social theory. Even though the question be heretical I do not see how it can be avoided. I wish to explain why the question is very much in order.

I think that thoughtful study shows conclusively that the concepts of our discipline are fundamentally sensitizing instruments. Hence, I call them "sensitizing concepts" and put them in contrast with definitive concepts such as I have been referring to in the foregoing discussion. A definitive concept refers precisely to what is common to a class of objects, by the aid of a clear definition in terms of attributes or fixed bench marks. This definition, or the bench marks, serve as a means of clearly identifying the individual instance of the class and the make-up of that instance that is covered by the concept. A sensitizing concept lacks such specification of attributes or bench marks and consequently it does not enable the user to move directly to the instance and its relevant content. Instead, it gives the user a general sense of reference and guidance in approaching empirical instances. Whereas definitive concepts provide prescriptions of what to see, sensitizing concepts merely suggest directions along which to look. The hundreds of our concepts—like culture, institutions, social structure, mores, and personality—are not definitive concepts but are sensitizing in nature. They lack precise reference and have no bench marks which allow a clean-cut identification of a specific instance and of its content. Instead, they rest on a general sense of what is relevant. There can scarcely be any dispute over this characterization.

Now, we should not assume too readily that our concepts are sensitizing and not definitive merely because of immaturity and lack of scientific sophistication. We should consider whether there are other reasons for this condition and ask particularly whether it is due to the nature of the empirical world which we are seeking to study and analyze.

I take it that the empirical world of our discipline is the natural social world of every-day experience. In this natural world every object of our consideration—whether a person, group, institution, practice or what not—has a distinctive, particular or unique character and lies in a context of a similar distinctive character. I think that it is this distinctive character of the empirical instance and of its setting which explains why our concepts are sensitizing and not definitive. In handling an empirical instance of a concept for purposes of study or analysis we do not, and apparently cannot meaningfully, confine our consideration of it strictly to what is covered by the abstract reference of the concept. We do not cleave aside what gives each instance its peculiar character and restrict ourselves to what it has in common with the other instances in the class covered by the concept. To the contrary, we seem forced to reach what is common by accepting and using what is distinctive to the given empirical instance. In other words, what is common (i.e. what the concept refers to) is expressed in a distinctive manner in each empirical instance and can be got at only by accepting and working through the distinctive expression. All of us recognize this when we commonly ask, for instance, what form does social structure take in a Chinese peasant community or in an American labor union, or how does assimilation take place in a Jewish rabbi from Poland or a peasant from Mexico. I believe that you will find that this is true in applying any of our concepts to our natural empirical world, whether it be social structure, assimilation, custom, institution, anomie, value, role, stratification or any of the other hundreds of our concepts. We recognize that what we are referring to by any given concept shapes up in a different way in each empirical instance. We have to accept, develop and use the distinctive expression in order to detect and study the common.

This apparent need of having to make one's study of what the concept refers to, by working with and through the distinctive or unique nature of the empirical instance, instead of casting this unique nature aside calls, seemingly by necessity, for a sensitizing concept. Since the immediate data of observation in the form of the distinctive expression in the separate instances of study are different, in approaching the empirical instances one cannot rely on bench marks or fixed, objective traits of expression. Instead, the concept must guide one in developing a picture of the distinctive expression, as in studying the assimilation of the Jewish rabbi. One moves out from the concept to the concrete distinctiveness of the instance instead of embracing the instance in the abstract framework of the concept. This is a matter of filling out a new situation or of picking one's way in an unknown terrain. The concept sensitizes one to this task, providing clues and suggestions. If our empirical world presents itself in the form of distinctive and unique happenings or situations and if we seek through the direct study of this world to establish classes of objects and relations between classes, we are, I think, forced to work with sensitizing concepts.

The point that I am considering may be put in another way, by stating that seemingly we have to *infer* that any given instance in our natural empirical world and its content are covered by one of our concepts. We have to make the inference from the concrete expression of the instance. Because of the varying nature of the concrete expression from instance to instance we have to rely, apparently, on general guides and not on fixed objective traits or modes of expression. To invert the matter, since what we infer does not express itself in the same fixed way, we are not able to rely on fixed objective expressions to make the inference.

Given current fashions of thought, a conclusion that concepts of social theory are intrinsically sensitizing and not definitive will be summarily dismissed as sheer nonsense by most people in our field. Others who are led to pause and give consideration to such a conclusion may be appropriately disquieted by what it implies. Does it mean that our field is to remain forever in its present state of vagueness and to forego the possibilities of improving its concepts, its propositions, its theory and its knowledge? This is not implied. Sensitizing concepts can be tested, improved and refined. Their validity can be assayed through careful study of empirical instances which they are presumed to cover. Relevant features of such instances, which one finds not to be covered adequately by what the concept asserts and implies, become the means of revising the concept. To be true, this is more difficult with sensitizing concepts than with definitive concepts precisely because one must work with variable instead of fixed forms of expression. Such greater difficulty does not preclude progressive refinement of sensitizing concepts through careful and imaginative study of the stubborn world to which such concepts are addressed. The concepts of assimilation and social disorganization, for instance, have gained more fitting abstraction and keener discrimination through insightful and realistic studies, such as those of W. I. Thomas and Robert E. Park. Actually, all that I am saying here is that careful and probing study of occurrences in our natural social world provide the means of bringing sensitizing concepts more and more in line with what such study reveals. In short, there is nothing esoteric or basically unusual in correcting and refining sensitizing concepts in the light of stubborn empirical findings.

It should be pointed out, also, that sensitizing concepts, even though they are grounded on sense instead of on explicit objective traits, can be formulated and communicated. This is done little by formal definition and certainly not by setting bench marks. It is accomplished instead by exposition which yields a meaningful picture, abetted by apt illustrations which enable one to grasp the reference in terms of one's own experience. This is how we come to see meaning and sense in our concepts. Such exposition, it should be added, may be good or poor—and by the same token it may be improved.

Deficiency in sensitizing concepts, then, is not inevitable nor irremediable. Indeed, the admitted deficiency in our concepts, which certainly are used these days as sensitizing concepts, is to be ascribed to inadequacy of study of the empirical instances to which they refer, and to inadequacy or their exposition. Inadequate study and poor exposition usually go together. The great vice, and the enormously widespread vice, in the use of sensitizing concepts is to take them for granted—to rest content with whatever element of plausibility they possess. Under such circumstances, the concept takes the form of a vague stereotype and it becomes only a device for ordering or arranging empirical instances. As such it is not tested and assayed against the empirical instances and thus forfeits the only means of its improvement as an analytical tool. But this merely indicates inadequate, slovenly or lazy work and need not be. If varied empirical instances are chosen for study, and if that study is careful, probing and imaginative, with an ever alert eye on whether, or how far, the concept fits, full means are provided for the progressive refinement of sensitizing concepts.

Enough has been said to set the problem of what is wrong with social theory. I have ignored a host of minor deficiencies or touched them only lightly. I have sought to pin-point the basic source of deficiency. This consists in the difficulty of bringing social theory into a close and self-correcting relation with its empirical world so that its proposals about that world can be tested, refined and enriched by the data of that world. This difficulty, in turn, centers in the concepts of theory, since the concept is the pivot of reference, or the gateway, to that world. Ambiguity in concepts blocks or frustrates contact with the empirical world and keeps theory apart in a corresponding unrealistic realm. Such a condition of ambiguity seems in general to be true of concepts of social theory.

How to correct this condition is the most important problem of our discipline insofar as we seek to develop it into an empirical science. A great part, if not most, of what we do these days does not touch the problem. Reflective cogitation on existing theory, the formulation of new theory, the execution of research without conceptual guidance or of research in which concepts are accepted uncritically, the amassing of quantities of disparate findings, and the devising and use of new technical instruments—all these detour around the problem.

It seems clear that there are two fundamental lines of attack on the problem. The first seeks to develop precise and fixed procedures that will yield a stable and definitive empirical content. It relies on neat and standardized techniques, on experimental arrangements, on mathematical categories. Its immediate world of data is not the natural social world of our experience but specialized abstractions out of it or substitutes for it. The aim is to return to the natural social world with definitive concepts based on precisely specified procedures. While such procedures may be useful and valuable in many ways, their ability to establish genuine concepts related to the natural world is confronted by three serious difficulties which so far have not been met successfully.

The other line of attack accepts our concepts as being intrinsically sensitizing and not definitive. It is spared the logical difficulties confronting the first line of attack but at the expense of forefeiting the achievement of definitive concepts with specific, objective bench marks. It seeks to improve concepts by naturalistic research,[2] that is by direct study of our natural social world wherein empirical instances are accepted in their concrete and distinctive form. It depends on faithful reportorial depiction of the instances and on analytical probing into their character. As such its procedure is markedly different from that employed in the effort to develop definitive concepts. Its success depends on patient, careful and imaginative life study, not on quick short-cuts or technical instruments. While its progress may be slow and tedious, it has the virtue of remaining in close and continuing relations with the natural social world.

The opposition which I have sketched between these two modes of attack sets, I believe, the problem of how the basic deficiency of social theory is to be addressed. It also poses, I suspect, the primary line of issue in our discipline with regard to becoming an empirical science of our natural social world.

NOTES

[1] There are two other legitimate and important kinds of social theory which I do not propose to assess. One of them seeks to develop a meaningful interpretation of the social world or of some significant part of it. Its aim is not to form scientific propositions but to outline and define life situations so that people may have a clearer understanding of their world, its possibilities of development, and the directions along which it may move. In every society, particularly in a changing society, there is a need for meaningful clarification of basic social values, social institutions, modes of living and social relations. This need cannot be met by empirical science, even though some help may be gained from analysis made by empirical science. Its effective fulfillment requires a sensitivity to new dispositions and an appreciation of new lines along which social life may take shape. Most social theory of the past and a great deal in the present is wittingly or unwittingly of this interpretative type. This type of social theory is important and stands in its own right.

A second type of theory might be termed "policy" theory. It is concerned with analyzing a given social situation, or social structure, or social action as a basis for policy or action. It might be an analysis of communist strategy and tactics, or of the conditions that sustain racial segregation in an American city, or of the power play in labor relations in mass production industry, or of the morale potential of an enemy country. Such theoretical analysis is not made in the interests of empirical science. Nor is it a mere application of scientific knowledge. Nor is it research inquiry in accordance with the canons of empirical science. The elements of its analysis and their relations have a nature given by the concrete situation and not by the methods or abstractions of empirical science. This form of social theorizing is of obvious importance.

[2] I have not sought in this paper to deal with the logic of naturalistic research.

CHAPTER 5

The Sociologist's Quest for Respectability

Marshall B. Clinard

Academic sociologists and those trained in sociology have a long university tradition, and even though we are sociologists and professors, we often fail fully to appreciate this tradition in our daily existence of teaching, research, and other roles. As professors we sometimes forget that we have a long and eminent tradition. We have positions of high status, a status reflected in an often-quoted Swedish statement that "the professor walks second only to the king, who walks next to God." Universities extend as far back as the ninth century, but they were largely specialized institutions dealing with medicine, law, and theology. As groups of schools, faculties, and colleges, universities date primarily from the twelfth and thirteenth centuries, following the accumulation of knowledge largely derived through the rediscovery of Aristotle, Arabian commentaries, and the study of the broader liberal arts. Many universities from which we trace our traditions have existed for as long as nine hundred years: Bologna (1088), the universities of Paris, Oxford, and Cambridge from the twelfth century; Prague (1348); Vienna (1365); Uppsala (1477); Mexico and San Marcos de Lima (1551); and Harvard (1636). Universities today, as compared with the past, have developed well-established innovations, such as the preparation of theses in place of disputations, seminars, electives, laboratories, and separate graduate schools.

In this long academic tradition, sociologists are fairly late arrivals on the university faculties; the first independent department of sociology in the world is generally considered to be at the University of Chicago in 1893. The first professional journal was established in 1895. It was not until the 1940's that the University of California and Princeton University recognized sociology as a separate academic discipline. Today nearly all universities in this country have departments of sociology, and they are rapidly being established abroad. Thus it is understandable that sociologists often tend to feel inferior to those in the more established physical sciences or even to the disciplines of eco-

This chapter was prepared as the presidential address at the Midwest Sociological Society meetings, April 22, 1966, Madison, Wisconsin, and was published in *The Sociological Quarterly*, 7: 399–412.

nomics, political science, and psychology. The sociologist continues to seek his own identify; those outside the profession, even in academic circles, are not sure what identity should be accorded him. This feeling has been enhanced by the tendency to equate sociology with social work, with the study of general environmental influences and, by journalists, with anything that resembles liberal humanitarianism. It has been difficult for the sociologist to delineate a distinctive scientific view of social phenomena, a difficulty often made more complex when certain economists, political scientists, psychologists, and even psychiatrists incorporate a sociological approach to their data. The achievement of respectability by sociologists has taken a long time, and the end is not yet in sight.

Today perhaps 12,000 persons identify professionally with the field of sociology in the United States; nearly 10,000 of them are members of the American Sociological Association, which was founded in 1905. The Midwest Sociological Society, nearly 30 years old, has over 800 members. There is an increasing demand for the teaching of sociological courses and for sociological research in areas such as industry, politics, and medicine. Salarywise, sociologists have advanced to the point where the occupation is generally financially respectable.

Perhaps one of the first major recognitions of sociologists occurred in the 1920's when the sociologist, William Fielding Ogburn, was appointed by the President's Committee on Recent Social Trends to direct a study whose planning implications were far-reaching, even though they were largely not implemented. Beginning in the 1930's, sociologists, particularly through the efforts of Carl Taylor, were recognized in the Department of Agriculture. In the late 1930's, Louis Wirth and other sociologists played leading roles in the pioneer studies of the Urbanism Committee of the National Resources Committee, particularly in the volume *Our Cities*. Had their findings and recommendations been applied, much would have been done to prevent our present urban chaos.

During the past five to ten years there have been a number of significant recognitions of our discipline. The National Science Foundation established a Division of Social Sciences which has been headed continuously by sociologists; sociologists are on the Behavioral Sciences Committee of the National Research Council of the National Academy of Sciences; sociologists serve on various study sections and training committees of various divisions of the National Institute of Health; they serve on the Basic Research Committee of the Office of Education, the Research Committee of the Social Security Administration, and on the President's Committee on Delinquency. The Ford, Rockefeller, and Russell Sage foundations have also helped increasingly to lend scientific respect to sociologists and sociological approaches to social phenomena.

SOME STATUS SYMBOLS OF SOCIOLOGICAL RESPECTABILITY

Despite these advances, many sociologists feel that their inherent qualities as scientists and teachers are not being sufficiently respected, esteemed, or considered as authoritative as are those in other disciplines. Consequently, at the personal level, sociologists often place undue emphasis on status symbols which are current in the academic community. Such symbols become the means of achieving scientific respectability. In their quest for status, probably too many sociologists still rely on flamboyant language, the clever wording of a concept, exhibitionism in ideas, quantitativeness in publication, the "research" label, quantitative methodology, grantsmanship, being a theoretician in the grand manner of being a professional politician rather than the more tedious role of real scholarship.

Numerical Count of Publications

One way for the sociologist to achieve respectability is to follow the age-old academic prescription of "publish or perish." What is published may be inconsequential; numbers alone count, even though one book or article may be a greater contribution than several. One excellent article may deliberately be split into several mediocre parts.

The "Research" Label

The label of "research" carries particularly high prestige among sociologists. In fact, they often use the word "research" as though it represents some unique charismatic power. In actual fact, research is simply any "investigation directed to the discovery of some fact by careful study of a subject."[1] Research is carried out in all fields: home economics, French, English, history, philosophy, etc. Some, of course, may wish to draw the line between research and scientific research. This again takes us into the realm of semantics, since particular usages often become questions of scientific design and technique. The important question about research is not the technique used, but the essential nature of the problem under investigation and the degree of its relevance to the search for adequate generalizations. Many sociologists do scientific research on problems of little scientific importance, whose only defense often has been that data were readily available. The basic issue is not "research," but the significance to sociology of the research problem under investigation. Without this consideration, respectability under the guise of "research" is a scientific farce, and, in the end, leaves sociology still in shambles. In fact, academic success often comes to those who neglect their assigned teaching duties in order to have more time for private professional interests.

This means, as Caplow and McGee have concluded, that "a great deal of foolish and unnecessary research is undertaken by men who bring to their investigation neither talent nor interest."[2]

The Quantitative Methodologist

Techniques of more precise measurement of associations among social phenomena have advanced tremendously in the past few years, and this has helped to advance sociology as a science. To many sociologists, however, to become known as a quantitative expert, a methodologist with mathematical overtones, or an expert with the new electronic computers is one of the short cuts to contemporary respectability. Whether knowledge of these skills alone makes one a creative scientist is a question which might well be directed to Charles Cooley, George Mead, Emile Durkheim, Georg Simmel, or Edwin H. Sutherland, if they were alive today. Theirs would be termed "soft sociology," since ideas and concepts derived from the workings of a deeply reflective original mind, using empirical data but without mathematical emphasis, are not as likely to be recognized as the real attributes of the scientific sociologist. One might equally argue that mere emphasis on methodology with mathematical overtones rather than the hard-core sociological concepts and principles is a "soft" way of developing a "hard" science.

Grantsmanship

Sociologists often gauge their scientific respectability by their successes in securing large training or research grants. Such "grantsmanship" may take precedence over the scientific question, or even their real interest in the problem. This sense of personal respectability achieved through obtaining a large grant is seldom marred by the fact that guidelines for scientific grants are still nebulous, personal influence with foundations or special government agencies still plays a role in securing some grants, and foundation or government agency committees often must dispose of large funds in the most equitable and expeditious manner possible. Logan Wilson wisely commented, in his *Academic Man,* that the "amount of money expended on a research project, to be sure, is no indication of its importance and real significance."[3]

Theoretician in the Grand Manner

System-building has always abounded in our discipline, as Logan Wilson has pointed out about professional prestige. "Though small amounts of prestige accrue bit by bit to the scholar who turns out monographs on subjects of no wide interest, the heights are not reached until a man has created a system and formed a school of followers."[4] For both builders and erudite followers of particular intricate systems, there has been an achievement of respectability, although it may be only a contemporary one.[5] C. Wright Mills has termed them "Grand Theorists" whose theories "all too readily become an elaborate and arid formalism in which the splitting of concepts and their endless rearrangement becomes the central endeavor."[6] System-builders attract many followers, particularly among the younger sociologists who achieve much satisfaction in memorizing and trying to interpret the works of the masters. All this reveals not the maturity of a discipline but often its immaturity as a real science of substantive empiric findings based on a series of related and more limited specific hypotheses and models.

The Professional Politician

Nearly all professional organizations have an inner clique or power structure: professional sociologists are no exception. Affiliation with this inner circle is another short cut to respectability, both within and outside of the academic community. This association with the power structure is sometimes warranted on the basis of professional achievements; more often, it is based on such other considerations as friendship and office-seeking techniques. Many sociologists who have made solid and permanent contributions have never held an important professional office or even been nominated to one.

The Absent Scholar

Finally, absence from the campus for committee work, lectures, or overseas assignments are marks of particular distinction among sociologists and impressive for others in the university community. It is immaterial whether what one is doing while absent is more important than being home, whether the committee or lecture assignment was promoted through personal rather than professional influence, or brings personal rather than scientific advancement. Mere absence from the campus in New York, Washington, or Timbuktu is a sure sign of sociological respectability.

Here I want to emphasize that I do not wish to imply that these considerations do not enter into the quest for respectability in other disciplines, nor that they are always inherently deleterious in their effects; my contention is simply one of degree, namely, the sociologist's insecure status in the academic world makes him more likely to pursue these ends and to be deluded into believing that he has achieved a solid scientific respectability as a consequence.

THE ACHIEVEMENT OF SOCIOLOGICAL RESPECTABILITY

The sociologist today is in a position to make even more rapid scientific progress because of the increasing build-up of sociological theory and research, the manifold opportunities provided him through advanced statistical techniques, and the application of electronic computers to sociological data. I should like to suggest, however, that the sociologist's difficulty in achieving respectability stems primarily not from his failure to make empiric studies or to emulate the more rigorous research techniques of the physical sciences; nor is his failure to achieve adequate recognition due to his failure to engage in building impressive systems to explain the larger society. If sociology is to achieve full respectability in the academic and larger world, sociologists need (1) more firsthand acquaintance with the data of the real world, (2) the raising of more significant questions and significant research problems about the social world around them, (3) a clearer recognition of the cultural variability of human behavior and its importance for scientific generalizations, and (4) wider recognition of the necessity to test more of their research findings by application to the social control of the world around them.

Acquaintance with the Data of Social Experience

Many inside and outside our profession have some skepticism about the professional sociologist's real acquaintanceship with the raw data of social experience. The sociologist may claim to be an expert on minorities, political sociology, industrial sociology, urban sociology, criminology, mental disorder, social change, or social stratification, with little, if any, firsthand experience with the data. He may never have talked with a lower-class Negro in Harlem or in Mississippi, met politicians, experienced at first hand an industrial plant or a slum, interviewed many delinquents, criminals or mental patients, or, if in social stratification, personally studied individuals from various social classes and occupations. Instead, he may rely upon mailed questionnaires and brief interviews, using census or secondary material from similar sources. Where pre-tests are done, they are likely to be limited in number and carried out by a research assistant.

Even the opportunities provided by graduate training for this type of firsthand experience appear to be decreasing rather then increasing.[7] Extensive knowledge in methodology and memorizing Parsons and Weber have largely been substituted for training and actual experience with social data. Graduate research today all too frequently involves the use of secondary data and the manipulation and tabulation of punch cards. Occasionally there are opportunities for brief personal interviews or brief pre-tests. Universities like Michigan that provide continuous field experience for students are the exception. Today's graduate students often seem reluctant or even embarrassed to become fully acquainted with the data to be investigated, or social phenomena in the raw, as was expected, for example, of all graduate students at Chicago twenty-five years ago. When I was engaged in a research study of the function of public drinking houses shortly after World War II my graduate seminar students were asked to make a comparative study of the social organization of two taverns. As the years progressed, I noticed more and more reluctance on their part to participate. This was curious, considering that there are more than 200,000 taverns in the United States, over 14,000 in Wisconsin, all of which appear to play an important role in lower-class neighborhoods. With regret I finally dropped experimenting with this sociological field experience.

The Significant Question

Greater acquaintance with the data of social experience would increase the sociologist's scientific respectability in many ways. First, he would see the whole man, the social group, as it really is and not compartmentalized on the questionnaire, schedule, or personality test, nor in an artificial small-group research laboratory. Man makes decisions, using a set of significant symbols in on-going social acts, and this fact about the essential nature of human behavior needs more recognition in research design. Many persons in the scientific community, and elsewhere in my judgment are critical of the sociologist's present ability to represent man's real world adequately; I believe that many sociologists are also concerned.

Second, if the sociologist had more firsthand acquaintance with the data of social experience he might be able to do research on more significant scientific problems. He would be more likely to ask significant questions and to raise important problems about human behavior, insisting that they take first place in scientific methodology as they should. As it is now, research is too often dictated by the availability of data, current scientific fashions, or by the possibility of a substantial research grant. Caplow and McGee, after surveying academic sociologists, have stated: "The multiplication of specious or trivial research has some tendency to contaminate the academic atmosphere and to bring knowledge itself into disrepute."[8] I do not mean to imply here, however, that significant scientific problems necessarily have to come out of firsthand experience.

An examination of any of our scientific journals or programs of our professional meetings will show that much research does not deal with significant problems of human behavior, that a significant question was not being answered because it was not being asked. Out of firsthand experience George Mead and Charles Cooley asked significant questions about the self, and they discovered answers that, with modifications, will last as long as sociology. Many significant questions for scientific research can be secured from the world around us; what Mills terms "sociological imagination," in the sense that the sociologist should have a meaningful relation to the scene in which he lives.[9] As Lindesmith, for example, studied drug addicts and related data, he asked the question why do some persons who take opiate drugs for a length of time not become addicted. As a result, he came up with a significant social psychological research problem.

Comparative Sociology

Scientific knowledge based on actual human experience in only one culture or society is often insufficient for the sociologist to achieve respectability. As a scientist he must attempt to discover processes applicable to the three billion persons in the more than 100 nations in this world, or to propose modifications of such generalizations in the light of subprocesses found in other societies. He must not delude himself that research based on a college sample, or on a particular American city, state, or region is a scientific generalization in the sense that it will predict beyond the limited data at hand. Very few of our professional papers carry the necessary qualifications in the title: "a college sample," "a Madison study," "a United States study"; pretentions or illusions of generalizations are great. Little of the Protestant Ethic exists in a Hindu country; much of the communist world appears to de-emphasize individualistic goals; Sweden's high rate of delinquency and other deviant behavior contradict the differential opportunity formulations of Cloward and Ohlin, a theory derived largely from the United States urban Negro slum.

Unless we, as sociologists, gather data from other societies and seek to explain contradictions in other cultures, we cannot expect others to have faith in our postulates or even in our contentions that we are a science. There are, fortunately, indications that a comparative sociology is slowly emerging, yet most sociologists in this country cling to the belief that the sociological principles they teach and discover are scientific generalizations and not a study of American or, at most, Western European society. Comparative knowledge is more advanced in the field of the economist, I believe, thus contributing a great deal to their status as a science. Some of our earlier, and important, sociologists like Sumner, Durkheim, Thomas, and Weber, saw the implications and necessity for a comparative approach.

Applied Sociology

Twenty-five years ago Robert S. Lynd emphasized, in his *Knowledge for What?* that "social science is not a scholarly arcanum, but an organized part of the culture which exists to help man in continually understanding and rebuilding his culture." He raised a number of important problems and stated a number of hypotheses which would help sociology to become a more applied science. Although sociology is most highly developed in the United States, its professional practitioners exercise relatively little power in government or elsewhere. In the world of the social sciences and outside this realm, respectability is accorded those disciplines whose practitioners exercise a real influence on decision-making functions or power in the larger society. This is certainly true of economics, public administration, clinical psychology, and to an increasing degree, anthropology. The increasingly wider use of sociologists in conducting research for business and industrial concerns, being members of psychiatric faculties, and in other research functions, while it is a useful step in this direction, is not the same as being in a position to make or to recommend policy decisions.

Today a total of only about 200 sociologists, probably half of them in purely research capacities, are employed as such by the federal government, most of them in the Bureau of the Census, the Department of Agriculture, the National Institute of Health, the Office of Education, and the National Science Foundation. In fact, recognition has been so limited that sociologists did not appear in the National Science Foundation Register of Scientific and Technical Personnel until 1964.[10] Relatively few sociologists have been employed in overseas work, while hundreds of academic economists have served abroad as consultants for various agencies and foundations. During 1956-1962 only 25 sociologists served abroad as consultants for the federal government, helping to make policy decisions for foreign countries, and an even smaller number served foundations. Fortunately, there are indications that this number is now increasing.

Only a handful of sociologists in the immense federal government are in positions to make or to recommend major policy decisions. In 1966 the highest-ranking sociologists are an assistant director of the Census Bureau, the head of a division in the National Science Foundation, two heads of major programs in the Office of Education, and one principal staff member of the President's Commission on Crime and Law Enforcement. A number of sociologists hold middle level positions. There is however, no sociological equivalent to the President's Council of Economic Advisors, a research agency which makes continuous economic policy decisions. While large numbers of economists, political scientists, lawyers, and even historians are brought in on policy advisory commissions at the highest government level, the sociologists generally continue to be ignored even in making policy decisions in such areas as government Civil Rights programs or the Poverty Program.

Many factors may account for the sociologist's lack of participation in policy making decisions. First, many persons who control power-making decisions do not know exactly what a sociologist is, and sometimes the vague and unnecessarily abstruse writing and seemingly insignificant problems studied by sociologists do not help to clarify this dilemma. Second, there is skepticism that the sociologist has real firsthand knowledge of the component elements and sensitivity to the data which must go into the decision-making process. In his 1963 ASA presidential address, Everett Hughes raised this perceptive question in commenting on the Civil Rights demonstrations: "A deeper question concerning sociology and social life lurks in the background:

Why did social scientists—and sociologists in particular—not foresee the explosion of collective action of Negro Americans toward immediate full integration into American society? It is but a special instance of the more general question concerning sociological foresight of and involvement in drastic and massive social changes and extreme forms of social action."[11]

Third, so far the sociologist has largely demonstrated so little interest in the application of his knowledge that it is hard to discover whether sociology is a science in the sense that its acquired knowledge can be used as actual controls in the world of reality. Thousands of research projects have been completed, innumerable articles and books published, and hundreds of theses and dissertations produced, yet many sociologists think that research has not been adequate to support an applied sociology. Some sociologists even regard themselves as so-called pure scientists and thus above sullying their professional reputations with anything so degrading as the direct application of their findings in the form of social control. Some may even go as far as to be proud of the fact that their "research is not good for anything."

A reluctance to make practical suggestions is easily understood. The sociologist is often unwilling to put his research knowledge on the line to discover whether it really has use. Despite his verbiage and claims that his discipline should be the recognized equal of the other social sciences, he fears he is in no position to undertake the preparation of analyses that may lead to social action. When the social scientist says, "Let's do more research," he often signifies his inability, when faced with a practical problem, to draw upon codified knowledge. He fears he might be identified with social work, a field with which he was associated for a long period and is still more often confused, and he is concerned with the negative effects on the development of the discipline that preoccupation with social action and social problems had early in the century.[12] He is fearful that he will receive no professional recognition for action work from his colleagues who conceive of his role as writing and research within an academic community. He has developed false images of the scientist forever detached and aloof from the world of practical reality, failing to see the more recent direction into applied areas being followed by other behavioral scientists. Despite elaborate theory-building, on the one hand, and preoccupation with quantitative techniques, which he feels will give him scientific respectability, the sociologist has probably had less first-hand experience with actual data of his science than any other. Not really knowing about, for example, slum dwellers, lower class Negroes, and politicians at first hand he understandably feels handicapped to devise action programs that may have considerable immediate consequences. Unlike the economist whose basic theory and concepts are better organized for application to social practice, the sociologist's knowledge is often too diffused and unorganized for such practical application.

Applied sociology involves more than simply the application of principles derived from pure science; it is the development of a body of knowledge and experience which can deal effectively with the problems of social and cultural change. In this respect, as Gouldner has pointed out, applied social scientists are more likely to use the concepts than the generalized propositions of their discipline, to find that not all concepts or theoretical models are equally applicable, that those most likely to be borrowed are those useful for producing change, and that when pure sociology does not provide adequate theoretical systems or concepts the applied sociologist will need to develop them himself.[13] The so-called pure sociologist who is interested in social change can learn a great deal, therefore, from the applied sociologist's efforts to bring about change whether it is an effort to change slum areas[14] or to modify some institutional system. Despite this fact, it is important to recognize that not all problems of applied sociology are pertinent to, or contribute to, the development of the science. Many cannot be formulated as scientific problems, and "any discipline has technical and internal problems that are important to resolve and deal with, if the field is to progress, but they may have no conceivable relationship to pressing social problems."[15]

Fortunately, some changes are taking place. The sociologist is becoming disturbed by his limited interest and ability to produce change; he realizes that scientific research, particularly in the social sciences, must try to render some accountability to society for its expenditure of manpower and financial assistance. In the past year three books have shown this interest: *Applied Sociology,* edited by Gouldner and Miller, *Sociology in Use,* by Valdes and Dean, and *Sociology in Action,* edited by Shostak.[16] There is also a forthcoming book, *The Uses of Sociology,* edited by Lazarsfeld, Sewell, and Wilensky.[17] These collections report actual attempts by sociologists to direct social change in concrete situations including applications of sociology to education, religion, health, community development, race relations, crime, law, poverty, political action, and urban areas such as the slum. Other sociologists are increasingly making explicit policy control recommendations in their particular areas of research, as for example, Lindesmith in his recent *The Addict and the Law.* Such a practical application of sociological research and theory to concrete situations may have salutary effects on the development of scientific sociology. It may force sociologists to be more precise and maintain closer contacts with reality. Actual application represents one of the most effective means of checking upon a research finding which, if proved to be inadequate, can then be revised or reconceptualized. If applied programs wait until theoretical and research knowledge is complete, "they will wait for an eternity, for theoretical knowledge is increased most significantly in the efforts of social control."[18] The sociologist's respectability—in the academic community, the outside world, and in his own view—will be greatly enhanced by his success in the achievement of some degree of control over the social forces around him through the application of his research findings.

NOTES

[1] *The Oxford University Dictionary,* p. 1712.

[2] Theodore Caplow and Reece J. McGee, *The Academic Marketplace* (New York: Basic Books, Inc., 1958), p. 221.

[3] Logan Wilson, *The Academic Man* (New York: Oxford University Press, 1942), p. 201.

[4] *Ibid.,* p. 207.

[5] For example, a recent volume which critically appraises Merton's neat and logical anomie formulation of deviant behavior has shown largely that it does not jibe with empiric evidence. Perhaps it would not even have been formulated had its advocate known more about actual deviant behavior. Marshall B. Clinard (ed.), *Anomie and Deviant Behavior: A Discussion and Critique* (New York: Free Press, 1964).

[6] C. Wright Mills, *Sociological Imagination* (New York: Oxford University Press, 1959), p. 23.

[7] Sibley in his comments on graduate training in research emphasizes experience in research methods rather than firsthand acquaintance with the data. Elbridge Sibley, *The Education of Sociologists in the United States* (New York: Russell Sage Foundation, 1963).

[8] Caplow and McGee, *op. cit.,* p. 221.

[9] Mills, *op. cit.*

[10] The 1964 National Register of Sociologists showed that of 2,703 listed, 76 per cent were in academic positions as compared with 41 per cent of economists. Janice A. Hopper, "Sociologists in the 1964 National Register of Scientific and Technical Personnel," *The American Sociologist,* 1: 71-78 (Feb., 1966). It is difficult to determine whether or not this sample is a representative one.

[11] Everett C. Hughes, "Race Relations and the Sociological Imagination," *American Sociological Review,* 28: 879-91 (Dec., 1963).

[12] Edwin H. Sutherland, "Social Pathology," *American Journal of Sociology,* 50: 429-36 (May, 1945).

[13] Alvin W. Gouldner, "Explorations in Applied Social Science," in Alvin W. Gouldner and S. M. Miller, *Applied Sociology: Opportunities and Problems* (New York: The Free Press, 1965), pp. 9-10.

[14] Marshall B. Clinard, *Slums and Community Development: Experiments in Self-Help* (New York: The Free Press, 1966).

[15] S. M. Miller, "Prospects: The Applied Sociology of the Center-City," in Gouldner and Miller, *op. cit.,* p. 447.

[16] Gouldner and Miller, *op. cit.;* Donald W. Valdes and Dwight G. Bean, *Sociology in Use: Selected Readings for an Introductory Course* (New York: Macmillan, 1965); Arthur B. Shostak (ed.), *Sociology in Action* (Homewood, Ill.: The Dorsey Press, 1966).

[17] Paul F. Lazarsfeld, William H. Sewell, and H. Wilensky (eds.), *Uses of Sociology* (New York: Basic Books, Inc., 1966).

[18] Alfred R. Lindesmith, *The Addict and the Law* (Bloomington: University of Indiana Press, 1965).

PART TWO

Field Work Roles:
Contact, Entrance, and Rapport

CHAPTER 6

The "Outsider's" Role in Field Study

H. M. Trice

This report is interested in adding to the growing body of knowledge about the "outsider's" role that is thrust upon a field researcher in almost all situations. Kluckhohn,[1] fifteen years ago, stated that "the investigator is never able to shake off entirely his role of outsider, and I am in accord with those who maintain that it is not advisable for him to do so. Some exceedingly valuable information comes to the outsider simply because he is one." Later Merton states that, in connection with a study of a planned community, "informants will not hesitate to make certain private views known to a disinterested outside observer—views which would not be expressed were it thought that they would get back to management; the outsider has 'stranger' value."[2]

The effectiveness of this strategy was recently demonstrated to the present writer in what seemed to be an almost impossible research situation. The research question concerned what experiences and attitudes discriminated alcoholics who had successfully affiliated with Alcoholics Anonymous from those alcoholics who had been unable to affiliate with A.A.

In an effort to develop meaningful hypotheses as well as data to test them, a difficult twofold rapport problem arose. Many alcoholics who had been unable to affiliate with A.A. were available at the Mendota State Hospital in Madison, Wisconsin. This was near the University of Wisconsin campus and thus accessible to the research. Also nearby was a large A.A. clubhouse with sufficient membership to provide alcoholic subjects who had successfully affiliated with A.A. for at least a year, during which time they had attended meetings at least twice a month (the bulk attended at least once a week). Thus, there was immediately available a population of both affiliates and nonaffiliates. The problem was to become accepted by both those alcoholics who were hospitalized and those who had successfully arrested their chronic drinking through Alcoholics Anonymous.

Only after repeated failure at both the hospital and the A.A. clubhouse did the research value of being an "outsider" occur to the writer. The first rapport efforts at the hospital were aimed at including "all levels" in the

This chapter was originally published in *Sociology and Social Research*, 41: 27-32.

research so that it would be well accepted by everyone involved. Consequently, numerous contacts were developed and maintained with front-office people in the hospital, psychiatrists, and ward personnel. At the same time, incoming alcoholics were contacted on the in-take wards and later, informally, in kitchens, sculleries, and on the grounds. These contacts produced a series of arranged interviews with a sample of alcoholics in which a high resistance to the research by the alcoholics was encountered. The gist of opposition centered around the belief that the writer was a "nut-doctor professor from the University who would find out if you were crazy or not."

At the same time that this resistance was arising, tentative efforts to develop acceptance by the A.A. group were under way. These, too, encountered high resistance, but for other reasons. Previous and recent researchers had left them with the impression that research was "useless" and "unintelligible." They did not know the outcome of the tests and interviews to which they had responded and were in no mood to be "studied" further. The experience calls to mind the statement by Mann to the effect that "human relations mistakes made by researchers with [industrial groups] live long lives. It is not uncommon to hear of accounts of poorly conducted studies years after those studies occurred—and even in some cases—after some of the persons who participated have gone to other jobs."[3] This resistance was coupled with a tendency to equate any social scientist with psychiatry. Psychiatrists were widely disliked among the group and a researcher was readily identified as one. Thus the researcher was often greeted with the half-antagonistic question, Are you a psychiatrist? Together, these two attitudes served to stymie acceptance, and the formal request by the researcher for voluntary participation in the study was greeted with only sparse response by the A.A. members.

At this point the research was almost abandoned due to the resistance at both hospital and A.A. clubhouse. However, it was decided to consult the literature on the problem to determine if something might be done. Except for the writers previously mentioned, little of a systematic nature was discovered, and those who did discuss it lamented the absence of a recognition of the problem. Rogler concluded that "such a methodological problem weighs as heavily on researchers as does the creation of a carefully reasoned conceptual framework or thorough familiarity with formal quantitative methods." Merton observed that a "deep silence cloaks many of the concrete problems found in field work," while Sewell was of the opinion that "unfortunately there has been little discussion in the professional journals of the basic field techniques currently being used in the study of social-psychological behavior." Finally, Mann insisted that "the experiences of field-workers have not been systematically reported and as a result, a whole area of methodological skills—the human relations skills which go with the social researchers' role—has remained relatively uncodified."

The suggestions in the literature to make use of the outsider role appealed to the writer because of the obvious fact that he had been given such a role by the subjects and made to fill it. Furthermore, the problem of time seemed to rule out any extensive effort to become accepted by shaking off the outsider label. The effort to constructively use the label was aimed at endowing the role with a neutrality and divesting it of the threat which it seemed to contain. This was attempted in three ways: (1) by insisting that it was *they* who had the information and "expertness," not the researcher; that he was merely the outside media through which their experience and knowledge could be woven together; (2) by studying, as closely as possible, the communication system among both hospitalized, nonaffiliated alcoholics, and active A.A. members. A knowledge of this system would afford an opportunity to disseminate the neutrality of the outsider role; (3) overt behavior consistent with "outsideness," i.e., by declaring emphatically that the researcher was *not* a part of treatment staff of the hospital and by staying away from all contacts with treatment personnel.

Upon executing this "about-face" there appeared to be a decided change in the degree of response to the outsider role at both the hospital and A.A. clubhouse. The first step in attempting to put it into effect was an assessment of how definitions of situations were transmitted among alcoholics. Basic to this consideration was the in-group nature of the relationship between alcoholics in both situations. At the hospital they separated themselves out from the "mentals" and were exceptionally sensitive about their nonpsychotic rating. A close solidarity developed on the basis of this commonality, facilitating the rapid exchange of any "definition of situation." Numerous informal discussions with these hospitalized alcoholics indicated further that a highly favorable or highly unfavorable definition of a situation was transmitted among them, rarely a tempered assessment; they formulated a "black or white" reaction and rapidly spread it. Further, there appeared to be some persons in both situations who had a wide variety of contacts and performed the liaison function for the "black or white" assessments. Their wide contacts and outgoing personality traits made for rapid transmission within a tight-knit group. Finally, there was an overlap between the communication system of the hospitalized alcoholics and the active A.A. members. There were a few liaison persons who were active in both. After locating these persons it was possible to instill in the communication system the neutral "outsider" definition of the researcher. By emphasizing with these liaison persons the simple, unvarnished research fact that they were the source of data about alcoholism and affiliation with A.A., that it was they who had experienced it and it was they from whom the researcher had to gain his knowledge, it was possible to give the outsider role a synthesizing definition.

Simultaneously, a studied effort was made to avoid all contacts with the treatment staff of the hospital. It was assumed that much of the resistance in both quarters arose from the identification of the researcher with this staff. These persons were the target for the projected hostility of most alcoholics. At the A.A. group they often served the same scapegoat function. Consequently, the outsider role of the researcher was retained by avoiding, scrupulously, any unnecessary association with the hospital staff. In this manner, the researcher remained an outsider, but a neutral one who was dependent upon the alcoholics for information about a meaningful subject, i.e., A.A. "Inside" implications were avoided, since there were no observations of contacts with "inside" persons except those who had the data.

The degree of acceptance apparently rose rapidly following the inauguration of those measures, since volunteers for exploratory interviews came forward in both hospital and A.A. club. Conceivably this might have happened without such efforts, but the speed of the acceptance after they were made and the high resistance before such rapport efforts were made lead to the conclusion that the rapport effort described had some appreciable effect.

These experiences led to an appraisal of the outsider role as a general technique to be considered as a possible approach in any field research situation. Certain advantages and disadvantages of the technique are suggested by the experiences narrated above. First, it seems probable that such a role for the researcher reduces the amount of time necessary to develop acceptance. To abandon the outsider role means that the researcher must attempt to develop "inside" roles that are understandable to the various levels of an organization. This requires more time and effort, since the researcher must seek out, by trial and error means, a role that is compatible with the situation. Furthermore, as is well known, any formal organization is honeycombed with face-to-face informal groups and congeniality groupings. "Outsideness" is an advantage, since the researcher can maintain a neutrality relative to these groupings. If, on the other hand, he attempts to abandon his outside role, he unwittingly becomes identified with one of the clique formations and finds it quite difficult to maintain his acceptance with various levels. Second, this "outsideness" seems to stimulate more uninhibited response from data-bearers, since the "inside" threat of transmittal to others in the organization is less with an outsider. However, this advantage places an extraordinary burden on the researcher to maintain strict confidence regarding all information imparted. Intense attention to this point is required, since confidants will be prone to test the degree of confidence actually held by the researcher.

Third, the deliberate acceptance of the outsider role operates to reduce the development of too much rapport. As Miller[4] has pointed out, field researchers often develop more rapport than is necessary. As a consequence, the acceptance grows to the point that it hinders the study. He reports that he had developed such a close relationship with union leaders that "some penetrating lines of inquiry had to be dropped. . . . To continue close rapport and to pursue avenues of investigation which appeared antagonistic to the union leaders was impossible." It would seem that the outsider role would tend to reduce this tendency. Even though acceptance of the researcher in this outside role does develop, he is still an outsider, leaving him freer to design his question in whatever direction he desires than if he attempted to minimize his "outsideness."

Finally, the utilization of the "outsider" role allows for a maintenance of objectivity that would become weakened if roles other than this one were attempted. It is a maxim of rapport development that the researcher make certain he is not allowing himself to be labeled as a representative of any group or interest, i.e., that he remain impersonal. It seems that when the outsider role is given a neutral flavor, it can be a most effective vehicle for securing this objectivity. It is difficult for the researcher to become emotionally involved in the viewpoint of any particular group if he continues to view himself as someone apart from the organization in which his research is taking place.

Despite these possible advantages, specific difficulties arise in the use of the role. Many researchers are overconcerned with their acceptance and find it difficult to remain an outsider. There is a mild compulsion to "be accepted," to feel secure in the data-gathering process. Consequently, it is hard for the researcher to think of remaining "outside." Especially is this the case if the researcher has been relatively unaware of the acceptance problem, only to be rudely awakened by intense resistance to him. The researcher with this experience is more apt to be oversensitive about acceptance and find it difficult to think of remaining an outsider during the research. If we add to this the fact that initially the outsider role will be interpreted by subjects as a possible threat of some kind, a compound disadvantage arises. It appears necessary to divest the role of this threat definition, at the same time replacing it with a neutrality definition. It is probable that this cannot always be done, and, even if it is accomplished, the researcher will not be aware of whether or not he has made the alteration. In short, the threat of an outsider may remain as the definition of the researcher's role, leaving him as stymied as before.

Further, if the outsider role limits the degree of acceptance, as has been observed, the researcher cannot define hypotheses in as sharp a manner as he could if he developed a more intense acceptance. He cannot allow the hypotheses concerning a question to grow from his knowledge of a field situation, since his outside role, regardless of how well developed it may be, hampers him in getting an intimate contact with the phenomenon involved. This may also lead to a suppression of vital data on the part of informants; they may partially respond but hold back attitudes, etc., that might be identified by the researcher if he were not in the outsider role.

Despite the various pros and cons in the situation, it seems possible to conclude that the use of the outsider role as a means of developing acceptance in the research situation is a technique to be considered by the field researcher. He will probably discover that the role is given him by the data-bearers and that it is more effective to turn this role assignment to his advantage than to try to remove it from his research activities.

NOTES

[1] Florence Kluckhohn, "The Participant Observer Technique in Small Communities," *American Journal of Sociology,* 46: 331-43.

[2] Robert K. Merton, "Selected Problems of Field Work in a Planned Community," *American Sociological Review,* 12: 304-12.

[3] Floyd C. Mann, "Human Relations Skills in Social Research," *Human Relations,* 4: 341ff.

[4] S. M. Miller, "The Participant Observer," *American Sociological Review,* 17: 97-99.

CHAPTER 7

Getting Individuals to Give
Information to the Outsider

Fred H. Blum

This paper deals with experience gained in the course of an action-research project which has been under way in Austin, Minnesota since 1948, at George A. Hormel & Company. The workers are organized in Local 9 of the United Packinghouse Workers of America, C.I.O. The objective of the project is to understand the ways in which these workers are related to the industrial and social process and to explore ways and means of establishing the kind of "inner" and "outer" relatedness which will allow them to develop their individual potentialities to the greatest extent. During the first two years field work was mainly concerned with getting acquainted and interviewing. Workers, the supervisory staff, management, and union officials were interviewed. During the third year group discussions with the workers and an experimental testing program were added.

Among the manifold questions which such an action-research project raises, this paper is concerned with two interrelated problems: (1) How can the social researcher, as an outsider, get valid data? (2) How can such data be obtained within a context of mutual understanding and willingness to collaborate in sharing information in a real social situation? These two problems will be explored in regard to information obtained from a sample of workers. We will focus mostly on the researcher's relationship to the workers. These issues also apply to some degree in relations with the supervisory staff, management and union officials.

ESTABLISHING A GOOD HUMAN CONTACT

The first problem is to establish some human contact with the people who become part of an action-research project. Since I was not only an outsider but a total stranger, it seemed to me the best way to get acquainted with the workers was to share their work in the factory. I used the only two contacts

This chapter was originally published by the Society for the Psychological Study of Social Issues, in *Journal of Social Issues*, 8: 35-42.

which I had in the community, a letter of introduction to the Personnel Director of the Company and to the President of the Union, to get permission to work in the plant. This permission was granted in a generous and most helpful manner. I could work wherever I wanted, as long as I wanted. Or I could just go in the plant and talk to the people. First I worked like any worker in a gang, staying about a week or two in each gang. After several months I worked only irregularly, relieving some worker or helping him as long as I felt it to be necessary or desirable. At times I only visited the plant and talked to people while they worked, or while we ate in the cafeteria.

INTERPRETING THE PROJECT

The research design was based on the idea that the most valuable information could be obtained from a relatively small group of workers who were to be sufficiently involved to become active participants in the project. Therefore the project was presented to them from the very beginning as a common undertaking in which they played as important a role as the researcher.

Sampling procedures were adapted to these principles. Instead of discovering typical attitudes through extensive sampling, they were to be discovered by intensive study of the interrelationship of the personality, attitudes, and social structures of a small group of participants. A one percent sample, stratified according to department, sex and age, was selected. Particular individuals who fitted this predetermined sample were selected by personal contact with the workers in the plant. Usually I worked in the department long enough to get acquainted with as many workers as the sample required. The first worker who fitted into the sample was asked to cooperate in the project. Eighty percent of the workers accepted, twenty percent declined.

I was perfectly frank and direct in informing the workers why I worked in the plant, what my objectives were and what I conceived their contribution to be:

I am working here because I want to write a story about your life and your work, and I believe that it is important for me to share your work and life as much as possible because I want you to share your experiences with me. . . . I am neither working for the company nor for the union, though both know of my intentions and approve of them. . . . The story I am writing is really a condensation and unification of all the stories you and your fellow workers will tell me. . . . In a way you are writing the story. . . . You have a unique set-up here and it is important for everybody to know about it; workers in other plants may be helped if people hear about this place. . . .

Such an appeal for a genuine cooperation from somebody who was willing to meet the workers on an equal level was effective.

INFORMAL SOURCES OF DATA

To share work with the workers proved not only to be a most significant starting point to induce them to give information, it was in itself a most valuable source of information. Remarks made during work and conversations between workers give clues and insights which cannot be obtained otherwise. During work, the researcher meets the worker in a situation in which the worker is stronger than the researcher, a relationship unlikely to be repeated in the course of the regular research relationship.

Another contact with workers in the factory yielded significant information. I met many workers during the meals which I took regularly in the cafeteria. In order to get some "representative" impression of workers' feelings and thoughts, I sat every day at a different table, moving systematically through the cafeteria. Conversations on everyday events and rumors can easily be picked up in this manner. First I simply listened to what workers had to say. Once I was sufficiently aware of their interests and concerns, I raised questions about topics which I was thinking of covering in the interview schedules and on which I needed to test reactions.

The human bond established in the factory, so necessary for any genuine involvement and participation, was systematically developed by visits to the homes. Some people become key "informants." A word of caution should be added in regard to data thus obtained. They should not be accepted at face value but must be carefully screened in the light of the nature of the researcher's relationship to the people and the motives which prompt certain people to give him information and others not to do so. Such a screening requires a high degree of consciousness from the researcher. Besides insight into personal relationships, the researcher must know something about the position of the people in the community and in the factory, the role they play, and the reactions of other people to them. Only a careful evaluation of information in the light of these factors can indicate their real meaning and significance as research data.

THE INTERVIEW-CONVERSATION

Those workers who were asked to cooperate on the project by spending some time with me outside the plant, and who accepted this invitation, were given a choice whether they wanted to come to my apartment or talk to me in their home. Practically all preferred the latter, a choice which I welcomed because it gave me a good opportunity to meet the worker's family.

When I came to the house of a worker, I initiated an informal conversation in which I explained why I was going to ask them a series of specific questions:

Ideally we should just talk, but in order to write one story from all the stories I hear, I must have comparable stories. It would take too long to get such stories without following a definite schedule. That's why I am going to ask you a series of questions. . . . If you do not feel like answering some of these questions, feel free to tell me. . . . I have no desire to pry into personal matters but I have to ask you all kinds of things in order to get to know you. . . .

At the same time, the interviewee was assured strictest secrecy: "What you are going to tell me is as confidential as if you were to talk to your minister (priest) or doctor. It is absolutely confidential."

At the preliminary stages of the field work, interviews were administered in the usual fashion. But in the attempt to create a permissive atmosphere I found myself becoming involved in a conversation during which I told the interviewee several things out of my own life. This departure from the regular interview procedure led to a notable change in atmosphere and a greater facility in obtaining information. This was a chance observation which led to the systematic development of the interview-conversation.

The interview-conversation, as developed in this project, is a rather unique combination of interviewing and exchanging information—a procedure which can best be explained by following the course of an interview. The informal conversation which began as indicated above, continued in this manner:

There is nothing I am going to ask you that I am not willing to answer myself. . . . You are entitled to know as much about my life as I want to know about yours. After I have asked you a series of questions about your younger years, I will tell you on my own what I have been doing during these years. . . . Other things you may want to know about me you have to ask on your own initiative.

The interview schedule began like a life history. The first ten questions refer to the environment and activities during childhood, socio-economic background, schooling, number of brothers and sisters, etc. After the worker answered these questions, I gave him a brief sketch of my own life. In this manner a real give-and-take is substituted for a one-way flow of information.

In order to assess the nature and the amount of the information received, it is important to know that the interview schedule covered such varied aspects as: relationship to fellow-workers, to the supervisory staff; perception of management; the meaning of work and leisure; attitudes toward the union and towards community affairs; the perception of society as well as participation in political matters; the role of religion; etc. Personal experiences, aspirations and needs were examined. The interview-conversation lasted from four to 14 hours with an average length of six hours.

The interview schedule was too long to be administered in one session. Therefore workers were asked, after the first three-hour session, to give another evening or afternoon. Only two out of 50 workers refused to continue the interview, one because he felt I was "really making a psychological study," the other because his wife did not want him to go on.

PROBLEMS OF POTENTIAL BIAS

What sources of potential bias are there in the technique of the interview-conversation? The interviewee may adjust his answers to those he believes the researcher to expect. He may be reticent in answering certain questions about which he assumes he has ideas very different from those of the interviewer. In order to avoid these dangers as much as possible, I limited the areas of mutual interchange of information to objective events, i.e. where I was born, where I went to school, etc. I did not volunteer my own ideas in regard to the work process and life in general. It is true that the workers sometimes asked me questions about controversial issues. And it is likely that some of my answers influenced the interviewee's response to similar or related questions which came up later in the interview. This, however, seems a much smaller risk than the bias which intrudes into interviews from conscious, or unconscious, reactions to the interviewer and to the questions asked. It is naive to assume that biases due to the personality of the interviewer and the nature of the questions asked could be avoided. Each interviewer is somehow stereotyped, and responded to accordingly. And each question evokes a certain emotional reaction which affects the interviewee's answers. By giving the interviewee a chance to ask questions, these factors are brought to the surface where the researcher can deal with them. The information given in an interview-conversation is, therefore, more easily studied for biases than the information given in the traditional type of interview. The questions asked will reveal to the researcher when the interviewee hesitated, when he had doubts about his answers, what answers may have been distorted, and what problems concern him most.

The nature and length of an interview-conversation raises another problem. It was found to be absolutely necessary to record on the spot whatever happened in an interview. I took notes all the time during the interview. I noted not only what the interviewee said, but also his behavior. Recording had a deterrent influence on some interviewee's willingness to give information. More than once a worker said, "but what I am telling you now is not for the record," implying or asking me directly not to write down what he said. Whether wire-recording would be less likely to evoke resistance than taking notes during an interview is a question which is unclear, and which is likely to depend on the nature of the particular interview situation.

Workers' remarks in regard to the "off-the-record" character of their statements raises the question as to what extent any of the information given in an interview can be considered to be more than a "for-the-record" statement. Even what may be called a good relationship from the point of view of the researcher has elements of mistrust and areas of defense. To get scientifically valid results, it seems better to take a rather pessimistic view of the data one secures and try to remedy it, rather than be overly optimistic and get trapped by the unavoidable pitfalls of interviewing.

CROSS-CHECKING AND VALIDATING INFORMATION

A first precaution is to construct the interview schedule in such a way that key issues are approached from different points of view. A well structured interview is likely to yield some time, often when least expected, the kind of information which gives a real understanding of attitudes. A long intensive interview is, by itself, a good way to get deeper insights rather than superficial, biased verbalizations. Indeed, it gives not only verbal responses but a whole behavior pattern. It is very difficult for an interviewee to "pretend" consistently for many hours of close contact. A well-trained and highly conscious interviewer will, therefore, get enough motivational clues, besides getting the kind of information which helps him to evaluate the data properly.

Valuable "off-the-record" information can be obtained by spending some time with the interviewee after the interviewee-conversation has been completed. At that time the interviewee is likely to "open up" and give new, useful information. More than once a worker commented on earlier questions or answers and said things which usually came as much as a surprise to the interviewer as they were to the interviewee.

PROBING FOR DEPTH

The skilled interviewer does not have to wait for the end of the interview to touch deeper levels. He may give a motivational interpretation to the interviewee and note his reaction. Though valuable information can be gained in this manner, this procedure has certain dangers which must be carefully met. The researcher may give a wrong interpretation and lose status and confidence. He may give a correct interpretation and arouse resistance or create a sympathetic identification. If personal problems are involved, the researcher may come too close to the role of the therapist. If social problems arise, his correct interpretation may give the interviewee the impression that he agrees, or it may lead to disappointments. In both cases the information received is vitiated. In order to avoid these pitfalls I have learned to abstain from stirring up "touchy" personal problems. And whenever I have given interpretations which implied value-judgments, I have made it perfectly clear that I ask this question only to get an understanding of the worker without expressing any agreement or disagreement with what has been said.

GROUP DISCUSSIONS

Problems of this kind, centering around the role of "taking a position" as a social scientist, become even more pronounced when group discussions are used to get information.

About one year after the field work had started, all those workers who had participated in interview conversations were called to a meeting in the city hall. This neutral place was chosen in preference to the union hall or company offices in order to stress the independent character of the research project. This meeting offered the first opportunity for the workers to get together as a group. Its purpose was to inform them about "what happened to the stories they told me." I gave them a non-technical but rather detailed description of the processing of the interviews, coding, etc. I asked for their participation in the interpretation and evaluation of the insights gained by the research and in the search to find means of changing the situation by making it more democratic. I suggested small group meetings, but left the size of the group and the number of meetings up to the workers. Questionnaires were distributed to find out what their feelings and ideas were.

As a result of this meeting and of the questionnaire, two groups were formed. One group met once a week, the other twice a month. These meetings took place in my apartment. They were open to all workers who had taken part in interview-conversations, as well as to their friends. They consisted of two hours of discussion followed by refreshments and informal conversations. These meetings, which took place for nearly a year, proved to be most valuable sources of information. The discussions were usually started by my reading some of my written material describing workers' attitudes towards some particular aspect of the work process. The workers' reactions to my analysis of the interview material were used to verify conclusions. Sometimes they led to certain reformulations or to further research. The group discussions were more than regular "feed-back" sessions. They were a preliminary step for a change experiment. But the information obtained in these sessions was of the greatest research significance. It touched deeper levels and gave insights not obtainable in interview-conversations. I believe that a development of group discussions into real group therapy will tap completely new sources of information for social research, besides becoming an important instrument for social change.

CONCLUSIONS

In concluding we may mention some general problems which arise whenever the process of information gathering touches deeper levels—in an interview-conversation or in group discussions. The basic problem is one of "coloring" of the communicated information by values, prejudices, likes and dislikes. This situation must be met individually; but there are certain general principles which must be emphasized. (1) The researcher must have the trust and confidence of the persons who give the information. (2) He must not only speak their language but he must have a human understanding and ability to penetrate a "world" different from his own. (3) He must be highly conscious of psychological dynamics.

These qualities are necessary preconditions for securing scientifically valid information. They are not easily acquired, but fortunately the researcher can in many ways benefit by the very fact of being an outsider. The outsider has to overcome distrust. But if he has given evidence that he does keep all information secret and is trusted as a human being he can get more information than an insider.

The ability to speak the language of the people who cooperate on an action-research project can best be obtained by sharing their life as much as possible. An outsider is at a disadvantage in this respect. But as far as his ability to understand different points of view is concerned, the outsider has many advantages. He is likely to have a wider experience with different personality types and various outlooks on life. And he is in a better position to maintain a certain "inner distance." It is important to realize that such an inner distance is as vital as the involvement of the researcher with the people. Unconscious reaction to the informant as a person or to his personal and social values vitiates the data. Frankness about values and clear-cut value positions also may invalidate the significance of information, if the situation is not properly met. But this is not likely to do as much damage as unconscious reactions, provided the researcher has a real understanding of different value positions, and provided he has enough psychological training to interpret and evaluate his material.

CHAPTER 8

Participant Observation As Employed in the Study of a Military Training Program

Mortimer A. Sullivan, Jr.
Stuart A. Queen
Ralph C. Patrick, Jr.

Until recently the Air Force included in its research and development planning an extensive social science program. This program, itself part of a larger and more elaborate organization devoted to the Air Force's personnel and training requirements, utilized in its studies classical experimental design, polling, the interview, and, occasionally, observation and the ethnographic or survey approach. There existed, however, certain aspects of the Air Force training situation which apparently could not adequately be understood through the use of these techniques. In particular, certain officers wished to gain a better notion of how basic and technical training were lived, understood, and felt by new airmen. Hence, after a year of preliminary study, a plan was drawn up and approved for the utilization of a participant-observer.[1]

The general purpose of the study was to gain insight into the motivations and attitudes of personnel (in training) as reflected in both their military and social behavior. Through such insight into airmen's own views and feelings it was hoped to find leads to new ways of reducing disciplinary problems (particularly AWOL), failures in the course of training, poor performance thereafter, and non-re-enlistment. To be sure, the Air Force had already studied these problems extensively and had already done something about them. There was no sense of abject failure, but rather an earnest desire to improve programs that had much to be said in their favor. Moreover, it was believed that observation, interviews, questionnaires, and the like, had been used to the point of diminishing returns, at least until some new leads might be turned up. Participant observation was therefore adopted for a pilot study in order to identify first, problems viewed by enlistees during basic and technical training, and second, new areas for research by other methods.

To accomplish this purpose it was decided that a research officer should "enlist" as a basic trainee. He would be a fullfledged member of the group

This chapter was originally published by the American Sociological Association in *American Sociological Review,* 23: 660–67.

under study, his identity, mission, and role as a researcher unknown to every one (except the investigators), even to his own commanding officer. This then became one of the few cases of real participant observation.

There were literally thousands of problems to overcome, not only in deciding how the study would be conducted, but also in determining how the participant-observer would be guided in his work, the things to be looked for or recorded if observed, the form reports should take, and how the data would be used after the study was completed. There were also less obvious difficulties arising from the mechanics involved and, of course, the problem of preparation for the role to be played by the participant-observer himself.

It was assumed that the recruit airman, having been drafted, enters the service with a structure of attitudes favorable to the service, or at least neutral to the Air Force and his place in it. There was evidence from previous research that during his service the airman's attitudes change, frequently turning against the Air Force. Thus the research problem posed was: What are the processes through which the recruit airman's attitudes toward the service and his place within it change, resulting often in behavior which is, from the organizational point of view, deviant?

The assumptions and frame of reference guiding the research were derived from general social science theory. The first guiding assumption was that membership in the American social system provides the airman with many predispositions toward nonconforming behavior in the armed forces, as well as predispositions toward conformity.[2] Second, we anticipated that there would be found patterns of behavior which might be called a sub-culture of the Air Force. We expected that this culture would include "unofficial" patterns different from the "official" expectations contained in the formal rules and regulations of the service, and that the recruit airman would acquire both the "unofficial" and the "official" patterns of the subculture.[3] Thirdly, we expected to find an "informal" social organization in addition to the formal organization imposed by Air Force Regulations. The recruit airman would be "socialized," presumably, during his training into the "informal" as well as the "formal" structure of the service. Finally, we hypothesized that certain aspects of the "unofficial" culture and the "informal" social structure of the Air Force would tend to increase the tendencies to non-conforming behavior already present in the airman. The method of participation observation would, we believed, be especially useful in revealing these patterns of "unofficial" culture and "informal" social structure which contribute to behavior which is, from the standpoint of the official Air Force, deviant.

PREPARATION FOR THE STUDY

The preliminary arrangements for the "enlistment" of the observer and the recording and transporting of data were well taken care of by high ranking Air

Force personnel. The provost marshal of the command for which the study was undertaken worked closely with those primarily concerned in providing the needed support and information, and the Air Force's social science agency which guided the study made available a capable member of its organization, a civilian sociologist, to oversee and coordinate the research.

Once the participant-observer was in the field the reporting burden fell primarily upon three men: the observer himself, and a sociologist and anthropologist who were available at a nearby university. The sociologist, in addition to research in urban culture, had conducted field work in the Cumberland mountains and undertaken a combination of research and administration in jails and prisons of California. The anthropologist had field experience among the Havasupai Indians and in a study of a South Carolina community. These men had been members of the Air Force in earlier days, the former in World War I and the latter as a master sergeant in World War II. The participant-observer, who had not undergone basic training before, was a twenty-six year old first lieutenant with undergraduate work in psychology and a year of graduate training. At the time of the study he was assigned as a research psychologist with the Air Force's personnel and training research organization. The personal compatability of the members of the "team" and their ability to realign their approaches to the problem were of major importance to the successful outcome of the study. The fact that each "team member" provided a distinctive perspective on the findings improved the chances of identifying useful data and interpreting them in ways that might be of value both to social scientists and to the Air Force. However, it decreased the probability that results could be fitted easily into any closed system or established school of thought.

Extensive requirements had to be met in order to make the study possible, including "enlistment," processing, assignment, and, finally, "discharge" of the participant-observer. Since the observer was to "enlist" under an assumed name, even his "existence" had to be verified. Such problems would probably have been insuperable were it not for the cooperation of key personnel in the highly structured military establishment.

The plan agreed upon was to have the participant-observer "enlist" in a northern city, undergo his first four weeks of basic training at an Air Force Base in the South, and attend a technical training school (an over-all time of four months). During the period in which the observer was in basic training, the problem of reporting was most difficult. Every minute of the trainee's waking time being allocated, it was necessary for hours to be taken from sleeping in order to write reports. Of equal importance, the observer's contacts with his associates were limited to a few visits by the Air Force's civilian sociologist and correspondence with the other team members. As a consequence, the observer was never certain whether his reports were adequate or whether he was "getting across" what he was observing.

Once the observer arrived at his technical training base he could meet with the other two team members. During the week, the observer took whatever notes he could, consolidating them each evening. On those weekends when he was able to leave the base, he transcribed his notes onto a dictating machine. Thereafter, he would meet, usually for eight to ten hours, with the other team members. Then the three researchers would discuss the preceding report, first as to what it meant itself, then as to how it fit into the overall picture as viewed at that time. Sometimes it was found that significant patterns of behavior could be agreed upon; at other times it was necessary to realign "team" thinking.

The team was very important to the participant-observer because it enabled him to keep the purpose of the study in sight. Aspects of the reports which were vague or which the observer mistakenly took for granted sometimes were cleared up during the weekend "conferences." At the same time, however, the conferences were difficult for the observer, because of the minor trauma experienced when he returned to the airman role.

In addition to the other team members, the provost marshal, and the Air Force's civilian sociologist, there were many individuals who contributed to the study. After the participant-observer left the South and arrived at the technical training base, he was told that an additional person had been informed of his presence and of his mission, a young chaplain who had had enlisted service in World War II and whose primary duty, in addition to ministerial responsibilities, was counseling newly arrived trainees. The chaplain contributed to the investigation not only through his familiarity with the training situation, but also by his personal interest in the problems of the observer. While the observer came to rely heavily upon the team for professional guidance whenever they met, he also depended upon the chaplain as his sole contact between meetings with the other team members.

The creation of a "new personality" for the observer was of some importance to the study. It would have been entirely possible for him to have "enlisted" and undergone training without disguising his name, age, or education. On the other hand, it appeared advantageous to provide the observer with an identity through which he might achieve a maximum of rapport with other trainees—most of whom, it was known, were under twenty years old and few of whom had any college education. Furthermore, a two-day meeting between the observer and William Foote Whyte and one of his "corner boys"[4] emphasized the value of prior knowledge of those who were to be observed.

For nine months before the beginning of the field study itself, the observer was coached in the ways of the adolescent sub-culture. A young airman was told the requirements of the study and given the job of creating a "new personality" for the observer. Dress, speech, and mannerism, as well as interests, attitudes, and general appearance were "corrected" by the observer's enthusiastic coach. On one occasion, the observer thought he had succeeded in meeting the requirements when he was told, "You look real tough, hey." But the coach quickly added, "You ain't supposed to look tough. You're supposed to look like you're *trying* to be tough, but you ain't supposed to be." So successful was the airman's tutoring that when the time for "enlistment" arrived, the recruiting sergeant (who did not know of the study) suggested that the observer not be accepted by the Air Force because by all appearances he was a juvenile delinquent. To make the observer's role further convincing, it was decided that his age would be reported as being nineteen instead of twenty-six. To accomplish this appearance, the observer underwent minor surgery and lost thirty-five pounds.

There was also the problem of providing the observer with an acceptable "cover" story. Here again, the "coach" was relied upon to suggest significant items which would help convince not only the other trainees but also the training personnel that the observer was genuine. The suggestions of the coach were painstakingly followed (even to the extent of using the name "Tom" which he said fit the observer). The following biographical "facts" were seemingly accepted and responded to by the other trainees. "Tom" was from a lower middle class, but potentially mobile, family. As a result of an automobile accident, in which Tom was driving, his father, a laborer who had started college but encountered "bad breaks," was killed. This left Tom's mother to support him (an only child). Tom wanted to quit high school but his mother persuaded him to get his diploma and tried to induce him to go to college. During an argument over this issue, Tom left home and went to Northern City from which he enlisted in the Air Force. Again the coach's advice was convincing. During an interview in the early stages of training, an Air Force neuro-psychologist identified the observer as having mild anxiety over "killing" his father, and suggested that he be reclassified.

In deliberately cultivating a second self the research observer was engaged in something superficially like intelligence work or espionage. But there was a very important difference in goal for, in this case, it was a general understanding of a significant sub-culture, the processes of its development and transmission to new recruits, and its effect on the official training program. It was not the indictment of anybody or the immediate change of anyone's behavior. In fact, the data were so safeguarded that they could not lead to disciplinary action against any of the men under study. Neither was the objective a general indictment or defense of the Air Force. It was simply to gather a body of previously unavailable information and to interpret it in a way that might be helpful both to the military and to social scientists.

A very important aspect of preparation for the field study, was the training of the observer for the job of reporting. On the one hand, there was very little detailed material on participant-observer reporting and, on the other, the observer had had no experience in field study. The former problem was considerably resolved by the meetings with Professor Whyte,[5] but the latter required many weeks of coordinated effort by the sociologist and anthropologist members of the team and the Air Force's civilian sociologist.

CONDUCT OF THE STUDY

As the study progressed, the observer felt that he had been well prepared for his job. Since there was a lag of only one week between the dictation of a report and discussion of it by the team, the observer could take quick advantage of comments, suggestions, and questions, all of which reassured the observer and lessened his uncertainty as to the adequacy of his reporting. The Air Force's civilian sociologist sat in with the team during several of its discussions and provided information on the progress of other aspects of the study.

The first month was the most hectic for the observer. Anyone familiar with military basic training will understand the extent to which the observer and his fellow airmen were caught up in a swirl of regimented activity. Whereas the observer had just undergone a nine month "prenatal" period of preparation for his new "life," the Air Force instructors undertook to assure him that he was "not a civilian any more . . . but in the Air Force." On the first day, the observer, in an attempt to demonstrate the "new personality" which he had worked so hard to develop, intentionally appeared to defy an order of an instructor. A short time later, the instructor told his men, "I have handled many hundreds of enlistees and I know my job. I have already spotted some of you that I'm going to have trouble with."

At first, when the training was roughest or when he was spoken to gruffly by an instructor, the observer attempted to reassure himself that he was really an Air Force officer. He even would say to himself, "If these people knew what my *real* rank was they'd certainly act differently toward me." Interestingly, this attitude was apparently shared by another trainee who told the observer, "Back home I was a big shot." It wasn't long, however, before the observer realized that it made no difference who he *really was* as long as those around him *thought* he was Tom, and that there was little consolation in "pretending" that he was anybody else. Just as the other trainees were legally bound by the training situation, so the participant-observer considered himself morally bound and he felt that there was little difference between their respective positions. With the passage of time, the observer "forgot" about his old self; there was only the ever-present note taking to remind him that he was not just another trainee. His role in the barracks brought him so closely in contact with the men and their problems that he sometimes lost perspective. Here, again, the team was important in reassuring the observer and helping him regain his objectivity.

Perhaps the most interesting phenomenon to the participant-observer was the ease with which he was able to carry out his role with the other trainees. The men not only accepted him and his cover story, but identified many aspects of his past as being similar to their own lives. The observer shared the sorrows and hopes of the other trainees and felt compelled to do his best out of loyalty to them. When the others learned of "tricks" by which to pass inspections or to give the appearance of doing a job which they had actually not done, the observer joined in and suffered no guilt for doing what he, as an officer, knew was "wrong." The observer is convinced that his complete integration into the trainees' sub-culture was essential for understanding and conveying the attitudes and problems which he reported. However, he also attaches importance to the professional guidance given by the other team members and the counsel and reassurance which they and the chaplain offered.

When the field study was completed, everyone who had been reading the reports felt that the effort had been successful; but this feeling had to be identified and codified. The reports were typed with a three inch margin so that the sociologist and anthropologist could make comments and point out significant items. This somewhat simplified the task of compiling key items, but it did not solve it. There remained the difficult job of reviewing each of the more than six hundred pages and listing those items which the team members thought most significant.

During the field study itself, the sociologist and anthropologist prepared memoranda pointing out critical aspects of the training environment with which they assumed their report would be concerned. This made it possible to develop categories or items which were believed to be sufficiently general (and significant) for consideration. Nevertheless, the three team members were faced with a mass of narrative and descriptive material, concrete, rich in detail, and vivid in language. For many weeks the team went over the items one by one. Because of their different training and experience and the unique requirements of this study, they found it necessary to develop a common language (common not only to them, but also to the people whose comments and views were expressed in the study). When it was agreed that the significant items had been identified, the sociologist and anthropologist prepared summaries of the seven stages into which they had divided the field study. The summaries were then sent to the Air Force sociologist who, together with the participant-observer, used them as the basis of their final report.

As indicated above, the "team" was able to identify many re-occurring items in the reports. Some of these were behavior patterns of trainees and instructors, others were attitudes toward military life. Since this paper concerns primarily the method by which the study was carried out, it will not be possible here (a further article is planned) to describe at any length the substantive results of the research. However, a brief general statement of the findings should be of value at this time.

SOME OF THE FINDINGS

As had been anticipated, the trainees' images of the Air Force and of themselves changed in the course of their experiences. In the strange world of basic training the men looked to their instructors, exclusively at first, for leadership and explanations of their day-by-day activities. Then, as the training took shape, as the trainees saw themselves becoming airmen, as they began to understand the structure of their environment, they learned how to meet the multitude of requirements with which they were faced. There then began an unending search for shortcuts, methods by which one job could be done more quickly so as to allow more time for doing a second, third, and fourth. In seeking shortcuts, the trainees learned that some things were never checked up on even though they were officially required, and others did not have to be done as long as the appearance of doing them was demonstrated. There were instances when it seemed that "the Air Force" *expected* the trainees to indulge in these "patterned evasions,"[6] and one who had learned the "trick" behind the requirement did not need to feel any guilt.

While in basic training patterned evasion was used almost exclusively as a means for keeping up with all the tasks required in the short time allowed, this was not the only benefit it could provide. After the trainees reached their technical training base, but before they were actually able to begin school (a period of about four weeks during which they were assigned to a "holding" squadron), one flight was able to make use of numerous evasions in order to win the highly competitive honor of best flight in the squadron, and with this honor went privileges. Although winning the title of "honor flight" required the men to out-work the other flights, the "out-working" also involved a certain amount of "out-foxing."

The trainees were naturally disappointed at having to wait several weeks after reaching their technical training base before actually starting school, and at having to perform a great deal of "KP" during that time, but they were probably more discouraged at finding that they were not yet members of the "real Air Force." Even after receiving their first stripe, the feeling that they were still basic trainees persisted. Once in technical school, the patterned evasions upon which they had come to depend had to be abandoned in many instances because the added requirement of attending classes made it necessary for the squadrons to function differently. There were still many of the original requirements in effect, but it was almost impossible to know which ones were "important" and which ones were not. Since the men were in what seemed to be an unstructured and fluctuating situation, they began to slip in meeting requirements. This resulted in periodic crackdowns, which themselves led to the renewed use of patterned evasions—this time, however, not for the purpose of winning "honor flight" or solely as a means of allowing time to get everything done (as in basic training), but rather as a technique for providing the men with more leisure time. They felt that their job was to do their best in technical school and that any time which they could save from their squadron (housekeeping) duties should be theirs to enjoy.

Certain men seemed to be able to cope with this problem better than others by virtue of their ability to separate the "testable" requirements from the "untestable" ones and to anticipate the crackdowns. Those who appeared to have rigid personalities never seemed to be able to structure the situation, nor to realize when they were spending their time on tasks which were never recognized. Such airmen, because of their inability to perceive subtle differences between situations, were most likely to get into trouble with both the official Air Force and the unofficial peer groups. The more adaptive airmen noticed that inspecting officers looked for certain things and not for others.

At four times during the field study, the men in the participant-observer's organizations were given a questionnaire which contained thirty-seven items intended to reflect the subject's attitudes toward aspects of their training and their image of the Air Force. The responses to these items, although often mysterious in themselves, were almost entirely explainable in terms of the field study reports. Significant increases were found in favorable responses given after the initial phase of basic training as compared with favorable responses given to the same items at the beginning of enlistment. While only an "educated guess" would suggest that this was due to the airmen's belief that "the worst was over," the field study demonstrated it. The highly consistent drop in favorable responses after technical training, as compared to responses before it, would probably have been unaccountable but for the mass of information which was available to describe the events of that period. The questionnaire, although inconclusive by itself, was of value to the study insofar as it confirmed in quantitative terms some of the findings of participant-observation research.

SIGNIFICANCE OF THE STUDY

Of course, a study of this type cannot, by itself, guarantee representativeness of samples nor afford rigorous testing of hypotheses. Its function seems to us to be that of supplementing other research procedures, turning up new leads for questioning, observation, and interpretation. The method of participant observation was adopted in this case only after responsible Air Force personnel believed they had obtained about all they could from general observation, questionnaires, and formal interviews. In addition, they suspected that airmen, like other human beings, could and did maintain "false fronts," often deceiving officers, researchers, and perhaps themselves. Here seemed to be a new approach that might probe beneath the surface in a revealing way. Now that the study has been completed, both responsible Air Force personnel and we ourselves believe that significant results were obtained.

Obviously no other study could duplicate our procedures in complete detail. But something of the sort could profitably be done, we believe, in the study of institutions such as prisons and hospitals. We suspect that heretofore most would-be participant-observers have been early "spotted" by the objects of study and thereby prevented from entering fully into the life of the group in question. This study has at least demonstrated that thorough-going participant observation is very difficult, but not impossible.

NOTES

1Participant observation is defined by Florence R. Kluckhohn as ". . . conscious and systematic sharing, insofar as circumstances permit, in the life-activities and, on occasion, in the interests and affects of a group of persons. Its purpose is to obtain data about behavior through direct contact and in terms of specific situations in which the distortion that results from the investigator's being an outside agent is reduced to a minimum." "The Participant-Observer Technique in Small Communities," *American Journal of Sociology*, 46 (November, 1940), 331.

2For some of the predispositions to non-conformity, see Talcott Parsons on youth culture, *Essays in Sociological Theory* (rev. ed.; Glencoe, Ill.: Free Press, 1954), pp. 91-93, 342-345; and Albert K. Cohen on the culture of the gang, *Delinquent Boys* (Glencoe, Ill.: Free Press, 1955), pp. 24-32.

3See John J. Honigmann, *Some Patterns of Bomb Squadron Culture*, Technical Report No. 9, Air Force Base Project (Chapel Hill, N.C.: Institute for Research in Social Science, n.d.).

4See William Foote Whyte, *Street Corner Society* (Chicago: University of Chicago Press, 1955).

5In addition to the meetings themselves, the participant-observer was considerably aided by reading Professor Whyte's account of his field study. For example:

"I had to balance familiarity with detachment or else no insights would have come. There were fallow periods when I seemed to be just marking time. Whenever life flowed so smoothly that I was taking it for granted, I had to try to get outside of my participating self and struggle again to explain the things that seemed obvious." *Ibid.*, p. 357.

6This useful concept is taken from Robin M. Williams, Jr., *American Society: A Sociological Interpretation* (New York: Knopf, 1952), pp. 357-366.

PART THREE

Collection of Data

CHAPTER 9

Interviewing Medical Students

Howard S. Becker

The values of any social group are an ideal which actual behavior may sometimes approximate but seldom fully embodies. To deal with the tension between ideal and reality conceptually, there are two possible polar attitudes toward values. Individuals may be idealistic, accepting the values warmly and wholeheartedly, feeling that everyone can and should live up to them and that they are both "right" and "practical." Or they may be cynical, conceiving the values as impossibly impractical and incapable of being lived up to; they may feel that anyone who accepts these values wholeheartedly deceives himself and that one must compromise in meeting the exigencies of daily life. The distinction, only one among many which might be made, is useful in a discussion of certain problems of which I have become aware in studying the social-psychological development of medical students.[1]

Probably most commonly, individuals feel both ways about the values of their group at the same time; or one way in some situations, the other way in others. In which of these moods are they likely to respond to the interviewer seeking sociological information? Or to turn attention to the interviewer himself: Which of these is he looking for in the people he talks to? Which kind of response is he concerned with eliciting?

Sociologists have had a penchant for the exposé since the days of muckraking. The interviewer is typically out to get "the real story" he conceives to be lying hidden beneath the platitudes of any group and is inclined to discount heavily any expressions of the "official" ideology. The search for the informal organization of the group reflects this, and Merton's dictum that sociology's distinctive contribution lies in the discovery and analysis of latent rather than manifest functions is a theoretical statement of this position.[2]

The interviewer must always remember that cynicism may underlie a perfunctory idealism. In many situations, interviewees perceive him as a potentially dangerous person and, fearing lest he discover secrets better kept from the outside world, resort to the "official line" in order to keep his inquisitive-

This chapter was originally published by the University of Chicago Press in *American Journal of Sociology*, 62: 199-201. Copyright © by the University of Chicago Press.

ness at bay in a polite way. The interviewer may circumvent such tactics by affecting cynicism himself, so that the interviewee is lulled into believing that the former accepts his own publicly disreputable view of things,[3] or by confronting him with the evidence of his own words or reported deeds which do not jibe with the views he has presented.[4] There may, perhaps, be other ways, for this area has not been well explored.

Convinced that idealistic talk is probably not sincere but merely a cover-up for less respectable cynicism, the interviewer strives to get beneath it to the "real thing." If he is using a schedule, he may be instructed or feel it necessary to use a "probe." An interview is frequently judged successful precisely to the degree that it elicits cynical rather than idealistic attitudes. A person interviewing married couples with an eye to assessing their adjustment would probably place less credence in an interview in which both partners insisted that theirs was the perfect marriage than he would in one in which he was told that "the honeymoon is over."

Important and justified as is the interviewer's preoccupation with the problem, it creates the possibility that he will either misinterpret idealism sincerely presented to him or, by his manner of questioning, fashion a role for himself in the interview that encourages cynicism while discouraging idealism. For the interviewer's manner and role can strongly affect what the interviewee chooses to tell him, as can the situation in which the interview is conducted.

In what follows I speak largely from my current experiences in interviewing medical students.

In interviewing medical students, the difficulty does not lie in eliciting cynical attitudes; such statements are likely to be made without much help from the interviewer. The real problem is quite different—that of making sure that one does not prevent the expression of more idealistic attitudes but helps the interviewee to say such things if he has them to say. Using the semicynical approach I have elsewhere described as useful in piercing the institutional idealism of schoolteachers,[5] in interviewing the students informally and casually in the midst of the student groups among whom I have done my participant observation, I failed to allow them much opportunity to give vent to their hidden personal idealism.

By being warm and permissive, by expressing idealistic notions one's self, and subtly encouraging their expression on the part of the student, one might well gather a set of data which would picture the student as wanting to "help humanity," uninterested in the financial rewards of medical practice, intrigued by the mysteries of science, bedeviled by doubts about his ability to make sound judgments in matters of life and death—a set of data, in short, which would draw heavily on this part of the student's repertoire of mixed emotions. If one saw students alone and was not with them as they went through their daily routine, he would be even more likely to get such an impression. The student cannot well express such thoughts to his fellows or in front of them, for the students are almost ritualistically cynical, and, more important perhaps, their attention is focused on immediate problems of studenthood rather than on problems which will be forced into immediate awareness only when, as young doctors, they assume full medical responsibility. By playing his role properly, the interviewer can help the student express this submerged part of his medical self and become a sounding board for his repressed better half.

As I began my field work, I fell into a relationship with the students which would have inhibited their expressing idealistic sentiments to me, even had I been operating with an "idealistic" frame of reference rather than the "realistic" one I in fact used. I was with them most of the time, attending classes with them, accompanying them on teaching rounds, standing by while they assisted at operations and in delivering babies, having lunch with them, playing pool and cards with them, and so on. This meant, in the first place, that I was with them mainly in larger groups where cynicism was the dominant language and idealism would have been laughed down; this fact colored more intimate and private situations. More subtly, in being around them so much, day after day, I was likely to see the inevitable compromises and violations of lofty ideals entailed by the student role. Could a student expect me to believe his statement that the patient's welfare should be a primary consideration for him (to take a hypothetical example) when he knew that I had seen him give less than his full time to his patients because of an impending examination?

My data give a quite different picture from that arrived at by our hypothetical "idealist" researcher. I finally became aware of the way I had been systematically underestimating the idealism of the men I was studying by finding evidences of it in my own field notes. Some men made almost continual implicit reference, in their comments about practicing physicians they had seen at work, to an extremely high and "impractical" standard of medical practice best typified by their clinical teachers. Others went to great lengths to acquire knowledge on specific topics required neither by their immediate practical interests as students nor by the more long-range material interests related to their medical futures. Particular patients seen on the hospital wards typified certain difficult dilemmas of medical idealism, and, faced with a concrete example, some students brought up their own heavily idealistic worries about what they might do if confronted with a similar dilemma when they became doctors.

Seeing this, I began deliberately encouraging the expression of such thoughts. I spent more time with students engaged in activities carried out alone, raising questions in a sympathetic fashion quite different from the manner I used in groups. I "kidded" them less, asked interestedly about topics in which they had an "impractical" interest, and so on. Not every student displayed strong "idealism"; a few, indeed, did not respond idealistically at all, no matter how hard I searched for it or what situations I attempted to search in. But I had now looked for it; if I missed it where it was in fact present, it was not because of aspects of my research role.

So, in the long run, I have both kinds of data on my interviewees. I have been fortunate in having long enough contact with them to get by another means the idealism I missed at first and so have ended with a picture of these men which includes both aspects of their selves. The technical moral to be drawn is perhaps that one might best assume that interviewees have both varieties of feelings about the values underlying the social relationships under study and be aware of and consciously manipulate those elements of role and situation which give promise of eliciting one sentiment or the other.

As always, the technical moral forces a theoretical moral as well. We may tend to assume too readily that our interviewees will be easily classified as "attitude types" and that they will be more or less consistent in their view of things germane to our study. It is, after all, such a theoretical assumption that accounts for the exposé, with its emphasis on uncovering the "real" attitudes, as well as for the opposite "Pollyanna" attitude, with its unquestioning belief that people are as good as they say they are. It may be more useful to start with the hypothesis that people may entertain each attitude, at one time or another, and let this notion inform a more flexible interviewing style.

NOTES

[1] This study is sponsored by Community Studies, Inc., of Kansas City, Missouri, and is being carried out at the University of Kansas Medical Center, to whose dean and staff we are indebted for their wholehearted co-operation. Professor Everett C. Hughes of the University of Chicago is director of the project.

[2] Robert K. Merton, *Social Theory and Social Structure* (Glencoe, Ill.: Free Press, 1949), p. 68.

[3] See Arnold M. Rose, "A Research Note on Interviewing," *American Journal of Sociology,* 51 (September, 1945), 143-44.

[4] See Howard S. Becker, "A Note on Interviewing Tactics," *Human Organization,* 12 (Winter, 1954), 31-32.

[5] *Ibid.*

CHAPTER 10

Initial Interaction of Newcomers in Alcoholics Anonymous: A Field Experiment in Class Symbols and Socialization

John F. Lofland
Robert A. Lejeune

This paper reports an exploratory field experiment on one aspect of one of the alcoholic therapy organizations, Alcoholics Anonymous. A.A. enjoys the reputation of being one of the more effective organizations in helping alcoholics arrest their sickness. Attention has naturally turned to the problem of why a larger number of alcoholics do not affiliate with A.A. (5,8). We are concerned with the sociological features of this problem and specifically with what features of the social structures of A.A. groups may facilitate or deter affiliation. Field observation in about half of the approximately seventy A.A. groups in the Manhattan Borough of New York City revealed that A.A. groups are quite heterogenous in their social class composition *across* groups but that *within* groups they are relatively homogeneous. This we took to be an important structural fact. It seems clear that members, to some extent, self-select themselves to groups of approximately their own social class level. However, beyond self-selection, we wondered on the one hand, if A.A. groups themselves differed by social class on their reception of new persons to A.A. and on the other hand if newcomers might not be received differentially depending on their own social class (6, pp. 39-40; 7, p. 115).

An alcoholic who is not in an institution may attend his first A.A. meeting in various ways. One of the more frequent ways is that he decides on his own, or through the advice of a friend, to try A.A. He enters his first meeting alone and without knowing anyone in the group or in A.A. We are concerned with this class of first contacts with A.A. and specifically with some of the properties of this phenomenon in large urban centers.

In an urban setting the objective social class ranks of actors have low visibility. In lieu of viewing the actual ranks which determine an actor's social

This chapter was originally published by the Society for the Study of Social Problems in *Social Problems,* 8: 102-11. The authors acknowledge the assistance of Morris Zelditch, Jr., Irving P. Gellman, Jerald T. Hage, and the students who took part in the experiment.

class, symbolic means of communicating social class occupancy develop. These social class symbols select for a given actor the social class that is to be imputed to another actor.[1] Alcoholics alone at their first A.A. meeting, where they know no one and before they have spoken to anyone, are in a situation where the "others" present must assign social class to them on the basis of a limited number of social class symbols, mainly those presented by the actor's clothes, postural behavior, grooming and ethnicity. Those social class symbols presented by one anonymous actor to another before they have spoken we shall call an actor's *presentation*. A.A. norms call on members to seek out those at meetings whom they perceive as newcomers. The decision by a member to approach a newcomer may well be, to a large extent, a function of the positive or negative evaluation by the members of the presentation of the newcomer. The latter's presentation may thus determine which newcomers become socialized into A.A. and which do not.

Newcomers, of course, have the option of initiating interaction with members, but most are probably not disposed to do so due to their unfamiliarity with A.A. and—if member accounts of their first meeting are at all general—because they come to their first meeting with feelings of fear and anxiety. We, therefore, assume that newcomers, though they may desire interaction with group members, are not likely to be the initiators of this interaction. On the basis of our field experience in A.A. we feel safe in saying that if there is to be interaction between members and newcomers at these first meetings, then in most cases the members must take the initiative.

The experiment reported below deals with three variables. Social class presentation of the group and social class presentation of the newcomer are the two independent variables and *initial socialization* of newcomers is the dependent variable. The experiment consisted in sending six male agents in different social class presentations to A.A. open meetings where they posed as alcoholic newcomers. We term the agent and group class level as "high" and "low" but by this we do not mean "high class" or "low class"; rather, that relative to one another the levels are high or low. Since the two independent variables are taken at two levels only, the experiment has four *conditions* (or treatments): 1. agents in low social class presentation attending low social class A.A. groups, 2. agents in low social class presentation attending high social class A.A. groups, 3. agents in high social class presentation attending low social class A.A. groups and 4. agents in high social class presentations attending high social class groups. The next section reports the methods of determining high and low A.A. groups, and is followed by a description of the content of the agents' treatments of the groups. Following these are the means of measuring initial socialization, the design employed to reduce extraneous variation, the results and a discussion of the results.

On the basis of the notion ubiquitous in sociology that actors of like ranks interact more than actors of unlike ranks, we, before undertaking the research, stated the general hypothesis that *if the newcomer and the A.A. group display similar social class presentations, then the initial socialization will be higher,* and conversely, *if the newcomer and the A.A. group display different social class presentations, then the initial socialization will be lower.*

RANKING THE GROUPS BY SOCIAL CLASS

Although we had reason to believe that A.A. groups in Manhattan were dispersed on social class composition, we wanted to be more precise and state more exactly the nature of these differences. During our field work we developed a series of direct observation indicators that appeared to specify, at least in part, the notion of social class as it is presented to the observer who has no more than simple observational knowledge. From these we built a weighted index, which is similar in its logical structure to Chapin's Living Room Scale (2). It should be made clear that the ranking of the groups was by the social class symbols they displayed. We assume that the symbols currently associated with specific social classes are not subject to such anomalous display (1, pp. 158-163), that any group's index score would have no correlation with the average objective class ranks of the people composing the group.

Our indicators fell into three main groups: 1. individual properties of A.A. group members (e.g., style of dress and grooming), 2. properties of the group's immediate action (e.g., amount of money in the collection plate and quantity and quality of food served after the meeting) and 3. properties of the meeting place (e.g., condition of floors and walls).

To help keep the sample homogeneous on variables other than social class, we decided to rank only those meetings that 1. started at 8:30 P.M., 2. were open meetings, 3. not in institutions, 4. were not discussion groups, 5. were 90 per cent or more "white" members. (There is racial self-segregation in A.A.), and 6. were attended by both sexes. In other words, we limited ourselves to what is known in A.A. as "typical A.A. meetings." At the time of the ranking, twenty-one groups met our specifications. We attended a meeting of each of the groups and independently scored them on the index. Apart from this, before calculating the score, we each gave the group an independent intuitive relative rank. No attempt was made in the intuitive ranking (or by the index) to assign the groups to social class categories, only to determine which groups stood higher or lower than others. As a further check, we asked an informant member of a Manhattan A.A. group to rank the groups in our sample by their social class. He was familiar with, and was able to rank, fourteen of the twenty-one groups. We found it interesting that the informant had never attended over half of the fourteen groups that he could confidently rank. We took this as an indication that specific groups have informal "statuses" in A.A. (reputations) with which he had become familiar as a result of being an A.A. member. He reported that some of these groups were referred to in A.A. as "snob groups," where piped music, showmanship and furs were the norm at the meetings, whereas other groups, often referred to as "real A.A.," were held in modest surroundings and were composed mostly of working and lower class members.

Five rankings of the meetings resulted. Table 1 presents the intercorrelations among the rankings.

The intercorrelations among the observers are all fairly high. The correlations with the informant are lower. Examination of the various rank orders reveals that the correlations are reduced by rather small rank shifts of the groups between the observers and the informants' ranks. The shifts are smallest at the extremes and larger for the ranks of the groups in the middle. Because of this, we took as our sample the six highest and the six lowest groups. There was no disagreement in delineating the extremes; the difference between the six highest and six lowest was quite striking. However, since we could not reliably or confidently order all of the groups *within* these extremes, they are treated as being simply *"high"* or *"low."*

THE MANIPULATED TREATMENTS: PRESENTATION AND ACTION

The manipulation we imposed upon the high and low groups consists in preparing the agents in certain presentations and having them perform in certain ways while they were in the meetings.

Presentation

It appears to us that there are four basic styles of male dress in contemporary urban society (1960), that these styles are, of course, seen in A.A., and that they are associated with certain broad social classes in U.S. society. To describe these styles exactly is a difficult and lengthy effort, but somehow most of us are able to discern them. The presentations that actors make are com-

Table 1. Intercorrelations among the Five Social Class Rankings
of A.A. Groups

| | Observer 1 | | Observer 2 | |
	Index	Intuitive	Index	Intuitive
Informant	.65*	.67*	.71*	.79*
Observer 1				
Index		.90	.86	.90
Intuitive			.83	.88
Observer 2				
Index				.89

All correlations computed by Kendall's Tau.
*Based on correlation of 14 groups; all others based on 21 groups.

posed of facts of so great a number and variety that delineation in terms of a few attributes is quite difficult.

We believe that each of the four types briefly described below are associated not only objectively but also perceptually in most people's inferences to social class from observing anonymous actors. Evidence of the perceptual association of types of actor presentation is outlined in Form and Stone (3).

Salient descriptive attributes of male presentation types:

I. *Upper-Middle and Upper Class:* well groomed, clean, latest style clothes (esp. suits and ties), subdued colored clothes, which are neatly pressed, of good quality, not worn and are of matching colors (using as criteria the present men's fashion advertisements).

II. *Lower-Middle Class:* less well groomed, clean, wearing suits and ties but of out-dated style, colors not so subdued, clothes showing some wear, fair to poor quality, less well pressed, articles of "clashing" colors.

III. *Working Class:* not so well groomed, clean, wash trousers, no suit coat (a waist jacket, usually) no ties, "clashing" colors.

IV. *Derelict:* poorly groomed, dirty, dirty wash pants, suit coat (usually out of style, worn, unpressed, dirty).

Since the Type IV presentation is confounded by the fact that occupants are usually older than any of our agents were, we choose to use the Type I and Type III presentations as the values on the variable of agent presentation. Type I is called the "high presentation" and Type III we call the "low presentation."

The agents themselves were all white male graduate students in sociology, primarily of upper-middle class origin and ranging in age from 24 to 34.

Action

Instructions for agent action at the meetings were of two kinds: what they were to do physically and what they were to say when interacting with a member.

Agents arrived alone at a meeting at 8:20. In the first week of a group's treatment they sat mid-way in the room in the center of a row of chairs on the right side. In the second week, they sat on the left side. They were carefully instructed not to initiate interaction with anyone and to sit through the meeting looking tense and uncomfortable. If they were contacted at any time they were serious and sincere, polite but not gracious. Following the end of the speaking, they went over to the literature table and browsed through the literature for five minutes. If no contact was made they went over to the main concentration of members where coffee was being served and stood around in the concentration for fifteen minutes. They did not take coffee or smoke during that time. If at the end of this period, there was no contact, they left the meeting. When contact was made, the agent was instructed to let his movement be directed by the member.

In connection with other work, we had field notes available on what went on in first contacts at A.A. meetings. From this we isolated the probes that the agents could expect when they were contacted. Our problem was, interestingly enough, not in passing the agents as alcoholic newcomers—this was more often than not assumed in interaction—but to give them *standard* responses that would not get them too involved with the members, but at the same time would not put off the members. The responses to probes on alcoholism, A.A. familiarity, where they lived, their marital status and their phone numbers were the same for all conditions. We made them as vague but as plausible as possible. The only item that changed was the occupation they gave if they were asked, which varied appropriately by high and low presentation. All agents used assumed "American" names. We role-played with the agents before their meetings to get them used to their status and familiarize them with their responses. In interaction, the burden of carrying the conversation forward was laid completely on the member. The agents were purposely bland, as one might expect in an alcoholic who is new to A.A.

MEASUREMENT

Three kinds of measurements were made on each visit to a group: 1. time spent in interaction with members, 2. number of persons in contact, and 3. interaction content.

Each agent was equipped with a cumulative pocket stop watch. He kept this in his pocket at the meeting and switched it on while someone was talking to him. The resulting figure was the group's total time in interaction with the agent in that trial (visit). The agent was instructed to consider himself in interaction when an individual was attending to him whether listening or talking or if he was part of a larger system (a dyad or larger in which actors addressed comments to him and/or to the group). If the conversation lulled but had the direct potential of resuming, he was to consider himself in interaction.

From the field notes of some twenty earlier observers in A.A., we developed a list of interaction content that appeared to be particularly relevant to the socialization of the newcomer. They were set up in dichotomous form so that the agent upon leaving the meeting could score whether each member said the item or not. A separate form was filled out for each member who interacted with the agent. In addition, other characteristics such as approximate age, sex and presentation type of interacting members were noted. The agents filled out the forms as soon as they left the meeting and arrived home. The next morning the forms and the qualitative characteristics of the visit were reviewed with one of us. Ideally, each agent would have carried a hidden recorder from which the content could have been scored more accurately and reviewed in detail. However, we found that this was not feasible.

THE DESIGN

To partial out the structural effects of group social class composition and agent presentation type, it was necessary to design the agents' visits to groups such that 1. meeting-specific variations (size, idiosyncratic members, etc.) apart from any effects of their social class composition, would not obscure the experimental manipulation and 2. agent-specific variations (age, physical features, personality, etc.) would not obscure the fact of their different presentations. In addition to these, the design had to be such that the possibility of the agent being seen in different presentations by the same members was minimized.

To reduce meeting-specific variation, each of the twelve meetings was treated (visited) with a high and a low agent. To reduce agent-specific factors each agent administered the four treatment conditions. On substantive grounds we decided that each agent should attend a meeting two weeks in a row, since he might not be recognized as a newcomer in the first visit or if he was, we could see how the members followed up contacts in the second visit. Time, economy and the possibility of the agent being seen by members in a different presentation led us to assign each of the six agents to four groups under each of the four conditions and to have him visit these four groups during two consecutive meetings, for a total of eight visits per agent. Thus each of the twelve groups was visited four times, twice (on consecutive weeks) by one low agent and twice by one high agent.

The experiment was executed in two two-week phases. In the first two weeks three of the agents administered high treatments and three low treatments. In the second two weeks they switched presentations. Also, in the first two weeks three of the low and three of the high groups received low treatments and the other three of the high and low groups received high treatments. In the second two weeks each group received the opposite treatment. The agents were rotated in this manner to help control for possible effects on agents due to the fact that they administered the high or low treatment first. Likewise, groups were allocated so that one half were first treated with high and one half with low to help control for any effect due to the order in which they were treated.

One visit by one agent in one presentation to one meeting is considered a trial; therefore, there are twelve replications (N = 48). The rotational patterns outlined above were set up formally; groups and agents were randomly assigned to them.

RESULTS

Before presenting the results we must specify more clearly our concept of socialization. If socialization is viewed in terms of the dimensions determining its effectiveness, and if we only consider the dimensions generic to A.A. groups, we may, for these purposes, specify one broad dimension determining effective socialization. Effective socialization into A.A. is defined as the newcomer maintaining relative sobriety and becoming active in some way in A.A. The dimension is a given A.A. group's *degree of activity directed toward linking the newcomer into the social system.* Amount and kind of activity are considered here simply as degree. At any point in time the dimension has a value. The unit used in speaking of the value of the dimension is one attendance by a newcomer to one meeting of an A.A. group. This value, which results from an attendance, we shall call an *activity outcome.*

We are concerned with *initial* activity outcomes. A reformulation of our hypothesis in these terms reads: If the newcomer and the A.A. group display similar (different) social class presentations, then higher (lower) initial activity outcomes will occur.

Our data are accurate on three indicators of the values of initial activity outcomes: 1. number of members interacting with the agent, 2. amount of time they spend in interaction and 3. amount of commitment they make to help the agent. The data trend on each of the three indicators, contrary to our expectations, does not support the hypothesis. As shown in Table 2, the agents interacted with 118 members[2] over the forty-eight trials,[3] of which sixty-four per cent were in the "incongruent status" conditions. The low agents in the low groups interacted with 24 per cent of the total members contacted and the high agents in the high groups had 12 per cent of the total. This relationship is significant by the X^2 test ($X^2 = 9.88$, $.01 > P > .001$). This, of course, could have been due to longer interactions in the congruent status conditions which would have precluded a large number of interactions. Table 3, which shows the total interaction times for each treatment condition,

Table 2. Percentage of A.A. Members Interacting with Agents in the Four Conditions*

	Relative Group Rank		
	Low	High	Total
Agent Presentation			
Low	24%	32%	56%
High	32%	12%	44%
Total	56%	44%	100% (118)

*$X^2 = 9.878$, $.01 > P > .001$

Table 3. Total Time A.A. Members Interacted with Agents
in the Four Conditions (in Minutes)*

Agent Presentation	LOW				HIGH					
Relative Group Rank	Low		High		Low		High		Total	
	Time	(%)	Time	(%)	Time	(%)	Time	(%)	Time	(%)
Time in interaction	97	(40)	155	(65)	115	(48)	42	(18)	409	(43)
Time not in interaction	143	(60)	85	(35)	125	(52)	198	(82)	551	(57)
Total time agents spent at meetings after speeches	240	(100)	240	(100)	240	(100)	240	(100)	960	(100)

*H = 6.36, .10 > P > .05 (Kruskal-Wallis Analysis of Variance by ranks of Group Interaction Times)

indicates that the relationship is the same as in Table 2, the number of members interacting. Table 3 shows the actual amount of time in interaction for all visits in each condition relative to possible amount of time in interaction. The incongruent status conditions have the higher proportion of time in interaction, but the difference between the high and low agents in the low groups is not great. The high agents in the low groups were in interaction 48 per cent of the time while the low agents in low groups were in interaction 40 per cent of the possible time. The most striking difference is between the agents in high and low presentation in the high meetings, where the low agents were in interaction 65 per cent of the possible time and the high agents 18 per cent of the possible time. The Kruskal-Wallis test on the ranks of the individual group's interaction times by treatment is not significant at the 5 per cent level (H = 6.36, .10 > p > .05). However, substantively, we judge differences of this magnitude to be important.

The interaction content between the members and the agents usually involved a number of the following topics: 1. giving information about: a. A.A., b. the members' way of working the program, c. their alcoholic backgrounds, and d. their non-A.A. statuses; 2. giving suggestions about: a. working the program, and b. the attitude the newcomer should take toward his alcoholism; and 3. seeking information about: a. the newcomer's familiarity with A.A., b. his alcoholic condition, and c. his non-A.A. statuses. On the content form, the number of times that most specific content items were reported as occurring in each condition was roughly proportional to the number of persons interacting in each condition. We had expected to do an analysis of the interaction content of the members by experimental condition **to** ascertain any class differences by group or agent presentation, but the N turned out to be small and the difficulties in measuring accuracy were such that we have little confidence in most of the differences.

Two of the items, on which accuracy was excellent due to their salience, were judged to be particularly important as indicators of initial activity outcomes. They were, the member giving the agent his phone number and inviting the agent out for coffee after meeting (agents politely declined). These are actions that commit members beyond the open meetings. On the basis of substantive knowledge of the norms of A.A., all members who gave phone numbers and/or asked the agent out for coffee are considered committed. Thirteen per cent of the total number of members committed themselves (Table 4).

The two presentations in the low groups and the high presentation in the high groups have about the same proportion of members committing themselves to the agents. Compared to approximately 7 per cent for these three conditions, the low agents in the high groups had 24 per cent of the members commit themselves. Although the relationship is the same as on the other measures, the difference is not statistically significant at the five per cent level by the X^2 test ($X^2 = 6.09$, $.20 > P > .10$).

Overall, the data indicate consistent differences in the initial activity outcomes of A.A. groups as a function of the social class level of the group and the class level of the newcomers' presentations. Although any general statement must be very tentative, for the present, we state that initial activity outcomes seem to be highest where the A.A. group is relatively high and the newcomers relatively low in social class. The outcome differences that exist between the response of the low groups to high and low newcomers are very small, but consistently the outcomes for the high presentation newcomers are

Table 4. Commitment: Number of A.A. Members Inviting Agents
Out for Coffee or Giving a Phone Number
in the Four Conditions*

Agent Presentation	LOW				HIGH					
Relative Group Rank	Low		High		Low		High			
	No.	(%)	No.	(%)	No.	(%)	No.	(%)	Total	(%)
Members committed	2	(7)	9	(24)	3	(8)	1	(7)	15	(13)
Members not committed	26	(93)	29	(76)	35	(92)	13	(93)	103	(87)
Total members	28	(100)	38	(100)	38	(100)	14	(100)	118	(100)

*$X^2 = 6.09$, $.20 > P > .10$

higher. The lowest activity outcomes occurred in the high groups where the newcomer is in high presentation.

DISCUSSION

We offer a *post factum* explanation as to why our hypothesis was not supported. First, all newcomers who are incongruent with the class level of the groups they attend are physically more visible. We suspect that lower class newcomers do not normally appear very often in the high groups, so that visibility is especially high for them. Further, the high presentation newcomers in the high groups have low visibility, lower even then the low newcomers in the low groups, by virtue of the confounding effect of the larger size of high groups. Most of the high groups had attendances of over one hundred persons while most low groups had attendances well under one hundred.[4] Operating together, these factors probably reduce the initial activity outcomes for the high groups in relation to the high presentation newcomers. Secondly, for the case of the low presentation newcomers in the high groups, we would say that the normative obligation on A.A. members to help other alcoholics is evoked with greater strength here because of the tendency to associate lower class presentation with the more acute need to be helped. In addition, it could be that some subtle cues still existed in the agents' presentations that conveyed to the members in the high groups that the agents were of a higher social class origin. Upper-middle class training and many years of higher education is indeed difficult to completely cover. However, we do not doubt that the agents were perceived as being *presently* of a lower class. We understand that among members of high groups there is particular concern with reclaiming alcoholics who have fallen in class rank. Third, for the case of the high presentation newcomers in the low groups, we suspect that members who are of a lower class derive some sense of importance from introducing a member of a higher social class to A.A. A.A. presents a system reference where the lower class member can, at least initially, be of higher rank by virtue of his length of time in the system.

In closing, we must note that only initial activity outcomes were dealt with in this experiment. We do not know the values of activity outcomes over time for different types of meetings. It may be that activity outcomes are quite different in later stages. On the newcomers' side of the process, we do not know how given newcomers *react* to given activity outcomes. Trice reports (5) that high activity outcomes contribute to effective socialization, but it also may be true that some newcomers are alienated by high activity, and prefer to be left alone—at least initially. We pose these problems as topics for further research.

NOTES

[1] This formulation is taken from Goffman (4). Form and Stone (3) have conducted a study indicating that symbols are used to infer social class and discuss which symbols are used to infer which classes.

[2] Member interactions lasting less than one minute in which the verbal content was no more than just asking directions, an "excuse me" in a crowd, asking the time of day, etc., were considered irrelevant to activity outcomes and not counted.

[3] In the analysis, the 48 visits are considered independent trials. We had hoped to study member follow up in second visits, but each second visit turned out to be a first visit in terms of contacts. The agents usually in the second week did not see those present who contacted them in the first week. Those few that they did see did not seem to notice the agent.

[4] This fact was controlled for in comparing effect of preparation by the equal treatment of all groups by all presentations.

REFERENCES

1. Barber, Bernard. *Social Stratification* (New York: Harcourt Brace, 1957).

2. Chapin, F. Stuart. *The Measurement of Social Status* (Minneapolis: University of Minnesota Press, 1933).

3. Form, William H. and Stone, Gregory P. "Urbanism, Anonymity and Status Symbolism," *American Journal of Sociology* LXII (March, 1957), 504-514.

4. Goffman, Erving. "Symbols of Class Status," *British Journal of Sociology,* 2 (December, 1951), 294-304.

5. Trice, Harrison M. "The Process of Affiliation with Alcoholics Anonymous," *Quarterly Journal of Studies on Alcohol,* 18 (March, 1957), 39-54.

6. —————. "Alcoholism: Group Factors in Etiology and Cure," *Human Organization* 15 (Summer, 1957), 33-40.

7. —————. "Alcoholics Anonymous," *The Annals of the American Academy of Political and Social Science,* 315 (January, 1958), 108-116.

8. —————. "The Affiliation Motive and Readiness to Join Alcoholics Anonymous," *Quarterly Journal of Studies on Alcohol,* 20 (June, 1959), 313-320.

CHAPTER 11

Human Relations Skills in Social Research

Floyd C. Mann

INTRODUCTION

Researchers in the social sciences have increasingly assumed their scientific responsibility for setting out in detail the technical operations which they use in doing research. They have not, however, given equal attention to detailing the human relations skills they have developed to handle the concrete inter-personal and intergroup problems encountered in social research. While we have made studies of many social roles, we have done little towards the analysis of the role of the social researcher. The experiences of field-workers have not been systematically reported; and as a result a whole area of method-ological skills—the human relations skills which go with the social researcher's role—has remained relatively uncodified.[1]

This inadequate codification of the researcher's skills has not been too important until recently. For as long as little field research was done, an occasional failure to exercise good judgment in working with others did not markedly affect the total population of research situations available to social scientists. We could—in a statistical sense at least—afford to leave some of our research subjects feeling that they had been human guinea pigs for the last time. However, as more and more researchers leave the campus to study people in relatively small, meaningful, *closed* systems of social relationships, it becomes imperative to reduce to a minimum the number of times we leave a hostile research situation behind us. It must be remembered that the rights and privileges accompanying the social researcher role can be given or with-held by those whom we study depending upon how we act.

There are a number of situations where these human relations skills are not so important. Where the researcher and his subjects have the same scien-tific values—as in the case where the subjects are students—those studied may be asked to accept almost any kind of a guinea pig experience for the sake of science. Where the researcher is working with people in groups which have

This chapter was originally published by Plenum Publishing Company Limited, in *Human Relations,* 4: 341-54, and was read before the annual meeting of the American Sociological Society, September 5-7, 1951, in Chicago. The author acknowledges the assistance of Helen Metzner.

little psychological meaning for them—as in the case where he has created a group for experimentation and will use it only to accomplish his research goal—he does not have to be so concerned with the points made here. Just the opposite is true for researchers working with people in groups which have great importance to them—such as the work group where the person spends a large proportion of his total day. A few bad interviews with members of an industrial plant become common knowledge to a large number of employees in the plant in a short period of time. Moreover, human relations mistakes made by researchers with these groups live long lives. It is not uncommon to hear of accounts of poorly conducted studies years after those studies occurred—and even—in some cases—after most of the persons who participated have gone to other jobs. It appears that researchers can afford fewer mistakes when working in relatively small closed systems of relationships than when working with people in less meaningful systems of relationships.

Researchers need to develop a better understanding of the skills of working with other people, not only to gain and maintain access to research situations, but also to accomplish the objectives of a particular study. The researcher's own actions are as much a part of the study design as the research instruments used. He becomes a factor in the study situation when he enters it. If a researcher seeks to assess the factors in an on-going situation which would normally not include him, it becomes important that he use skills which will minimize the effect of his presence. It is necessary to use the same skills to minimize his presence if he wishes to do a change experiment. The researcher can afford to have only those factors he is trying to change operating in such an experiment, not his particular personality or behavior.

The objectives of this paper are:

1. to call attention to the importance of codifying this area of methodological skills,

2. to review some of the human relations skills which are already being used by researchers, and

3. to suggest several procedures by which training in these skills can be given to social scientists.

DEVELOPING AN UNDERSTANDING OF THE ROLE OF SOCIAL RESEARCHER

When the researcher plans to work with people who have little conception of what a social researcher does, it is necessary for him to build their understanding of this role. He must recognize that while his subjects may not have any real clear notion of the researcher role, they do have some bases on which to predict what he will be like and how he will act. These are generally centered around such characteristics as age, sex, race, perceived class, and other factors which have some cue stimulus value. The expectations that others receive from these cues may limit markedly what a researcher can do in the early phases of a project.

Two examples will make this clearer. When we first began a study in a large public utility, we found that the age role expectations of the people in that organization put us at a disadvantage. Few people in a public utility can expect to obtain positions of major responsibility until they have served long in the organization. It was disturbing to some, therefore, when they saw that a relatively young group was to have major responsibility for a company-wide study of human relations. This problem was compounded by the fact that one phase of the study was to deal with the ways in which the major functional units and the managers in charge of these units related their operations and themselves to one another. While these plant expectations concerning age and relative responsibility affected our acceptance by some people at the outset in the study, it was possible with the help of those whose age characteristics were more consistent with the role expectations of the plant to build personal acceptance over a period of time.

In a study of human relations in a laundry, Robert Bain (2) reports he learned near the end of his study that he had never completely established his role as a researcher with the women in the plant. But instead the women had at times placed him in what approached "a mother-son type of relationship." Since the women had had no experince with a social researcher, they had responded to him in role relationships which they did understand. Some of them looked upon him as an imaginary son they might have had going through college and whom they would have expected other mothers to help if they could.

While we have very little evidence from the literature that researchers have given much attention to the limitations which these role expectations have placed on their research role, it is probable that we frequently take these expectations into account implicitly in doing our research work. Our evaluations of the expectations of potential research subjects affect our own choice of studies, to what students or associates we give or withhold support for undertaking certain investigations, how we assign interviews, our use of language, the way we dress, etc.

The researcher role identification problem must indeed be great for some of the people with whom we work. There are numerous tell-tale phrases in our monographs which suggest the magnitude of this problem. West (16) points out that since he was living with the county agent who was a "government man," this led some people to believe that West was "investigating the WPA" or collecting information about "all the old crimes" in the county. And even after he had attempted to lessen the hostility to his work by paying for a full column description of his research intentions, the few people who did seek him out brought "old objects and documents" and asked just what he was trying to find out. Since people frequently fear or are at least suspicious of others whom they cannot place in an occupational niche with which they are familiar, it is clear that we need to learn how to develop quickly in others an understanding of the job of social researcher. We need to do much more at the beginning of any research project than we have in the past towards clarifying what our research values and objectives are, how we plan to go about getting our data, and how long the study will take.

DEVELOPING AN UNDERSTANDING OF THE OBJECTIVES AND VALUES OF RESEARCH

Some of the most important skills that the researcher must develop in dealing with other people have their origin in the researcher role requirement of objectivity. A researcher must learn how to maintain balanced relationships with all groups in his research situation. He can, and should of course, use certain institutional supports to obtain and keep an objective role as a researcher. Being associated with an academic institution and working towards the completion of a program of research which will for its ultimate success be dependent upon the support of all groups are two such obvious supports. These, however, are not enough. The researcher himself must see that he is not talking too frequently with one group, that he is not allowing himself to be tagged as management's boy, as labor's tool, or as a staff man in a running battle between the line and staff.

Moreover, it is the researcher's responsibility to develop in those who are cooperating with him an understanding of the meaning of objectivity in the research role. He should demonstrate through his behavior as well as words the meaning and the necessity of maintaining this role as impartial outsider. With experience the researcher can learn to recognize and use test situations, which one party or another has engineered as a test of his sincerity, to demonstrate by action what objectivity means. Some of the best writing which has been done concerning these skills has been by the Tavistock group and need only be referred to here (8).

It is not enough that the researcher develop in himself and others a deep understanding of the objectivity role he plays. He must also demonstrate his adherence to the values of "fair play" and respect for the other person. Much that goes on early in any researcher-client or researcher-subject relationship may be understood as an attempt by each party to find out what the values of the other are. This is accompanied by the implicit questions—Shall I trust this person? Is this a person who will misuse me in the interest of gaining his ends?

There are a number of specific ways by which the researcher can demonstrate his respect for the other person. He can, for example, be careful never to violate any anonymity and confidentiality pledges which he makes.

This means more than simply watching what he says to others. It means—if he is doing research in an industrial plant—that he will provide a location for his research team outside of the regular working space of the organization where they can talk freely about what they are hearing in interviews. He will caution his associates about talking of their work on elevators, in the halls, etc., and he will see that locks on cases of confidential materials and even waste paper baskets are policed at certain phases of a project.

PARTICIPATION AND COMMUNICATION—MEANS OF DEVELOPING UNDERSTANDING

There are also numbers of more general procedures open to the researcher to establish some understanding of the values and objectives of his work. Participation and involvement provide mechanisms by which the process of research may actually become cooperative, and they simultaneously present the maximum safeguards against either the researcher or the research subjects being used by one another or by a third party. The two-way flow of communication between social researcher and research subjects—which is inherent in any real attempt at participation—provides an important opportunity for both parties to make a thorough analysis of the problems of doing a particular study. The research subjects can do some testing of the fundamental aims of the researcher; the researcher can, through this testing, check whether or not he understood as well as he thought he had all of the implications of doing such research.

1. Involving Leaders

From the very beginning of a study the researcher must encourage participation and involvement. This starts with his initial contacts with the authority figures in the relevant social systems. With respect to these initial contacts Merton (10) has pointed out that we have long known that the most effective point of entry into a community is through the top levels of status, authority, and prestige. He cites the work of the Webbs and Malinowski as evidence of the first real understandings of this methodological fact.

The importance of involvement of the leaders is stressed by Whyte (17) in the following quotation:

"I found that in each group I met there was one man who directed the activities of his fellows and whose word was authority. Without his support, I was excluded from the group; with his support, I was accepted. Since he had to take the responsibility of vouching for me, I made a practice of talking with him quite frankly about the questions in which I was interested. When his friends questioned him, he knew much more about me than they did, and he was, therefore, in a position to reassure them."

Another example comes from West's work in which he pointed out that the final acceptance of his role as investigator-resident of Plainville came slowly and only after he had gained the cooperation of one particular man. He was a "politician" who had great ability in manipulating rumor and opinion. After this man become convinced of the value of West's work he vouched for West's "safety" as a repository of confidences and arranged numerous interviewing situations. West emphasized that this man through the same techniques he employed in any "political" manipulation, set rumor to working *for* West, rather than against him. Warner and Hunt (15) sought out a prominent and important local leader who helped them by introducing them to other civic leaders and friends.

These cases show the importance of involving people who have high status and authority in a community. The logic behind this action is clear. Researchers are normally not members of the groups which they want to study—they are seen as an "outsider" and, therefore, usually viewed with suspicion. They must, therefore, gain the acceptance of those who hold either formal or informal leadership positions within the community so that the formal and informal channels of communications can be set to working in the researcher's favor. We do not have evidence in the literature of many instances when the researcher openly by-passed the formal or informal leadership structure of the group which he proposed to study. We do know, however, from a Festinger, Cartwright study of rumor (5) that researchers attempting to change the level of participation in a housing project must be extremely careful of how the rise of new leaders is perceived by the old leaders of a community.

Research situations in which the social scientist is interested more often than not have more than one authority structure within them. In such instances it is necessary to devise procedures whereby the researcher obtains the cooperation of all groups, does not by-pass the leadership of any group, or become identified with any one group. When confronted with this type of problem in attempting to initiate a research project in a planned housing community having two hierarchies of authority, Merton (10) employed "a procedure of dual entry." This meant that the research team "made virtually simultaneous but independent contacts on the two levels of management and residents."

This account of a dual entry portrays well the type of problem that we, as researchers, must learn to face and master if we wish to study problems of overlapping memberships or controversial issues where the lines of adherence are sharply drawn. Merton used this particular procedure to establish his research team with independent status—fully dissociated from management.

The researcher should avoid finding himself in the position of having a member of one faction question him as to whether he has seen members of the other faction. He should state his interest in developing an objective status and openly declare whom he has seen and is planning to see. There are two important reasons for taking this position: 1. the channels of informal communication in small communities are very complicated and occasionally amazingly efficient at getting the right bit of information to the right place for the basis of an exceedingly embarrassing question, 2. and more importantly, if the members of one faction see that you are willing to work with them to engineer a particular objective, they cannot but later question your motives and wonder if they are being engineered.

Researchers doing studies in industrial settings are continually confronted with the problem of how to gain the confidence of several factions which are more or less suspicious of one another: management and union, line and staff, supervisors and employees, etc. In doing our studies in the Human Relations Program of the Survey Research Center we have come to use not only the procedure of multiple entry, but attempt through a research committee structure which we create in each situation to broaden the range of participation to include representatives of all populations which are likely to be interested and affected by the study. We make it clear to both management and the union, for example, that we will not be interested in doing a particular piece of research unless both agree not only to give us their support but to work with us actively on the project. Specifically this active participation ranges from help in framing certain research objectives and planning for the utilization of the research findings to the time consuming tasks of question construction and phrasing. Participation in research by the representatives of the different factions appears to be one of the best devices available to the social researcher to assure himself that he will take and retain the proper objectivity role.

2. Involving All Members of Research Situation

The researcher must not only gain acceptance of the formal and informal leaders of the relevant power structures in which he wishes to work for, as Gardiner and Whyte (6) have suggested, such sanction in itself is not enough to assure general acceptance of the researcher and his project. In a large hierarchical organization, for example, the researcher must involve all people who are likely to be affected by the study. In our study in a public utility we started this process by informing people of the study and its objectives from almost the very beginning, and we also attempted to involve in the planning of the study all the people who would have the responsibility for making use of the findings months later. This was done in different ways and with varying intensity at different levels in the organization. Lower levels of management and the employees were initially less intensively involved in this process of communication, and we relied on the organization's regular channels of information. We found subsequently that we could not assume that because the top hierarchy knew all about the study that they would make this information available to others. Information that was passed along was selected and distorted to fit the understanding of those at each key point in the communication system. This experience probably means that the researcher cannot afford to rely on others to communicate correctly certain essential facts about his work. He, himself, must assume the responsibility for getting the major points about the study objectives across to people at all levels. This he can do by making sure that these key facts are written and in the hands of those delegated to help in this communication process. If it is feasible, the researcher should go further than this and provide the research subjects with a chance to talk out any doubts they may have as to the study. But this latter is, of course, often difficult to arrange.

A partial answer to the problem of inadequate communication about a study through the formal channels is to use the informal channels of communication. During our first two weeks of interviewing we attempted to use the grapevines to establish full understanding and increase confidence in our research project: We assumed that each person who showed up for an interview would not only have some questions of his own about the study but that he would also have questions suggested by several of his close associates with whom he ate, shared rides and company gossip. Our interviewing schedules were arranged during the first two weeks, therefore, to allow each interviewer to seek out and answer fully any questions or reservations that the interviewee had. Our interviewers not only reviewed briefly the purpose of the interview, but what the over-all study objectives were, who we were, and how the data were going to be processed and analyzed. He encouraged the interviewee to raise any questions which he might have. This cost us some ten to twenty minutes at the beginning of each interview for about two weeks, but we felt it gave us a chance to get the informal channels of communication working for us within the company.

Another way of increasing the understanding of research goals and objectives is to work research problems through jointly. The researcher who enlists the help of others is putting himself in a different psychological relationship than one who is certain he knows how others feel and barges ahead without seeking advice. Whyte (17) learned that it was not only important to help members of the gang he was studying as individuals, but that it was even more important to his social position to *ask them* to help him. Bain's experience in attempting to collect sociometric information (2) likewise suggests the value of seeking help in obtaining emotionally loaded data. As a part of his measurements Bain wanted to obtain interpersonal choice and rejection data from workers. When he found it would be difficult to obtain this information from workers during working hours, he asked permission of a second group to interview them personally in their homes to secure information of a more confidential nature than he had gathered previously. A rumor immediately sprang up that it was now all clear why he had been in the plant, that he was merely trying to find out who likes and dislikes each other. When through a chance meeting with the person who was spreading the rumor, he explained why he needed the data, that he had probably made a mistake in the way he had introduced that phase of the study, *and asked for advice,* the whole problem disappeared. Other researchers could undoubtedly cite numerous cases where putting the other person in the role of expert has helped to clear and smooth the way long after the situation seemed past repair. The implicit recognition of another person's status by seeking his help has long been known to be important in getting along with people.

The researcher must not only be concerned with establishing an understanding of his role at the beginning of any study, but he must be continually concerned with maintaining his understanding. He will need to be continually interpreting for others how changes in the situation are or are not related to his behavior. Since it is frequently necessary to stay in a research situation a relatively long time, researchers must remember that as the situation changes —even though they may have nothing to do with these changes—this may affect the way others now look at them. Therefore, the role of the researcher is a dynamic one. The researcher who like Robert Bain (2) was working in a university laundry when the management began initiating a lay-off does not need to be reminded of this. Researchers should be constantly aware of the fact that they are potential scapegoats, and must guard against being autistically perceived and reacted to.

Gardiner and Whyte (6) tell of an incident which underlies the importance of the researcher maintaining interaction with both management and workers. They suggest that it may be necessary to continue to consult with and keep getting "the true picture" from those with whom the researcher has his first plant contact long past the time when the researcher may feel it is necessary for his own understanding of the situation.

In the case that Gardiner and Whyte cite, the researcher was brought into the plant with the support of a plant manager. The first interviews were with him, he assumed the responsibility for getting the researcher properly introduced at the next lower level, etc. As the researcher carried the interviewing to successively lower levels during a two-month period, he noticed a decided change in the manager's attitude toward him.

Since the early contacts with the manager had been frequent and informal, the researcher probably felt no need to check back occasionally to see how the manager was perceiving the way in which the research operation was unfolding. The manager, however, had been on the job only five months and knew that some supervisors and workers were strongly hostile to him. Gardiner and Whyte point out that "subsequent interviews showed he felt the researcher was not interviewing the 'right' people, that he was not getting 'the true picture' of the situation." The researcher's presence was, therefore, no longer welcome, as far as the manager was concerned. Gardiner and Whyte conclude by noting "Had the manager been consulted regularly for advice on people to be interviewed and for his statement of 'the true picture' it seems unlikely that this estrangement would have developed."

We have also found that the general tone of interpersonal relations between the researcher and those with whom he is working becomes increasingly better with each opportunity for two-way communications. The more frequent the contacts the more chance there is to share experiences and work out problems together. It must be realized that between contacts non-shared experiences may reduce the level of mutual understanding. The drop is seldom so great that the researcher must start all over again to build the relationship. But it is equally seldom that the researcher can start off on the same level with the person as when he last talked to him. The researcher interested in maintaining a social research laboratory in which he has a maximum degree of freedom to do research may find the time investment in frequent interaction heavy. It is, however, a necessary cost in doing research on people in social organizations which have real psychological relevance for them. We also feel that the time cost involved in re-establishing relationships after a long lapse of contact is more costly than small regular investments in the maintenance of good relations.

Participation, involvement, and communication are important human relations skills for the researcher. Joint working relationships with those who are studied frequently increase the quality of research and simultaneously the probability that socially beneficial action will grow out of the research. The action research literature (3, 9, 13) shows clearly the importance of using joint participation in research as a means of insuring that survey findings will be employed in making changes. Not enough recognition, however, has been given to the value of participation in research which is not designed to lead into a particular action program.

DEVELOPING AN UNDERSTANDING OF RESEARCH INSTRUMENTS

There are a number of specific techniques that a researcher can employ to develop an understanding in others of how a social scientist goes about his work and what instruments he uses. The anthropologists have emphasized the usefulness of map making in this respect. "Making a map" is a recognized job that people understand and accept. In an industrial setting, for example, it provides the researcher with an opportunity to establish relationships and talk with the workers about the study while doing something they understand. Map making is often a highly productive activity in that it is simultaneously useful for building understanding and acceptance of the social researcher and in providing needed ecological information on work positions, processes, and work flow. Perhaps equally important, it provides an inexperienced researcher with an activity which allows him to increase or decrease the number of researcher-subject contacts as he feels necessary to gain confidence in his own abilities to establish working relations in his new role. In reporting on human relations problems in observing behavior of boys and girls at summer camps, Polansky *et al.* (8) state they attempted to handle some of the fears the children might have of people in the unknown role of observer by having the observer "working" with observation instruments as the children arrived at the camp. James West (6) reports that *as* he interviewed his first informant in the afternoons under a shady tree in the yard "passers-by gradually got accustomed to the fact that I sometimes worked with a notebook." We have found it useful in our studies to inform supervisors and employees as to how we work by having pictures showing the different phases of a research project —questionnaire construction, administration, interviewing, machine analysis, etc.—published in the company and employee organizations papers. These pictures are usually accompanied by sample questionnaire items and short explanations of what a social research team does.

THE "COST" OF USING HUMAN RELATIONS SKILLS

While most social scientists will agree that participation, involvement, and communication are important, many would want to question whether the time costs involved are worth while. These human relations skills need to be used not only to gain and maintain access to research situations but to get data of maximum validity. Much that has been emphasized in this paper pertains to the larger problem of validity. Researchers frequently have some choice about the extent to which they adhere to the requirements of rigorous design. They can either conceal the objectives of the study from those with whom they work, or they can involve their subjects in the research. Allowing subjects to have no knowledge of study objectives may result in taking heavy risks that subjects will be suspicious and, therefore, more likely to give "safe" answers from their point of view. Subjects who are aware of the researcher's goals will be more likely to say how they actually see the situation. There is no final answer here, but it should be noted that under some conditions the use of human relations skills may be cheap in terms of study validity.

THE TRAINING OF HUMAN RELATIONS SKILLS

The majority of the researchers who attempt to do research today have good training in theoretical conceptualization and technical methods. They have not, however, been given much training, at the action level, in human relations skills. The preceding sections indicate that we already know quite a bit about what works and what will not work in this area. This suggests that we should initiate more formal training in this area than we have had in the past.

There are numbers of different procedures which might be used for the teaching of these skills. A combination of the following three would be exceedingly powerful: 1. actual field experience, 2. use of case-book materials, and 3. role-playing.

Researchers acquire judgment and understanding in the use of these human relations skills mainly from experience. There is, of course, no substitute for actual field experience and the interpersonal and intergroup problems which accompany these operations. It is, therefore, imperative that every senior researcher provide opportunities for his assistants to participate in the analysis and attempted solutions of these problems as often as possible. Much more training can be done in this area than has been up to now. Senior researchers all too frequently operate on the assumption that there are two distinct classes of problems associated with a project—those which are technical and can be delegated to assistants, and those which are "going to be difficult human relations problems" and are of concern only to him as project administrator. Thinking such as this of course results in subordinates getting a maximum of technical skills training and a minimum of the human relations skills training required for the social researcher role.

While there is no substitute for real experience, it is obvious that a collection of the human relations problems encountered by researchers in the past would go a long way toward equipping students and fellow researchers to handle human relations problems as they arise. We need to build up a professional literature on these problems. Aberle (1) has suggested the development of such "Case Books." Relatively little has been written in this area, and as he points out for every experience written up, however briefly, there are many more buried in the minds of those who have had these kinds of experiences.

The failure to record these kinds of experiences constitutes a real loss. The skills which have been worked out by the researchers who have encountered some of these problems before us have remained unique to the individuals concerned or to a small group of close students.

We seldom write about our successes in this area perhaps because we feel these represent things that all social scientists just naturally know. And of course we never write about failures, unless we are ingenious enough to turn a particular failure into a success by shifting the objective of a study. Few of us have the security and professional status to allow us to admit such mistakes, even though we recognize that the reporting of such failures might serve a useful function in preventing a repetition of such a misstep by some future researchers.

Aberle's suggestion that cases should be collected and published in the form of a case book appears to be an excellent way around the several facets of the anonymity problem. Stripping the cases of their research situation identification, will reduce the likelihood of violating professional confidences, destroying carefully built relationships within research groups and between research groups and the research participants.

Case material such as this would easily lead to something other than orthodox classroom teaching of these skills. The students could not only have all the advantages of the "case method" of instruction—in which the student is constantly being presented with different concrete situations—but the instructor could supplement these teachings with concrete demonstrations and applications to specific situations that social researchers are likely to encounter. Such role-playing might well be a small part of the training of social science graduates. Working through simulated research situation problems would, of course, quickly demonstrate the extent to which the student had gained full behavioral understanding of these human relations skills. Role-playing has been found to be particularly important in giving participants and observers a real opportunity to explore the various facets of the problems they may actually be called upon to handle at a later date.

One further word about these human relations skills. The researcher who regards these skills simply as a bag of tricks—a means to gain his own ends—will probably sooner or later defeat himself. Researchers—like others who use these skills to manipulate others—are usually found out. Once found out the researcher will, of course, find it doubly difficult to regain the confidence of those with whom he is working. This does not mean that these skills should not be used. There is nothing amoral or immoral about the possession and use of these skills. The question that the researcher who uses these skills must continually ask himself is "Have I given the other person a chance to say no?"

The skills that have been emphasized in this paper are things that we *"know"* at the verbal level. We *teach* them in our courses about human behavior. But we frequently do not use them in our own dealings with others as researchers. It has been the objective of this paper to call attention to this area of research skills. Methodologists in the social sciences may in the future need to be as concerned with these human relations skills as they have been in the past with the technical and analytical skills required for social research.

NOTE

[1] The notable exceptions to this are papers by Gardiner and Whyte (6), Merton (10), Sewell (14), and Bain(2).

BIBLIOGRAPHY

1. Aberle, D. F. "Introducing preventive psychiatry into a community." *Human Organization,* 1950, *9* (No. 3), 5-9.

2. Bain, R. K. "The researcher's role: a case study." *Human Organization,* 1950, *9* (No. 1), 23-28.

3. Chein, I., Cook, S. W., and Harding, J. "The use of research in social therapy." *Human Relations,* 1948 (Vol. 1, No. 4), 497-511.

4. Elmer, G. A. "Maintaining rapport necessary for reliability in industrial research." *American Sociological Review,* 1951, *16* 91-93.

5. Festinger, L., Cartwright, D., *et al.* "A study of rumor: its origin and spread." *Human Relations,* 1948 (Vol. 1, No. 4), 464-486.

6. Gardiner, B. B., and Whyte, W. F. "Methods for the study of human relations in industry." *American Sociological Review,* 1946, *11* 506-512.

7. Hutte, H. A. "Experiences in studying social psychological structures in industry." *Human Relations,* 1949 (Vol. 2, No. 2), 115-192.

8. Jaques, E. *The Changing Culture of a Factory.* London: Tavistock Publications, 1951.

9. Krech, D., issue ed. "Action and research—a challenge." *Journal of Social Issues,* 1946, *2* (No. 4).

10. Merton, R. K. "Selected problems of field work in the planned community." *American Sociological Review,* 1947, *12* 304-312.

11. Polansky, N., *et al.* "Problems of interpersonal relations in research on groups." *Human Relations,* 1949 (Vol. 2, No. 2), 281-291.

12. Schuler, E. A. *Rural sociological research needs in the Middle West.* December 1949 (mimeographed).

13. Sellitz, C., and Wormser, M. H., issue eds. "Community self-surveys: an approach to social change." *Journal of Social Issues,* 1949, *5* (No. 2).

14. Sewell, W. H. "Field techniques in a social psychological study in a rural community." *American Sociological Review,* 1949, *14* 718-726.

15. Warner, W. L., and Lunt, P. S. *The Social Life of a Modern Community.* Vol. 1, "Yankee City Series," New Haven: Yale University Press, 1941.

16. West, J. *Plainville, U.S.A.* New York: Columbia University Press, 1945.

17. Whyte, W. F. *Street Corner Society.* Chicago: University of Chicago Press, 1943.

CHAPTER 12

Participant Observation and Interviewing: A Comparison

Howard S. Becker and Blanche Geer

The most complete form of the sociological datum, after all, is the form in which the participant observer gathers it: An observation of some social event, the events which precede and follow it, and explanations of its meaning by participants and spectators, before, during, and after its occurrence. Such a datum gives us more information about the event under study than data gathered by any other sociological method. Participant observation can thus provide us with a yardstick against which to measure the completeness of data gathered in other ways, a model which can serve to let us know what orders of information escape us when we use other methods.

By participant observation we mean that method in which the observer participates in the daily life of the people under study, either openly in the role of researcher or covertly in some disguised role, observing things that happen, listening to what is said, and questioning people, over some length of time.[1] We want, in this paper, to compare the results of such intensive field work with what might be regarded as the first step in the other direction along this continuum: the detailed and conversational interview (often referred to as the unstructured or undirected interview).[2] In this kind of interview, the interviewer explores many facets of his interviewee's concerns, treating subjects as they come up in conversation, pursuing interesting leads, allowing his imagination and ingenuity full rein as he tries to develop new hypotheses and test them in the course of the interview.

In the course of our current participant observation among medical students,[3] we have thought a good deal about the kinds of things we were discovering which might ordinarily be missed or misunderstood in such an interview. We have no intention of denigrating the interview or even such less precise modes of data gathering as the questionnaire, for there can always be good reasons of practicality, economy, or research design for their use. We simply wish to make explicit the difference in data gathered by one or the

This chapter was originally published by The Society for Applied Anthropology, in *Human Organization,* 16: 28-32. The authors acknowledge the assistance of R. Richard Wohl and Thomas S. McPartland.

133

other method and to suggest the differing uses to which they can legitimately be put. In general, the shortcomings we attribute to the interview exist when it is used as a source of information about events that have occurred elsewhere and are described to us by informants. Our criticisms are not relevant when analysis is restricted to interpretation of the interviewee's conduct *during the interview,* in which case the researcher has in fact observed the behavior he is talking about.[4]

The differences we consider between the two methods involve two interacting factors: the kinds of words and acts of the people under study that the researcher has access to, and the kind of sensitivity to problems and data produced in him. Our comparison may prove useful by suggestive areas in which interviewing (the more widely used method at present and likely to continue so) can improve its accuracy by taking account of suggestions made from the perspective of the participant observer. We begin by considering some concrete problems: learning the native language, or the problem of the degree to which the interviewer really understands what is said to him; matters interviewees are unable or unwilling to talk about; and getting information on matters people see through distorting lenses. We then consider some more general differences between the two methods.

LEARNING THE NATIVE LANGUAGE

Any social group, to the extent that it is a distinctive unit, will have to some degree a culture differing from that of other groups, a somewhat different set of common understandings around which action is organized, and these differences will find expression in a language whose nuances are peculiar to that group and fully understood only by its members. Members of churches speak differently from members of informal tavern groups; more importantly, members of any particular church or tavern group have cultures, and languages in which they are expressed, which differ somewhat from those of other groups of the same general type. So, although we speak one language and share in many ways in one culture, we cannot assume that we understand precisely what another person, speaking as a member of such a group, means by any particular word. In interviewing members of groups other than our own, then, we are in somewhat the same position as the anthropologist who must learn a primitive language,[5] with the important difference that, as Icheiser has put it, we often do not understand that we do not understand and are thus likely to make errors in interpreting what is said to us. In the case of gross misunderstandings the give and take of conversation may quickly reveal our mistakes, so that the interviewee can correct us; this presumably is one of the chief mechanisms through which the anthropologist acquires a new tongue. But in speaking American English with an interviewee who is, after all, much like us, we may mistakenly assume that we have understood him and the error be small enough that it will not disrupt communication to the point where a correction will be in order.

The interview provides little opportunity of rectifying errors of this kind where they go unrecognized. In contrast, participant observation provides a situation in which the meanings of words can be learned with great precision through study of their use in context, exploration through continuous interviewing of their implications and nuances, and the use of them oneself under the scrutiny of capable speakers of the language. Beyond simply clarifying matters so that the researcher may understand better what people say to each other and to him, such a linguistic exercise may provide research hypotheses of great usefulness. The way in which one of us learned the meaning of the work "crock," as medical students use it, illustrates these points.

I first heard the word "crock" applied to a patient shortly after I began my field work. The patient in question, a fat, middle-aged woman, complained bitterly of pains in a number of widely separated locations. When I asked the student who had so described her what the word meant, he said that it was used to refer to any patient who had psychosomatic complaints. I asked if that meant that Mr. X——, a young man on the ward whose stomach ulcer had been discussed by a staff physician as typically psychosomatic, was a crock. The student said that that would not be correct usage, but was not able to say why.

Over a period of several weeks, through discussion of many cases seen during morning rounds with the students, I finally arrived at an understanding of the term, realizing that it referred to a patient who complained of many symptoms but had no discoverable organic pathology. I had noticed from the beginning that the term was used in a derogatory way and had also been inquiring into this, asking students why they disliked having crocks assigned to them for examination and diagnosis. At first students denied the derogatory connotations, but repeated observations of their disgust with such assignments soon made such denials unrealistic. Several students eventually explained their dislike in ways of which the following example is typical: "The true crock is a person who you do a great big workup for and who has all of these vague symptoms, and *you really can't find anything the matter with them.*"

Further discussion made it clear that the students regarded patients primarily as objects from which they could learn those aspects of clinical medicine not easily acquired from textbooks and lectures; the crock took a great deal of their time, of which they felt they had little enough, and did not exhibit any interesting disease state from which something might be learned, so that the time invested was wasted. This discovery in turn suggested that I might profitably investigate the general perspective toward medical school which led to such a basis for judgment of patients, and also suggested hypotheses regarding the value system of the hospital hierarchy at whose bottom the student stood.

At the risk of being repetitious, let us point out in this example both the errors avoided and the advantages gained because of the use of participant observation. The term might never have been used by students in an ordinary interview; if it had, the interviewer might easily have assumed that the scatological term from which it in fact is descended provided a complete definition. Because the observer saw students on their daily rounds and heard them discussing everyday problems, he heard the word and was able to pursue it until he arrived at a meaningful definition. Moreover, the knowledge so gained led to further and more general discoveries about the group under study.

This is not to say that all of these things might not be discovered by a program of skillful interviewing, for this might well be possible. But we do suggest that an interviewer may misunderstand common English words when interviewees use them in some more or less esoteric way and not know that he is misunderstanding them, because there will be little chance to check his understanding against either further examples of their use in conversation or instances of the object to which they are applied. This leaves him open to errors of misinterpretation and errors of failing to see connections between items of information he has available, and may prevent him from seeing and exploring important research leads. In dealing with interview data, then, experience with participant observation indicates that both care and imagination must be used in making sure of meanings, for the cultural esoterica of a group may hide behind ordinary language used in special ways.

MATTERS INTERVIEWEES ARE UNABLE OR UNWILLING TO TALK ABOUT

Frequently, people do not tell an interviewer all the things he might want to know. This may be because they do not want to, feeling that to speak of some particular subject would be impolitic, impolite, or insensitive, because they do not think to and because the interviewer does not have enough information to inquire into the matter, or because they are not able to. The first case—the problem of "resistance"—is well known and a considerable lore has developed about how to cope with it.[6] It is more difficult to deal with the last two possibilities for the interviewee is not likely to reveal, or the interviewer to become aware, that significant omissions are being made. Many events occur in the life of a social group and the experience of an individual so regularly and uninterruptedly, or so quietly and unnoticed, that people are hardly aware of them, and do not think to comment on them to an interviewer; or they may never have become aware of them at all and be unable to answer even direct questions. Other events may be so unfamiliar that people find it difficult to put into words their vague feelings about what has happened. If an interviewee, for any of these reasons, cannot or will not discuss a certain topic, the researcher will find gaps in his information on matters about which he wants to know and will perhaps fail to become aware of other problems and areas of interest that such discussion might have opened up for him.

This is much less likely to happen when the researcher spends much time with the people he studies as they go about their daily activities, for he can see the very things which might not be reported in an interview. Further, should he desire to question people about matters they cannot or prefer not to talk about, he is able to point to specific incidents which either force them to face the issue (in the case of resistance) or make clear what he means (in the case of unfamiliarity). Finally, he can become aware of the full meaning of such hints as are given on subjects people are unwilling to speak openly about and of such inarticulate statements as people are able to make about subjects they cannot clearly formulate, because he frequently knows of these things through his observation and can connect his knowledge with these half-communications.

Researchers working with interview materials, while they are often conscious of these problems, cannot cope with them so well. If they are to deal with matters of this kind it must be by inference. They can only make an educated guess about the things which go unspoken in the interview; it may be a very good guess, but it must be a guess. They can employ various tactics to explore for material they feel is there but unspoken, but even when these are fruitful they do not create sensitivity to those problems of which even the interviewer is not aware. The following example indicates how participant observation aids the researcher in getting material, and making the most of the little he gets, on topics lying within this range of restricted communication.

A few months after the beginning of school, I went to dinner at one of the freshman medical fraternities. It was the night non-resident members came, married ones with their wives. An unmarried student who lived in the house looked around at the visitors and said to me, "We are so much in transition. I have never been in this situation before of meeting fellows and their wives."

This was just the sort of thing we were looking for—change in student relationships arising from group interaction—but I failed in every attempt to make the student describe the "transition" more clearly.

From previous observation, though, I knew there were differences (other than marriage) between the non-residents and their hosts. The former had all been elected to the fraternity recently, after house officers had gotten to know them through working together (usually on the same cadaver in anatomy lab). They were older than the average original member; instead of coming directly from college, several had had jobs or Army experience before medical school. As a group they were somewhat lower in social position.

These points indicated that the fraternity was bringing together in relative intimacy students different from each other in background and experience. They suggested a search for other instances in which dissimilar groups of students were joining forces, and pointed to a need for hypotheses as to what was behind this process of drawing together on the part of the freshmen and its significance for their medical education.

An interviewer, hearing this statement about "transition," would know that the interviewee felt himself in the midst of some kind of change but might not be able to discover anything further about the nature of that change. The participant observer cannot find out, any more than the interviewer can, what the student had in mind, presumably because the student had nothing more in mind than this vague feeling of change. (Interviewees are not sociologists and we ought not to assume that their fumbling statements are attempts, crippled by their lack of technical vocabulary, to express what a sociologist might put in more formal analytic terms.) But he can search for those things in the interviewee's situation which might lead to such a feeling of transition.

While the participant observer can make immediate use of such vague statements as clues to an objective situation, the interviewer is often bothered by the question of whether an interviewee is not simply referring to quite private experiences. As a result, the interviewer will place less reliance on whatever inferences about the facts of the situation he makes, and is less likely to be sure enough of his ground to use them as a basis for further hypotheses. Immediate observation of the scene itself and data from previous observation enable the participant observer to make direct use of whatever hints the informant supplies.

THINGS PEOPLE SEE THROUGH DISTORTING LENSES

In many of the social relationships we observe, the parties to the relation will have differing ideas as to what ought to go on in it, and frequently as to what does in fact go on in it. These differences in perception will naturally affect what they report in an interview. A man in a subordinate position in an organization in which subordinates believe that their superiors are "out to get them" will interpret many incidents in this light though the incidents themselves may not seem, either to the other party in the interaction or to the observer, to indicate such malevolence. Any such mythology will distort people's view of events to such a degree that they will report as fact things which have not occurred, but which seem to them to have occurred. Students, for example, frequently invent sets of rules to govern their relations with teachers, and, although the teacher may never have heard of such rules, regard the teachers as malicious when they "disobey" them. The point is that things may be reported in an interview through such a distorting lens, and the interviewer may have no way of knowing what is fact and what is distortion of this kind; participant observation makes it possible to check such points. The following is a particularly clear example.

Much of the daily teaching was done, and practical work of medical students supervised, in a particular department of the hospital, by the house residents. A great deal of animosity had grown up between the particular group of students I was with at the time and these residents, the students believing that the residents would, for various malicious reasons, subordinate them and embarrass them at every opportunity. Before I joined the group, several of the students told me that the residents were "mean," "nasty," "bitchy," and so on, and had backed these characterizations up with evidence of particular actions.

After I began participating daily with the students on this service, a number of incidents made it clear that the situation was not quite like this. Finally, the matter came completely into the open. I was present when one of the residents suggested a technique that might have prevented a minor relapse in a patient assigned to one of the students; he made it clear that he did not think the relapse in any way the student's fault, but rather that he was simply passing on what he felt to be a good tip. Shortly afterward, this student reported to several other students that the resident had "chewed him out" for failing to use this technique: "What the hell business has he got chewing me out about that for? No one ever told me I was supposed to do it that way." I interrupted to say, "He didn't really chew you out. I thought he was pretty decent about it." Another student said, "Any time they say anything at all to us I consider it a chewing out. Any time they say anything about how we did things, they are chewing us out, no matter how God damn nice they are about it."

In short, participant observation makes it possible to check description against fact and, noting discrepancies, become aware of systematic distortions made by the person under study; such distortions are less likely to be discovered by interviewing alone. This point, let us repeat, is only relevant when the interview is used as a source of information about situations and events the researcher himself has not seen. It is not relevant when it is the person's behavior in the interview itself that is under analysis.

INFERENCE, PROCESS AND CONTEXT

We have seen, in the previous sections of this paper, some of the ways in which even very good interviews may be astray, at least from the perspective of the field observer. We turn now to a consideration of the more general areas of difference between the two methods, suggesting basic ways in which the gathering and handling of data in each differ.

Since we tend to talk in our analyses about much the same order of thing whether we work from interviews or from participant-observational materials, and to draw conclusions about social relations and the interaction that goes on within them whether we have actually seen these things or only been told about them, it should be clear that in working with interviews we must necessarily infer a great many things we could have observed had we only been in a position to do so. The kinds of errors we have discussed above are primarily errors of inference, errors which arise from the necessity of making assumptions about the relation of interview statements to actual events which may or may not be true; for what we have solid observable evidence on in the first case we have only secondhand reports and indices of in the second, and the gap must be bridged by inference. We must assume, when faced with an account or transcription of an interview, that we understand the meaning of the everyday words used, that the interviewee is able to talk about the things we are interested in, and that his account will be more or less accurate. The examples detailed above suggest that these assumptions do not always hold and that the process of inference involved in interpreting interviews should always be made explicit and checked, where possible, against what can be discovered through observation. Where, as is often the case, this is not possible, conclusions should be limited to those matters the data directly describe.

Let us be quite specific, and return to the earlier example of resident-student hostility. In describing this relationship from interviews with the students alone we might have assumed their description to be accurate and made the inference that the residents were in fact "mean." Observation proved that this inference would have been incorrect, but this does not destroy the analytic usefulness of the original statements made to the fieldworker in an informal interview. It does shift the area in which we can make deductions from this datum, however, for we can see that such statements, while incorrect factually, are perfectly good statements of the perspective from which these students interpreted the events in which they were involved. We could not know without observation whether their descriptions were true or false; with the aid of observation we know that the facts of the matter are sometimes quite different, and that the students' perspective is strong enough to override such variant facts. But from the interview alone we could know, not what actually happened in such cases, but what the students thought happened and how they felt about it, and this is the kind of inference we should make. We add to the accuracy of our data when we substitute observable fact for inference. More important, we open the way for the discovery of new hypotheses for the fact we observe may not be the fact we expected to observe. When this happens we face a new problem requiring new hypothetical explanations which can then be further tested in the field.

Substitution of an inference about something for an observation of that thing occurs most frequently in discussions of social process and change, an area in which the advantages of observation over an extended period of time are particularly great. Much sociological writing is concerned, openly or otherwise, with problems of process: The analysis of shifts in group structure, individual self-conception and similar matters. But studies of such phenomena in natural social contexts are typically based on data that tell only part of the story. The analysis may be made from a person's retrospective account, in a single interview, of changes that have taken place; or, more rarely, it is based on a series of interviews, the differences between successive interviews providing the bench marks of change. In either case, many crucial steps in the process and important mechanisms of change must be arrived at through inferences which can be no more than educated guesses.

The difficulties in analyzing change and process on the basis of interview material are particularly important because it is precisely in discussing changes in themselves and their surroundings that interviewees are least likely or able to give an accurate account of events. Changes in the social environment and in the self inevitably produce transformations of perspective, and it is characteristic of such transformations that the person finds it difficult or impossible to remember his former actions, outlook, or feelings. Reinterpreting things from his new perspective, he cannot give an accurate account of the past, for the concepts in which he thinks about it have changed and with them his perceptions and memories.[7] Similarly, a person in the midst of such change may find it difficult to describe what is happening, for he has not developed a perspective or concepts which would allow him to think and talk about these things coherently; the earlier discussion of changes in medical school fraternity life is a case in point.

Participant observation does not have so many difficulties of this sort. One can observe actual changes in behavior over a period of time and note the events which precede and follow them. Similarly, one can carry on a conversation running over weeks and months with the people he is studying and thus become aware of shifts in perspective as they occur. In short, attention can be focused both on what has happened and on what the person says about what has happened. Some inference as to actual steps in the process or mechanisms involved is still required, but the amount of inference necessary is considerably reduced. Again, accuracy is increased and the possibility of new discoveries being made is likewise increased, as the observer becomes aware of more phenomena requiring explanation.

The participant observer is both more aware of these problems of inference and more equipped to deal with them because he operates, when gathering data, in a social context rich in cues and information of all kinds. Because he sees and hears the people he studies in many situations of the kind that normally occur for them, rather than just in an isolated and formal interview, he builds an evergrowing fund of impressions, many of them at the subliminal level, which give him an extensive base for the interpretation and analytic use of any particular datum. This wealth of information and impression sensitizes him to subtleties which might pass unnoticed in an interview and forces him to raise continually new and different questions, which he brings to and tries to answer in succeeding observations.

The biggest difference in the two methods, then, may be not so much that participant observation provides the opportunity for avoiding the errors we have discussed, but that it does this by providing a rich experiential context which causes him to become aware of incongruous or unexplained facts, makes him sensitive to their possible implications and connections with other observed facts, and thus pushes him continually to revise and adapt his theoretical orientation and specific problems in the direction of greater relevance to the phenomena under study. Though this kind of context and its attendant benefits cannot be reproduced in interviewing (and the same degree of sensitivity and sense of problem produced in the interviewer), interviewers can profit from an awareness of those limitations of their method suggested by this comparison and perhaps improve their batting average by taking account of them.[8]

NOTES

[1] Cf. Florence R. Kluckhohn, "The Participant Observer Technique in Small Communities," *American Journal of Sociology*, 46 (Nov., 1940), 331-43; Arthur Vidich, "Participant Observation and the Collection and Interpretation of Data," *American Journal of Sociology*, 60 (Jan., 1955), 354-60; William Foote Whyte, "Observational Field-Work Methods," in Marie Jahoda, Morton Deutsch, and Stuart W. Cook (eds.), *Research Methods in the Social Sciences* (New York: Dryden Press, 1951), Vol. 2, 393-514, and *Street Corner Society* (enlarged ed.; Chicago: University of Chicago Press, 1955), pp. 279-358.

[2] Two provisos are in order. In the first place, we assume in our comparison that the hypothetical interviewer and participant observer we discuss are equally skilled and sensitive. We assume further that both began their research with equally well formulated problems, so that they are indeed looking for equivalent kinds of data.

[3] This study is sponsored by Community Studies, Inc., of Kansas City, Missouri, and is being carried out at the University of Kansas Medical Center, to whose dean and staff we are indebted for their wholehearted cooperation. Professor Everett C. Hughes of the University of Chicago is director of the project.

[4] For discussion of this point, see Thomas S. McPartland, *Formal Education and the Process of Professionalization: A Study of Student Nurses* (Kansas City, Missouri: Community Studies, Inc., 1957), pp. 2-3.

[5] See the discussion in Bronislaw Malinowski, *Magic, Science, and Religion and Other Essays* (Glencoe: The Free Press, 1948), pp. 232-38.

[6] See, for example, Arnold M. Rose, "A Research Note on Interviewing," *American Journal of Sociology*, 51 (Sept., 1945), 143-44; and Howard S. Becker, "A Note on Interviewing Tactics," *Human Organization*, 12: 4 (Winter, 1954), 31-32.

[7] Anselm L. Strauss, "The Development and Transformation of Monetary Meanings in the Child," *American Sociological Review*, 17 (June, 1952), 275-86, and *An Essay on Identity* (unpublished manuscript), *passim*.

[8] We are aware that participant observation raises as many technical problems as it solves. (See, for instance, the discussions in Morris S. Schwartz and Charlotte Green Schwartz, "Problems in Participant Observation," *American Journal of Sociology*, 60 (Jan., 1955), 343-53, and in Vidich, *op. cit.*) We feel, however, that there is considerable value in using the strong points of one method to illuminate the shortcomings of another.

CHAPTER 13

Comment on "Participant Observation and Interviewing: A Comparison"

Martin Trow

I

Insofar as the paper by Becker and Geer says: "Participant observation is a very useful way of collecting data, and here are some illustrations to show how useful we found it in one study," I can take no issue with them. On the contrary, I profited from their discussion of the method and their illustrations of its use.

But, unfortunately, Becker and Geer say a good deal more than that. In their first paragraph they assert that participant observation, by virtue of its intrinsic qualities, "gives us more information about the event under study than data gathered by any other sociological method." And since this is true, "it provides us with a yardstick against which to measure the completeness of data gathered in other ways. . . ."

It is with this assertion, that a given method of collecting data—*any* method—has an inherent superiority over others by virtue of its special qualities and divorced from the nature of the problem studied, that I take sharp issue. The alternative view, and I would have thought this the view most widely accepted by social scientists, is that different kinds of information about man and society are gathered most fully and economically in different ways, and that the problem under investigation properly dictates the methods of investigation. If this is so, then we certainly can use other methods of investigation as "yardsticks" against which to measure the adequacy of participant observation for the collection of certain kinds of data. And my impression is that most of the problems social scientists are studying seem to call for data gathered in other ways than through participant observation. Moreover, most of the problems investigated call for data collected in several different ways, whether in fact they are or not. This view seems to me implied in the commonly used metaphor of the social scientist's "kit of tools" to which he turns to find the methods and techniques most useful to the prob-

This chapter was originally published by the Society for Applied Anthropology, in *Human Organization*, 16: 33-35.

lem at hand. Becker and Geer's argument sounds to me very much like a doctor arguing that the scalpel is a better instrument than the forceps—and since this is so we must measure the forceps' cutting power against that of the scalpel.

Much of the paper by Becker and Geer is devoted to measuring "the interview" against the yardstick of "participant observation." To make the "contest" between interviewing and participant observation a fair one, the authors make the proviso (footnote 2) that they are employed by men who are equally competent, and who start with equally well formulated problems, "so that they are indeed looking for equivalent kinds of data." I would assume, on the contrary, that interviewing and participant observation would rarely produce "equivalent" kinds of data, and should not be asked to, but rather produce rather different kinds of data designed to answer quite different kinds of questions about the same general phenomenon. Here again we have Becker and Geer's view of the forceps as a rather poor kind of cutting instrument.

But if I respectfully decline to enter debate on the question of whether the scalpel is a better instrument than the forceps (unless it is rather closely specified "for what")—nevertheless, it may be useful to consider some of the assumptions about the nature of social research out of which such an unreal question can emerge.

II

The first thing that struck me on reading this paper is its oddly parochial view of the range and variety of sociological problems. To state flatly that participant observation "gives us more information about the event under study than . . . any other sociological method" is to assume that all "events" are directly apprehensible by participant observers. But what are some of the "events" that sociologists study? Is a national political campaign such an "event"? Is a long-range shift in interracial attitudes an "event"? Is an important change in medical education and its aggregate of consequences an "event"? Are variations in suicide rates in different social groups and categories an "event"? If we exclude these phenomena from the definition of the term "event" then we exclude most of sociology. If we define "event" broadly enough to include the greater part of what sociologists study, then we find that most of our problems require for their investigation data of kinds that cannot be supplied by the participant observer alone.

But the answer of the participant observation enthusiast, if I read Becker and Geer correctly, would be "that is all very true, but very sad. Many students do require the gathering of data in all kinds of defective and suspect ways, but the closer they approximate to participant observation, and the more frequently they check their findings against those of participant observation, the better." To deal with this, let us for the moment drop the whole question of scalpel *versus* forceps, and consider one or two specific research studies, and the ways their data bear on their questions. This may allow us at least to raise what I feel is a far more fruitful set of questions: What kinds of problems are best studied through what kinds of methods; what kinds of insights and understandings seem to arise out of the analysis of different kinds of data; how can the various methods at our disposal complement one another? I can hardly attempt to contribute to the systematic discussion of these questions in a short "rebuttal" paper, but we can perhaps at least restate the questions in connection with some illustrative evidence.

The central problem of a recent study of the organization and internal politics of a trade union[1] was to explain the development, and especially the persistence, of a two party system within the union's political structure. To this end the research team examined a variety of documents, conducted various kinds of unstructured, focused, and highly structured interviews, examined voting records, and also engaged in participant observation.

Among the problems that we confronted was that of assessing the degree of legitimacy imputed to the party system by various groups and social categories within the union. This, I maintain, we could not have done at all adequately through participant observation. Let us leave aside the question, clearly not within the grasp of the participant observer, of whether the several hundred union officers and "leaders" were more or less inclined to think the party system a good thing in its own right as compared with the ten thousand men in a local or the one hundred thousand men in the international union we were studying. More to the point is the fact that the workings of the party system inhibited direct expressions of hostility to the system. In the ordinary give and take of conversation in the shop, party meeting, club meeting, informal gatherings after hours, such expressions were not likely to be expressed; they violated strongly held norms, and called down various kinds of punishments. It was only when we interviewed leaders individually and intensively that we could get some sense of the reservations that they held about the party system, how widely and strongly those reservations were held, and thus could make some assessment of those sentiments as a potentially disruptive force in the party system. It is true, as Becker and Geer point out, that men will do and say things in their customary activities and relationships that point to factors which might be wholly missed in the course of an interview—and where these things come to the attention of a participant observer he gains insights thereby. But the converse is also true, though perhaps not as widely recognized: Ordinary social life may well inhibit the casual expression of sentiments which are actually or potentially important elements in the explanation of the social phenomena under study. And participant observation is a relatively weak instrument for gathering data on sentiments, behaviors, relationships which are normatively proscribed by the group under observation.

I might note in passing that we gained useful insights into some of the mechanisms operating to sustain this union's political system through our observations at union meetings, party meetings, and during ordinary working days (and nights) spent in the shops. But these insights only took on full meaning in light of much other knowledge about that organization and its social and political structure that had been gained in other ways.

A recent study in the sociology of medicine—the field from which Becker and Geer draw their own illustrations—emphasizes the need for the widest variety of research methods in attacks on comprehensive problems.[2] The index to the volume in which the first reports of this study are published list, under the heading "Methods of social research," the following sources of information used: diaries; documentary records; intensive interviews; observation; panel techniques; questionnaires; sociometry. Most of the papers in this volume deal with problems that could not have been studied solely through direct observation. One paper, for example, deals with the question of the processes by which medical students select their profession.[3] The author finds, among other things, that the occupation of the student's father was an important element in how and when he made that decision. Becker and Geer argue that the interview is not a good source of information "about events that have occurred elsewhere and are described to us by informants." But surely certain important facts about a man's early life experience—and these include what his father did for a living—can be reported quite accurately to an interviewer or on a questionnaire, and give the analyst invaluable data for the analysis of the forces and processes involved in the choice of a profession or occupation. But the bearing of one's father's occupation, or of one's religion, on attitudes and behaviors may never emerge in the ordinary course of events which the participant observer apprehends. Moreover, it is just not true, as Becker and Geer suggest, that the interview is a reliable source of information only regarding the interviewer's conduct *during the interview.* The amount of information people can tell us, quite simply and reliably, about their past experience is very great; and it is only in light of that information, I would maintain, that we can frequently understand their behaviors in the "here and now" that the participant observer is so close to.[4]

True, if we imagine that interviews can deal with past events only through questions of the sort: "Now, why did you choose medicine as a career?" then we may indeed worry about the distortions in reporting information retrospectively. But this effort to make the respondent do the analysis for the sociologist is not the only, and almost certainly not the best, way to assess the bearing of prior events on past or current decisions.

III

We all profit, as I have from this paper, when social scientists broaden our knowledge of the special strengths of the methods which they have found useful and in the use of which they have acquired expertise. The danger lies in the kind of exclusive preoccupation with one method that leads to a systematic neglect of the potentialities, even the essential characteristics, of another. Becker and Geer seem to display this neglect when they contrast participant observation with "the interview." But with some exceptions, the data gathered by the interviewer are not usually embodied in "the interview" taken one at a time, but in the series of interviews through which a body of comparable data has been gathered. It is all of the comparable interviews, with their analysis, that must be compared with participant observation, and not the interviews taken one at a time. The charge is frequently made, and Becker and Geer repeat it, that the interview (and especially the highly structured survey interview) is a very "crude" instrument for collecting data—its artificiality and directedness ensure that much of the "richness" of social life as it is lived passes through its meshes. I would argue that there is more than one way to gain knowledge of the richness, the subtlety and infinite variety, of social life, and that sufficiently sensitive and intensive analysis of "crude" survey data is one such way. Durkheim, whose data in his study of suicide was even "cruder" and further removed from the "rich experiential context" than that of the survey analyst, nevertheless adds much to our understanding of some of the most subtle and complex aspects of social life. How much a social scientist can add to our understanding of society, I submit, is more a product of the way he defines his problem, the questions he brings to his data, and the adequacy of his data to answer his questions and suggest new ones, than it is of how "close," in a physical sense, he gets to the social life he is studying. And this, I think, is as true for social scientists who gather most of their data through participant observation, as for those who use that method to supplement others, and for those who use it not at all.

It is no disparagement of the legitimate uses of participant observation to suggest that some of the uncritical enthusiasm and unwarranted claims for it show what seems to be a certain romantic fascination with the "subtlety and richness" of social life, and especially with "cultural esoterica," the ways very special to a given group. But it seems to me profoundly mistaken to search for the special essence of a method of data collection, and appraise it in terms of its ability to directly reflect this "subtlety and richness." As social scientists, our business is with describing and explaining social phenomena; our judgment of the usefulness of data is properly made against the criterion; how much does this help us understand the phenomenon we are studying? It may well be that participant observation is more successful than any other method in gathering data on the "cultural esoterica" of a group. But this is not a good in itself; the question remains, is this information useful, and importantly useful, for our purposes? And that of course will depend on our purposes. The correlative question is equally important: could the matters which these esoteric cultural items point to—the matters we are *really* interested in—have been learned in other, and perhaps more economical, ways? I suspect that very often they can. But at the very least the question should be raised more often than it is.

The argument the authors make for the superiority of participant observation comes finally to an expression of a preference for what can be observed "directly" over what we must make inferences about. But the authors' strong commitment to observation leads them, I believe, to an unnecessarily dim, and basically incorrect, view of the process of inference in social science. All interpretations of data, however collected—through observations, interviews, or whatever—involve inferences regarding their meaning and significance. We confuse ourselves if we believe that the people whose behavior we are concerned with, whether we observe them or interview them, can themselves provide an adequate explanation of their own behavior. That is our job, and the participant observer makes inferences from the data he collects just as the survey analyst makes inferences from the data collected for him. The data gathered by participant observers are still data, despite the perhaps misleading circumstance that the participant observer usually both gathers and interprets the data himself, and to a large degree simultaneously.[5] But the data he collects are not a substitute for the interpretive inference. We all forget that at our peril.

The fact that social scientists are constantly making inferences from their data does not especially disturb me, as it does Becker and Geer. Our progress in social science will come not through an effort to get "closer" to the source of data, and thus try to minimize or do away with the process of inference by dissolving it back into data collection and somehow apprehending reality directly. That simply isn't possible. Our progress will come as we are increasingly able to develop systems of theoretically related propositions— propositions which are "checked" at more and more points against data collected through a variety of means. The inferences that we make from data, and the theory from which they derive and to which they contribute, may indeed be nothing more than "educated guesses"—but that is the nature of scientific theory. Our aim is to make them increasingly highly educated guesses. We cannot evade that fate, which is the fate of science, through reliance on a wrongly conceived participant observation which apprehends social reality "directly."

IV

Every cobbler thinks leather is the only thing. Most social scientists, including the present writer, have their favorite research methods with which they are familiar and have some skill in using. And I suspect we mostly choose to investigate problems that seem vulnerable to attack through these methods. But we should at least try to be less parochial than cobblers. Let us be done with the arguments of "participant observation" *versus* interviewing—as we have largely dispensed with the arguments for psychology *versus* sociology— and get on with the business of attacking our problems with the widest array of conceptual and methodological tools that we possess and they demand. This does not preclude discussion and debate regarding the relative usefulness of different methods for the study of specific problems or types of problems. But that is very different from the assertion of the general and inherent superiority of one method over another on the basis of some intrinsic qualities it presumably possesses.

NOTES

[1] S. M. Lipset, M. A. Trow, and J. C. Coleman, *Union Democracy* (Glencoe: The Free Press, 1956).

[2] R. K. Merton, George Reader, and P. L. Kendall, eds., *The Student-Physician* (Cambridge, Mass.: The Harvard University Press, 1957). See especially George Reader, "The Cornell Comprehensive Care and Teaching Program," section on "Methods," pp. 94-101.

[3] Natalie Rogoff, "The Decision to Study Medicine," in Merton, Reader, and Kendall, eds., *op. cit.,* pp. 109-131.

[4] This suggests, more generally, that participant observation *by itself* is most nearly satisfactory in studies of small, isolated, relatively homogeneous populations, such as primitive tribes, where variations in the character of early life experience, and the effects of those variations on present sentiments and behaviors, are not so great. Where variations in experience outside the arena being observed are great, we must, for most problems, turn to other methods of data collection to learn about them.

[5] This involves special strengths and hazards, a matter which has been discussed extensively elsewhere, and also in the paper by Becker and Geer and their references.

CHAPTER 14

"Participant Observation and Interviewing": A Rejoinder

Howard S. Becker and Blanche Geer

We read Martin Trow's "Comment"[1] on our "Participant Observation and Interviewing: A Comparison"[2] with interest and profit. An unfortunate ambiguity in key terms led Trow to misinterpret our position radically. We would like to clear up the confusion briefly and also to discuss a few interesting questions raised in his argument.

Trow believes us to have said that participant observation is the best method for gathering data for all sociological problems under all circumstances. We did not say this and, in fact, we fully subscribe to his view "that different kinds of information about man and society are gathered most fully and economically in different ways, and that the problem under investigation properly dictates the methods of investigation." We did say, and now re-iterate, that participant observation gives us the most complete information about social events and can thus be used as a yardstick to suggest what kinds of data escape us when we use other methods. This means, simply, that, if we see an event occur, see the events preceding and following it, and talk to various participants about it, we have more information than if we only have the description which one or more persons could give us.

Perhaps Trow accused us of insisting on "the general and inherent superiority" of participant observation, when, in fact, we did not, because he misunderstood the sense in which we meant it to be used as a "yardstick." We did not mean that the *value* of any method used for any purpose must be assessed by such a comparison. Since completeness is obviously not the only criterion one would apply to data gathered by any method—relevance, accuracy, and reproducibility are others that come immediately to mind—a discussion centered on this criterion does not imply any claim for general superiority. But, if comparison with participant observation can make one aware of what kinds of data may be lost by use of another method, it seems to us that a conscientious researcher would want to assess his data by a systematic

This chapter was originally published by The Society for Applied Anthropology, in *Human Organization,* 16: 39-40.

consideration of the points we raised rather than by an offhand dismissal of the problem.

It is possible Trow thought we were arguing the general superiority of participant observation because he misunderstood our use of the word "event." We intended to refer only to specific and limited events which are observable, not to include in the term such large and complex aggregates of specific events as national political campaigns. Naturally, such events are not "directly apprehensible" by an observer. But to restate our position, the individual events of absorbing information about an election, discussing it with others, and deciding which way to vote are amenable to observation. It is the information that one gets about these events, and then combines in order to arrive at generalizations, which one might want to examine for completeness by the yardstick of participant observation.

We evidently failed to make the flexible nature of participant observation clear enough to prevent Trow from concluding that we are claiming a great deal for a restricted technique. As we and others have used it, it does not preclude private conversations with members of the group under observation as opportunities for such conversation arise. These conversations are in many ways the functional equivalent of an interview and can be used to get the same sort of information. Thus, even though "ordinary social life may well inhibit the casual expression" of deviant attitudes, the participant observer can uncover such attitudes.[3] Again, to avoid misunderstanding, we do not believe all information is accessible to a participant observer.

Finally, Trow misunderstands our view of the role of inference in social science. We do not wish to do away with inference by getting closer to the source of the data. But we would like to distinguish between inferences about things which can only be discovered by observation. Since social systems, for instance, are not directly observable, but can only be characterized by inference from data which are themselves observable, such inferences are not only necessary but inevitable. But the question of whether to rely on inference for information on points which could be settled by observation is a pragmatic one, to be decided by the importance of the inference, the degree of our confidence in it, and the difficulty of making the necessary observations. Many circumstances may decide us to infer certain facts rather than find them out directly, but the inference can never be more accurate than the observation and may be less so. Analysts of projective tests are able to infer the sex of a subject from the protocol alone with great accuracy, but there are still better and easier ways to do it.

None of what has been said should obscure the fact that we do not argue that participant observation should be used in all studies, but simply that it is possible to tell by comparison with the data it produces what data is lost by use of another method. Whether the loss is important or not depends on the character of the problem under investigation; whether the loss is unavoidable or too expensive to avoid is a practical, not a logical, problem. Though our paper did not touch on the problem, it may be appropriate for us to state here the kind of problem participant observation is most suited to. Briefly, it is the problem in which one is more interested in understanding some particular group or substantive social problem rather than in testing hypotheses about the relations between variables derived from a general theory. These two aims are naturally not mutually exclusive, but many studies are particularly focused in one or another of these directions. In the study aimed at understanding substantive problems, the greatest difficulties lie in discovering appropriate problems for soicological analysis and in discovering valid indicators for theoretical variables. Participant observation is particularly useful in meeting these difficulties. Also, when one wishes to construct a model of the social systems of an organization, a technique which allows one to see the interrelations of elements of that system in action is especially helpful.

NOTE

[1] *Human Organization,* 16: 3 (Fall, 1957), 33-35.
[2] *Ibid.,* 28-32.
[3] An account of our own use of such techniques is found in Howard S. Becker, "Interviewing Medical Students," *American Journal of Sociology* (Sept., 1956), 199-201. Numerous examples can be found in William Foote Whyte, *Street Corner Society* (Enlarged ed.; Chicago: The University of Chicago Press, 1955), *passim.*

PART FOUR

Analysis of Data

CHAPTER 15

Training in Field Relations Skills

Stephen A. Richardson

As knowledge of the human relations skills involved in social research increases, the development of procedures whereby these skills can be effectively taught to students in social science becomes important.

The ideas and methods reported in this paper are based on a university course in field research methods in social science. In this course, training is given in field relations skills, field observation, and interviewing. Further research is essential both in making explicit the skills involved in field relations in social science, and in evaluating the methods of teaching these skills, before training in them can be given effectively. However, this report of training methods now in use may be taken as a first step towards such systematization.

THE NEED FOR SYSTEMATIC TRAINING
IN FIELD RELATIONS SKILLS

The skills of field relations in social science research have been learned by most field workers through trial and error. There are a number of reasons why it is too costly to continue to rely upon this form of training. (1) Social scientists have an ethical responsibility to minimize the social or personal damage that may result from their field research activities. (2) A number of potentially able field workers if unprepared for their initial exposure to field work are likely to experience serious failures or unpleasant experiences which will discourage them from further attempts at field work. (3) In long range studies of organizations and small communities, one cannot afford to jeopardize good field relations by using students who have had no preparation for field work. (4) The use of inexperienced and unsuitable field workers is a heavy and often a wasteful drain on research funds.

This chapter was originally published by The Society for the Psychological Study of Social Issues, in *The Journal of Social Issues,* 8: No. 3, 43-50. The author acknowledges the assistance of the staff and advisory committee of the Field Methods Training Program sponsored by the Cornell University Social Science Research Center.

It is the thesis of this article that suitable preliminary classroom training and supervised field practice can minimize the need for trial and error learning in a practical field situation. Moreover, such preliminary course training can serve a number of other useful purposes. (1) It allows the student an opportunity to determine whether he likes field work and has aptitude in the needed field relations skills. (2) It allows the teaching staff an opportunity to make a tentative assessment and selection of students for further training. (3) It allows the student to "try out" his ideas on field relations skills in a devised situation rather than in one which might jeopardize an actual field situation.

GENERAL PLAN OF THE TRAINING COURSE

This one-semester course is planned to give preliminary training in skills of field relations, field observation, and interviewing. It is limited to twelve students who have had no prior field work experience but are trained in the social science disciplines. Three staff members share the teaching of the course and at times other faculty members are invited to participate in class sessions.

Training takes place both in the classroom and in the field. During the early part of the semester, most of the time is devoted to classroom work, planning an actual field project in which the class will be divided into three teams, and moving into the field. As field activities increase classroom work decreases. Toward the end of the semester, field work is terminated, and the final work of the course is carried out in the classroom.

Throughout the course, the aim is to compare the experience and skills gained by the class with those of field workers who have worked in widely differing types of organizations and communities. This enables the students to check the experience of other workers against their own and allows for the continuing development and testing of generalizations which may prove of value in later field experiences.

For carrying out the practice field project the class is divided into three teams, each made up of a staff member and four students. The teams work in separate but comparable organizations in order that a common problem can be selected and comparisons made between the organizations. We have a number of reasons for believing that students can learn more by working in small teams than on individual projects. The team method has three advantages: (1) It allows students and a staff member to share the same experiences and gain from each others' insights and skills. (2) It allows for a better coverage of organizational activities and the interviewing of more individuals than is possible by a single student with the limited time he can spend in the field. (3) Working in small teams results in better class morale than working on individual projects. (4) It provides some experience in working with and between research teams. This experience should be of value to students since an increasing amount of research is being carried out by teams of field workers.

Discussions of individual field projects are held by the teams separately and opportunities are given for students to have individual sessions with their staff member. Meetings of the whole class are held to present materials from diverse field projects, to give training in specific skills, and to hear reports and make comparisons of the progress of the three field teams.

THE SELECTION OF AN ORGANIZATION
FOR PRACTICE FIELD WORK

In selecting a place for practice field work, the two major alternatives are organizations connected with the university and off-campus organizations in the locality. This choice will largely depend on whether the university is located in an urban or a rural setting. Both alternatives have advantages and disadvantages worth considering. The campus has the advantage that it is easily accessible, that it provides a wide variety of organizations and activities, and that fellow students are fairly tolerant of the mistakes that field work trainees are likely to make. It has the disadvantage of being made up of people who are similar to the trainees in background, age, speech, and manner. The students may be placed in a position of studying their friends, a situation which has attendant dangers; or of studying organizations about which they will have widely varying prior knowledge and in some cases active membership.

When selecting an organization in the locality surrounding the university, we have found the following criteria useful as a guide: (1) An organization whose leaders can be told the purpose of the training course, and whose members are agreeable to the idea of having students observe their meetings and talk to them about their organization. (2) An organization in which the group meets regularly and frequently enough to give students sufficient practice field work. (3) An organization of sufficient complexity to supply opportunities for studying a variety of groups and sub-groups and how they relate to the total organization. (4) An organization which is sufficiently divorced from the everyday life of students so that no student will have intimate prior knowledge of the organization. (5) An organization whose membership fulfills at least one of the following requirements: it cuts across social, economic, and intellectual boundaries; it is outside the intellectual orbit of the university; and the ages of its members are different from the student group.

AN OUTLINE OF FIELD RELATIONS SKILLS
TAUGHT IN THE COURSE

The following outline of the field relations skills provides a framework within which descriptions of a number of classroom teaching techniques can be placed. The outline was developed through interviewing a large number of field workers about completed research projects in order to explore the skills required in field relations.

1. The ethics of social science field work.

2. General and specific knowledge of an organization which should be obtained before entering the field.

3. Sources from which information about an organization or a community may be obtained.

4. Making the decision with whom to make the first contacts inside or outside of the research area.

5. Making the initial contacts in the research area.

6. Structuring of the field worker's role.

7. Offering incentives for cooperation to people in the organization or community.

8. Deciding the sequence of research activities and timing this sequence.

9. Choosing sponsors and informants in the research area.

10. Dealing with rumors encountered while in the field concerning field workers and the research project.

11. Reporting research progress and findings to persons in the organization or community.

ILLUSTRATIONS OF THE TASK SITUATIONS USED IN FIELD RELATIONS TRAINING

General Knowledge of Organizations or Communities Required before Entering the Field. The following task was given as a written problem. It was designed to see what sort of general knowledge of a small community each student possessed. It has also been used as the basis for discussion in which a member of the research staff who had first-hand experience with such a problem was present to answer questions and evaluate the various suggestions made.

You have been called in by a university group to help them solve a problem which they have encountered in their research. They have been doing a community study in which their primary focus is the processes by which community problems are approached. For a year the field workers have been observing meetings of organizations. They soon plan to conduct a survey in which they will contact one person in every household in the community. They intend to continue their work in the community for another two years.

The problem is posed by the fact that they have five hundred dollars which they must donate to the community. This money was provided by the foundation as part of the grant for the study, with no specifications as to how the money should be donated except that it must be given in some way to the community by December thirty-first. It is now mid-October. An important consideration for the research group is to give the money in such a way as to best insure their continued acceptance by the entire community for the next two years. You have been given a short summary of the background of the problem as follows:

The research group is interested in finding out how a community solves its problems. For this reason the researchers wish to minimize their influence on community affairs.

The community being studied is a township which includes a small village, population about two thousand. The village is governed by an elected body, the Village Board, and the township is governed by another elected body, the Town Board. These groups raise taxes and support services such as road maintenance, police and fire departments. The research group is not clear as to how authority is divided between these two groups.

There are a great many voluntary organizations in the community, among the most active of which are the Better Business Bureau, the Grange (farmers' organization), the Parent-Teacher Association, and the Women's Republican Club. The research group has observed that the most influential men in the community are Mr. Jamison, a lawyer; Mr. Hopkins, the editor of the local newspaper; Mr. Hooper, the owner of the local telephone company; and Mr. Shinwell, a prosperous dairyman.

Different members of the research group have suggested that the most pressing needs in the community seem to be road improvement, recreational facilities for children after school hours and during the summer, beautification of the village, and incentives (e.g., house and office) to bring a dentist to town.

You, as an objective outsider, have been asked to write a report on this problem for the research group. Your report should emphasize the considerations to be taken into account in making the decision about how to donate the money rather than a specific proposal as to how to donate it. You may find that you need more information than is included in the short summary which you have been given as background material. If so, include these questions in the report, explaining why you want the information.

Making the Initial Contacts in the Research Area. Here is an illustrative task for this area of training:

You are interested in making a study of relations between workers and management in a non-unionized industrial plant. You also want to study relations between the plant and the community. After some investigation you decide that Backtown would be a suitable community for the study. It has the following characteristics: (a) The population of the town is 2000. (b) There is only one industrial plant in the town which hires predominantly semi- and unskilled workers. (c) The town is geographically isolated from other work centers, and there are few jobs in Backtown not directly related to the one industry. (d) Local management is reputed to have a tight control over the community affairs. (e) Local management is under the close direction of an absentee owner, Mr. Harvey, and his central staff. (f) The community is made up of long established New Englanders who are Protestant, and French Canadian Catholics who immigrated to Backtown at the beginning of this century. (g) Several unions have made unsuccessful attempts to organize the plant. (h) There are rumors that Mr. Harvey is considering transferring the plant to the South.

You decide it is essential to gain Mr. Harvey's consent before you can begin the study. His office is in New York City. Write a letter to him asking for an appointment to see him. Your purpose in seeing him will be to gain his permission for the research.

On a separate sheet from the letter explain why you wrote the letter as you did and why you think it will be effective. Were there any other alternatives you considered using?

Here is a second training task in this same area.

You are to imagine you are a research director at Hilltop University in the Department of Sociology and Anthropology. The project you are directing is making a study of race relations in a number of large cities throughout the United States. Funds for the project were obtained from the Federal Foundation. Today you arrive at Great City to begin a study which is to last three weeks.

It is your practice to phone the Mayor and make an appointment to see him. You are to phone Mayor Hetherington at his office. (A phone number is given which all students know is an extension on the University exchange, along with a specific date and time to make the call.) The purpose of your call is to speak to Mayor Hetherington and make an appointment to see him either tomorrow or the following day. This problem consists only of the phone call. Keeping the appointment is not included. Please be sure you make your call exactly at the hour at which you are instructed to call.

For teaching purposes your phone call will be tape recorded. This recording will be treated confidentially in the same way as all other data gathered from you.

[In this task the part of the mayor was played by a research worker who had considerable experience in dealing with this specific problem. The following questions were used by the mayor and his secretary in a flexible manner depending on the particular phone call.]

Secretary: Who is calling please?

Secretary: Just what did you want to talk with Mayor Hetherington about?

Secretary: Just one moment. I'll let you talk to the mayor.

Mayor: Hello.

Mayor: I'm terribly busy this week. We're right in the middle of preparing our budgets for the city council. I wonder if the City Manager couldn't answer any questions you have.

Mayor: What sort of things do you want to find out about?

Mayor: What organization did you say you represent?

Mayor: About how long will it take?

Mayor: Well, alright . . . It'll have to be sometime next week. What does your schedule look like next week?

Mayor: Well, how would 3 P.M. next Tuesday be?

Terminate call.

From the experience gained by the students in carrying out these two tasks and from an analysis by the students and staff of the results, some useful generalizations can be made on how to write letters and make phone calls under actual field conditions. The staff members can role-play the phone call and then repeat the call incorporating suggestions made after the students have criticized the first call.

Gaining Knowledge of an Organization before Beginning Field Work. Early in the course it was decided in which organization in a nearby community the class would like to carry out a practice field project which would involve the three teams. A resident in this community was then chosen who knew this organization but was not himself a member, who possessed an intimate knowledge of this community, and who was sympathetic to the purposes of the course. He was visited by a staff member who explained the nature of the training course and the reasons for selecting the particular organization in his community. He was then asked if he would attend a meeting of the class to allow the class to question him about the community and the organization. He accepted and the class questioned him to obtain what information they felt was necessary in order to proceed in translating the proposed project into active field work. After the visitor left, the class discussed what they had learned and how this information could be utilized in starting the field project. Because of the striking difference in the nature of the discussion during and after the local resident's visit to the class, it would also have been valuable to discuss what limitations were placed on the questions and answers by the roles of the visitor and the class members.

The Structuring of the Field Worker's Role. The following task situation was given to the students as preparation for the types of questions which are asked field workers about themselves and their work when they are in the field.

The staff members of the course prepared a sociodrama which depicted the closing stages of a committee meeting. The type of committee and the problems discussed resembled as closely as possible those the students were going to observe in practice field work. Before the sociodrama was performed the students were instructed that they were to consider themselves as observers at this committee meeting. They are given a summary of the types of information that they would have obtained had they observed the meeting from the start, e.g., the agenda, and the names and status of the committee members. The students were also told that when the business of the committee ended refreshments would be served. (This fits in well with our established custom of tea during the seminar session.) The committee members and the students were to remain in their roles during tea. At this time the committee members would talk informally with the students. The sociodrama was then enacted and followed by the tea, at which time the committee members chatted with the students and asked such questions as "What are you *really* getting out of this?" "Where are you from?" "Will we get anything out of this study?" "How much are you telling people about this?" When the role playing session was ended the types of questions and answers were then discussed by the class. It was stressed to the students that in an actual field situation most people are too shy, well-mannered, or kindly to ask such embarrassing questions and that it is extremely unlikely that they will meet such a barrage of questions in such a short time span in the field.

Presenting Completed Field Projects. (This presentation can cover any of the points in the outline of field relations skills.) In order to supplement the experience gained by the students in practice field work, classroom sessions have been held when an experienced field worker from a completed project was asked to attend. He briefly outlined the purpose of his field project and gave enough information about the organization and community to allow the class to begin questioning him on the field relations aspect of the field work. It has been found better to restrict the questioning to the same stage of the project as is being currently carried out by the class in their field work, rather than to cover all aspects of field relations. If two or three such visitors are invited, each with very different types of projects, at the beginning of the class, the visitors can be later brought back for further questioning on the field relations skills required at later stages in their and the class's projects. After such sessions the various presentations are discussed and an attempt is made to derive useful generalizations.

Interviewing Skills. Skills needed in interviewing have not been discussed in this paper. However, the research relations aspects of interviewing cannot be ignored during field relations training. One technique that can be used is to create a standardized situation which permits the class to conduct and evaluate trial interviews.[1] This technique can best be illustrated by an example.

A group of students' wives were asked to act as a committee to discuss the subject of how "marriage" should be taught at a university. At the end of half an hour they were asked to make some recommendations that could be considered in developing a course or series of talks on marriage to be given at the university. The discussion was tape recorded and notes were taken by two trained observers. Five days later the students' wives were asked to return and were told that the purpose of the initial committee meeting was to create a life situation which could be carefully recorded by various mechanical means, and that now a number of students would be interviewing them to find out what happened at the meeting. Each student wife was interviewed successively by a number of students. The interviews were also tape recorded. After each interview the informant answered a number of questions concerning her reactions to the interviewer and to the interview. Independently the records of the interviews were played over, and the staff members noted any aspects of the interview which might have affected good research relations with the informant. These were then compared with the informants' evaluation of the interviews. Subsequently a conference was held between a staff member and the student, during which the interview was played over and the interviewing techniques discussed.

Great care must be taken in these sessions to induce a balance between anxiety and reassurance so that the student will not be too discouraged, and will be able to learn from the experience. The willingness of the student to receive criticism appears to be greater if before the student's interview some of the staff members conduct demonstration interviews and these are discussed and freely criticized by the students.

Students should be warned about the ill effects that may result from not setting limits upon the type of information obtained in a first interview; e.g., statements concerning hostilities, attachments, and dependencies should not be probed or encouraged. Examples of this over-rapid establishment of rapport can be given by means of a tape recording or acting out of an interview especially written and acted to point up the problem.

CONCLUSION

The evaluation of the students who have been taught by means of the methods described in this paper has been favorable. An objective evaluation of the methods described herein is not possible at this time. The question of how to transmit effectively the human relations skills required in field work is precisely the focus of the Field Methods Training Program research which is now underway.

NOTE

[1] This technique is used primarily for teaching the variety of skills needed in interviewing.

CHAPTER 16

Participant Observation and the Collection and Interpretation of Data

Arthur J. Vidich

The practical and technical problems as well as many of the advantages and disadvantages of participant observation as a data-gathering technique have been well stated.[1] We propose to discuss some of the effects on data of the social position of the participant observer. The role of the participant observer and the images which respondents hold of him are central to the definition of his social position; together these two factors shape the circumstances under which he works and the type of data he will be able to collect.

In a broad sense the social position of the observer determines *what* he is likely to see. The way in which he sees and interprets his data will be largely conditioned by his theoretical preconceptions, but this is a separate problem with which we will not be concerned.[2]

What an observer will see will depend largely on his particular position in a network of relationships. To the extent that this is the case, this discussion of relatively well-known but frequently unstated observations is not purely academic. The task assumes the necessity of less concern with methodological refinements for handling data after they are collected and more concern with establishing canons of validity and the need, too, for a better balance between the standardization of field techniques and the establishment of standards for the evaluation of field data according to their source and the collector.

BROADER RELEVANCE OF PARTICIPANT OBSERVATION

As a technique, participant observation is central to all the social sciences. It has been singled out and treated as a rather specialized field approach with peculiar problems of its own, but this has obscured the extent to which the various social sciences depend upon it. Participant observation enables the research worker to secure his data within the mediums, symbols, and experiential worlds which have meaning to his respondents. Its intent is to prevent imposing alien meanings upon the actions of the subjects. Anthropologists dealing with cultures other than their own have consciously recognized and utilized the technique as a matter of necessity. Experimental psychologists who try their own instruments out on themselves as well as psychiatrists who undergo analysis are practicing a form of participant observation for much the same purpose as the anthropologist.

The sociologist who limits his work to his own society is constantly exploiting his personal background of experience as a basis of knowledge. In making up structured interviews, he draws on his knowledge of meanings gained from participation in the social order he is studying. He can be assured of a modicum of successful communication only because he is dealing in the same language and symbolic system as his respondents. Those who have worked with structured techniques in non-Western societies and languages will attest to the difficulty encountered in adjusting their meanings to the common meanings of the society investigated, a fact which highlights the extent to which the sociologist is a participant observer in almost all his work.[3]

In view of this widespread dependence upon participant observation as a source of data and as a basis for giving them meaning, a discussion of the factors which condition data obtained by this method is warranted.

Our source of immediate experience is the Springdale community of Upstate New York.[4] Experience as a participant observer in one's own culture sets the major problems of this technique into clearer focus. The objectification and self-analysis of the role of the participant observer in one's own society has the advantage that communication is in the same language and symbolic system.

FORMATION OF RESPONDENT IMAGES OF THE PARTICIPANT OBSERVER

Whether the field worker is totally, partially, or not at all disguised, the respondent forms an image of him and uses that image as a basis of response. Without such an image the relationship between the field worker and the respondent, by definition, does not exist.

The essential thing in any field situation is the assumption of some position in a structure of relationships. The position is assumed not only by various types of participant observers but by all interviewers. The undisguised interviewer establishes his personal identity or the identity of the organization he works for and, hence, makes himself and the questions he asks plausible to his respondent. In disguised interviewing, including that of the totally disguised participant observer, a plausible role is no less important even though it may be more complex and more vaguely defined; but the first concern remains the assumption of a credible role. Likewise the totally disguised social scientist, even as genuine participant, is always located in a given network of relationships.

Every research project is in a position partly to influence image formation by the way it identifies itself. However, these self-definitions are always dependent on verbalizations, and, at best, the influence they have is minimal unless supported overtly by the research worker. Field workers are well aware that the public is likely not to accept their statements at face value; gossip and talk between potential respondents when a research program first enters the field attests to this fact. This talk places the research worker in the context of the values, standards, and expectations of the population being studied, and its effect is to establish the identity of the field worker in the eyes of the public.

There is tremendous variation from field situation to field situation in the assignment of identity to the field worker. In the usual anthropological field situation he is identified as a trader, missionary, district officer, or foreign spy—any role with which the native population has had previous contact and experience. In time these ascriptions can and do change so that the anthropologist, for example, may even gain an identity within a kinship structure:

> He was assigned on the basis of residence to an appropriate Kwoma lineage and, by equation with a given generation, was called "younger brother" or "father" or "elder uncle," depending on the particular "kinsman" who addressed him. Having found a place for Whiting in the kinship, the Kwoma could orient their social behavior accordingly.[5]

In every case the field worker is fitted into a plausible role by the population he is studying and within a context meaningful to them. There seem to be no cases where field workers have not found a basis upon which subjects could react toward them. This is true even in the face of tremendous language barriers. Moreover, the necessary images and the basis for reaction which they provide are not only always found, but they are demanded by the mere fact of the research worker's intrusion into the life of his subjects. Even when a field worker is ejected, the image and meaningful context exists.

SOCIAL ROLE OF THE PARTICIPANT OBSERVER

Once he is placed in a meaningful context, the social position of the researcher is assured. His approach to the social structure is subsequently conditioned by his position.

Obviously the ascription and the assumption of a plausible role are not the equivalent of placing the participant observer in the experiential world of his subjects. Indeed, this impossibility is not his objective. For to achieve the experience of the subject, along with the baggage of perceptions that goes along with it, is to deny a chance for objectivity. Instead, an observer usually prefers to keep his identity vague; he avoids committing his allegiance—in short, his personality—to segments of the society. This is true even when he studies specialized segments of mass societies and organizations. In this case the observer may deliberately antagonize management, for example, in order to gain the confidence of the union or segments of it. However, within the union he has further to choose between competing factions, competing leaders, or leadership-membership cleavages. The anthropologist integrated into a kinship system or class faces the same problem. Eventually, no matter the size of the group he is studying, the observer is forced to face the problem of divided interests. He is "asked" to answer the question, "Who do you speak for?" and it is an answer to this question which, in the interests of research, he avoids.

Consequently, the observer remains marginal to the society or organization or segments of them which he studies. By his conscious action he stands between the major social divisions, not necessarily above them, but surely apart from them. Occupationally concerned with the objectification of action and events, he attempts to transcend all the local cleavages and discords. In avoiding commitments to political issues, he plays the role of political eunuch. He is socially marginal to the extent that he measures his society as a non-involved outsider and avoids committing his loyalties and allegiances to segments of it. This is not hypocrisy but rather, as Howe has noted of Stendhal, it is living a ruse.[6] Being both a participant and an observer is "the strategy of having one's cake and eating it too": "Deceiving the society to study it and wooing the society to live in it." His position is always ambivalent, and this ambivalence shapes the character of the data he secures and the manner of securing them.

THE PARTICIPANT OBSERVER'S DATA

All the information which the participant observer secures is conditioned by the meaningful context into which he is placed and by his own perspective as shaped by his being socially marginal. Together these circumstances greatly affect the kind of data he can get and the kind of experience he can have. The meaningful context into which he is placed by the public provides the latter with their basis for response, and his marginality specifies the order of experience possible for him.

To the extent that the observer's data are conditioned by the basis upon which subjects respond to him, the anthropologist studying another culture has one important advantage. He can justifiably maintain an attitude of naïveté and on this basis exploit his situation as a stranger to the fullest possible extent. Indeed, it is relatively easy to breach local customs and standards and still maintain a tenable research position in the society. This naive attitude cannot be assumed in working in his own culture, for the simple reason that the respondent cannot accept it as plausible. In fact, the difficulty of securing data may be increased by the "ethnocentrism" of some respondents who assume that their own experiences are similar to those of others. Yet with the increased complexity, specialization and pluralization of roles in American society, the social science observer is likely to have had no direct contact at all with whole ranges of experience. With the exception of his professional world (and partly because of his professionalization), he is something of a stranger in his own society without being in a position to exploit his innocence. He has the disadvantage of living in a society in which his experience is limited, while, at the same time, he is regarded as a knowledgeable member of all segments of it.

If the participant observer seeks genuine experiences, unqualifiedly immersing and committing himself in the group he is studying, it may become impossible for him to objectify his own experiences for research purposes; in committing his loyalties he develops vested interests which will inevitably enter into his observations. Anthropologists who have "gone native" are cases in point; some of them stop publishing material entirely.[7] And all anthropologists have learned to make appropriate compensation in data interpreted by missionaries, traders, and government officials, no matter how excellent the material may be.

In practice, the solution to the dilemma of genuine versus spurious experiences is to make use of individuals who are socially marginal in the society being studied. In almost any society in this postcolonial and specialized age, the observer is likely to find persons with a penchant for seeing themselves objectively in relation to their society, such as the traveled Pacific Islander and the small-town "intellectual." But they differ from the social scientist in one important respect: a portion of their experience, no matter how much it is subsequently objectified, has been gained within the society under study. When the social scientist studies a society, he characteristically makes his first contacts with these marginal persons, and they will vary according to his interests and the identity he claims for himself. Even when the observer tries to avoid the marginal individuals, he is nevertheless sought out by them. This is not unfortunate, for these types are a bridge, perhaps the most important one, to the meanings of the society. It is they who provide him with his first insights into the workings of the society. The sociologist studying his own society is, to varying degrees according to the relation between his background of experience and his object of study, his own bridge. Without such a bridge, without at least an interpreter or one lone native who can utter a word or two in another language, the observer would have no basis for approaching his data. The social marginality of the participant observer's role with all the limitations it imposes provides a basis for communication and, hence, ultimately, for understanding.

FIELD TACTICS AND DATA EVALUATION

When the participant observer sets out to collect his data, he is faced with two types of problems: the tactical problem of maneuver in the field and the evaluation of the data. The two problems are related in that the data to be evaluated are conditioned by the field tactics. The discussion of them will be limited to selected problems central to the technique of participant observation: the tractical problem of conformity or nonconformity, the observer's experience as related to the imputation of meaning and the formulation of categories, and the significance of participant observation to the study of social change.

Conformity or nonconformity to local standards and styles of living when engaging in field research is a relevant issue only in so far as the choice affects the research. Conformity is always conformity to specified standards and implies nonconformity to other possible standards. Almost all societies or groups in the contemporary world present alternative forms of behavior based on differing internal standards. Consequently it is hardly possible to conform to the standards of an entire society, and, hence, to follow a general policy of conformity is to follow no policy at all. Any policy which is designed to guide the field worker's actions must be based on a deliberate judgment as to which sources of information must be used to secure data. In the adopting of standards necessary to keep these sources open, other sources are likely to be alienated and closed off, or data from them may be distorted.

Moreover, conscious conformity to any standards, at best, is "artificial," for the participant observer does not commit himself to the point of genuine partisan action. In the interests of objectivity this is necessarily the case. In failing to make genuine commitments, he reveals his socially marginal position and the outside standards upon which he acts. In these terms the old argument posed by Radin, who said, "For any anthropologist to imagine that anything can be gained by 'going native' is a delusion and a snare," and by Goldenweiser, who said of sharing the lives of the natives and participating in their culture, "The more successful an anthropologist is in doing this, the better foundation he has laid for his future work,"[8] is no argument at all. The decision to assume standards and values or the degree to which participation is required is best made on the basis of the data to be collected and not on the basis of *standard* field practice.

The related tactical problem of conscious identification with groups, causes, or issues can be treated similarly. Complete and total neutrality is extremely difficult, if not impossible, to assume even where research considerations seem to demand it. By virtue of his research, no matter how transitory and irrespective of the exact dimensions of his marginal position, the investigator must react to the actions of his respondents. Neutrality even to the point of total silence is a form of reaction and not only will be considered as such by all parties to the conflict but also implies a specific attitude toward the issue—being above it, outside it, more important than it, not interested in it. Whatever meanings respondents attach to neutrality will, henceforth, be used as a further basis for response. This is true even when respondents demand an opinion or approval in structured interview situations. Failure to make a commitment can create resentment, hostility, and antagonism just as easily as taking a stand. In both cases, but each in its own way, relationships will be altered and, hence, data will be affected.

The data secured by the participant observer, except in so far as he reports personal experiences, cannot be independent of his subjects' ability and willingness to report. He is obliged to impute meaning to both their verbal and their nonverbal actions. His own experiences, though genuine, are at best vicarious approximations of those of his respondents; he never completely enters their world, and, by definition, if he did, he would assume the values, premises, and standards of his subjects and thereby lose his usefulness to research except as another subject. If the action observed is purely physical—the daily, routine physical movements of an individual, for example—the observer-interpreter cannot understand its meaning unless he communicates with the person involved in the action and gains insight into its meaning for the actor. Of course, studying within the meanings of his own society gives the observer a background of standardized meanings on which to draw. One knows that a man walking down the street at a certain time every morning is probably going to work. But the action of Raymond in *One Boy's Day*[9] was observed precisely because it was not known. In more complicated action in a segment of society in which the observer does not have experience, he gains it vicariously by talking with others and in that way secures almost all his data.

The respondent, on the other hand, is not necessarily able to verbalize his experiences, and, as attested to by psychoanalysis, it is quite probable that he will not understand their meaning. The greater the social distance between the observer and the observed, the less adequate the communication between them. Hence, as stated above, the observer's data are determined by the subjects' ability and willingness to report. Since he cannot duplicate their experience, he cannot draw his conclusions from his own marginal experiences. He always operates in the borderland of their experience and, hence is still faced with the problem of *imputing* meaning to their actions. Whereas his subjects base their own interpretations and evaluations on folklore, religion, myth, illusion, special and vested interests or even on the basis of local standards of social analysis, the social science observer-analyst uses the independent and extraneous standards of science.

The participant-observation technique has been offered as one of the best techniques on which to base prearranged observational and structured interview categories. The assumption is that, with his greater familiarity with the respondents' experiences and their meanings, the participant observer is in the best position to draw up meaningful categories. However, with the passage of time and the assumption and ascription of new roles and statuses, his perspective on the society is constantly changing. His marginal position allows him more social movement by virtue of which his perceptions will change with time, particularly as he gains greater and greater familiarity. Categories which initially seemed meaningful later on may appear superficial or even meaningless. Moreover, as long as he remains a participant observer, his social marginality undergoes continuous redefinition. As a result any categories he formulates in advance or at any given time will seem inadequate later when his social perspective has changed.[10] Attempts to establish categories into which directly observed actions can be classified threaten to reduce the action to static entities which influence later observations, a condition which the technique of participant observation is designed to avoid. Indeed, it is this last condition which makes participant observation most suitable to the study of social change.

The technique of participant observation more than any other technique places the observer closer to social change as it takes place in a passing present. Change, as measured by the succession of days and hours rather than by years or arbitrary measures, takes place slowly. The desire of, and necessity for, individuals is to act in terms of what is possible in specific immediate situations. The immediacy of social change to those who are involved in the moving present tends to obscure their perspective on it: a continuous altering of his memories and definitions of reality makes the individual involved un- aware of change. The participant observer is also involved in these changes, but, by his marginal position and his conscious effort to objectify himself, he achieves a measure of noninvolvement. Hence, his perspective is conditioned by considerations other than involvement. If the participant observer changed his perspective in phase with continuous changes in reality, he too could not see the change. For as long as changes in perspective accompany changes in reality, the change is likely not to be recognized. The participant who studies change as an observer must therefore maintain a perspective outside and independent of change. Noninvolvement helps to prevent the alteration of memory structures and permits the observer to see cumulative changes.

To refresh his memory, the participant observer can turn to his records. But, if his perspective has changed with time, he may disregard or discount early notes and impressions in favor of those taken later. Field notes from two different periods in a project may, indeed, be one of the more important means of studying change. Instead, what probably happens is that the field worker obscures change by treating his data as though everything happened at the same time. This results in a description from a single perspective, usually that held just before leaving the field, but redefined by the rereading of his notes.

CONCLUSIONS

Data collection does not take place in a vacuum. Perspectives and perceptions of social reality are shaped by the social position and interests of both the observed and the observer as they live through a passing present. The participant observer who is committed to relatively long periods of residence in the field experiences a continuous redefinition of his position. In this context the respondent's basis of response, as conditioned by his image of the observer, changes in accordance with new images based on the changing definitions of the observer's position. These forces influence the data.

A valid evaluation of data must necessarily include a reasonably thorough comprehension of the major social dimensions of the situation in which data were collected. The social positions of the observer and the observed and the relationship between them at the time must be taken into account when the data are interpreted. To fail to take account of these conditions is to assume an equivalence of situations which does not exist and leads to distortion.

To the extent that a participant observer can participate and still retain a measure of noninvolvement, his technique provides a basis for an approach to the problem of validity. The background of information which he acquires in time makes him familiar with the psychology of his respondents and their social milieu. With this knowledge he is able to impose a broader perspective on his data and, hence, to evaluate their validity on the basis of standards extraneous to the immediate situation. To accomplish this, it is necessary that the participant observer be skeptical of himself in all data-gathering situations; he must objectify himself in relation to his respondents and the passing present. This process of self-objectification leads to his further alienation from the society he studies. Between this alienation and attempts at objective evaluation lies an approach to the problem of validity.

NOTES

[1] See especially the following: Florence R. Kluckhohn, "The Participant Observer Technique in Small Communities," *American Journal of Sociology,* 46 (November, 1940), 331-43; William F. Whyte, *Street Corner Society* (Chicago: University of Chicago Press, 1943), pp. v-x, and also his "Observational Field-Work Methods" in Marie Jahoda, Morton Deutsch, and Stuart W. Cook (eds.), *Research Methods in the Social Sciences* (New York: Dryden Press, 1951), Vol. 2, 393-514; Marie Jahoda *et al.* "Data Collection: Observational Methods," in Marie Jahoda *et al.* (eds.), *Research Methods,* Vol. 1, Chap. V; Benjamin D. Paul, "Interview Techniques and Field Rela-

tions," in A. L. Kroeber *et al.* (eds.), *Anthropology Today: An Encyclopedic Inventory* (Chicago: University of Chicago Press, 1953), pp. 430-51; and Edward C. Devereux, "Functions, Advantages and Limitations of Semi-controlled Observation" (Ithaca, N.Y.: Staff Files, "Cornell Studies in Social Growth," Department of Child Development and Family Relationships, Cornell University, 1953).

[2] Oscar Lewis has devoted considerable attention to this problem. See especially his *Life in a Mexican Village: Tepoztlan Restudied* (Springfield: University of Illinois Press, 1951) and "Controls and Experiments in Field Work," in Kroeber *et al.* (eds.), *Anthropology Today*, pp. 452-75.

[3] F. C. Bartlett's "Psychological Methods and Anthropological Problems," *Africa*, 10 (October, 1937), 401-19, illustrates this problem.

[4] This work was conducted under the sponsorship of the Department of Child Development and Family Relationships in the New York State College of Home Economics at Cornell University. It is part of a larger project entitled "Cornell Studies in Social Growth" and represents an outgrowth of a study in the determinants of constructive social behavior in the person, the family, and the community. The research program is supported in part by grants from the National Institute of Mental Health, United States Public Health Service, and the Committee on the Early Identification of Talent of the Social Science Research Council with the aid of funds granted to the Council by the John and Mary R. Markle Foundation.

[5] Benjamin D. Paul in Kroeber *et al.* (eds.), *Anthropology Today*, p. 434.

[6] Irving Howe, "Stendhal: The Politics of Survival," in William Phillips and Philip Rahv (eds.), *The Avon Book of Modern Writing* (New York: Avon Publishing Co., 1953), pp. 60-61.

[7] Paul, in Kroeber *et al.* (eds.), *Anthropology Today*, p. 435, names Frank Cushing as one.

[8] Both quoted in Paul, Kroeber *et al.* (eds.), *Anthropology Today*, p. 438.

[9] Roger G. Barker and Herbert F. Wright, *One Boy's Day* (New York: Harper & Bros., 1951).

[10] These changes in circumstances refer not only to his position in the society he studies but also to the professional society with which he works and changes in research focus.

CHAPTER 17

An Abortion Clinic Ethnography

Donald W. Ball

Traditionally, the study of deviant behavior, however defined, has suffered from a lack of primary data. Materials available to students of various forms of deviance have usually been, in some degree, removed from the actual phenomena under investigation. Thus all too often reports dealing with unconventional social behavior and/or its organization have been based on official statistics produced by variously concerned agencies and on self-reports by the apprehended violators of formal rules and regulations. Neither of these sources is likely to produce an unbiased sample of deviant actors, their actions, and the social organization of these phenomena.[1]

An alternative method of pursuing the study of deviance, one rarely utilized, is to develop contacts with unapprehended deviants themselves, i.e. to go directly to unconventional actors and their subcultures; it is only with such procedures that the natural context of deviance can be studied without the skewedness typical of the usual sources of data.[2] The report which follows is an effort of this alternative: an attempt to utilize actual direct contact with deviant actors in their natural habitat—in this case an abortion clinic—in order to shed light on selected aspects of this relatively unstudied area of social life.[3]

More specifically, what follows is an effort to describe ethnographically certain aspects of a particular abortion clinic, especially as such data may illuminate the presentational strategies employed by an habitually deviant establishment in its dealing with a situationally deviant clientele.

For the clinic's staff, participation in an action legally defined as deviant, i.e. criminal abortion, is habitual; that is to say, it is regularly repeated on a routine, business-like basis. For patrons, however, participation is occasional, irregular, and frequently a once-in-a-lifetime engagement in this form of deviance. Most of them are members of otherwise law abiding cul-

This chapter was originally published by the Society for the Study of Social Problems, in *Social Problems,* 14: 293-301, and portions of it were presented to the panel on Medical Sociology, Pacific Sociological Association meetings, Vancouver, British Columbia; April 7, 1966. The author acknowledges the assistance of Stanford Lyman, Theodore Ravetz, and Carma Westrum Coon.

174

tures. Unlike the staff, their involvement in this deviant setting is not an aspect of a career, but an accidental consequence of an unwanted pregnancy.

In the context of the clinic, therefore, the deviant transaction ordinarily is enacted by two kinds of actors: those habitually involved in such exchanges, i.e. the staff; and those only situationally deviant, the otherwise conventional actors in their clinic-related roles as patrons. It becomes of some interest, then, to consider how the clinic manages and fosters impressions for this audience constituted of actors drawn from outside its habitually deviant, abortion-oriented sub-culture, and some of the characteristics of such strategies. Put another way, the focus herein will be upon techniques used by the clinic to key itself to the demands and expectations of a patronage drawn from the conventional culture.

Suffice to say, strictures of confidence prevent any elaborate discussion of method, problems of access, etc. Let it be noted, however, that the materials reported and interpreted herein are based upon: 1) sufficiently lengthy observation of a clinic's routine (exclusive of specifically medical procedures, which are not strictly relevant to the problem) to establish the patterns of its everyday functioning; 2) extensive interviews with a necessarily small number of patrons, some of whom were also observed within the clinic; and 3) limited discussions with some of the clinic's non-medical staff. Additionally, supplementary and confirmatory data have been drawn from interviews with individuals who have utilized other similar facilities. Unfortunately, any more detailed methodological description would, not surprisingly, violate promises of anonymity guaranteed to the subjects involved; for similar reasons, no direct quotations will be presented.[4]

BACKGROUND

The clinic studied is located, along with several like establishments, in a border town along the California-Mexico line. Its staff includes two practitioners or abortionists, ostensibly physicians, the younger of whom is in an apprentice relationship to the senior man; a practical nurse; a receptionist-bookkeeper; a combination janitress and custodian; a chauffer-errand boy; and a telephone-appointments secretary.

As costs for such procedures go, the clinic is a relatively expensive one, with fees averaging $500 per abortion. The rate is somewhat less for other medical personnel and students, who are eligible for a discount; and more for persons desiring post-operative overnight observation, or else beyond the tenth week of pregnancy. In terms of finances, the clinic studied is probably representative of others catering to a middle and upper-middle class clientele.

In order to obtain a better picture of the establishment, a brief natural history of a typical involvement between clinic and patron is useful at this point.

Preliminarily, it should be recognized that the ideal-typical practitioner-patient model is not appropriate for the analysis of abortion. Like veterinarians and pediatricians, abortionists frequently have patients for whom financial, if not moral, responsibility is an aspect of the role of some other person, i.e. a client. For abortionists such clients include boyfriends, husbands, and parents. Along with persons such as accompanying friends, they comprise for the patient what might be classified as *supportive others:* persons attending the clinic along with the patient in order to provide psychological support and reinforcement in this crisis situation. Not surprisingly, it is rare for a patient to go to the clinic completely alone, without some morally supportive other. Thus, within the context of abortion, the typical practitioner-patient dyad usually becomes a triad, comprising practitioner, patient, and supportive other.[5]

After referral, usually by a physician, less often by friend or acquaintance, the patron makes original contact with the clinic by telephone. The typically tentative, noncommital, but implicitly urgent communication of the patron is immediately treated in a matter-of-fact manner by the telephone girl. In appropriate middle class speech patterns she asks the length of the pregnancy, extolls the skills of the staff, sets up a tentative appointment, and discusses the fee and its mode of payment. Treating as routine the patron's problem helps minimize anxiety inherent in such situations. Parallel to this is a "medicalization" of the situation, also helping to disarm the patron vis-à-vis the deviant nature of the proposed transaction; at all times, the terminology is that of conventional medicine and surgery. Later, ordinarily two or three days prior to the appointment, the patron again calls the clinic, this time to get confirmation of date and time.

Usually patrons spend the night before their appointment at a hotel or motel near the clinic. Early in the morning of the scheduled date they call the clinic once again, this time to get directions to the only then revealed place of rendezvous where they are picked up and transported to the clinic by one of the staff members in a large, late model station wagon.

It is at this time that patrons find that they are not alone in their dilemma as there are also several others picked up at the same time, filling the station wagon to capacity. Although propinquity might argue for it, there is little deliberate interaction among the patrons during the ride to the clinic, uncertainty effectively immobilizing them in this ambiguous situation.

Upon arrival at the clinic site, where the wagon and all related cars of the staff are hidden from street view, the patrons are ushered into a large, well furnished waiting room. The clinic itself resembles a roomy private home, both externally and internally in its non-medical areas, and is located in a prestigious residential neighborhood.

Once in, the patrons find seats for themselves and settle into a waiting period of hushed expectancy. Conversation is limited to patients and their respective supportive others, i.e. to those previously known to one another. After a short interval of perhaps five minutes, the receptionist appears and calls out the name of the first patient. The pair, patient and receptionist, then retire out of sight of the remaining patrons and into the medical wing of the clinic.

The first stop in the medical wing is an office. After first explaining the procedure in explicitly medical terminology, the receptionist shifts to her bookkeeper role and requests the fee (in cash or traveler's checks) from the patient, frequently finding that it is being held by an accompanying supportive other still in the waiting room. Following this discussion and collection of the fee, the patient is then sent to a bathroom, well appointed in terms of luxury rather than gynecology, to remove her street clothes and put on a surgical gown. Once gowned, the patient is directed to the room where the actual abortion will take place.

Those specifically involved in the procedure include, in addition to the patient, the two practitioners, senior and apprentice, and a practical nurse. Although an anesthetic is administered, at no time is the patient allowed to lose consciousness; a necessity born of the possible need for quick removal in the event of visitation by legal agents. Immediately upon completion of the procedure the patient leaves the table and is sent to another room to rest for fifteen minutes to an hour and a half. Finally, after receiving medication and instruction regarding post-operative care from the receptionist, the patient and any supportive others are returned to the site of the original rendezvous and thus to their conventional worlds.

ANALYSIS

With this brief, oversimplified picture it is now possible to turn to more specifically sociological concerns: the aforementioned presentational strategies which make up what may be called, for the clinic, a *rhetoric of legitimization*.

Sociologically, a rhetoric is a vocabulary of limited purpose; that is to say, it is a set of symbols functioning to communicate a particular set of meanings, directed and organized toward the representation of a specific image or impression. Such vocabularies are not only verbal but also include visual symbols such as objects, gestures, emblems, etc.[6]

In the case of the clinic the rhetoric operates to subvert the conventional world's view of abortion, and to generate a picture of legitimate activity. Fundamentally, the question thus becomes: What techniques are utilized via this rhetoric to *neutralize* the context of deviance in which the clinic operates, so as to enhance parallels with conventional medical and social situations and thus derive a kind of "rightness" or legitimization.[7] How, in other words, are the setting and actions *qua* impressions manipulated to maximize the clinic's image over and above successful performance of its task and contradict the stereotypic stigma of deviance? Specifically, how does the clinic 1) minimize the possibilities of trouble with frightened or recalcitrant patrons; 2) generate the patron satisfaction necessary for referral system maintenance; and 3) present an image which will provide the most favorable self image or identity for the actors involved, whether patron or staff?[8]

For conceptual purposes, the clinic's rhetoric of legitimization may be treated by employing Goffman's delineation of *front* and its constituents of setting, appearance, and manner,[9] originally a framework for analyzing the presentation of self, it seems extendible to the strategies of establishments and institutions as well.

Essentially, front consists of those communications which serve to define the situation or performance for the audience: standardized expressive equipment including *setting,* the spatial/physical background items of scenery in the immediate area of the interaction; *appearance,* the sign-vehicles expressing the performer's social status or type; and those expressions which warn of a performer's demeanor, mood, etc., i.e. *manner.*

Examining each of these elements for evidence of how they are manipulated to make up a rhetoric will show the central themes and dimensions of the clinic's presentational strategies. Although the combination of the conceptions of rhetoric, neutralization, and front produces an admittedly loose theoretical scheme, the character of the data does not suggest the need for further rigor.

Setting

A paramount feature of the clinic's rhetoric is its physical and spatial characteristics. Especially important for patrons generally is the stereotype-contradicting waiting room, the first impression of the clinic itself—and the dominant one for supportive others. The waiting room is likely to be the only room in which the supportive others will be present during their entire visit to the clinic, save the possibility of a short interval in the office if they happen to be holding the fee, a frequent occurrence, especially if the other is also a client.

Spatially, the waiting room is L-shaped and extremely large; approximately 75 feet long and 50 feet wide at the base leg. Its size is accentuated by the fact that most of the room is sunken about three feet below other floor levels. Fully and deeply carpeted, well furnished with several couches, arm chairs, large lamps, and tables, the room speaks of luxury and patron consideration, also implied by the presence of a television set, a small bar, and a phonograph, in addition to the usual magazines present in waiting room situations.

Both the size of the room and the placement of the furniture function to provide private islands which need not be shared; space is structured so as to create withdrawal niches for each set of patrons. Couches and chairs are arranged along the walls of the room, maximizing distance between groupings and minimizing the possibilities of direct, inter-group eye-contact between the various patron-sets who, despite their shared problem and the recently experienced forced propinquity of the ride to the clinic, tend to keep their anxieties private. Thus, interaction among patrons in the waiting room is closed, confined to patients and their own accompanying supportive others only.

Turning to the medical wing: The picture is a far cry from the shabby and sordid image of "kitchen table abortion" drawn in the popular press; it is one of modern scientific medicine, and with it comes assurance to the patient. Once the patient has donned a gown, her next stop is the operating room, a designation used without exception by the staff. In addition to a gynecological table, the room contains familiar (to the lay patient) medical paraphernalia: surgical tools, hypodermic syringes, stainless steel pans and trays, bottles and vials enclosing various colored liquids, capsules, pills, etc.–props effectively neutralizing the negative stereotypes associated with abortion as portrayed in the mass media.

After the procedure has been completed, the patient is moved from the scientific arena of the operating room and back again into luxury. As is the waiting room, the rooms in which the patients spend their short period of post-operative rest are expensively furnished.

Ultimately, after resting, the patient returns to the waiting room and, for most, to supportive others, and receives a final post-operative briefing before being returned to the rendezvous site. Parenthetically it may be noted that throughout the entire episode piped-in music has prevaded every room in which patrons are present.

In terms of setting, the clinic presents itself as not unlike a small hospital albeit with a decorator-designed interior. For patient and supportive others the scenery and props have functioned to communicate an image of assurance and protection through the devices of cost and luxury along with scientific medicine, to minimize the deviant nature of the transaction, and to emphasize positive cultural values, thus efficiently countering the stereotypic image.

Appearance and Manner

A widespread device for visibly differentiating various social categories or types is clothing.[10] Items of dress may function as insignia or uniforms to label the persons so garbed as members of particular social groups, occupations, etc. Such institutionalized symbols act as both identifiers and identities; to be attired in certain ways is to be a certain kind of person, not only in the eyes of the audience, but also in terms of the actor's perception of himself. Dress is an integral aspect of social identity.

So it is with the staff of the clinic: practitioners, patient, nurse—all wear the appropriate symbols, from the layman's point of view, of dress for surgically centered roles. White tunics are worn by the practitioners; the patient is surgically gowned; the nurse and even the janitress wear white uniform dresses. This element of the rhetoric is highlighted at the beginning of the procedure when both practitioners ostentatiously don surgical gloves, visibly emphasizing their, and the clinic's, concern with the necessities of asepsis. This ritualistic activity also serves to forcefully identify these actors in their roles as defined by the rhetoric.

The medical model is further underscored by the pre-operative medical history which is taken and recorded upon a standard, multi-carboned form (the destiny of those duplicate copies is unknown). Actions such as this, along with dress, provide major modes of stressing the medical legitimacy of the clinic, its staff, and its task.

From the receptionist on up through the clinic's hierarchy, behavior, particularly verbal, emphasizes medical and professional aspects of the clinic's operation. Nowhere is this more apparent than in the area of vocabulary; it is strictly medical, with no effort either made or implied to speak down to the less knowledgeable lay patron. It is also noteworthy that at no time is the word abortion used in the presence of a patron; rather, it is referred to as the operation, the procedure, or as a D and C (dilation and curettage). Similarly, as noted above, the room in which the procedure takes place is at all times designated by the staff as the operating room.

Other elements of staff behavior which further the medical impression are 1) the post-operative consultation and medication which effectively contrast with the popular view of abortion as an "off-the-table-and-out" procedure, and 2) the presence of an apprentice practitioner and its obvious analogy, at least to the medically sophisticated, with a teaching hospital. For the patient, the teaching aspects of the senior practitioner's role help to generate confidence in his skill, a matter which is verbally reinforced by other staff members in their interactions with the patrons.

As with appearance, the manner of the staff is essentially directed toward the medical elements of the clinic's rhetoric; their demeanor is professional at all times, with one exception. This exception is the receptionist-bookkeeper, whose role is, by definition, outside the strictly medical aspects of the clinic. As a result, freed of the obligations of professional mien, the receptionist is able to interact with patrons in a reassuring and supportive manner; in effect, her presentation of the rhetoric is through expressive strategies, while the manner of other staff members is more instrumentally oriented.[11]

Before turning to the central themes engendered among the patrons by the clinic's rhetorical strategies, it may be well to at least take note of some flaws in the presentation, even though they may escape the usual patron's attention. These may be considered under the general rubrics of pseudo-sterility and miscellaneous delicts.

Pseudo-Sterility

Although ostentation is the rule as regards the emphasis of aseptic and antiseptic precautions, there are also omissions less readily obvious. It will be recalled that measures apparently designed to minimize infection and also at the same time maximize parallels with legitimate medicine included the wearing of tunics by the practitioners, their donning of surgical gloves prior to the procedure, and the display of the tools and paraphernalia of medicine and surgery in the operating room.

It should be pointed out that, aseptically, tunics are no substitute for full surgical gowns, that full precautionary tactics would also include items such as face masks, caps, etc.; and that it is highly irregular for an operating room to lack an autoclave (for the sterilization of instruments) and changeable covering for the table, and for surgical instruments to stand on display, exposed to the air for long periods of time. Additionally, it may be noted that the portion of the pre-operative medical history which is taken by the senior practitioner is recorded by him after his elaborate display of putting on the surgical gloves—a less than ideal practice for sterility.

These breaches of standard procedure suggest that much of what is passed to the lay patron as concern with aseptic and antiseptic practices is actually rhetoric, designed to communicate to the audience a standard of medical rigor which does not in fact exist.

Miscellaneous Delicts

Within this category are included additional practices at variance with the fostered impression.

Perhaps the most glaring of these is the lack of privacy afforded the patient in comparison with more conventional medical settings. The fact that patients are handled in groups, and moved and serviced in what in comparison with a hospital is a small and not systematically designed space, leads to a good deal of enforced contact between patients and staff involved in various stages of the process. Of necessity this leads to invasions of privacy, at least as perceived by patients accustomed to more traditional medical situations. Thus, for instance, the room used as an office also doubles as a resting room, and a patient lying there for post-operative rest may suddenly find herself witness to a financial transaction as a later-scheduled patron pays the fee; the resting patient is thus treated, in effect, as an object, becoming, in Goffman's phrase, a non-person,[12] i.e. an actor not accorded the usual deferences given as minimal acknowledgements of a person's moral worth simply by virtue of the person's being human.

Also of interest is the function of the music, piped into every room including the one for the procedure. When the patrons first arrive at the clinic the music is quiet, soothing, and relaxing in style; but with the entrance of the first patient into the medical wing, the tempo and timbre increase. The volume of the music then operates to drown out any untoward sounds which might emanate from the medical wing and alarm those patrons still in the waiting room.

Another delict involves the marked contrast in vehicles used in picking up and returning patrons to the rendezvous. In keeping with the symbolism of cost and luxury presented to the prospective patron, the station wagon which brings them to the clinic is an expensive late model. By contrast, for the return to the rendezvous, which is not done en masse as is the initial pick up, and by which time presentational strategies are less necessary, the car driven by the chauffer-errand boy is in an old, rather decrepit foreign sedan of low cost and questionable reliability.

Another item at variance with traditional medical procedures is the emphasis, especially by the practitioners, on the necessity of the patient's cooperation to assure the procedure's success. The patient is in effect invited, if not commanded, to become an active participant in the ongoing activity.[13] She is told, for instance, of the desirability of her concentrating on other matters, e.g. "think of something else and all will go smoothly and rapidly." This assigning an active role to the patient stands in marked contradiction to her objectification as regards matters of privacy, and implies expediency as a more central concern of the clinic's operation than is patient welfare.

Finally, it may be noted that though the practitioners are verbally represented by others on the staff as physicians, gynecologists; in fact, no evidence of medical training in the form of certificates or diplomas is available for patron scrutiny.

DISCUSSION

From this selective ethnographic description of various aspects of the clinic's front, two broad dimensions appear essential to its rhetoric of legitimization: 1) luxury and cost, and 2) conventional medical practices and procedures. It is these two themes which are emphasized in the clinic's efforts to neutralize its aura of habitual deviance before an audience of situationally deviant patrons drawn from the world of conventional culture. Thus, the rhetoric draws its vocabulary from meaningful and positive values of the patron's culture.

Within these two valued themes, four elements may be specified as contributing to the two broader dimensions of luxury and cost and conventional medicine: cleanliness, competence, conventionality, and concern for the patron.

Cleanliness and competence are both elements of the instrumental aspects of medicine. Albeit with significant flaws, unrecognized by most lay patrons anyway, the clinic's presentational strategies enhance these impressions, if not to the same extent their actualities. The obvious symbols of dress and equipment are presented to the patient in the medical wing of the clinic where anxiety and uncertainty are high. The symbols are readily recognizable and imply the conventionality of the situation; they provide, in effect, a set of familiar expectations drawn from past experience with legitimate medicine. In a similar allaying manner, the practitioner's skill and competence is repeatedly voiced by the staff from the time of the initial telephone contact until the beginning of the actual abortive procedure itself.

Conventionality here means a realization of the middle class values of most patrons. One of these values is, of course, a positive view of professional medicine, a view which the clinic attempts to exploit. Throughout the patron's experience with the clinic, parallels with this model are highlighted; but it is in another area that this element of the rhetoric functions most effectively.

This is the waiting room setting. The obvious expense, comfort, and general decor of this room are such as to disarm all but the most fearful and suspicious patron. This room and the first impressions it presents are such as to immediately link the clinic to the safe, known world of respectable middle class conventionality. In the process of this linkage, the clinic is, in the patron's perception, divorced from the usually illicit image conjured by abortion; if not rendered totally respectable, the clinic is at least brought within the context of the definitions and expectations of mundane, everyday experience. Because of its crucial location in the process, being the patron's first direct exposure to the clinic milieu, it is fair to say that this room is the most successful presentational strategy in the clinic's legitimizing rhetoric.

The comfort of the waiting room is but one of the forms of expression of concern for the patron which help to create a legitimitizing presentation. Other strategies include the telephone girl's supportive routinization of the patron's problem at the time of the initial contact; the similarly solicitous demeanor of the receptionist; and the post-operative consultation. This involves not only the dispensing of drugs to facilitate the patient's convalescence, but also a brochure specifically detailing an expected course of progress and steps to be taken in case of complications.

By demonstrating concern, the clinic affirms its subscription to the values of its patrons, and thus asserts its basically conventional nature, i.e. the congruence of its operation with the norms of those upon whom its income relies.

All of these factors combine to help construct a rhetoric of legitimacy: a set of presentational strategies which allows the clinic to minimize problems inherent in typically anxious and fearful patrons, and thus to function more effectively; and in addition to generate the reputation necessary for an establishment of its kind, dependent upon referrals from physicians.

Additionally, whether manifest or latent, the rhetoric also has consequences for the identities of the actors involved. Both habitual deviants, the staff, and situational deviants, the patrons, are able to partake of the rhetoric so as to enhance their own self images. The rhetoric helps the staff define their participation in the clinic's habitually deviant activities, despite the occasional flaws, as involvement in a professionally operating establishment with the trappings of conventional medicine. For patrons, though they too are admittedly involved in a deviant situation, the rhetoric blunts this hard truth. By accepting the presentational strategies as part of the clinic's image, the patron is allowed to define the situation through the symbols drawn from his conventional everyday experience. Thus, for both patron and staff alike, the rhetoric allows for a minimization of the threat to identity which is built into their illicit transaction.

Unfortunately, the confidential nature of this research does not allow one of the usual canons of science to be met, i.e. that regarding exact replication; and no claim regarding the typicality of the clinic described herein can be made. Hopefully, however, the materials have shed some light on a relatively little known area of social behavior. Given the incidence of abortion, it may be hoped that similar analyses can be conducted by others.[14] Additionally, it may be suggested that the concept of rhetoric provides a useful tool for examining the dramas of social life, whether deviant or conventional, spontaneous or routine, unusual or mundane.

NOTES

[1] The sources of bias in official statistics are too well known to require citation, e.g. differentials in organizational actions, variances in definitions, etc.; to deal with apprehended violators only is to study the *technically unskilled* and the *politically unconnected*.

[2] See the penetrating discussion of the ethical problems involved in this method by Ned Polsky, quoted in Howard B. Becker, *Outsiders* (New York: The Free Press of Glencoe, 1963), pp. 171-172.

[3] For a recent summary which demonstrates how little is known see Edwin M. Schur, *Crimes Without Victims* (Englewood Cliffs, N.J.: Prentice-Hall, 1965), pp. 11-16.

[4] For those interested in procedural minutiae as criteria of validity, the only answer can be: Go out and replicate using your own design. Though precise comparisons would not be possible, such confirmation or refutation would be most desirable.

[5] In this discussion the general label patron will be used in reference to patients, clients, and supportive others, unless reference is specifically limited to one of the roles in this category.

[6] The concept of rhetoric as used herein is similar to but independent of the work of Kenneth Burke. As a theoretical point it should be noted that rhetorics are not necessarily the same thing as ideologies, although this may empirically be the case. The conceptual difference between the two is that rhetoric speaks to communication, both style and content, while ideology refers to perception and justification in terms of the ideologue's conception of the relevant portions of the world. It is quite conceivable that individual actors will utilize a rhetoric without any ideological convictions as regards its validity, but with a recognition of its pragmatic efficacy; and similarly, that ideological dedication does not automatically assume any developed rhetoric to attempt its maintenance or furtherance.

[7] Compare Gresham M. Sykes and David Matza, "Techniques of Neutralization: A Theory of Delinquency," *American Sociological Review,* 22 (December, 1967), 664-670, where the analysis is individual rather than institutional; also Matza, *Delinquency and Drift* (New York: John Wiley and Sons, 1964).

[8] The second and third problems are, in effect, special cases of the first. Minimization of trouble is not motivated by fear of patron complaints to legal agents, which would involve the complainants in admitting complicity, but by desire to maintain referrals and enhance self images. Additionally, such minimization produces a smoother, easier work-flow for the staff; a similar rationale in conventional medical settings sometimes dictates the use of general anesthetics when, in terms of patient pain, locals would be adequate.

[9] Erving Goffman, *The Presentation of Self in Everyday Life* (Garden City, N.Y.: Doubleday Anchor, 1959), pp. 22-30. This scheme formed the observational framework for data collection as well as a perspective for preparing the data.

[10] Mary Ellen Roach and Joanne Bubolz Eicher (eds.), *Dress, Adornment, and the Social Order* (New York: John Wiley and Sons, 1965).

[11] Excluded from this consideration is the telephone girl who is never in face-to-face interaction with the patrons but is also supportive in her demeanor.

[12] Goffman, *The Presentation of Self, op. cit.,* pp. 151-152.

[13] See the discussion of the patient as basically helpless and passive in Talcott Parsons, *The Social System* (Glencoe, Ill.: The Free Press, 1951), pp. 439-447. An alternative approach is indicated in Robert Leonard's work. See his several papers in James Skipper, Jr. and Leonard, *Social Interaction and Patient Care* (Philadelphia: J. P. Lippincott, 1965).

[14] A step in this direction is the dissertation (in progress) of Nancy L. Howell, "Information Channels and Informal Networks in the Distribution of Source Information," Department of Social Relations, Harvard University.

PART FIVE

Problems of Validity and Reliability

CHAPTER 18

Problems of Inference and Proof
in Participant Observation

Howard S. Becker

The participant observer gathers data by participating in the daily life of the group or organization he studies.[1] He watches the people he is studying to see what situations they ordinarily meet and how they behave in them. He enters into conversation with some or all of the participants in these situations and discovers their interpretations of the events he has observed.

Let me describe, as one specific instance of observational technique, what my colleagues and I have done in studying a medical school. We went to lectures with students taking their first two years of basic science and frequented the laboratories in which they spend most of their time, watching them and engaging in casual conversation as they dissected cadavers or examined pathology specimens. We followed these students to their fraternity houses and sat around while they discussed their school experiences. We accompanied students in the clinical years on rounds with attending physicians, watched them examine patients on the wards and in the clinics, sat in on discussion groups and oral exams. We ate with the students and took night calls with them. We pursued interns and residents through their crowded schedules of teaching and medical work. We stayed with one small group of students on each service for periods ranging from a week to two months, spending many full days with them. The observational situations allowed time for conversation and we took advantage of this to interview students about things that had happened and were about to happen, and about their own backgrounds and aspirations.

Sociologists usually use this method when they are especially interested in understanding a particular organization or substantive problem rather than demonstrating relations between abstractly defined variables. They attempt to

This chapter was originally published by The American Sociological Association, in *American Sociological Review,* 23: 652-60, and has developed out of problems of analysis arising in a study of a state medical school. The study was sponsored by Community Studies, Inc., of Kansas City, Missouri. The author acknowledges the assistance of Blanche Geer and Alvin W. Gouldner.

make their research theoretically meaningful, but they assume that they do not know enough about the organization *a priori* to identify relevant problems and hyphotheses and that they must discover these in the course of the research. Though participant observation can be used to test *a priori* hypotheses, and therefore need not be as unstructured as the example I have given above, this is typically not the case. My discussion refers to the kind of participant observation study which seeks to discover hypotheses as well as to test them.

Observational research produces an immense amount of detailed description; our files contain approximately five thousand single-spaced pages of such material. Faced with such a quantity of "rich" but varied data, the researcher faces the problem of how to analyze it systematically and then to present his conclusions so as to convince other scientists of their validity. Participant observation (indeed, qualitative analysis generally) has not done well with this problem, and the full weight of evidence for conclusions and the processes by which they were reached are usually not presented, so that the reader finds it difficult to make his own assessment of them and must rely on his faith in the researcher.

In what follows I try to pull out and describe *the basic analytic operations carried on in participant observation,* for three reasons: to make these operations clear to those unfamiliar with the method; by attempting a more explicit and systematic description, to aid those working with the method in organizing their own research; and, most importantly, in order to propose some changes in analytic procedures and particularly in reporting results which will make the processes by which conclusions are reached and substantiated more accessible to the reader.

The first thing we note about participant observation research is that analysis is carried on *sequentially,*[2] important parts of the analysis being made while the researcher is still gathering his data. This has two obvious consequences: further data gathering takes its direction from provisional analyses; and the amount and kind of provisional analysis carried on is limited by the exigencies of the field work situation, so that final comprehensive analyses may not be possible until the field work is completed.

We can distinguish three distinct stages of analysis conducted in the field itself, and a fourth stage, carried on after completion of the field work. These stages are differentiated, first, by their logical sequence: each succeeding stage depends on some analysis in the preceding stage. They are further differentiated by the fact that different kinds of conclusions are arrived at in each stage and that these conclusions are put to different uses in the continuing research. Finally, they are differentiated by the different criteria that are used to assess evidence and to reach conclusions in each stage. The three stages of field analysis are: the selection and definition of problems, concepts, and indices; the check on the frequency and distribution of phenomena; and the incorporation of individual findings into a model of the organization under study.[3] The fourth stage of final analysis involves problems of presentation of evidence and proof.

SELECTION AND DEFINITION OF PROBLEMS, CONCEPTS, AND INDICES

In this stage, the observer looks for problems and concepts that give promise of yielding the greatest understanding of the organization he is studying, and for items which may serve as useful indicators of facts which are harder to observe. The typical conclusion that his data yield is the simple one that a given phenomenon exists, that a certain event occurred once, or that two phenomena were observed to be related in one instance; the conclusion says nothing about the frequency or distribution of the observed phenomenon.

By placing such an observation in the context of a sociological theory, the observer selects concepts and defines problems for further investigation. He constructs a theoretical model to account for that one case, intending to refine it in the light of subsequent findings. For instance, he might find the following: "Medical student X referred to one of his patients as a 'crock' today."[4] He may then connect this finding with a sociological theory suggesting that occupants of one social category in an institution classify members of other categories by criteria derived from the kinds of problems these other persons raise in the relationship. This combination of observed fact and theory directs him to look for the problems in student-patient interaction indicated by the term "crock." By discovering specifically what students have in mind in using the term, through questioning and continued observation, he may develop specific hypotheses about the nature of these interactional problems.

Conclusions about a single event also lead the observer to decide on specific items which might be used as indicators[5] of less easily observed phenomena. Noting that in at least one instance a given item is closely related to something less easily observable, the researcher discovers possible shortcuts easily enabling him to observe abstractly defined variables. For example, he may decide to investigate the hypothesis that medical freshmen feel they have more work to do than can possibly be managed in the time allowed them. One student, in discussing this problem, says he faces so much work that, in contrast to his undergraduate days, he is forced to study many hours over the weekend and finds that even this is insufficient. The observer decides, on the basis of this one instance, that he may be able to use complaints about weekend work as an indicator of student perspectives on the amount of work they have to do. The selection of indicators for more abstract variables occurs in two ways: the observer may become aware of some very specific phenomenon first and later see that it may be used as an indicator of some larger class of phenomena; or he may have the larger problem in mind and search for specific indicators to use in studying it.

Whether he is defining problems or selecting concepts and indicators, the researcher at this stage is using his data only to speculate about possibilities. Further operations at later stages may force him to discard most of the provisional hypotheses. Nevertheless, problems of evidence arise even at this point, for the researcher must assess the individual items on which his speculations are based in order not to waste time tracking down false leads. We shall eventually need a systematic statement of canons to be applied to individual items of evidence. Lacking such a statement, let us consider some commonly used tests. (The observer typically applies these tests as seems reasonable to him during this and the succeeding stage in the field. In the final stage, they are used more systematically in an overall assessment of the total evidence for a given conclusion.)

The Credibility of Informants

Many items of evidence consist of statements by members of the group under study about some event which has occurred or is in process. Thus, medical students make statements about faculty behavior which form part of the basis for conclusions about faculty-student relations. These cannot be taken at face value; nor can they be dismissed as valueless. In the first place, the observer can use the statement as evidence *about the event,* if he takes care to evaluate it by the criteria an historian uses in examining a personal document.[6] Does the informant have reason to lie or conceal some of what he sees as the truth? Does vanity or expediency lead him to mis-state his own role in an event or his attitude toward it? Did he actually have an opportunity to witness the occurrence he describes or is hearsay the source of his knowledge? Do his feelings about the issues or persons under discussion lead him to alter his story in some way?

Secondly, even when a statement examined in this way proves to be seriously defective as an accurate report of an event, it may still provide useful evidence for a different kind of conclusion. Accepting the sociological proposition that an individual's statements and descriptions of events are made from a perspective which is a function of his position in the group, the observer can interpret such statements and descriptions as indications of the individual's perspective on the point involved.

Volunteered or Directed Statements

Many items of evidence consist of informants' remarks to the observer about themselves or others or about something which has happened to them; these statements range from those which are a part of the running casual conversation of the group to those arising in a long intimate tete-a-tete between observer and informant. The researcher assesses the evidential value of such statements quite differently, depending on whether they have been made independently of the observer (volunteered) or have been directed by a question from the observer. A freshman medical student might remark to the observer or to another student that he has more material to study than he has time to master; or the observer might ask, "Do you think you are being given more work than you can handle?" and receive an affirmative answer.

This raises an important question: to what degree is the informant's statement the same one he might give, either spontaneously or in answer to a question, in the absence of the observer? The volunteered statement seems likely to reflect the observer's preoccupations and possible biases less than one which is made in response to some action of the observer, for the observer's very question may direct the informant into giving an answer which might never occur to him otherwise. Thus, in the example above, we are more sure that the students are concerned about the amount of work given them when they mention this of their own accord than we are when the idea may have been stimulated by the observer asking the question.

The Observer-Informant-Group Equation

Let us take two extremes to set the problem. A person may say or do something when alone with the observer or when other members of the group are also present. The evidential value of an observation of this behavior depends on the observer's judgment as to whether the behavior is equally likely to occur in both situations. On the one hand, an informant may say and do things when alone with the observer that accurately reflect his perspective but which would be inhibited by the presence of the group. On the other hand, the presence of others may call forth behavior which reveals more accurately the person's perspective but would not be enacted in the presence of the observer alone. Thus, students in their clinical years may express deeply "idealistic" sentiments about medicine when alone with the observer, but behave and talk in a very "cynical" way when surrounded by fellow students. An alternative to judging one or the other of these situations as more reliable is to view each datum as valuable in itself, but with respect to different conclusions. In the example above, we might conclude that students have "idealistic" sentiments but that group norms may not sanction their expression.[7]

In assessing the value of items of evidence, we must also take into account the observer's role in the group. For the way the subjects of his study define that role affects what they will tell him or let him see. If the observer carries on his research incognito, participating as a full-fledged member of the group, he will be privy to knowledge that would normally be shared by such a member and might be hidden from an outsider. He could properly interpret his own experience as that of a hypothetical "typical" group member. On the other hand, if he is known to be a researcher, he must learn how group members define him and in particular whether or not they believe that certain kinds of information and events should be kept hidden from him. He can interpret evidence more accurately when the answers to these questions are known.

CHECKING THE FREQUENCY AND DISTRIBUTION OF PHENOMENA

The observer, possessing many provisional problems, concepts, and indicators, now wishes to know which of these are worth pursuing as major foci of his study. He does this, in part, by discovering if the events that prompted their development are typical and widespread, and by seeing how these events are distributed among categories of people and organizational sub-units. He reaches conclusions that are essentially quantitative, using them to describe the organization he is studying.

Participant observations have occasionally been gathered in standardized form capable of being transformed into legitimate statistical data.[8] But the exigencies of the field usually prevent the collection of data in such a form as to meet the assumptions of statistical tests, so that the observer deals in what have been called "quasi-statistics."[9] His conclusions, while implicitly numerical, do not require precise quantification. For instance, he may conclude that members of freshman medical fraternities typically sit together during lectures while other students sit in less stable smaller groupings. His observations may indicate such a wide disparity between the two groups in this respect that the inference is warranted without a standardized counting operation. Occasionally, the field situation may permit him to make similar observations or ask similar questions of many people, systematically searching for quasi-statistical support for a conclusion about frequency or distribution.

In assessing the evidence for such a conclusion the observer takes a cue from his statistical colleagues. Instead of arguing that a conclusion is either totally true or false, he decides, if possible, how *likely* it is that his conclusion about the frequency or distribution of some phenomenon is an accurate quasi-statistic, just as the statistician decides, on the basis of the varying values of a correlation coefficient or a significance figure, that his conclusion is more or less likely to be accurate. The kind of evidence may vary considerably and the degree of the observer's confidence in the conclusion will vary accordingly. In arriving at this assessment, he makes use of some of the criteria described above, as well as those adopted from quantitative techniques.

Suppose, for example, that the observer concludes that medical students share the perspective that their school should provide them with the clinical experience and the practice in techniques necessary for a general practitioner. His confidence in the conclusion would vary according to the nature of the evidence, which might take any of the following forms: (1) *Every* member of the group said, *in response to a direct question,* that this was the way he looked at the matter. (2) *Every* member of the group *volunteered* to an observer that this was how he viewed the matter. (3) *Some given proportion* of the group's members either *answered* a direct question or *volunteered* the information that he shared this perspective, but none of the others was asked or volunteered information on the subject. (4) Every member of the group was asked or volunteered information, but *some given proportion said* they viewed the matter from the differing perspective of a prospective specialist. (5) No one was asked questions or volunteered information on the subject, but *all members were observed to engage in behavior* or to make other statements from which the analyst *inferred* that the general practitioner perspective was being used by them as a basic, though unstated, premise. For example, all students might have been observed to complain that the University Hospital received too many cases of rare diseases that general practitioners rarely see. (6) *Some given proportion* of the group *was observed* using the general practitioner perspective as a basic premise in their activities, but *the rest of the group* was not observed engaging in such activities. (7) *Some proportion* of the group *was observed* engaged in activities implying the general practitioner perspective while *the remainder* of the group was observed engaged in activities implying the perspective of the prospective specialist.

The researcher also takes account of the possibility that his observations may give him evidence of different kinds on the point under consideration. Just as he is more convinced if he has many items of evidence than if he has a few, so he is more convinced of a conclusion's validity if he has *many kinds* of evidence.[10] For instance, he may be especially persuaded that a particular norm exists and affects group behavior if the norm is not only described by group members but also if he observes events in which the norm can be "seen" to operate—if, for example, students tell him that they are thinking of becoming general practitioners and he also observes their complaints about the lack of cases of common diseases in University Hospital.

The conclusiveness which comes from the convergence of several kinds of evidence reflects the fact that separate varieties of evidence can be reconceptualized as deductions from a basic proposition which have now been verified in the field. In the above case, the observer might have deduced the desire to have experience with cases like those the general practitioner treats from the desire to practice that style of medicine. Even though the deduction is made after the fact, confirmation of it buttresses the argument that the general practitioner perspective is a group norm.

It should be remembered that these operations, when carried out in the field, may be so interrupted because of imperatives of the field situation that they are not carried on as systematically as they might be. Where this is the case, the overall assessment can be postponed until the final stage of postfield work analysis.

CONSTRUCTION OF SOCIAL SYSTEM MODELS

The final stage of analysis in the field consists of incorporating individual findings into a generalized model of the social system or organization under study or some part of that organization.[11] The concept of social system is a basic intellectual tool of modern sociology. The kind of participant observation discussed here is related directly to this concept, explaining particular social facts by explicit reference to their involvement in a complex of interconnected variables that the observer constructs as a theoretical model of the organization. In this final stage, the observer designs a descriptive model which best explains the data he has assembled.

The typical conclusion of this stage of the research is a statement about a set of complicated interrelations among many variables. Although some progress is being made in formalizing this operation through use of factor analysis and the relational analysis of survey data,[12] observers usually view currently available statistical techniques as inadequate to express their conceptions and find it necessary to use words. The most common kinds of conclusions at this level include:

(1) Complex statements of the necessary and sufficient conditions for the existence of some phenomenon. The observer may conclude, for example, that medical students develop consensus about limiting the amount of work they will do because (a) they are faced with a large amount of work, (b) they engage in activities which create communication channels between all members of the class, and (c) they face immediate dangers in the form of examinations set by the faculty.

(2) Statements that some phenomenon is an "important" or "basic" element in the organization. Such conclusions, when elaborated, usually point to the fact that this phenomenon exercises a persistent and continuing influence on diverse events. The observer might conclude that the ambition to become a general practitioner is "important" in the medical school under study, meaning that many particular judgments and choices are made by students in terms of this ambition and many features of the school's organization are arranged to take account of it.

(3) Statements identifying a situation as an instance of some process or phenomenon described more abstractly in sociological theory. Theories posit relations between many abstractly defined phenomena, and conclusions of this kind imply that relationships posited in generalized form hold in this particular instance. The observer, for example, may state that a cultural norm of the

medical students is to express a desire to become a general practitioner; in so doing, he in effect asserts that the sociological theory about the functions of norms and the processes by which they are maintained which he holds to be true in general is true in this case.

In reaching such types of conclusions, the observer characteristically begins by constructing models of parts of the organization as he comes in contact with them, discovers concepts and problems, and the frequency and distribution of the phenomena these call to his attention. After constructing a model specifying the relationships among various elements of this part of the organization, the observer seeks greater accuracy by successively refining the model to take account of evidence which does not fit his previous formulation;[13] by searching for negative cases (items of evidence which run counter to the relationships hypothesized in the model) which might force such revision; and by searching intensively for the interconnections *in vivo* of the various elements he has conceptualized from his data. While a provisional model may be shown to be defective by a negative instance which crops up unexpectedly in the course of the field work, the observer may infer what kinds of evidence would be likely to support or to refute his model and may make an intensive search for such evidence.[14]

After the observer has accumulated several partial-models of this kind, he seeks connections between them and thus begins to construct an overall model of the entire organization. An example from our study shows how this operation is carried on during the period of field work. (The reader will note, in this example, how use is made of findings typical of earlier stages of analysis.)

When we first heard medical students apply the term "crock" to patients we made an effort to learn precisely what they meant by it. We found, through interviewing students about cases both they and the observer had seen, that the term referred in a derogatory way to patients with many subjective symptoms but no discernible physical pathology. Subsequent observations indicated that this usage was a regular feature of student behavior and thus that we should attempt to incorporate this fact into our model of student-patient behavior. The derogatory character of the term suggested in particular that we investigate the reasons students disliked these patients. We found that this dislike was related to what we discovered to be the students' perspective on medical school: the view that they were in school to get experience in recognizing and treating those common diseases most likely to be encountered in general practice. "Crocks," presumably having no disease, could furnish no such experience. We were thus led to specify connections between the student-patient relationship and the student's view of the purpose of his professional education. Questions concerning the genesis of this perspective led to discoveries about the organization of the student body and communication among students, phenomena which we had been assigning to another part-model. Since "crocks" were also disliked because they gave the student no opportunity to assume medical responsibility, we were able to connect this aspect of the student-patient relationship with still another tentative model of the value system and hierarchical organization of the school, in which medical responsibility plays an important role.

Again, it should be noted that analysis of this kind is carried on in the field as time permits. Since the construction of a model is the analytic operation most closely related to the observer's techniques and interests he usually spends a great deal of time thinking about these problems. But he is usually unable to be as systematic as he would like until he reaches the final stage of analysis.

FINAL ANALYSIS AND THE PRESENTATION OF RESULTS

The final systematic analysis, carried on after the field work is completed, consists of rechecking and rebuilding models as carefully and with as many safeguards as the data will allow. For instance, in checking the accuracy of statements about the frequency and distribution of events, the researcher can index and arrange his material so that every item of information is accessible and taken account of in assessing the accuracy of any given conclusion. He can profit from the observation of Lazarsfeld and Barton that the "analysis of 'quasi-statistical data' can probably be made more systematic than it has been in the past, if the logical structure of quantitative research at least is kept in mind to give general warnings and directions to the qualitative observer."[15]

An additional criterion for the assessment of this kind of evidence is the state of the observer's conceptualization of the problem at the time the item of evidence was gathered. The observer may have his problem well worked out and be actively looking for evidence to test an hypothesis, or he may not be as yet aware of the problem. The evidential value of items in his field notes will vary accordingly, the basis of consideration being the likelihood of discovering negative cases of the proposition he eventually uses the material to establish. The best evidence may be that gathered in the most unthinking fashion, when the observer has simply recorded the item although it has no place in the system of concepts and hypotheses he is working with at the time, for there might be less bias produced by the wish to substantiate or repudiate a particular idea. On the other hand, a well-formulated hypothesis makes possible a deliberate search for negative cases, particularly when other knowledge suggests likely areas in which to look for such evidence. This kind of search requires advanced conceptualization of the problem, and evidence gathered in this way might carry greater weight for certain kinds of conclusions. Both procedures are relevant at different stages of the research.

In the post field work stage of analysis, the observer carries on the model building operation more systematically. He considers the character of his conclusions and decides on the kind of evidence that might cause their rejection, deriving further tests by deducing logical consequences and ascertaining whether or not the data support the deductions. He considers reasonable alternative hypotheses and whether or not the evidence refutes them.[16] Finally, he completes the job of establishing interconnections between partial models so as to achieve an overall synthesis incorporating all conclusions.

After completing the analysis, the observer faces the knotty problem of how to present his conclusions and the evidence for them. Readers of qualitative research reports commonly and justifiably complain that they are told little or nothing about the evidence for conclusions or the operations by which the evidence has been assessed. A more adequate presentation of the data, of the research operations, and of the researcher's inferences may help to meet this problem.

But qualitative data and analytic procedures, in contrast to quantitative ones, are difficult to present adequately. Statistical data can be summarized in tables, and descriptive measures of various kinds and the methods by which they are handled can often be accurately reported in the space required to print a formula. This is so in part because the methods have been systematized so that they can be referred to in this shorthand fashion and in part because the data have been collected for a fixed, usually small, number of categories—the presentation of data need be nothing more than a report of the number of cases to be found in each category.

The data of participant observation do not lend themselves to such ready summary. They frequently consist of many different kinds of observations which cannot be simply categorized and counted without losing some of their value as evidence—for, as we have seen, many points need to be taken into account in putting each datum to use. Yet it is clearly out of the question to publish all the evidence. Nor is it any solution, as Kluckhohn has suggested for the similar problem of presenting life history materials,[17] to publish a short version and to make available the entire set of materials on microfilm or in some other inexpensive way; this ignores the problem of how to present *proof.*

In working over the material on the medical school study a possible solution to this problem, with which we are experimenting, is a description of the natural history of our conclusions, presenting the evidence as it came to the attention of the observer during the successive stages of his conceptualization of the problem. The term "natural history" implies not the presentation of every datum, but only the characteristic forms data took at each stage of the research. This involves description of the form that data took and any significant exceptions, taking account of the canons discussed above, in presenting the various statements of findings and the inferences and conclusions drawn from them. In this way, evidence is assessed as the substantive analysis is presented. The reader would be able, if this method were used, to follow the details of the analysis and to see how and on what basis any conclusion was reached. This would give the reader, as do present modes of statistical presentation, opportunity to make his own judgment as to the adequacy of the proof and the degree of confidence to be assigned the conclusion.

CONCLUSION

I have tried to describe the analytic field work characteristic of participant observation, first, in order to bring out the fact that the technique consists of something more than merely immersing oneself in data and "having insights." The discussion may also serve to stimulate those who work with this and similar techniques to attempt greater formalization and systematization of the various operations they use, in order that qualitative research may become more a "scientific" and less an "artistic" kind of endeavor. Finally, I have proposed that new modes of reporting results be introduced, so that the reader is given greater access to the data and procedures on which conclusions are based.

NOTES

[1] There is little agreement on the specific referent of the term *participant observation*. See Raymond L. Gold, "Roles in Sociological Field Observations," *Social Forces*, 36 (March, 1958), 217-223, for a useful classification of the various procedures that go by this name. Our own research, from which we have drawn our illustrations, falls under Gold's type, "participant-as-observer." The basic methods discussed here, however, would appear to be similar in other kinds of field situations.

[2] In this respect, the analytic methods I discuss bear a family resemblance to the technique of *analytic induction*. Cf. Alfred Lindesmith, *Opiate Addiction* (Bloomington: Principia Press, 1947), especially pp. 5-20, and the subsequent literature cited in Ralph H. Turner, "The Quest for Universals in Sociological Research," *American Sociological Review*, 18 (December, 1953), 604-611.

[3] My discussion of these stages is abstract and simplified and does not attempt to deal with practical and technical problems of participant observation study. The reader should keep in mind that in practice the research will involve all these operations simultaneously with reference to different particular problems.

[4] The examples of which our hypothetical observer makes use are drawn from our own current work with medical students.

[5] The problem of indicators is discussed by Paul F. Lazarsfeld and Allen Barton, "Qualitative Measurement in the Social Sciences: Classification,

Typologies, and Indices," in Daniel Lerner and Harold D. Lasswell, eds., *The Policy Sciences: Recent Developments in Scope and Method* (Stanford: Stanford University Press, 1951), pp. 155-192; "Some Functions of Qualitative Analysis in Sociological Research," *Sociologica*, 1 (1955), 324-361 (this important paper parallels the present discussion in many places); and Patricia L. Kendall and Paul F. Lazarsfeld, "Problems of Survey Analysis," in R. K. Merton and P. F. Lazarsfeld, eds., *Continuities in Social Research* (Glencoe, Ill.: Free Press, 1950), pp. 183-186.

[6]Cf. Louis Gottschalk, Clyde Kluckhohn, and Robert Angell, *The Use of Personal Documents in History, Anthropology, and Sociology* (New York: Social Science Research Council, 1945), pp. 15-27, 38-47.

[7]See further, Howard S. Becker, "Interviewing Medical Students," *American Journal of Sociology*, 62 (September, 1956), 199-201.

[8]See Peter M. Blau, "Co-operation and Competition in a Bureaucracy," *American Journal of Sociology*, 59 (May, 1954), 530-535.

[9]See the discussion of quasi-statistics in Lazarsfeld and Barton, "Some Functions of Qualitative Analysis," pp. 346-348.

[10]See Alvin W. Gouldner, *Patterns of Industrial Bureaucracy* (Glencoe, Ill.: Free Press, 1954), pp. 247-269.

[11]The relation between theories based on the concept of social system and participant observation was pointed out to me by Alvin W. Gouldner. See his "Some Observations on Systematic Theory, 1945-55," in Hans L. Zetterberg, ed., *Sociology in the United States of America* (Paris: UNESCO, 1956), pp. 34-42; and "Theoretical Requirements of the Applied Social Sciences," *American Sociological Review*, 22 (February, 1957), 92-102.

[12]See Alvin W. Gouldner, "Cosmopolitans and Locals: Toward an Analysis of Latent Social Roles," *Administrative Science Quarterly*, 2 (December, 1957), 281-306, and 3 (March, 1958), 444-480; and James Coleman, "Relational Analysis: The Study of Social Structure with Survey Methods," mimeographed.

[13]Note again the resemblance to analytic induction.

[14]See Alfred Lindesmith's discussion of this principle in "Comment on W. S. Robinson's 'The Logical Structure of Analytic Induction,'" *American Sociological Review*, 17 (August, 1952), 492-493.

[15]"Some Functions of Qualitative Analysis," Lazarsfeld and Barton, p. 348.

[16]One method of doing this, particularly adapted to testing discrete hypotheses about change in individuals or small social units (though not in principle limited to this application), is "The Technique of Discerning," described by Mirra Komarovsky in Paul F. Lazarsfeld and Morris Rosenberg, eds., *The Language of Social Research* (Glencoe, Ill.: Free Press, 1955), pp. 449-457. See also the careful discussion of alternative hypotheses and the use of deduced consequences as further proof in Lindesmith, *Opiate Addiction*, *passim*.

[17]Gottschalk, Kluckhohn, and Angell, *Personal Documents*, pp. 150-156.

CHAPTER 19

Looking Backward: Case Studies on the Progress of Methodology in Sociological Research

Irwin Deutscher

The problem of validity has tended to receive short shrift in the social sciences. At least, this appears to be true when we compare it with the attention devoted to the problem of reliability. Following the customary distinction, the concept of validity addresses itself to the truth of an assertion that is made about something in the empirical world. The concept of reliability, on the other hand, concentrates on the degree of consistency in the observations obtained from the devices we employ: interviewers, schedules, tests, documents, observers, informants. Although it is possible to create an abstract mathematical relationship between validity and reliability, the relationship between the two concepts is asymmetric, i.e., measurement can be consistently in error as well as consistently correct and therefore a high degree of realiability can be achieved anywhere along the continuum between absolute invalidity and absolute validity.[1]

The sources of our "obsession with reliability" as I have referred to it elsewhere (1966: 241-242) are at least partly identifiable:

1. We are indeed faced with serious problems not only of instability in our measuring instruments but of instability of the populations we are attempting to measure. This dual instability compounds our problem, since we cannot always be certain of the extent to which discrepant readings on our instruments are a result of instrument error and the extent to which they are a result of the innate cussedness of our research subjects, who frequently insist on changing their minds—changing both their attitudes and their behaviors—and, therefore, changing their responses to our delicately balanced instruments. Since it is not possible, except by chance alone, to obtain high validity in conjunction with low reliability, this is a problem of no mean

This chapter was originally published by the American Sociological Association, in *The American Sociologist,* 4: 34-42. It is a revised version of a paper prepared under a National Science Foundation senior postdoctoral fellowship at the University of California, Berkeley, and read at the annual meeting of the Pacific Sociological Association, in Vancouver, British Columbia in April, 1966.

importance. One reason, then, for our concentration on problems of reliability is that they are central to our successful pursuit of knowledge about
human behavior.

2. The sociology of knowledge provides clues to another source of our
concern with problems of reliability. During the 1930's, those sociologists who
were most committed to objective empirical research embarked upon a
crusade to achieve scientific respectability for the discipline, which at that
time suffered considerable contempt both within the universities and outside.
This crusade manifested itself in an effort to purify sociology of its association with do-gooders, on the one hand, and, on the other, a self-conscious
pursuit of methodological rigor along lines analogous to what was perceived as
The Scientific Method. Problems of reliability were amenable to attack within
this framework. A body of technology already existed and could easily be
developed further. We know now how to measure reliability and we know
how to improve it and, most important, we can obtain clear, convincing, and
reproducible evidence of the precise extent to which our methodological refinements increase our confidence in the reliability of our data. We can measure our improvements in measurement and we can measure them well and
that is a very satisfying accomplishment—one upon which a scientist in any
discipline can look with pleasure and approval.

3. Finally, we have been able to concentrate on reliability while simultaneously neglecting validity, because we have developed certain concepts that
encourage us to do so. The idea of the operational definition is a device
precisely designed to eliminate the problem of validity. When we define the
object of our interest to be the phenomenon our instrument is measuring, we
need no longer worry about validity. Etzioni (1965: 943) provides an example
of how operational definitions can divert us from our intended purposes:

[Lewis Richardson] sought to discover whether an increase in armaments
increases or decreases national security. As armaments cannot be totaled, he
used, instead, sums spent on arms. As security cannot be neatly quantified, he
used the number of casualties in the wars that followed periods of arming.
Thus, rather than answer the question he set out to answer—one of vital
importance—he discovered how much it costs to kill a soldier!

More recent conceptual innovations that achieve the same end as the
operational definition are the notions of "intrinsic validity," "construct
validity," and "face validity," which assure us that we may be content with
the validity of an instrument if the items of which it is composed appear
reasonably to represent the object of our interest (Gulliksen, 1950; Cronback
and Meehl, 1955).

Although such explanations may be plausible in that they help us to
understand why we have not concentrated on the problem of validity, they do
not obviate the need for independent verification that our conclusions do

indeed reflect the empirical phenomena we claim—that they are valid. Several types of criteria can be employed for the establishment of validity. This paper reports the results of applying one of them to a problem of general theoretical relevance in social psychology and particular substantive relevance in inter-group relations.

I will compare three studies conducted by different investigators, in different places, with different sets of subjects at three points in time. None of these studies is a rigorous replication of the others, although two of them are similar in technique and instrumentation. It should be recognized that this similarity weakens the power of evidence of validity, since, to the extent that different studies replicate each others' methods, concordance between their results must be viewed as evidence of reliability rather than of independent validation.[2]

In conjunction with their relative independence of one another, these three studies have in common a primary concern for the question of the relationship between verbal attitudes toward an object and overt action toward that same object. In addition, the object selected by each of the three investigators for testing the relationship between attitude and behavior is a racial minority group sometimes subject to prejudice and discrimination. In all three studies, the respondents are members of the dominant Caucasian majori-ty. These studies were reported in the professional journals in 1934, 1958, and 1965. The investigators conducting the intermediate study are aware of and refer to the earlier study. The investigator conducting the last study is aware of and refers to both the earlier studies. Let us examine the progress of three decades of sociological pursuit of answers to the same question.

THE THREE CASES

For clarity of presentation and for other reasons that will become apparent later, I will refer to the three investigations as Study X, Study Y, and Study Z. Study X "is concerned with the relationship between verbal attitudes as expressed through response items on an attitude questionnaire and subsequent behavior." The investigator is interested ultimately in achieving prediction of behavior from written attitude scores. The attitude of his female subjects is obtained by asking them if they would be willing to pose for hypothetical photographs with Negro men. A graded series of conditions under which the pictures would be used, ranging from strictly scientific use to propaganda, provides a "scale" from which an estimate of prejudice is made. Selected subjects are asked at a later point if they would be willing to cooperate with a psychological testing agency by permitting their photos actually to be taken with Negroes. Under these supposedly real conditions, the subjects are asked to sign a series of photographic releases, that series being graded along the same lines as the conditions earlier described in the attitude scale. As the author puts it, "attitude objects (items on the questionnaire) [are] identical to the behavior observed (the signing of photographic releases)."

Although this cleverly indirect technique for establishing the relationship between attitude and behavior may be superior to the crude empirical descriptions typical of an earlier era of sociological research, it suffers from at least five types of defects, all of which tend to be typical of studies done at that time. The first of these is the primary concern with prediction, a primitive scientific notion that assumes a direct, uninterrupted, straight-line flow of behavior. The idea of such simple cause and effect relationships between two variables has been by and large discarded in the philosophy of science.[3]

Herbert Blumer has argued repeatedly that prediction of a later phase of a social act is not possible on the basis of knowledge of an earlier phase. As Blumer points out, the act is a process in constant development: it is being constructed. The earlier dimension tapped (for example, attitudes toward Dingbats) does not determine any later dimension that may be tapped (for example, overt action toward a Dingbat). The determination is made during the course of the intervening period and may be heavily influenced by factors in the immediate situation in which the act or attitude is called forth.

Science is concerned with "input" and "output" only in marginal ways. Its central concern is understanding "why" and "how"—what goes on *inside* the black box! If prediction is closely akin to magic, I suspect that control is more nearly a problem of politics. The most effective and economic means of controlling human behavior is probably through coercion—whether military or otherwise and whether real or threatened. Moral questions aside, it is both expensive and inefficient to attempt to apply social science to the control of human behavior.

The second defect is related to the sample. It is small and select, consisting of thirty-four eighteen- and nineteen-year-old girls enrolled in an introductory sociology course at a state university. The selectivity is compounded by the fact that only volunteers from among those who took the attitude test were exposed to the behavior test. The investigator concedes that his subjects have had few or no contacts with members of the minority group during their young lives, therefore leaving some doubt as to the salience of the research situation to them.

The third problem area relates to the lack of power in a research design that incorporates no form of control group. Under these conditions, it is impossible to draw experimental conclusions, i.e., there is no basis for comparison between those who do and do not receive the experimental treatment. In addition, by submitting samples of Negro males, Negro females, and white males to the two tests, it would be possible to obtain estimates of the amount of variance attributable to sex, race, and interaction between them.

Assumptions about the scalability of the seven items in the two presumed scales raise a fourth question. There is no evidence whether or not or to what degree these items do, in fact, form a scale. Related to this problem is the question of how large a discrepancy between ratings on the attitude scale and on the behavior scale can be assumed to represent an inconsistency. The author reports that 59 per cent of the girls had discrepancies of two or more intervals between attitude and behavior. A 2-point discrepancy on a 7-point scale is not necessarily indicative of gross inconsistency. In addition, it has been demonstrated empirically that unit interval gaps at one end of an attitude scale are not necessarily the same size as the same unit gaps at the other end of the same scale (Jordan, 1965). This is not very powerful evidence. It suggests, at best, that discrepancies *may* frequently occur between attitude and behavior.

The fifth, and final, type of defect apparent in Study X lies in the statistical treatment of the data. Numerous assumptions are required by the statistical procedures without evidence that these assumptions are met, and there is considerable loss of degrees of freedom resulting from the grouping of data and from other computational procedures. Furthermore, the use of the statistics selected is questionable. One of these is a 3-by-3 chi-square analysis. Reasonable interpretation of a 2-by-2 chi-square matrix is difficult enough; the 3-by-3 is much more problematic. In this analysis, frequencies of less than 5 would be expected in 7 of the 9 cells. Although there is nothing magic about the number 5, it is customary procedure to limit chi-square analysis to tables in which at least five observations are expected to occur in each cell.[4]

The other statistic employed is the simple Pearsonian coefficient of correlation. This is questionable under conditions where the author has already posited nonlinearity and where two variables are correlated that by definition are limited in their fluctuations between 1 and 7. On the basis of tests employing these two statistics, the investigator concludes that "neither test showed the variables to be significantly related, thus confirming the hypothesis that individuals with either positive or negative verbal attitudes do not necessarily act in accord with those attitudes in an overt situation. . . ." In what appears to be a direct contradiction of his conclusion, the author states in a footnote that if his sample had been larger, the differences would probably have been significant.

Let us turn to Study Y, which was reported in 1958. It, too, addresses itself to the relationship between verbal attitudes and overt acts, and its design closely parallels that of Study X. The two studies are, however, sufficiently different so that they cannot be considered replications. These investigators are primarily methodologically oriented. They observe that "in the face of the steady stream of studies of the verbal dimension of attitudinal behavior, the paucity of investigations of the overt-action correlates of such verbal behavior is indeed striking." Their major goal is the development of standardized situations or instruments "enabling the investigator to quantify, on a positive-negative continuum, an acceptance or avoidance act for a set of subjects, with other conditions held constant."

The behavioral test is identical with that employed in Study X: a request to have the subject's picture taken with a Negro and to sign a graded series of releases for the use of the picture. The identity ends here. In this study, the attitudinal dimension is derived from an occupational social-distance scale that asks for acceptance or rejection of a large number of occupations when the incumbents are white and when they are Negro. The sum of the differences of ratings of Negroes and whites provides a prejudice score. Extreme prejudiced and unprejudiced groups were identified, and a multi-factor matching procedure resulted in matched samples of 23 prejudiced and 23 unprejudiced undergraduate sociology students. Measures of attitude toward and behavior toward the minority group were available for 46 subjects.

Using as criteria the five types of defects derived from my hindsight analysis of Study X, what kinds of progress are represented in Study Y? First, there is an explicit rejection of the problem of prediction coupled with a determination to reduce apparent methodological difficulties in sociological research. Although this is a beginning of awareness, there remains in Study Y an implicit assumption of a direct, if nonlinear, relationship between an independent and a dependent variable. It is difficult to shake the notion of simple cause and effect.

The second area of weakness in Study X revolved around the nature of the sample. Although still small in Study Y, there is an increase in sample size—from 34 subjects to 46. In Study Y the sexes are equally represented, and the introduction of a matching procedure reduces the probability of self-selective differences between prejudiced and unprejudiced volunteers. Although this Midwestern university is further south than the one in Study X and has a less liberal tradition, the salience of the questions to the subjects remains problematic, especially in terms of the perceived consequences of their responses.

The lack of controls, our third criterion, remains a serious problem. Although some controls become possible in Study Y, since both sexes are represented and other matching factors appear equally in both the prejudiced and the unprejudiced groups, no analyses of these are reported by the investigators. More important, neither Study X nor Study Y attempts to control for any effect it may have created when it administered the original verbal test. With the benefit of hindsight we can see how these investigators could have greatly improved the power of their evidence by subjecting an untreated control group to the behavioral test.

The fourth problem area centered on the scales and the arbitrary designation of what constitutes a discrepancy. In Study Y the issue of scalability is treated self-consciously. The derivation of the rank order of the scale is described and its validity argued on the basis of a high rate of agreement among a panel of expert judges. Although no scale analysis is possible because of sample limitations, high transitivity is reported: only three irregularities in the cumulative feature of the instrument occur in the forty-six cases. Only extreme prejudiced and unprejudiced scorers are used, and the subjects are classified behaviorally according to whether or not they signed the releases at a level above or below the mean of the total sample. As a result of these innovations in classifying both attitude and behavior, the problem disappears of arbitrarily assuming that a two-point discrepancy on the scales reflects inconsistency.

The fifth type of defect, related to unsubstantiated statistical assumptions and to losses of degrees of freedom resulting from grouping of data and computations, remains a problem in Study Y as it was in Study X. However, to the extent that the weak correlation analysis employed in Study X does not appear in Study Y, the latter achieves some reduction in the number of assumptions. This parsimonious achievement may, however, be nullified by the need in Study Y to assume that the differences in rating the Negro and white occupations are additive, and by the loss of additional degrees of freedom consequent to computing the mean level at which photographic releases were signed. The application of chi-square analysis in Study Y represents a clear improvement over the misuse of that same technique in Study X. In spite of the larger sample, these investigators hold their chi-square down to a 2-by-2 matrix and manage to achieve sufficient frequencies in each cell.

On the basis of the chi-square analysis, Study Y reaches the opposite conclusion from Study X: "In this situation, there was clearly a greater tendency for the prejudiced persons than the unprejudiced to avoid being photographed with a Negro. The relationship is significant, suggesting some correspondence in this case between attitudes measured by verbal scales and an acceptance-avoidance act toward the attitude object." This conclusion is followed immediately by a qualification: "In spite of the statistical significance, however, there were some prejudiced persons who signed the agreement without hesitation at the highest level, as well as some unprejudiced persons who were not willing to sign at any level. Thus the relationship between verbal and overt attitudinal dimensions is not a simple one-to-one correspondence."

Unfortunately, in spite of the fact that the probability is 99 out of 100 that the distribution in the Study Y chi-square table is attributable to something other than chance (presumably to the relationship between attitude and behavior), the fact remains that 30 per cent of the cases are deviant: 14 of the 46 subjects were either prejudiced people who showed a high level of willingness to sign releases or unprejudiced people who showed an unwillingness to sign releases. With some improvement in methodological sophistication, the evidence becomes more credible, but it remains relatively weak and inconclusive.

Study Z, the last of our trilogy, provides a radical innovation in the experimental design. Like Studies X and Y, it seeks to document the relationship between verbal attitudes and overt acts toward members of a minority racial group. In this study, the investigator employs confederates who are visually identifiable as "non-whites." The confederates seek to obtain services from entrepreneurs who are actually operating businesses. Two hundred and fifty-one such behavioral observations were made and the acceptance-avoidance result recorded. From among these, 128 attitude observations were obtained by allowing a six-month time lapse and then sending each of the entrepreneurs a questionnaire in which he was asked if he would service members of the minority group in his establishment. Let us expose Study Z to the five criteria used to evaluate Studies X and Y.

It will be recalled that Study X had a primary commitment to a primitive notion of prediction. In Study Y we find an explicit effort to set aside the notion of prediction, although many of its concomitant assumptions remain implicit. Study Z openly challenges the theoretical tenability of posing a causal relationship between attitude and behavior toward the same object. Attitude and behavior, it argues, are discrete phenomena that are theoretically independent of each other. It is unreasonable, the author suggests, to posit a prediction of behavior on the basis of attitudes. In spite of his efforts, however, he, like the rest of us, finds it difficult not to think in the causal terms with which we have all been deeply imbued.

The sample in Study Z consists not of 34 or 46 captive undergraduates, but of 128 mature adults engaged in the conduct of responsible business. The number is not only larger but the probability of self-selectivity is considerably less. Studies X and Y both coerced their total samples to participate in the verbal dimension of the study (at least, neither investigator reports any refusal of students to cooperate with that phase of the study), but both permitted voluntary withdrawal from the overt behavior test. Study Z, on the other hand, is designed to coerce the total sample to participate in the behavioral test (every entrepreneur is confronted with an acceptance-avoidance choice he must make) but permits voluntary refusal to respond to the verbal test. With this difference in mind and also the fact that the Study Y sample was reduced by the matching procedure as well as by noncooperation, the percentages of voluntary withdrawal for Studies Y and Z can be compared. (Study X reports only that the girls were told that "participation is completely voluntary." There is no indication of how many subjects did not volunteer.)[5] Voluntary withdrawal (i.e., refusal to participate) in Study Y was 81.6 per cent; in Study Z it was 49.0 per cent. To the extent that rates of voluntary withdrawal of subjects provide an index of self-selectivity, Study Z is far less self-selective in its sample than the other investigation.

The universe from which the Study Z sample is drawn also represents an improvement in sampling procedures. We no longer have undergraduate students for whom the verbal dimension holds no salience and the behavioral dimension is doubtful in this respect. The Study Z sample is drawn from a population that must make choices both in terms of intent and in terms of action they perceive as having real consequences in the conduct of their daily activities.

The Study Z design, unlike the other two, permits the use of a non-treated sample for control purposes. A sample of establishments which had not been tested on the behavioral dimension, and which was matched with the experimental sample by quality and geographic locale, received the same verbal inquiry. The distribution of responses from both treatment and control groups was nearly identical. This control over the effect of the treatment itself represents an important methodological improvement over Studies X and Y.

Since Study Z allows only an acceptance or a rejection on both the overt action dimension and the verbal attitude dimension, the problems of scaling, scalability, arbitrary assignments of the number of discrepancy units that are assumed to indicate an inconsistency, computations of means, grouping of data, use of only extreme scorers, and the many assumptions that must accompany these techniques *are all eliminated* from Study Z. This represents a massive step forward in assumptional parsimony.

As great as this achievement is, it is carried still further in the analytic techniques employed in Study Z. The need to make unsubstantiated statistical assumptions no longer exists and the loss of degrees of freedom resulting from computational procedures is eliminated. Of the 251 establishments confronted with the acceptance-avoidance choice of action, all but one chose to accept. Of the 128 of those responding to the verbal test, only 1 chose an unqualified acceptance (over 90 per cent of the establishments chose to reject on the verbal test, with the remainder providing qualified responses). The visible weight of this evidence regarding the inconsistency of attitude and behavior vis-à-vis a racial minority is so great and so obvious that neither statistical approximations nor probability estimates are required to interpret the results. The ambiguity in conclusions of Studies X and Y resulting from the high frequencies of deviant cases disappears in Study Z. This time the data permit only one clear-cut conclusion regarding the hypothesis.

Recapitulating, Study Y, as judged by at least five broad criteria, shows some methodological improvement over Study X, and somewhat greater confidence can be placed in its conclusions. The great increase in the power of evidence based on methods that are demonstrably superior along several lines comes with Study Z. It would be well if we could take pride in this accelerating curve of progress. I submit, however, that, instead of pride, it should give us cause for concern. Up to this point, I have deliberately avoided identifying these three studies. I will do so now. Study X, the first one described, was reported in *1965* by Lawrence Linn; Study Y appeared back in *1958* as an article by Melvin DeFleur and Frank Westie; *Study Z, the apex of our achievement, was published in 1934 by Richard LaPiere.*[6] To the extent that the analysis of the relative merits of these three studies is correct, we have suffered a dramatic methodological regression during the thirty-one-year time lapse covered by them.

CONCLUSIONS: WHAT VALIDATES WHAT?

In the case analysis above, I have deliberately attempted to mislead the reader regarding the chronological order of the three studies. This deception was designed to dramatize the argument. In order to protect the disguise, I neglected to mention that the racial minority dealt with by LaPiere in Study Z was Chinese rather than Negro, as was true of Studies X and Y. Whether the prejudice and discrimination toward the Chinese in the 1930's was of the same nature as those postured toward the Negro minority in the fifties and sixties remains a moot question (and, incidentally, a question not entertained by the investigators in Studies X and Y). There are, however, a number of field studies dealing with attitudes and behaviors toward Negroes that appear to validate LaPiere's Chinese study (Lohman and Reitzes, 1954; Kutner et al., 1952; Saenger and Gilbert, 1950). Theoretical bases for the independence of prejudice attitudes and discriminatory acts have also been effectively established (Rose, 1956).

It is possible that Linn's study may be superior in some respects to that of DeFleur and Westie. For example, Linn relates attitude and behavior more directly to the same object and, by carrying the photography farce a step further than DeFleur and Westie did, he confronts his subjects more directly with the overt action decision. Linn also introduces a different dimension into his analysis as a result of his attention to the *direction* of discrepancy between attitude and behavior. I am unable to find the two later studies superior to the pioneer project in any respect. It is possible that another analyst, employing other criteria, could identify ways in which the LaPiere study suffers in comparison with the two later ones.[7]

Although they acknowledge the existence of the LaPiere study, DeFleur and Westie offer no criticism of it. Linn, on the other hand, chooses to attack LaPiere on two fronts:

> ... it must be pointed out that the LaPiere study has certain methodological problems which reduce the validity of the results and which make a comparison of attitudes and action less credible. First, the questionnaire which he used to measure attitudes toward the Chinese dealt with general prejudice indices and was *not* necessarily comparable to the behavior situation in the study. Secondly, LaPiere's presence with the couple probably had a considerable biasing effect. Much different results would have been obtained had the couple gone across the country alone (1965: 354).

These two criticisms are difficult to understand. LaPiere reports that every establishment that had been confronted by the Chinese couple received the question: "Will you accept members of the Chinese race as guests in your establishment?" In what way is the question not comparable to the behavior situation? The fact that half the subjects also were asked questions about other ethnic groups for comparative purposes does not alter the response distributions (LaPiere, 1934: 234, cf. cols. 1 and 2 in Table I). The influence of the investigator's role on the phenomenon he is studying is a persistent problem in social science research. LaPiere made a deliberate effort to control for experimenter effect by remaining out of sight and forcing the Chinese to conduct negotiations alone whenever possible. His behavioral data are classified according to the presence or absence of the investigator and are so reported (1934: 235, Table II).

There is no denying that this is an important problem and, despite LaPiere's valiant efforts to exercise control over it, it remains uncertain to what extent experimenter effects persist in his study. The nature of the obligations—the unwritten contract—between experimenter and student subjects is a matter of serious concern to some social psychologists (Campbell, 1957; Milgram, 1964: 142, Orne, 1962).[8] One experimenter, for example, reports that, in his efforts to find a task that would easily discourage subjects for purposes of a planned experiment, he was unable to devise anything so odious and frustrating that his student subjects would give it up in a reasonable length of time. They felt so obligated to fulfill their obligation to science and to the experimenter that even the most apparently senseless tasks were perceived as having hidden importance (Orne, 1962: 777). Neither DeFleur and Westie nor Linn seem aware of the possible obligations felt by undergraduate sociology students taking a test on racial attitudes administered by their sociology professors. Neither Study X nor Study Y reports an effort to control for this potential effect; Study Z does.

The relative amount of confidence we are able to have in the conclusions of these three studies raises serious questions about validity tests based upon independent verification in contemporary sociology. With the current state of our methods, we cannot assume that a later study necessarily validates or invalidates an earlier study. It would indeed be an error to assume that Linn's 1965 study could either validate or invalidate LaPiere's 1934 study *under any conditions. If* Linn had been correct in his challenges to LaPiere's methods, then the LaPiere study would have to be treated as if it did not exist. It would make no difference whether there was agreement or disagreement between the Linn and LaPiere findings. With LaPiere's study completely discounted, any relationship between the two sets of findings must be attributed to chance and the Linn study becomes the baseline for future efforts at validation. To achieve validation we need to obtain evidence by means of at least two independent methods, both of which are tenable.[9]

The question of what validates what is a sticky one even under the best of conditions, when the results of two studies disagree. Which of the two is "invalid"? Campbell (1955), for example, is able to show a correlation of +.90 between the morale rankings of submarine crews as measured on an "expensive and extensive" questionnaire and as ranked by informants who knew all the crews. Since the two methods provided independent answers to the same question and those answers were nearly identical, we have evidence that our information is valid. But let us suppose that Campbell had discovered a low or negative correlation. What then? Perhaps one body of data is valid; perhaps the other one is; perhaps neither of them is. It would appear that, although we can achieve evidence of validity when there is agreement, we are unable to demonstrate where the source of invalidity lies when there is disagreement. It might be argued that if we have three or more independent tests and if the three are of equal veracity, and if there is agreement between two and disagreement with the third, then we can assume that the third is invalid—that the majority rules.

The three studies analyzed in this paper provide an example of at least one hypothetical difficulty with this democratic position. Let us suppose that Studies X and Y had agreed with each other and had reached radically different conclusions from Study Z (which, fortunately, they did not). We would then have considered Z invalid—largely on the basis of the fact that X and Y outnumber Z and on the basis of our faith in "progress." That is, we would assume that the more recent the investigation, the more refined its methods, and the more confidence we can place in its conclusions. It has been demonstrated above that this faith in "progress" is unwarranted.

It is also possible that when the results of two independent techniques disagree, *neither is valid.* Employing as their criteria the ultimate evidence of validity—direct observation of the behavior in question—Freeman and Ataov (1960) find no correlation between direct and indirect indexes of the behavior and no correlation between either index and the behavior itself. Their neat little validity study suggests one solution to the validity testing problem: the problem of validity disappears when we have direct observation of the actual phenomenon we are attempting to approximate with our measuring instruments. Herein lies one source of the power of LaPiere's evidence: he records direct observations of behavior under actual conditions of social interaction that are a real segment of the flow of everyday behavior of the actors.[10]

Validity poses a serious problem when we use instruments designed to provide estimates of hypothetical behavior. If, instead, our data consist of direct behavioral observations, the problem of validity becomes negligible. We then become free to concentrate on important problems of reliability.[11] Thus, in the case of LaPiere, we know that he observed what he intended to observe, but we are not certain how accurately he observed it. It is not a difficult task to determine the extent to which different observers will make the same observations. Replication becomes an important and legitimate pursuit under these conditions, rather than the meaningless game it is under conditions where validity is indeterminate. As Ehrlich and Rinehart (1965) have demonstrated in their analysis of a highly reliable stereotype measuring instrument which has been employed as a standard tool since 1933, we can be consistently wrong and, as a consequence, consistently misunderstand human behavior.

NOTES

[1] The paradigm may be expressed as follows: When reliability is high, validity may be either high or low, but when reliability is low, validity must be low. Empirically observed cases of low reliability associated with high validity must be attributed either to chance or to a hidden (unrecognized and unintended) dimension of reliability in the instrument. It follows that any mathematical formula which expresses validity as a direct function of reliability, or vice versa, must be in error.

Joseph Gutenkauf has convinced me that, in fact, whether a problem is one of reliability or of validity depends on the purpose of the investigator.

[2] In a replication, we have evidence only that the same methods obtain the same results when employed by different investigators. We have evidence of validity only to the extent that the investigators employ methods that are independent of each other.

[3] For the enlightenment of the very young and the very old, a brief extension of my view of "prediction" may be helpful. Some introductory textbooks continue to retain in their definition of "science" the criterion of "prediction and control." Prediction is, in fact, more closely related to magic than it is to science. One may accurately predict without ever understanding why the prediction works. Malaria, for example, could be related to the presence of stagnant water in warm climates and effectively brought under control with no knowledge of the particular breed of mosquito that carried it, much less any knowledge of what that mosquito carried. This is effective and valuable social action in the public health arena; it has nothing to do with science. Nehemia Jordan, in a personal communication, puts it this way:

"Imagine the green man from Mars coming in his space ship and giving us the gift we have all been looking for—the perfect computer. The computer is an unopenable black box with two slots, one for inputting the questions and the other for outputting empirical predictions to observable events. Perfect prediction is observed. Does this toll the death knoll for science? Not at all. The scientists of the existing disciplines will be compelled to try to figure out why the predictions are correct. And a new science will undoubtedly develop to try to answer the most burning question of them all. The name of this science will be a Graeco-Latin neologism which will mean: 'How the hell does this damn black box work?'"

[4] This is a reasonable custom, since large differences in the chi square can result from relocation of a single observation under such conditions. This problem is most serious in small matrices, with the likelihood of distortion decreasing as a number of degrees of freedom increases.

[5] We know only that the attitude test was administered to ten discussion sessions in introductory sociology and that "the students who were asked to volunteer were all of the eighteen- and nineteen-year-old girls who had previously responded to the attitude questionnaire."

[6] The line of continuity created by Studies X, Y, and Z continues beyond the point where the present analysis terminates. For example, the reader may wish to determine for himself whether Fendrich's recent work (1967a, 1967b) represents continued methodological regression or a reversal of that trend.

[7] Linn (1965: 355) believes his study to be superior to the other two and states that "the DeFleur and Westie study is methodologically superior to its predecessors . . . ," including LaPiere.

[8]I have discussed this issue in some detail in a chapter in a forthcoming volume (1969).

[9]In what is possibly a gentlemanly avoidance of the issue, one group of scholars (SSRC, 1964), attempting to relate field studies and laboratory experiments in social psychology, have offered another alternative: without denigrating either type of evidence, they conclude that the findings based on these two types of studies are simply not "commensurate."

[10]It is not my intention to deny the "reality" of any observed behavior —including the behavior of students in experimental situations such as those reported in Studies X and Y. It may be possible to derive valid conclusions from those two experiments regarding the behavior of subjects under experimental conditions. Only Study Z, however, permits valid conclusions regarding the behavior of members of a dominant group toward members of a minority group.

[11]There are a number of hints in the literature regarding possible models for field study (Kohn and Williams, 1956) as well as theoretical rationale (Becker, 1958).

REFERENCES

Becker, H. S. 1958. "Inference and proof in participant observation." *American Sociological Review*, 23 (December) 652-659.

Campbell, D. T. 1957. "Factors relevant to the validity of experiments in social settings." *Psychological Bulletin*, 54 (July) 297-312.

————. 1955. "The informant in quantitative research." *American Journal of Sociology*, 60 (January) 339-342.

Cronbach, L. J., and Meehl, P. E. 1955. "Construct validity in psychological tests." *Psychological Bulletin*, 52 (July) 281-302.

DeFleur, M., and Westie, F. R. 1958. "Verbal attitudes and overt acts: an experiment on the salience of attitudes." *American Sociological Review*, 23 (December) 667-673.

Deutscher, I. 1969. "Evil companions and naughty behavior: some thoughts and evidence bearing on a folk hypothesis." In Jack Douglas and Robert A. Scott (eds.), *Deviance*. New York: Basic Books (forthcoming).

————. 1966. "Words and deeds: social science and social policy." *Social Problems*, 13 (Winter) 235-254.

Ehrlich, H. J., and Rinehart, J. W. 1965. "A brief report on the methodology of stereotype research." *Social Forces*, 43 (May) 564-575.

Etzioni, A. 1965. "Mathematics for sociologists?" (a communication). *American Sociological Review*, 30 (December) 943-945.

Fendrich, J. M. 1967a. "Perceived reference group support: racial attitudes and overt behavior." *American Sociological Review*, 32 (December) 960-970.

————. 1967b. "A study of the association among verbal attitudes, commitment and overt behavior in different experimental situations." *Social Forces*, 45 (March) 347-355.

Freeman, L. C., and Atoav, T. 1960. "Invalidity of indirect and direct measures of attitude toward cheating." *Journal of Personality,* 28 (December) 443-447.

Gulliksen, H. 1950. "Intrinsic validity." *American Psychologist,* 5 (October) 511-517.

Jordan, N. 1965. "The 'asymmetry' of 'liking' and 'disliking': a phenomenon meriting further reflection and research." *Public Opinion Quarterly,* 29 (Summer) 315-322.

Kohn, M. L., and Williams, R. M. 1956. "Situational patterning and intergroup relations." *American Sociological Review,* 21 (April) 164-174.

Kutner, B., Wilkins, C., and Yarrow, P. B. 1952. "Verbal attitudes and overt behavior regarding racial prejudice." *Journal of Abnormal and Social Psychology,* 47 (July) 649-652.

LaPiere, R. 1934. "Attitudes vs. actions." *Social Forces,* 13 (March) 230-237.

Linn, L. S. 1965. "Verbal attitudes and overt behavior: a study of racial discrimination." *Social Forces,* 43 (March) 353-364.

Lohman, J., and Rietzes, D. 1954. "Deliberately organized groups and racial behavior." *American Sociological Review,* 19 (June) 342-348.

Milgram, S. 1964. "Group pressure and action against a person." *Journal of Abnormal and Social Psychology,* 69 (August) 137-143.

Orne, M. T. 1962. "On the social psychology of the psychological experiment: with particular reference to demand characteristics." *American Psychologist,* 17 (November) 776-783.

Rose, A. M. 1956. "Intergroup relations vs. prejudice: pertinent theory for the study of social change." *Social Problems,* 4 (October) 173-176.

Saenger, G., and Gilbert, E. 1950. "Customer reaction to the integration of Negro sales personnel." *International Journal of Opinion and Attitude Research,* 4 (Spring) 57-76.

SSRC. 1964. "Narrowing the gap between field studies and laboratory experiments in social psychology: a statement by the summer seminar." *Items,* 8 (December).

CHAPTER 20

Some Methodological Problems of Field Studies

Morris Zelditch, Jr.

The original occasion for this paper was a reflection on the use of sample survey methods in the field: that is, the use of structured interview schedules, probability samples, etc., in what is usually thought of as a participant-observation study. There has been a spirited controversy between, on the one hand, those who have sharply criticized field workers for slipshod sampling, for failing to document assertions quantitatively, and for apparently accepting impressionistic accounts—or accounts that the quantitatively minded could not distinguish from purely impressionistic accounts;[1] and, on the other hand, those who have, sometimes bitterly, been opposed to numbers, to samples, to questionnaires, often on the ground that they destroy the field workers' conception of a social system as an organic whole.[2]

Although there is a tendency among many younger field workers to accent criticisms made from the quantitative point of view,[3] there is reason to believe that the issue itself has been stated falsely. In most cases field methods are discussed as if they were "all of a piece."[4] There is, in fact, a tendency to be either *for* or *against* quantification, as if it were an either/or issue. To some extent the battle lines correlate with a relative concern for "hardness" versus "depth and reality" of data. Quantitative data are often thought of as "hard," and qualitative as "real and deep"; thus if you prefer "hard" data you are for quantification and if you prefer "real, deep" data you are for qualitative participant observation. What to do if you prefer data that are real, deep, *and* hard is not immediately apparent.

A more fruitful approach to the issue must certainly recognize that a field study is not a single method gathering a single kind of information. This approach suggests several crucial questions: *What* kinds of methods and *what* kinds of information are relevant? How can the "goodness" of different methods for different purposes be evaluated? Even incomplete and imperfect answers—which are all that we offer here—should be useful, at least in helping

This chapter was originally published by the University of Chicago Press, in *American Journal of Sociology*, 67: 566-76. Copyright © by University of Chicago Press. The author acknowledges the partial support given this investigation by funds from Columbia University's Documentation Project for Advanced Training in Social Research.

to restate the issue. They also pose, order, and to some extent resolve other issues of field method so that in pursuing their implications this paper encompasses a good deal more than its original problem.

THREE TYPES OF INFORMATION

The simplest events are customarily described in statements predicting a single property of a single object at a particular time and in a particular place. From these descriptions one may build up more complex events in at least two ways. The first is by forming a configuration of many properties of the same object at the same time in the same place. This may be called an "incident." A more complex configuration but of the same type would be a sequence of incidents, that is, a "history."

A second way to build up more complex events is by repeating observations of a property over a number of units. Units here can be defined formally, requiring only a way of identifying events as identical. They can be members of a social system or repetitions of the same type of incident at different times or in different places (e.g., descriptions of five funerals). The result is a frequency distribution of some property.

From such information it is possible to deduce certain underlying properties of the system observed, some of which may be summarized as consequences of the "culture" of S (S stands here for a social system under investigation). But at least some portion of this culture can be discovered not only by inference from what is observed but also from verbal reports by members of S—for example, accounts of its principal institutionalized norms and statuses. The rules reported, of course, are to some extent independent of the events actually observed; the norms actually followed may not be correctly reported, and deviance may be concealed. Nevertheless, information difficult to infer can be readily and accurately obtained from verbal reports. For example, it may take some time to infer that a member occupies a given status but this may readily be discovered by asking either him or other members of S.

We thus combine various types of information into three broad classes.

Type I: Incidents and Histories. A log of events during a given period, a record of conversations heard, descriptions of a wedding, a funeral, an election, etc. Not only the actions observed, but the "meanings," the explanations, etc., reported by the participants can be regarded as part of the "incident" insofar as they are thought of as data rather than actual explanations.

Type II: Distributions and Frequencies. Possessions of each member of S, number of members who have a given belief, number of times member m is observed talking to member n, etc.

Type III: Generally Known Rules and Statuses. Lists of statuses, lists of persons occupying them, informants' accounts of how rules of exogamy apply, how incest or descent are defined, how political leaders are supposed to be chosen, how political decisions are supposed to be made, etc.

This classification has nothing to do with what is *inferred* from data, despite the way the notion of reported rules and statuses was introduced. In particular, more complex configurations of norms, statuses, events which are "explained" by inferring underlying themes or structures involve a level of inference outside the scope of this paper: the classification covers only information *directly* obtained from reports and observations. Moreover, this classification cuts across the distinction between what is observed by the investigator and what is reported to him. Although Type III consists only of reports, Types I and II include both observations by the investigator himself *and* reports of members of *S*, insofar as they are treated as data. Later we talk of an event as seen through the eyes of an informant, where the investigator trusts the informant as an accurate observer and thinks of the report as if it were his own observation. Now, however, interest is focused not on the facts of the report but rather on what the report reveals of the perceptions, the motivations, the world of meaning of the informant himself. The report, in this case, does not transmit observational data; it is, itself, the datum and so long as it tells what the person reporting thinks, the factual correctness of what he thinks is irrelevant. (This is sometimes phrased as making a distinction between *informants* and *respondents,* in the survey research sense.) Thus Type I includes both observations (what we see going on) and the statements of members telling what they understand the observed events to mean, which is regarded as part of the event. In a somewhat different way, Type II also includes both reports (e.g., an opinion poll) and observations (e.g., systematically repeated observations with constant coding categories).

THREE TYPES OF METHOD

It is possible to make a pure, logically clear classification of methods of obtaining information in the field, but for the present purpose this would be less useful than one that is, though less precise, rather closer to what a field worker actually does.

Two methods are usually thought of as characteristic of the investigator in the field. He invariably keeps a daily log of events and of relatively casual, informal continuous interviews, both of which go into his field notes. Almost invariably he also develops informants, that is, selected members of *S* who are willing and able to give him information about practices and rules in *S* and events he does not directly observe. (They may also supply him with diaries, autobiographies, and their own personal feelings; i.e., they may also function as respondents.) Contrary to popular opinion, almost any well-trained field worker also keeps various forms of census materials, records of systematic observations, etc., including a basic listing of members of *S*, face-sheet data on them, and systematically repeated observations of certain recurrent events. Many field workers also collect documents; however, we will classify field methods into only three broad classes which we conceive of as primary. These are:

Type I. Participant-observation. The field worker directly observes and also participates in the sense that he has durable social relations in *S*. He may or may not play an active part in events, or he may interview participants in events which may be considered part of the process of observation.

Type II. Informant-interviewing. We prefer a more restricted definition of the informant than most field workers use, namely that he be called an "informant" only where he is reporting information presumed factually correct about others rather than about himself; and his information about events is about events in their absence. Interviewing during the event itself is considered part of participant-observation.

Type III. Enumerations and Samples. This includes both surveys and direct, repeated, countable observations. Observation in this sense may entail minimal participation as compared with that implied in Type I.

This classification excludes documents on the ground that they represent resultants or combinations of primary methods. Many documents, for example, are essentially informant's accounts and are treated exactly as an informant's account is treated: subjected to the same kinds of internal and external comparisons, treated with the same suspicions, and often in the end, taken as evidence of what occurred at some time and place from which the investigator was absent. The fact that the account is written is hardly important. Many other documents are essentially enumerations; for example, personnel and cost-accounting records of a factory, membership rolls of a union, tax rolls of a community.

TWO CRITERIA OF "GOODNESS"

Criteria according to which the "goodness" of a procedure may be defined are:

1. *Informational adequacy,* meaning accuracy, precision, and completeness of data.
2. *Efficiency,* meaning cost per added input of information.

It may appear arbitrary to exclude validity and reliability. Validity is excluded because it is, in a technical sense, a relation between an indicator and a concept, and similar problems arise whether one obtains information from an informant, a sample, or from direct observation. Construed loosely, validity is often taken to mean "response validity," accuracy of report, and this is caught up in the definition of informational adequacy. Construed more loosely yet, validity is sometimes taken as equivalent to "real," "deep" data, but this seems merely to beg the question. Reliability is relevant only tangentially; it is a separate problem that cuts across the issues of this paper.

FUNDAMENTAL STRATEGIES

Certain combinations of method and type of information may be regarded as formal prototypes, in the sense that other combinations may be logically reduced to them. For example: Instead of a sample survey or enumeration, an informant is employed to list dwelling units, or to estimate incomes, or to tell who associates with whom or what each person believes with respect to some issue. The information is obtained from a single informant, but he is treated *as if he himself* had conducted a census or poll. More generally, in every case in which the information obtained is logically reducible to a distribution of the members of S with respect to the property a, the implied method of obtaining the information is also logically reducible to an enumeration. The enumeration may be either through direct observation (estimating the number of sheep each Navaho has by actually counting them; establishing the sociometric structure of the community by watching who interacts with whom), or through a questionnaire survey (determining household composition by questioning a member of each household, or administering a sociometric survey to a sample of the community). If an informant is used, it is presumed that he has himself performed the enumeration. We are not at the moment concerned with the validity of this assumption in specific instances but rather in observing that regardless of the actual way in which the information was obtained, the logical and formal character of the procedure is that of a census or survey.

Suppose an informant is asked to describe what went on at a community meeting which the observer is unable to attend; or a sample of respondents is asked to describe a sequence of events which occurred before the observer entered S. In either case his reports are used as substitutes for direct observation. Such evidence may, in fact, be examined critically to establish its accuracy—we begin by assuming the bias of the reports—but it is presumed that, having "passed" the statements they become an objective account of what has occurred in the same sense that the investigator's own reports are treated as objective, once his biases have been taken into account. The informant, one usually says in this case, is the observer's observer; he differs in no way from the investigator himself. It follows that the prototype is direct observation by the observer himself.

The prototype so far is not only a formal model; it is also a "best" method, efficiently yielding the most adequate information. In learning institutionalized rules and statuses it is doubtful that there is a formal prototype and all three methods yield adequate information. Here we may choose the *most efficient* method as defining our standard of procedure. To illustrate: We wish to study the political structure of the United States. We are told that the principal national political figure is called a "president," and we wish to know who he is. We do not ordinarily think of sampling the population of the United States to obtain the answer; we regard it as sufficient to ask one well-informed member. This question is typical of a large class of questions asked by a field worker in the course of his research.

A second example: Any monograph on the Navaho reports that they are matrilineal and matrilocal. This statement may mean either of two things:

1. All Navaho are socially identified as members of a descent group defined through the mother's line, and all Navaho males move to the camp of their wife's family at marriage.

2. There exists a set of established rules according to which all Navaho are supposed to become socially identified as members of a descent group defined through the mother's line, and to move to the camp of their wife's family at marriage.

The truth of the first interpretation can be established only by an enumeration of the Navaho, or a sample sufficiently representative and sufficiently precise. It is readily falsified by exceptions, and in fact there *are* exceptions to both principles. But suppose among thirty Navaho informants at least one says that the Navaho are patrilineal and patrilocal. If this is intended to describe institutionalized norms as in (2) above, we are more likely to stop using the informant than we are to state that there are "exceptions" in the sense of (1) above. We might sample a population to discover the motivation to conform to a rule, or the actual degree of conformity, but are less likely to do so to establish that the rule *exists,* if we confront institutionalized phenomena. This also constitutes a very large class of questions asked by the field worker.

ADEQUACY OF INFORMANTS FOR VARIOUS PROBLEMS IN THE FIELD

It does not follow from the definition of a prototype method that no other form of obtaining information can suffice; all we intend is that it *does* suffice, and any other method is logically reducible to it. Further, comparison with the prototype is a criterion by which other forms can be evaluated. In considering the adequacy in some given instance of the use of an informant as the field worker's surrogate census, for example, we are interested primarily in whether he is likely to know enough, to recall enough, and to report sufficiently precisely to yield the census that we ourselves would make. Comments below, incidentally, are to be taken as always prefixed with the phrase, "by and large." It is not possible to establish, at least yet, a firm rule which will cover every case.

The Informant as a Surrogate Censustaker

A distinction must again be made between *what* information is obtained and how it is obtained. It is one thing to criticize a field worker for not obtaining a frequency distribution where it is required—for instance, for not sampling mothers who are weaning children in order to determine age at weaning—and another to criticize him for not obtaining it *directly* from the mothers. If the field worker reports that the average age at weaning is two years and the grounds for this is that he asked an informant, "About when do they wean children around here?" it is not the fact that he asked an informant but that he asked the wrong question that should be criticized. He should have asked, "How many mothers do you know who are now weaning children? How old are their children?"

The critical issue, therefore, is whether or not the informant can be assumed to have the information that the field worker requires, granting that he asks the proper questions. In many instances he does. In some cases he is an even better source than an enumerator; he either knows better or is less likely to falsify. Dean, for example, reports that workers who are ideologically pro-union, but also have mobility aspirations and are not well-integrated into their factory or local unions, are likely to report attending union meetings which they do not in fact attend.[5] She also shows that, when *respondent-reported* attendance is used as a measure of attendance, this tends spuriously to increase correlations of attendance at union meetings with attitudes toward unions in general, and to reduce correlations of attendance at union meetings with attitudes more specifically directed at the local union. The list of those actually attending was obtained by an observer, who, however, had sufficient rapport with officers of the local to obtain it from them.[6] Attendance, largely by "regulars," was stable from meeting to meeting so that the officers could have reproduced it quite accurately.[7]

On the other hand, there are many instances in which an informant is *prima facie* unlikely to be adequate, although no general rule seems to identify these clearly for the investigator. The nature of the information—private versus public, more or less objective, more or less approved—is obviously relevant, yet is often no guide at all. Some private information, for example, is better obtained from informants, some from respondents. The social structure of S, particularly its degree of differentiation and complexity, is also obviously relevant. An informant must be in a position to know the information desired, and if S is highly differentiated and the informant confined to one part of it, he can hardly enumerate it. Probably in order to discover attitudes and opinions that are relatively private and heterogeneous in a structure that is relatively differentiated, direct enumeration or sampling should be used.

The Informant as a "Representative Respondent"

An "average" of a distribution is sometimes obtained not by asking for an enumeration by the informant, nor even by asking a general question concerning what people typically do; sometimes it is obtained by treating the informant as if he were a "representative respondent." The informant's reports about himself—perhaps deeper, more detailed, "richer," but nevertheless like those of a respondent in a survey rather than an informant in the technical sense—stand in place of a sample. Where a multivariate distribution is thought of, this person is treated as a "quintessential" subject, "typical" in many dimensions. Some field workers speak favorably of using informants in this way, and it is likely that even more of them actually do so.

Since, as yet, we have no really hard and fast rules to follow, it is possible that in some cases this is legitimate; but, by and large, it is the most suspect of ways of using informants. It is simply a bad way of sampling. The legitimate cases are probably of three types: first, as suggestive of leads to follow up; second, as illustration of a point to be made in a report that is verifiable on other grounds. But in this second case the proviso ought to be thought of as rather strict; it is not sufficient to "have a feeling" that the point is true, to assume that it is verifiable on other grounds. The third case is perhaps the most legitimate, but is really a case of using informants to provide information about generally known rules: for example, using informants to collect "typical" genealogies or kinship terms, the assumption being that his kin terms are much like those of others (which is not always true, of course) and his genealogy sufficiently "rich"—this being the basis on which he was chosen—to exhibit a wide range of possibilities.

The Informant as the Observer's Observer

The third common use of the informant is to report events not directly observed by the field worker. Here the investigator substitutes the observations of a member for his own observation. It is not simply interviewing that is involved here, because participant observation was defined earlier as including interviewing on the spot, in conjunction with direct observation. Thus, some of the most important uses of the informant—to provide the meaning and context of that which we are observing, to provide a running check on variability, etc.—are actually part of participant observation. It is the use of informants as if they were colleagues that we must now consider.

Such a procedure is not only legitimate but absolutely necessary to adequate investigation of any complex structure. In studying a social structure by participant observation there are two problems of bias that override all others, even the much belabored "personal equation." One results from the fact that a single observer cannot be everywhere at the same time, nor can he be "everywhere" in time, for that matter—he has not been in S forever, and will not be there indefinitely—so that, inevitably, something happens that he has not seen, cannot see, or will not see. The second results from the fact that there exist parts of the social structure into which he has not penetrated and probably will not, by virtue of the way he has defined himself to its members, because of limitations on the movement of those who sponsor him, etc. There has never been a participant-observer study in which the observer acquired full knowledge of all roles and statuses through his own direct observation, and for that matter there never will be such a study by a single observer. To have a team of observers is one possible solution; to have informants who stand in the relation of team members to the investigator is another. The virtue of the informant used in this way, is to increase the accessibility of S to the investigator.

EFFICIENCY OF SAMPLING FOR VARIOUS PROBLEMS IN THE FIELD

Sampling to Obtain Information about Institutionalized Norms and Statuses

It has already been argued that a properly obtained probability sample gives adequate information about institutionalized norms and statuses but is not very efficient. Two things are implied: that such information is *general* information so that any member of S has the same information as any other; and that the truth of such information does not depend solely on the opinions of the respondents—the information is in some sense objective.

The first of these implications is equivalent to assuming that S is homogeneous with respect to the property a, so that a sample of one suffices to classify S with respect to it. It then becomes inefficient to continue sampling. The principal defect in such an argument is a practical one: By what criterion can one decide S is homogeneous with respect to a without sampling S? There are two such criteria, neither of which is wholly satisfactory. The first is to use substantive knowledge. We would expect in general that certain norms are invariably institutionalized, such as incest and exogamy, descent, inheritance, marriage procedures, patterns of exchange of goods, formal structure of labor markets, etc. We may assume a priori, for example, that a sample of two hundred Navaho is not required to discover that marriage in one's own clan is incestuous. But the pitfall for the unwary investigator is that he may stray beyond his substantive knowledge or apply it at the wrong time in the wrong place.

A second is to employ a loose form of sequential sampling. Suppose, for example, that we ask an informed male in S whom he may marry, or whom any male may marry. He answers, "All who are A, but no one who is B." We ask a second informant and discover again that he may marry all who are A, but no one who is B. We ask a third, a fourth, a fifth, and each tells us the same rule. We do not need to presume that the rule is actually obeyed; that is quite a different question. But we may certainly begin to believe that we have found an institutionalized norm. Conversely, the more variability we encounter, the more we must investigate further. The pitfall here is that we may be deceived by a homogeneous "pocket" within which all members agree but which does not necessarily represent all structural parts of S. For this reason we try to choose representative informants, each from a different status group. This implies, however, that we are working outward from earlier applications of this dangerous principle; we have used some informants to tell us what statuses there are, thereafter choosing additional informants from the new statuses we have discovered.

The second implication—that in some sense the truth of the information obtained depends not on the opinions of respondents but on something else that is "objective" in nature—simply paraphrases Durkheim: institutions are "external" to given individuals, even though they exist only "in" individuals; they have a life of their own, are *sui generis*. Illustrating with an extreme case: a "belief" of S's religion can be described by an informant even where neither he nor any living member of S actually believes it, although if no member ever did believe it we might regard the information as trivial. In other words, this type of information does not refer to individuals living at a given time, but rather to culture as a distinct object of abstraction. It is this type of information that we mean by "institutionalized norms and statuses." It bears repeating at this point that if one Navaho informant told us the Navaho were patrilineal and patrilocal, we would be more likely to assume he was wrong than we would be to assume that the Navaho had, for the moment, changed their institutions.

Sampling to Obtain Information about Incidents and Histories

If we had the good fortune to have a report from every member of S about what happened in region R at time T, would it really be good fortune? Would we not distinguish between those in a position to observe the event and those not? Among those who had been in the region R itself, would we not also distinguish subregions which provided different vantage points from which to view the event? Among those viewing it from the same vantage point, would we not distinguish more or less credible witnesses? Enumeration or not, we would apply stringent internal and external comparisons to each report in order to establish what truly occurred. Formally, of course, this describes a complex technique of stratification which, if carried out properly, would withstand any quantitative criticism. But if all the elements of a decision as to what is "truth" in such a case are considered, it is a moot point how important enumeration or random sampling is in the process.[8]

Informants with Special Information

Some things happen that relatively few people know about. A random sample is not a sensible way in which to obtain information about these events, although it is technically possible to define a universe U containing only those who do know and sample from U. A parallel case is the repetitive event in inaccessible parts of a social structure. A social structure is an organized system of relationships, one property of which is that certain parts of it are not readily observed by members located in other parts. There is a considerable amount of relatively esoteric information about S. It may be satisfactory from a formal point of view to regard S as consisting in many universes U_i, each of which is to be sampled for a different piece of information, but again the usefulness of such a conception is questionable, particularly if most U_i contain very few members.

EFFICIENCY AND ADEQUACY OF PARTICIPANT OBSERVATION FOR VARIOUS PROBLEMS IN THE FIELD

Ex Post Facto Quantitative Documentation

Because certain things are observed repeatedly, it sometimes occurs to the field worker to count these repetitions in his log as quantitative documentation of an assertion. In such cases, the information obtained should be subjected to any of the canons by which other quantitative data are evaluated; the care with which the universe is defined and the sense in which the sample is representative are particularly critical. With few exceptions, frequency statements made from field logs will *not* withstand such careful examination.

This sharp stricture applies only to ex post facto enumeration or sampling of field logs, and it is because it is ex post facto that the principal dangers arise. Events and persons represented in field logs will generally be sampled according to convenience rather than rules of probability sampling. The sample is unplanned, contains unknown biases. It is not so much random as haphazard, a distinction which is critical. When, after the fact, the observer attempts to correlate two classes of events in these notes very misleading results will be obtained. If we wish to correlate a and b it is characteristic of such samples that "a" will be more frequently recorded than "*not-a*," and "a *and* b" more frequently than "*not-a and b*" or "a *and not-b*." As a general rule, only those data which the observer actually intended to enumerate should be treated as enumerable.

There are, of course, some valid enumerations contained in field notes. For example, a verbatim account kept of all meetings of some organization is a valid enumeration; a record kept, in some small rural community, of all members of it who come to the crossroads hamlet during a year is a valid enumeration. These will tend, however, to be intentional enumerations and not subject to the strictures applicable to ex post facto quantification. A much rarer exception will occur when, looking back through one's notes, one discovers that without particularly intending it, every member of the community studied has been enumerated with respect to the property a, or that almost all of them have. This is likely to be rare because field notes tend not to record those who do *not* have the property *a*, and, of all those omitted in the notes, one does not know how many are *not-a* and how many simply were not observed. If everyone, or almost everyone, can be accounted for as either *a* or *not-a,* then a frequency statement is validly made.[9] But, if such information were desired in the first place, participant observation would clearly be a most inefficient means of obtaining it.

Readily Verbalized Norms and Statuses

It is not efficient to use participant observation to obtain generally known norms and statuses so long as these can be readily stated. It may take a good deal of observation to infer that which an informant can quickly tell you. Participant observation would in such cases be primarily to check what informants say, to get clues to further questions, etc. It is, of course, true that the concurrent interviewing involved in participant observation will provide the information—it is necessary to make sense out of the observations—but it comes in bits and pieces and is less readily checked for accuracy, completeness, consistency, etc.

Latent Phenomena

Not all norms and statuses can be verbalized. Consequently, there remains a special province to which participant observation lays well-justified claims. But certain misleading implications should be avoided in admitting them. Because such phenomena may be described as "latent"—as known to the observer but not to the members of *S*—it may be concluded that *all* latent phenomena are the province of participant observation. This does not follow. The term "latent" is ambiguous; it has several distinct usages, some of which do not even share the core meaning of "known to the observer, unknown to members." Lazarsfeld, for example, refers to a dimension underlying a series of manifest items as a "latent" attribute; it cannot be observed by anyone, and is inferred by the investigator from intercorrelations of observables. But the members of *S* may also make these inferences. (They infer that a series of statements classify the speaker as "liberal," for example.) The most advanced techniques for searching out such latent phenomena are found in survey research and psychometrics, not in participant observation.

These are matters of inference, not of how data are directly obtained. The same is true of the discovery of "latent functions." Often the observer is aware of connections between events when the members of *S* are not, even though they are aware of the events themselves. But again, relations among events are not the special province of any one method; we look for such connections in *all* our data. In fact, owing to the paucity and non-comparability of units that often plague the analysis of field notes, it might be argued that participant observation is often incapable of detecting such connections. The great value of participant observation in detecting latent phenomena, then, is in those cases in which members of S are unaware of actually observable events, of some of the things they do, or some of the things that happen around them, which can be directly apprehended by the observer. Any other case requires inference and such inference should be made from *all* available data.

SUMMARY AND CONCLUSION

Figure 1 offers a general summary.

With respect to the problem with which this paper originated the following conclusion may be drawn: Because we often treat different methods as concretely different types of study rather than as analytically different aspects of the same study, it is possible to attack a field study on the ground that it ought to be an enumeration and fails if it is not; and to defend it on the ground that it ought to be something *else* and succeeds only if it is. But, however we classify types of information in the future—and the classification suggested here is only tentative—they are not all of one type. True, a field report is unreliable if it gives us, after consulting a haphazard selection of informants or even a carefully planned "representative" selection, a statement such as, "All members of S believe that . . ." or "The average member of S believes that . . ." *and* (1) there is variance in the characteristic reported, (2) this variance is relevant to the problem reported, *and* (3) the informants cannot be seriously thought of as equivalent to a team of pollsters, *or* (4) the investigator has reported what is, essentially, the "average" beliefs of his *informants*, as if

Methods of Obtaining Information

Information Types	Enumerations and Samples	Participant Observation	Interviewing Informants
Frequency Distributions	Prototype and best form	Usually inadequate and inefficient	Often, but not always, inadequate; if adequate it is efficient
Incidents, Histories	Not adequate by itself; not efficient	Prototype and best form	Adequate with precautions, and efficient
Institutionalized Norms and Statuses	Adequate but inefficient	Adequate, but inefficient, except for unverbalized norms	Most efficient and hence best form

Figure 1

they were a representative, probability sample of respondents. But to demand that every piece of information be obtained by a probability sample is to commit the researcher to grossly inefficient procedure and to ignore fundamental differences among various kinds of information. The result is that we create false methodological issues, often suggest quite inappropriate research strategies to novices, and sometimes conceal real methodological issues which deserve more discussion in the literature—such as how to establish institutionalized norms given only questionnaire data. It should be no more satisfactorily rigorous to hear that everything is in some way a sample, and hence must be sampled, than to hear that everything is in some sense "whole" and hence cannot be sampled.

NOTES

[1] See Harry Alpert, "Some Observations on the Sociology of Sampling," *Social Forces,* 31 (1952), 30-31; Robert C. Hanson, "Evidence and Procedure Characteristics of 'Reliable' Propositions in Social Science," *American Journal of Sociology,* 63 (1958), 357-63.

[2] See W. L. Warner and P. Lunt, *Social Life of a Modern Community* (New Haven, Conn.: Yale University Press, 1941), p. 55; Conrad Arensberg, "The Community Study Method," *American Journal of Sociology,* 60 (1952), 109-24; Howard Becker, "Field Work among Scottish Shepherds and German Peasants," *Social Forces,* 35 (1956), 10-15; Howard S. Becker and Blanche Geer, "Participant Observation and Interviewing; A Comparison," *Human Organization,* 16 (1957), 28-34; Solon Kimball, "Problems of Studying American Culture," *American Anthropologist,* 57 (1955), 1131-42; and A. Vidich and J. Bensman, "The Validity of Field Data," *Human Organization,* 13 (1954), 20-27.

[3] See particularly Oscar Lewis, "Controls and Experiments in Field Work," in *Anthropology Today* (Chicago: University of Chicago Press, 1953), p. 455n.; also cf. Howard S. Becker, "Problems of Inference and Proof in Participant Observation," *American Sociological Review,* 23 (1958), 652-60; Elizabeth Colson, "The Intensive Study of Small Sample Communities," in R. F. Spencer (ed.), *Method and Perspective in Anthropology* (Minneapolis: University of Minnesota Press, 1954), pp. 43-59; Fred Eggan, "Social Anthropology and the Method of Controlled Comparison," *American Anthropologist,* 56 (1954), 743-60; Harold E. Driver, "Statistics in Anthropology," *American Anthropologist,* 55 (1953), 42-59; Melville J. Herskovitz, "Some Problems of Method in Ethnography," in R. F. Spencer (ed.), *op. cit.,* pp. 3-24; George Spindler and Walter Goldschmidt, "Experimental Design in the Study of Culture Change," *Southwestern Journal of Anthropology,* 8 (1952), 68-83. And see the section "Field Methods and Techniques" in *Human Organization,* esp. in its early years and its early editorials. Some quantification has been characteristic of "field" monographs for a very long time; cf. Kroeber's *Zuni Kin and Clan* (1916). Such classics as *Middletown* and the *Yankee City* series are studded with tables.

[4] A significant exception is a comment by M. Trow directed at Becker and Geer. Becker and Geer, comparing interviewing to participant observation, find participant observation the superior method and seem to imply that it is superior for all purposes. Trow insists that the issue is not correctly formulated, and that one might better ask: "What kinds of problems are best studied through what kinds of methods; . . . how can the various methods at our disposal complement one another?" In their reply, Becker and Geer are more or less compelled to agree. See Becker and Geer, "Participant Observation and Interviewing: A Comparison," *op. cit.;* Trow's "Comment," *Human Organization,* 16 (1957), 33-35; and Becker and Geer's "Rejoinder," *Human Organization,* 17 (1958), 39-40.

[5] L. R. Dean, "Interaction, Reported and Observed: The Case of One Local Union," *Human Organization,* 17 (1958), 36-44.

[6] *Ibid.,* p. 37n.

[7] *Ibid.*

[8] None of this applies to *repeated* events. If we are interested in comparing several repetitions of the same event, generalizing as to the course that is typical, care must be taken in sampling the events.

[9] We may make a less stringent requirement of our notes, using what might be called "incomplete" indicator spaces. Briefly, if we wish to classify all members of S with respect to the underlying property A, and behaviors a, b, c, d . . . , all indicate A, then it is sufficient for our purpose to have information on *at least one* of these indicators for each member of S. For some we might have only a, for some only b, etc., but we might have one among the indicators for all members, even though not the same one for all members; and thus be able to enumerate S adequately.

PART SIX

Ethical Problems in Field Studies

CHAPTER 21

Some Ethical Problems in Modern Fieldwork

J. A. Barnes

I. INTRODUCTION

Many people maintain that social anthropology and other empirically based social sciences would advance faster if they were modelled more closely on the natural sciences or on mathematics. There are two parts to this view. On the one hand we are urged to use concepts and methods of analysis closer akin to those of the natural sciences, on the other we are told that we should collect our empirical data in what is thought to be a more systematic and objective way. Here I am not concerned with the first issue, whether mathematics or atomic physics are better analytical models for social science than history or geology. My point of departure is the second issue. Can we behave in the field in essentially the same way as we would in a laboratory, looking down a microscope or watching through a one-way screen; or, since this is generally admitted to be a policy of perfection, should we in the field at least try to get as close as possible to laboratory conditions of work? I hope to show that this aim can lead to poorer, not better, research and that effective fieldwork in part depends on realizing how the field situation differs from the natural science laboratory.

Any empirical inquiry is likely to have several objectives, some theoretical, others practical, but usually one objective has precedence over the others. My discussion is restricted to scientific or academic research, where the main commitment of the investigator is to his discipline, to the acquisition and dissemination of knowledge. The problems I shall discuss present themselves in different guise when the primary research goals are administrative, therapeutic, educative or ameliorative, and their examination under these conditions lies outside the scope of this paper.

I refer to the field investigator as an ethnographer, a convenient neutral term, whether the people he is studying are tribesmen or townsmen, preliterate or industrialized, and whether he thinks of himself as sociologist or social anthropologist or both.

This chapter was originally published by Routledge & Kegan Paul, Ltd. and the London School of Economics in the *British Journal of Sociology,* 14: no. 2, 118-34.

II. COLONIAL AND POST-COLONIAL CONDITIONS

Many decades ago ethnographic fieldwork did usually take place under conditions similar to those met with in natural science. For example, when Haddon and his colleagues on the Cambridge expedition worked on the islands of the Torres Straits in northern Queensland in 1898 their methods of investigation were similar to those used in the natural sciences in which many of them had been trained. The field of inquiry was perceived as exterior to themselves, something which could be observed by an outsider without significant distortion. The lives of the islanders were thought not to be seriously disturbed by the presence of the ethnographic team, though in its reports the effects of prolonged missionary activity are discussed briefly. Information was collected mainly in interviews, using "jargon" English as a medium. Ceremonies were observed in essentially the same spirit as artifacts and physical characteristics were measured and depicted. Some attention was paid to European influence and somewhat unexpectedly there is an account of the courts set up by the Queensland government; but it is clear from the reports that European administrators, traders and missionaries did not form part of the field of study. They constituted, as it were, boundary conditions of the area under investigation. The research work was not aimed at influencing the future of the Torres Straits islanders. The islanders were not expected to read the reports of the expedition, nor, I think, was the Queensland government expected to be interested in them except as a disinterested contribution to knowledge; in any case, thirty-seven years elapsed before the last research report appeared. The names, marriages and totems of the islanders were given in the published genealogies.[1] In brief, the Torres Straits islanders were under the microscope and Haddon and his colleagues were looking down the tube at them.

These methods and assumptions were typical of ethnographic work done by avowed anthropologists until, say, 1925. Even Malinowski, despite the tremendous changes he brought about in fieldwork methods, still regarded the Trobriands as though it was a laboratory. The effects of missionary and administrative contacts on the Trobriands were marginal to his work and he was not much concerned with any effects his published work might have on the islanders or on the Papuan administration. He wrote in 1930:

> On the islands of the Pacific, though I was pursued by the products of the Standard Oil Company, weekly editions, cotton goods, cheap detective stories, and the internal combustion engine in the ubiquitous motor launch, I was still able with but little effort to re-live and reconstruct a type of human life moulded by the implements of the stone age, pervaded with crude beliefs and surrounded by a wide, uncontaminated open stretch of nature.[2]

Nowadays the picture is different. The ethnographer is usually greatly interested in the relationships existing between the community or system he is studying and the wider world. He knows that his own presence will affect the behaviour of people round him and he seeks to minimize or control this effect. He may discuss his manuscript with some of his informants before he publishes, and he knows that his published words may be read not only by government, missions and other outsiders but also by the people he has been studying. He is aware that what he writes may well become the basis for action designed to alter what he describes and will therefore either take special steps to prevent this happening or, alternatively, he will seek consciously to influence and even to take responsibility for such action.[3] Typically, in the old days informants and other actors in the ethnographic picture were given their real names, even though some of their actions might be described in Latin, whereas nowadays informants and others are given disguised names but their actions are described in plain English. The innocent daughters of the metropolitan reader, if they still exist, are no longer considered. Instead, regard is paid to the susceptibilities of people who may see their own private lives in print, and to the law of libel, the provisions of the Official Secrets Act and similar legislation.

Fieldwork during what we might call the colonial period was based on several assumptions that have been abandoned. The boundaries of the field of study were clear, and for the most part only non-Western peoples were studied. Inquiries were aimed at increasing knowledge rather than prompting local action, and although the knowledge acquired might have practical applications, these were ancilliary. It was quite legitimate to seek support from governments, both metropolitan and colonial, as appropriate patrons for disinterested research. The ethnographer took for granted that the observations and records he made did not significantly disturb the behaviour of the people studied. In the classical mechanics of the nineteenth century it was assumed that physical observations could be made without affecting the objects observed and in much the same way ethnographers assumed that in their researches there was no direct feed-back from them to their informants. Published research reports were intended to interest professional colleagues and the metropolitan public rather than the colonial administrator, and only rarely reached members of the tribes concerned.

These assumptions are now obsolete. Firstly, the ethnographer's field of study is enlarged so that even when focusing on an illiterate tribe he gives some attention to outside agencies. Secondly, the focus of study is no longer always an illiterate tribe but may be a community many of whose members can read, write letters to the newspapers and learned periodicals, and even sue the ethnographer if need be, and who may be his fellow-citizens. Thirdly, the ethnographer hopes not only to publish generalized statements about customary behaviour but also to describe the actions of individuals whom, for purposes of exposition, he must identify in some way; and these actions may be, in some eyes, reprehensible or illegal. Fourthly, administrators and others realize that ethnographic publications may include statements construable as criticism of their activities, and hence are more cautious about giving information.

This last change was impressed on me early in my own fieldwork in Rhodesia. I went with a colleague to call on the bishop of an area where there were many European planters. We were both firm believers in non-directive interview techniques and keen to make the best use of our first bishop as an informant. As the interview progressed non-directively, the bishop grew puzzled, until finally he asked, "And where do you intend to farm?" I answered, "We are not planters. My friend is a psychologist and I am an anthropologist." The bishop smiled with comprehension and replied, "Then we must be very careful what we say."

In brief, the division between those under the microscope and those looking scientifically down the eye-piece has broken down. There may still be an exotic focus of study but the group or institution being studied is now seen to be embedded in a network of social relations of which the observer is an integral if reluctant part.[4] Significant action in this social field is not restricted to the period the ethnographer spends working in the field. It begins when he first makes plans to visit his field location and continues at least until the time when his published work is discussed by the people he has studied.

III. SPONSORS

In this new situation the ethnographer faces problems of right conduct that were absent in the colonial period. One serious problem is what attitude the ethnographer should adopt towards those in authority. Before fieldwork can be begun almost anywhere in the world, permission must be obtained from some authority or other. Sometimes permission is required from a plurality of mutually antagonistic authorities. It is commonly believed that ethnographers experience more difficulty in this matter than do their colleagues in the natural sciences. If we assert that ethnographic research can be of value to an enlightened administration, we should not be surprised that less enlightened administrators exaggerate its dangers. Some field workers treat the establishment of relations with government as merely a necessary formality, even if a lengthy one. Thus Keesing, writing about fieldwork in Oceania, says:

The prospective investigator does well not only to have his institutional credentials in order, but also to stress them in applications for visas, special entry permits, and any other needed approvals.

Clearances, as well as courtesy, often require a complex series of contacts by correspondence, to be followed by personal calls. The anthropologist should be able to curb his impatience here because of his professional awareness of the importance of ceremonious behaviour, and of the functions of elaborate hierarchical and other patterned social structures.[5]

This formulation gives cold comfort and misses the point. The investigator's professional training should enable him to realize that what is more important than the ceremonial or bureaucratic delays of the administration is its power to prevent him from doing any work at all in its territory. And here the dilemma comes. In the colonial situation it was well realized that, for example, in a tribe with a chief, his co-operation was necessary to ensure the success of fieldwork. Usually this was not a serious problem. Behind the ethnographer was the support of the colonial administration, so that it was difficult or dangerous for the chief to resist the ethnographer openly. Appropriate gifts could smooth the way, for in the main the ethnographer's activities, if incomprehensible to the chief, did not threaten his position in any way. Though the ethnographer might not approve of, say, the arbitrary power wielded by the chief, or of the tribal subjection of women, or of the moral code and religious ideas of the people, he did not try to alter what he saw. Instead, he tried to understand and explain without passing moral judgments of his own. For the most part, this is still the accepted style of working, but now we are not sure over how wide an area we have to suspend moral judgments and to refrain from action. If it is wrong to influence the tribesman, is it wrong to influence the administration? For research purposes we want to study some at least of the actions of the administration; must we, therefore, treat the administration as though it were another savage tribe? Or is the administration a body to which we can appeal in the name of science; or again, is it a constitutional body in which we have rights or for which we have responsibilities? Or can we treat with the administration on two levels, seeking intellectual and logistic support at a high administrative level while at the same time endeavouring not to become identified with the administration at the local level? Do these problems arise in all field research or only when some aspect of administrative activity is one of the principal topics under investigation?

Spillius has discussed many of these issues at length[6] and I would merely reiterate his plea for a dispassionate view of colonial government as a social system. Yet an intellectual appreciation of the aims and methods of a colonial government does not entail approval of its methods, and the problem of how much and in what ways the ethnographer should seek its support still remains.

This dilemma is easier to solve in practice when fieldwork is undertaken in territory controlled by an administration that is entirely foreign to the investigator. Under these circumstances he is likely to have very little influence and is entirely dependent on the co-operation of the foreign administration. The ethnographer will then often try to make his research work appear harmless rather than useful. But when research is planned in some territory with which the ethnographer, or the institution supporting him, has some connection, a choice is open. The whole-hearted co-operation of the administration can either be consciously sought or carefully avoided, or some intermediate position adopted. Clearly the main consideration will be the attitude of the group being studied towards its administrators.

Relationships to the administration do not impinge merely at the point of getting or not getting an entry permit. We all hope that we shall win the confidence of our informants, but when this confidence extends to confidential administrative documents, we have to walk warily. When we are told in confidence that A is not really the father of B, we decide how to make use of this information principally by reference to our own professional ethics, ill-defined though these are. But when we are told "official" secrets other considerations enter, for the administration has effective sanctions to protect its interests. The ethnographer has to be clear from the start that co-operation with the administration may entail obligations as well as advantages.

It may be hazardous for the ethnographer to become identified with the administration, or with any one segment of the society he is studying. Yet without sponsorship at all he may be in difficulties. Informants in subordinate or insecure positions may be unwilling to co-operate unless responsibility for the ethnographer's presence has been taken by someone in authority. If there is no one at all to indicate to the community that the ethnographer has his approval, the research worker may have to explain his presence, describe his objectives and methods, and allay suspicion in each fresh context and with each new informant. In some field situations, particularly in towns, the ethnographer may well go out of his way to look for some publicly recognized organization enjoying wide-spread support that can act as his local sponsor. Yet such bodies do not always exist and the field worker may have to resign himself to explaining over and over again what he wants to do.

IV. MORAL JUDGMENTS IN THE FIELD

Under the microscope there could be no moral judgments. They had their code and we had ours, and the two never met.[7] There was a double standard of morality, one for informants in their world and the other for the ethnographer, the society he belonged to, his colleagues and his readers. Furthermore, in the colonial era before the advent of "development," even the administration's ideas of right and wrong impinged on the lives of its dependent peoples only in a limited number of contexts. But if tribesmen, administration and ethnographer are now all part of one social system, this inter-cultural ethical indifference disappears. More and more of the daily lives of tribesmen becomes subject to legal and moral evaluation by the administration, even though their respective codes differ widely. More and more the ethnographer finds himself in situations in which he cannot avoid evaluating the actions of his informants in terms of his own moral code. If he refrains from acting on these evaluations, it is because of the way he has defined his role as a scientific investigator and not because of the cultural gulf between him and his informants. But sometimes he cannot refrain. For example, we often find that many of the social actions taken in a tribal community are regarded as illegal by the administration.[8] These practices may have their origin in pre-contact conditions, or they may have evolved during colonial times or they may be directly linked with attempts to change or subvert the existing regime. The ethnographer is in a quandary. He may feel he has a duty to the administration to report illegalities. Even if he does not think he has this duty, the administration may think he has. The ethnographer may equally well feel that he has a duty to his informants to conceal his knowledge from the administration. He may feel a duty to the ideals of scientific inquiry not to intervene in the field situation, and yet the same sense of duty may require him to publish the facts of this illegal activity if this forms part of the basis of his analysis of social life, even if he disguises his evidence. Participation in community activities may involve the ethnographer himself in illegal acts. In extreme situations the ethnographer may well consider that, quite apart from any duty he may feel towards administration, informants, or science, his own personal values override other considerations; surely all of us would try to intervene to save a life. Spillius has described clearly his own intervention on Tikopia during a famine and the consequences this had for his role as a research worker.[9] But there are many situations that are not so clear cut, and the ethnographer is often under continual pressure from his informants, and sometimes from the administration, to intervene on their behalf.[10] No simple formula can apply to all circumstances. The ethnographer has to define his role, or try to do so, so that he can retain the good will of his informants and of the administration, continue to gain the flow of information essential to his research task, and yet remain true to his own basic values. This ideal may not always be possible and the ethnographer has to decide which of these desiderata he should forego. If he supplies information in confidence to the administration or some other body, he must be aware that though he may be on his guard against betraying his informants, when he himself becomes an informant, his confidence may be betrayed, either by accident or design.[11]

V. ROLE DEFINITION

Difficulties in role definition arise continually because of the multiplicity of contexts in which most ethnographers hope to make their observations. Some ethnographers may still hire informants by the hour and even follow an office routine beginning with the first informant at nine o'clock in the morning and pausing for a coffee break when informants may smoke.[12] Many of the problems discussed here do not arise when research inquiries are made in this way. Another method of working, springing from quite different premises, also limits contact between the investigator and the object of his inquiries. In the

Glacier project, an investigation into certain aspects of the social life of a London factory, correct roles for the research team were carefully worked out, but it was emphasized that outside the research situation members of the team had no relevant role at all. Jaques writes:

... the Research Team has limited its relationship with members of the factory to strictly formal contacts which have to do with project work publicly sanctioned by the Works Council ... this has meant refusing invitations to people's homes, to play tennis on the factory's courts, to discuss with individual members of a group occurrences which took place earlier at a meeting, and many other activities which could be construed as outside the terms of reference.[13]

Here the model of the natural science laboratory has been discarded in favour of the psychiatric clinic with group therapy in progress.

Both these methods where extra-professional contacts are shunned seem incompatible with the conventional ethnographic method of inquiry epitomized in Evans-Pritchard's classic phrase: "to get to know well the persons involved and to see and hear what they do and say."[14] By the first method, the ethnographer collects his information only in the artificial context of formal interviews and neglects opportunities for direct observation. The second method may be appropriate when the boundaries of the research field are agreed and distinct, but in many field inquiries there are no terms of reference agreed to by all parties and there is no representative body like a Works Council able to give formal approval to research activities. Furthermore, the ethnographer usually limits himself to observing and understanding and does not primarily aim to assist the group he is studying to see its own difficulties more clearly and to take action to overcome them; he does cast himself in the role of therapist. Only through informal association with his informants can he gain the rich flood of complex and conflicting information he needs; yet unequivocal identification with one faction may dry up the flow of information from all others. Sometimes it may be unwise to play tennis with the District Officer, to drink beer with one lineage and not with another, to attend a sacrifice to the ancestors but to stay away from Mass; sometimes it may be even harder to do both. A neutral role can often be defined so that the ethnographer can observe conflict situations from more than one standpoint and his neutrality may still entail twenty-four hours work a day.

In some field situations the ethnographer may have little latitude in defining his role for it will be done for him. Most commentators on fieldwork methods caution the ethnographer against becoming too closely identified with one faction within the community he is studying, although I think that this danger is often exaggerated. Yet if there is a major cleavage between the administration and the local community, it may be difficult for the ethnographer to find a neutral position where he can retain the confidence of both sides. In some recent situations (particularly in Africa) government approval has implied for the people that the ethnographer was a spy, while positive approval by the people has implied for the government that he was subversive. Similar difficulties have been encountered in the study of factories, where management approval has implied trade union suspicion, and vice versa.[15] In their study of Deep South, Davis and Gardner, one a Negro and the other a White, worked each on his own side of the colour line,[16] but this division of labour would be impossible in many field studies and the ethnographer has to try to straddle the cleavage. Even in situations of severe social conflict some community of interest remains and it may still be possible to do effective fieldwork even in situations where, to give a recent example, informants are fined in court for speaking to the ethnographer. But in some situations of conflict there are no neutral roles and impartial social inquiry is impossible.

Two ways have been suggested for avoiding these difficulties in role definition. One is to do research covertly. Many of us might say simply that this is dishonest and inexcusable. Yet it is not uncommon for an ethnographer, when trying to explain the purpose of his work to tribesmen and to administrators, to stress those aspects that seem innocuous such as, say, the collection of legends and of information on technology, rather than topics such as land tenure and social control, which are more likely to be controversial. This is in fact an attempt to disguise our main interests.[17] I well remember the surprise with which a District Officer greeted my naive remark that I was studying him too, and I think I was more circumspect thereafter. Clearly there are limits of comprehension that make necessary some kind of modified statement of one's research aims when talking to different audiences. But completely misleading statements of intentions will come home to roost with publication, and even if the ethnographer is by then well removed from his scene of study, the reputation of the profession suffers.

In completely covert research the ethnographer seeks his information while ostensibly filling some quite different role. The absence of any suitable alternative role for a visiting scientist in many tribal situations is probably the reason why covert research has not received more discussion among anthropologists. Covert research can sometimes yield results that are significant and which could perhaps not be obtained in any other way: *When Prophesy Fails,* by Festinger and others, a study of a small sect in the Middle West of the United States awaiting the destruction of the earth, is an outstanding example. Yet in my view this method is simply dishonest and we should not use it. Furthermore, I think we should say that we will not undertake covert research. If we wish to enjoy public support as a responsible profession we must not only avoid acting as spies even in the best causes; we must make it clear in advance that we will not act in this way.

The other method is to come completely out into the open, state one's neutral position in advance, and endeavour to get both sides to accept one as an intercalary figure. This procedure has been followed with success in several studies of industrial situations. However, an essential feature of these investigations seems to be a long period of preliminary negotiation during which the investigator gains acceptance from both the management and the trade unions. Only after this does fieldwork start in earnest. A procedure of this kind is obviously impracticable where the fieldwork is to be carried on among illiterate or unsophisticated people living thousands of miles away who may not be organized in an hierarchical structure. Yet the ethnographer may well endeavour to move into a neutral role as his fieldwork progresses. In particular he may prefer to facilitate the exchange of ideas between administration and people rather than give direct advice to one side about how to deal with the other.

VI. PUBLICATION

Research work that does not lead to published reports is usually a waste of time and money. Yet, when we publish, our eye is more often on our colleagues than on our informants. Articles may sometimes lie unnoticed in the decent obscurity of learned journals, but books find their way far into the bush and if they are not always well understood they are easily misunderstood. Some may say that no harm is likely to be done if people see themselves described in print. Indeed, the fieldworker is sometimes recommended to win the support of his tribal informants by saying that he is trying to write a book about them. Other tribes are already in the books; don't they want to be honoured in the same way?[18] Yet in research in Western society the usual procedure is to disguise the identity of individuals, locations and times, and this is done at the request of informants. Why this difference?

There are two questions to answer. Why and when should we try to minimize the effects that publication may have on the field situation? If we want to minimize effects, how can it best be done?

Ethnographic and other sociographic publications find their way back into the field. Even the Trobriand Islanders know of Malinowski's books and one of them has reported that Malinowski did not understand their system of clans and chiefs.[19] At one extreme, Rattray's books on Ashanti have become authorities accepted by Ashanti courts. At the other, in the community in the United States described by Vidich and Bensman under the pseudonym of Springdale, it is said that no further research will be possible for "many, many years."[20] The first effect may be good, the second is obviously bad. In general every field situation should be kept open for possible future research. Even if everyone in the community knows of A's misdeeds, he and they may not relish seeing them recorded for posterity. As Whyte points out with reference to the Springdale affair, there is a significant difference between public knowledge circulating orally in a community and stories appearing in print.[21] Furthermore, if actions are illegal according to a set of regulations imposed from outside or are regarded by outsiders as particularly reprehensible, this may be a strong additional reason for protecting the actors.[22] When publishing in the hope that action may be taken the ethnographer needs to be sure that the expected action is wanted by those who provided him with information; but in not publishing lest action might be taken the ethnographer has to consider his obligations to those who have supported his research and to the profession to which he belongs.

One way of controlling the effect of publication is to make sure that those affected agree to what is being said about them. The number of people who may possibly be affected by the publication of the results of a social inquiry is immense, and if the ethnographer tried to get unanimity he would certainly publish nothing. In practical terms all that can be done is to clear the manuscript with those most closely concerned. Two groups of people are typically involved: the administration, to whom the ethnographer is probably beholden for much confidential information as well as innumerable services such as hospitality, transport, advice and companionship; and certain key informants. With some justification, we tend to regard censorship by government as sinister and regrettable; at the same time we may regard discussion of draft manuscripts with informants as scientific and enlightened. Yet administrations are much harder to disguise than individuals, and are particularly sensitive to criticism in those territories where articulate opposition is not yet accepted as normal and legitimate. On the other hand administrators are capable of defending their own interests much more effectively than are private citizens and hence the effects of anthropological publication rarely constitute a serious threat to them. I hope that I am not alone in maintaining the old-fashioned view that governments should exist only to serve their peoples and I would argue that it would be regrettable if ethnographers were able to publish only manuscripts approved by the administration. Individuals are, for the most part, relatively defenceless and our duty towards them is consequently greater.

There are two situations in which informants may be asked to comment on a manuscript before publication. They may be asked merely to check the accuracy of the statements. This is an admirable though not always feasible procedure and need not concern us further. In addition, informants may be asked if they will agree to statements about themselves appearing in print. Their privacy is being invaded, their confidences revealed and they are asked to agree to this, either because they are indifferent or because what is described they now regard as past history.[23] Bott worked through her manuscript with two of her London couples and found that this procedure resulted, among other things, in more confidential material becoming available for publication.[24] This lengthy procedure entails further contact between ethnographer and informants after the main research has been concluded, and is impossible in many field situations. It requires a level of sophistication for the informants not too far removed from that of the investigator, and an awareness of the consequences of appearing in print. Nevertheless, it may well sharpen the understanding of the investigator as well as reassure the informant.

On the other hand, it may not be easy to find the appropriate body with whom to discuss a manuscript. A factory is a corporate body with a hierarchical structure and hence it was possible for Jaques and his colleagues to find groups in the factory able to take responsibility for approving his manuscript. Bott's couples took responsibility for the sections of her book which concerned themselves. But in a study of a stateless society, or of a village community, there may be no representative bodies who can act for the whole, and the whole may be too large for each individual to be approached. If there are several factions in a community, approval by one faction may well imply rejection by the others. The faction fight would be continued over the manuscript while the poor ethnographer waits in vain to get something into print.

One way of protecting informants from the effects of publication is to give them pseudonyms. Sometimes the names of individuals are disguised, sometimes places and times. Even the tribal name may be concealed,[25] and in at least one instance[26] the identification of time and place has been further impeded by using a pseudonym for the author. Case material is sometimes distorted in presentation, and there is then a particularly onerous responsibility on the writer both to ensure that none of the details altered is likely to be significant, and to indicate that distortion has been introduced. Often these disguises are only partly successful; informants can usually recognize themselves. But perhaps that does not matter much if strangers cannot recognize them. For what are the undesirable effects of publication? Bott's couples did not want their neighbours to know they were in her book.[27] Festinger and his colleagues say that they disguised their informants to protect them from the curiosity of unsympathetic readers.[28] Both these studies were made in industrial societies enjoying self-government, and unwelcome publicity may well be the most serious danger there. But under tribal conditions there may be others, including the possibility of criminal prosecution or of being put at a political disadvantage. Mead and others have mentioned the dangers of publishing undisguised accounts of tribal practices which may later become illegal,[29] but some socially significant actions are already illegal. Publication of such material obviously calls for great care by the ethnographer, and it may be necessary to delay publication for some years if the interests of informants are to be adequately protected.

With publication we run the risk of making public that which our informants would prefer to keep secret. The limits of privacy vary with time and place. Informants may object to a great variety of disclosures; women readers looking at photographs of sacred objects reserved for men; initiation procedures revealed to the uninitiated; details of tabooed characteristics such as income, sexual behaviour, medical histories; reprehensible actions as well as good deeds done by stealth. Where laboratory condition prevail, a promise can sometimes be made to ensure that publication of secret material will not affect secrecy within the society studied. For instance, permission has sometimes been given by aboriginal groups in Australia for the filming of secret ceremonies on condition that the films will not be shown to mixed audiences in Australia, where aboriginal women might be present. Where publication takes place within the group studied, the investigator has to be guided by the tolerance of his informants. In Britain we often assume that individuals do not wish others to know details of their income and expenditure. Income tax returns, where these details are set out, are well guarded and after a number of years are burnt, never becoming part of the public records. On the other hand if a man appears in court, or is involved in an accident, we expect his name to appear in the newspaper. Yet in Norway details of income and tax assessed for each individual are published annually, while in rural areas the policy is to report court cases and accidents anonymously. There are cultural fashions in secrecy and publicity, and they change through time. It is easier than it was a hundred years ago to publish medical and sexual information about individuals. The procedure followed by Bott and her colleagues enabled her informants to accept in print statements about their own personalities which previously they had not accepted consciously at all. But although the area of tolerance may be growing, the ethnographer may always be left with a problem. Some of the actions he has to describe and analyse are bound to be despicable, immoral, illegal or reprehensible, and most of the people concerned will prefer to keep them unheralded and unsung. In the semi-therapeutic relationships established by both Bott and Jaques, individuals and groups may be enabled to realize the truth about themselves and acquiesce in its publication; but the ethnographer has also to work with unregenerate social systems whose on-going activity contains significant amounts of deception, self-deception and secrecy. Even while the research is going on, the field inquiries may stimulate or force members of the community studied to look closely at aspects of their common life they normally repress or ignore. The authors of *Crestwood Heights,* while their research was in progress, made partial reportings to the community of tentative findings, which, they say, were in many cases "deeply disturbing, not to say shocking" to their informants.[30] Publication, with its potentially wider audience, may be even more disturbing. Francis Williams has recently argued that the press has a social function "to cut public figures down to size" and to show "that even great men often have feet of clay."[31] Would we argue that the ethnographer has the function of showing that the bullroarer is only a slab of wood, that the masked figure is not an ancestor but a neighbour in disguise, and that the chief who can do no wrong is as venial as his subjects? In others words, if we protect our informants, is it right to expose the myths of their institutions?

Some writers have maintained that social scientists have a duty to do research and to publish the results even if some informants find this unpleasant.[32] Vidich and Bensman argue that

... if social science is to have some kind of independent problems and identity and, if a disinterested effort is to be made to solve these problems, a certain number of social scientists, presumably residing at universities, must be willing to resist the claims for planned, popular, practical research.[33]

Vidich clearly regards the research he did at Springdale as part of this disinterested effort. The pseudonyms he gave to the individuals he mentions in his book were not effective in Springdale itself, for, after the book had been published, the individuals concerned drove in procession in a Fourth of July pageant wearing masks and bearing the names given to them by Vidich.[34] The disturbance caused in Springdale seems to be justified for Vidich and Bensman by the research done, and they assert that "Negative reaction to community and organizational research is only heard when results describe articulate, powerful and respected individuals and organizations."[35]

This observation may well be empirically correct, and perhaps explains why Festinger and his colleagues do not find it necessary in their book to discuss the ethics of covert research, although they give a detailed account of their methods of inquiry. Their investigation was conducted without the consent or knowledge of the group studied. The authors told their informants that they were "businessmen," and two of their assistants said falsely that they had had supernatural experiences. Notes were made in secret, and magnetic tapes made by the group were copied by the investigators. The authors write: ". . . we faced as much a job of detective work as of observation."[36]

This attitude towards research contrasts sharply with that adopted, for example, by Evans-Pritchard when he found it difficult to gain information on the training of witchdoctors by direct inquiry. His personal servant became a pupil and from him Evans-Pritchard got his information. He writes: "we acted straightforwardly in telling him [the witchdoctor] that his pupil would pass on all information to me" and he notes that the witchdoctors well understood that the pupil "was a sponge out of which I squeezed all the moisture of information which they put into it."[37] Yet even the limited and reluctant co-operation Evans-Pritchard got from his informants may not have many analogues in situations where the written word is better known. Despite the deception practised by the Festinger team, were their informants harmed by this? How many of us have not written down afterwards information that we dare not record openly? Even if some harm was done to Festinger's informants, is this justified by the scientific value of the book that reports the research?

Shils draws a careful distinction between private and public life, and argues that it is right to make inquiries in the public domain, as he defines it, even if illegalities are thereby exposed and popular myths refuted. Outside the public domain, on the other hand, the investigator should be most careful not to abuse the individual's right to privacy.[38] This distinction between public and private is however often difficult to apply in tribal societies and in face-to-face communities in the modern world.

Vidich and Bensman say that negative reactions are heard only from powerful groups of informants, and argue that this should not prevent us from carrying on research among such people. I argue differently. Negative reactions, by which I take it they mean annoyance, disillusionment with the investigators and opposition to further inquiries, may be heard only when the group studied is powerful and articulate, but there seems every reason for assuming that similar sentiments develop among weak and inarticulate groups of informants if they are treated in the same way. Their protests may be unheard and ineffective, but this does not permit us to ignore them. The groups we study are often far from articulate, powerful or respected and we should therefore be particularly on our guard to ensure that we do not betray the trust our informants have placed in us.

In fact we know almost nothing about the effects of publication, negative or positive. Most monographs tell us a good deal about preparations for the field research and the way in which it was carried on, perhaps even how the manuscript was checked, but there the story stops. Only in a second edition is it possible to report on the effects, if any, of publication. We hear more of the scandals, when unapproved publication of tribal secrets, private misdeeds or government blunders has led to overt hostility towards further visits from investigators, and less of those instances where publications have been well received by those persons described in them. Whyte's account, in the second edition of *Street Corner Society,* of the local effects of his book[39] indicates that publication does not necessarily ensure publicity. It also suggests that the ethnographer should reconcile himself to becoming inevitably somewhat of a disappointment to his informants.

As professional sociologists and anthropologists we have an abiding interest in seeing that we are regarded as responsible professionals by all those we work with, and the interests of the profession outlast those of the specific investigation or investigator. A professional code of ethics would not make any easier the solution of the many problems discussed here, but it might at least remind ethnographers that these problems do have to be solved and cannot be ignored. The "wide uncontaminated open stretch of nature," postulated by Malinowski, no longer separates our informants from the wide world or from us, and we have to allow for this.

NOTES

[1] Cambridge anthropological expedition, *Reports* (Cambridge, 1904–35), Vols. 1, 5 and 6.

[2] B. Malinowski, "The Rationalization of Anthropology and Administration," *Africa*, 1930, Vol. 3, p. 406.

[3] Cf. E. D. Chapple, "The Applied Anthropologist—Informal or Professional," *Human Organization*, Vol. 11, No. 2, pp. 3-4; L. P. Mair, *Studies in Applied Anthropology* (London, 1957).

[4] Cf. C. Lévi-Strauss, "Introduction à l'oeuvre de Marcel Mauss," in M. Mauss, *Sociologie et anthropologie* (Paris, 1950), p. xxvii.

[5] F. M. Keesing, *Field Guide to Oceania* (Washington, 1959), p. 16.

[6] J. Spillius, "Natural Disaster and Political Crisis in a Polynesian Society," *Human Relations*, Vol. 10, pp. 123-25.

[7] Cf. E. E. Evans-Pritchard, "Applied Anthropology," *Africa*, Vol. 16, p. 92; E. A. Shils, "Social Inquiry and the Autonomy of the Individual" in D. Lerner, ed., *The Human Meaning of the Social Sciences* (New York, 1959), p. 116.

[8] Cf. W. F. Whyte, *Street Corner Society* (enlarged ed.; Chicago, 1955), pp. 312-17.

[9] Spillius, *op. cit.*, pp. 18ff.

[10] Cf. B. Gallin, "A Case for Intervention in the Field," *Human Organization*, Vol. 18, pp. 140-44.

[11] Cf. Goodenough in Keesing, *op. cit.*, p 5n.

[12] Cf. M. I. Hilger, "An Ethnographic Field Method," in R. F. Spencer, ed., *Method and Perspective in Anthropology* (Minneapolis, 1954), pp. 26-33; J. F. Holleman, *African Interlude* (Capetown, 1958), pp. 34-37.

[13] E. Jaques, *The Changing Culture of a Factory* (London, 1951), pp. 14-15.

[14] J. Pitt-Rivers, *People of the Sierra* (London, 1954), p. x.

[15] J. Gullahorn and G. Strauss, "The Fieldworkers in Union Research," *Human Organization*, Vol. 13, No. 3, pp. 28-33.

[16] W. L. Warner and A. Davis, "A Comparative Study of American Caste," in E. T. Thompson, ed., *Race Relations and the Race Problem* (Durham, N.C., 1939), p. 234.

[17] Cf. E. Colson, *The Makah Indians* (Manchester, 1953), pp. vi-viii; Holleman, *op. cit.;* M. Mead, *The Changing Culture of an Indian Tribe* (New York, 1932), p. 16; Shils, *op. cit.*, p. 123.

[18] Cf. Keesing, *op. cit.*, p. 28.

[19] M. Groves, "Trobriand Island Clans and Chiefs," *Man*, Vol. 56, p. 164.

[20] R. Risley, "'Freedom and Responsibility in Research': Comments," *Human Organization*, Vol. 17, No. 4, p. 5.

[21] W. F. Whyte, "Freedom and Responsibility in Research: The 'Springdale' Case," *Human Organization*, Vol. 17, No. 2, p. 1.

[22] Cf. E. E. Evans-Pritchard, *Witchcraft, Oracles and Magic among the Azande* (Oxford, 1937), p. 511.

[23] Cf. Jaques, *op. cit.*, p. xvi.

[24] E. Bott, *Family and Social Network* (London, 1957), p. 47.

[25] E. Colson, "The Assimilation of an American Indian Group," *Rhodes-Livingstone Journal*, Vol. 8, p. 1n.; Mead, *op. cit.*, pp. xi, 16.

26 J. West, *Plainville, U.S.A.* (New York, 1945).

27 Bott, *op. cit.,* p. 11.

28 L. Festinger and others, *When Prophesy Fails* (Minneapolis, 1956), p. vi.

29 M. Mead and others, "Report of the Committee on Ethics," *Human Organization,* Vol. 8, No. 2, pp. 20-21.

30 J. R. Seeley and others, *Crestwood Heights* (New York, 1956), p. 24.

31 F. Williams, "The Right to Know," *Twentieth Century,* Vol. 170, p. 15.

32 Cf. Holleman, *op. cit.,* p. 253.

33 A. Vidich and J. Bensman, "'Freedom and Responsibility in Research': Comments," *Human Organization,* Vol. 17, No. 4, p. 5.

34 Whyte, *op. cit.,* p. 1.

35 Vidich and Bensman, *op. cit.,* p. 4.

36 Festinger and others, *op. cit.,* p. 25.

37 Evans-Pritchard, *op. cit.,* pp. 151, 153.

38 Shils, *op. cit.,* pp. 130-38.

39 Whyte, *op. cit.,* pp. 342-58.

CHAPTER 22

A Comment on Disguised Observation
in Sociology

Kai T. Erikson

At the beginning of their excellent paper on the subject, Howard S. Becker and Blanche Geer define participant observation as "that method in which the observer participates in the daily life of the people under study, either openly in the role of researcher or covertly in some disguised role...."[1]

The purpose of this paper is to argue that the research strategy mentioned in the last few words of that description represents a significant ethical problem in the field of sociology. In point of sheer volume, of course, the problem is relatively small, for disguised participant observation is probably one of the rarest research techniques in use among sociologists. But in point of general importance, the problem is far more serious—partly because the use of disguises seems to attract a disproportionate amount of interest both inside and outside the field, and partly because it offers a natural starting point for dealing with other ethical issues in the profession.

In recent years, a handful of studies have been reported in the literature based on the work of observers who deliberately misrepresented their identity in order to enter an otherwise inaccessible social situation. Some of these studies have already provoked a good deal of comment—among them, for instance, the cases of the anthropologist who posed as a mental patient by complaining of symptoms he did not feel,[2] the sociologists who joined a gathering of religious mystics by professing convictions they did not share,[3] the Air Force officer who borrowed a new name, a new birth date, a new personal history, a new set of mannerisms and even a new physical appearance in order to impersonate an enlisted man,[4] and the group of graduate students who ventured into a meeting of Alcoholics Anonymous wearing the clothes of men from other social classes than their own and the facial expressions of men suffering from an unfortunate disability.[5]

In taking the position that this kind of masquerading is unethical, I am naturally going to say many things that are only matters of personal opinion;

This chapter was originally published by the Society for the Study of Social Problems in *Social Problems,* 14: no. 4, 366-73, and was read at the annual meetings of the Society in Chicago, 1965.

and thus the following remarks are apt to have a more editorial flavor than is usual for papers read at professional meetings. But a good deal more is at stake here than the sensitivities of any particular person, and my excuse for dealing with an issue that seems to have so many subjective overtones is that the use of disguises in social research affects the professional climate in which all of us work and raises a number of methodological questions that should be discussed more widely.

I am assuming here that "personal morality" and "professional ethics" are not the same thing. Personal morality has something to do with the way an individual conducts himself across the range of his human contacts; it is not local to a particular group of persons or to a particular set of occupational interests. Professional ethics, on the other hand, refer to the way a group of associates define their special responsibility to one another and to the rest of the social order in which they work. In this sense, professional ethics often deal with issues that are practical in their application and limited in their scope: they are the terms of a covenant among people gathered together into a given occupational group. For instance, it may or may not be ethical for an espionage agent or a journalist to represent himself as someone he is not in the course of gathering information, but it certainly does not follow that the conduct of a sociologist should be judged in the same terms; for the sociologist has a different relationship to the rest of the community, operates under a different warrant, and has a different set of professional and scientific interests to protect. In this sense, the ethics governing a particular discipline are in many ways local to the transactions that discipline has with the larger world.

The argument to be presented here, then, is that the practice of using masks in social research compromises both the people who wear them and the people for whom they are worn, and in doing so, violates the terms of a contract which the sociologist should be ready to honor in his dealings with others. There are many respects in which this is true, but I will be dealing here in particular with the relationship between the sociologist and a) the subjects of his research, b) the colleagues with whom he works, c) the students he agrees to teach, and d) the data he takes as his subject matter.

The first of these points has to do with the responsibilities a sociologist should accept toward other institutions and other people in the social order. It may seem a little cranky to insist that disguised observation constitutes an ugly invasion of privacy and is, on that ground alone, objectionable. But it is a matter of cold calculation to point out that this particular research strategy can injure people in ways we can neither anticipate in advance nor compensate for afterward. For one thing, the sheer act of entering a human transaction on the basis of deliberate fraud may be painful to the people who are thereby misled; and even if that were not the case, there are countless ways in which a stranger who pretends to be something else can disturb others by failing to understand the conditions of intimacy that prevail in the group he has tried to invade. Nor does it matter very much how sympathetic the observer is toward the persons whose lives he is studying: the fact of the matter is that he does not *know* which of his actions are apt to hurt other people, and it is highly presumptuous of him to act as if he does—particularly when, as is ordinarily the case, he has elected to wear a disguise exactly because he is entering a social sphere so far from his own experience.

So the sheer act of wearing disguises in someone else's world may cause discomfort, no matter what we later write in our reports; and this possibility raises two questions. The first, of course, is whether we have the right to inflict pain at all when we are aware of these risks and the subjects of the study are not. The second, however, is perhaps more important from the narrow point of view of the profession itself: so long as we suspect that a method we use has at least *some* potential for harming others, we are in the extremely awkward position of having to weigh the scientific and social benefits of that procedure against its possible cost in human discomfort, and this is a difficult business under the best of circumstances. If we happen to harm people who have agreed to act as subjects, we can at least argue that they knew something of the risks involved and were willing to contribute to that vague program called the "advance of knowledge." But when we do so with people who have expressed no readiness to participate in our researches (indeed, people who would presumably have refused if asked directly), we are in very much the same ethical position as a physician who carries out medical experiments on human subjects without their consent. The only conceivable argument in favor of such experimentation is that the knowledge derived from it is worth the discomfort it may cause. And the difficulties here are that we do not know how to measure the value of the work we do or the methods we employ in this way, and, moreover, that we might be doing an extraordinary disservice to the idea of detached scholarship if we tried. Sociologists cannot protect their freedom of inquiry if they owe the rest of the community (not to mention themselves) an accounting for the distress they may have inadvertently imposed on people who have not volunteered to take that risk.

The second problem with disguised observation to be considered here has to do with the sociologist's responsibilities to his colleagues. It probably goes without saying that research of this sort is liable to damage the reputation of sociology in the larger society and close off promising areas of research for future investigators. This is true in the limited sense that a particular agency—say, for example, Alcoholics Anonymous—may decide that its integrity and perhaps even its effectiveness was violated by the appearance of sociologists pretending to be someone else and deny access to other students who propose to use an altogether different approach. And it is also true in the wider sense that any research tactic which attracts unfavorable notice may help diminish the general climate of trust toward sociology in the community as a whole. So long as this remains a serious possibility, the practice of disguised observation becomes a problem for everyone in the profession; and to this extent, it is wholly within the bounds of professional etiquette for one sociologist to challenge the work of another on this score.

This objection has been raised several times before, and the answer most often given to it is that the people who are studied in this fashion—alcoholics or spiritualists or mental patients, for example—are not likely to read what we say about them anyway. Now this argument has the advantage of being correct a good deal of the time, but this fact does not prevent it from being altogether irrelevant. To begin with, the experience of the past few years should surely have informed us that the press is more than ready to translate our technical reports into news copy, and this means that we can no longer provide shelter for other people beyond the walls of our own anonymity. But even if that were not the case, it is a little absurd for us to claim that we derive some measure of protection from the narrowness of our audience when we devote so much time trying to broaden it. The fact is that we are increasingly reaching audiences whose confidence we cannot afford to jeopardize, and we have every right to be afraid that such people may close their doors to sociological research if they learn to become too suspicious of our methods and intentions.

The third objection to be raised here, if only as a note in passing, concerns the responsibilities the profession should accept toward its students. The division of labor in contemporary sociology is such that a considerable proportion of the data we use in our work is gathered by graduate students or other apprentices, and this proportion is even higher for research procedures that require the amount of energy and time necessary for participant observation. Of the dozen or more observers who took part in the studies I have cited, for example, all but one was a graduate student. Now a number of sociologists who have engaged in disguised observation have reported that it is apt to pose serious moral problems and a good deal of personal discomfort, and I think one might well argue that this is a heavy burden to place on any person who is by our own explicit standards, not yet ready for professional life. I am not suggesting here that students are too immature to make a seasoned choice in the matter. I am suggesting that they should not be asked to make what one defender of the method has called "real and excruciating moral decisions" while they are still students and presumably protected from the various dilemmas and contentions which occupy us in meetings like this—particularly since they are so likely to be academically, economically, and even psychologically dependent upon those elders who ask them to choose.[6]

The fourth objection I would like to raise here about the use of undercover observation is probably the most important—and yet the most remote from what is usually meant by the term "ethics." It seems to me that any attempt to use masquerades in social research betrays an extraordinary disrespect for the complexities of human interaction, and for this reason can only lead to bad science. Perhaps the most important responsibility of any sociologist is to appreciate how little he really knows about his intricate and elusive subject matter. We have at best a poor understanding of the human mind, of the communication signals that link one mind to another, or the social structures that emerge from those linkages—and it is the most arrant kind of over-simplification for us to think that we can assess the effect which a clever costume or a few studied gestures have on the social setting. The pose might "work" in the sense that the observer is admitted into the situation; but once this passage has been accomplished, how is he to judge his own influence on the lives of the people he is studying? This is a serious problem in every department of science, of course, and a good deal of time has been devoted to its solution. But the only way to cope with the problem in even a preliminary way is to have as clear a picture as possible of the social properties that the observer is introducing into the situation, and this is altogether impossible if we ourselves are not sure who he is. We can *impersonate* other modes of behavior with varying degrees of insight and skill, but we cannot *reproduce* them; and since this is the case, it seems a little irresponsible for a sociologist to assume that he can enter social life in any masquerade that suits his purpose without seriously disrupting the scene he hopes to study.

When people interact, they relate to one another at many different levels at once, and only a fraction of the messages communicated during that interchange are registered in the conscious mind of the participant. It may be possible for someone to mimic the conventional gestures of fear, but it is impossible for him to reproduce the small postural and chemical changes which go with it. It may be possible for a middle-class speaker to imitate the broader accents of lower-class speech, but his vocal equipment is simply not conditioned to do so without arousing at least a subliminal suspicion. It may be possible for a trained person to rearrange the slant of his body and re-set his facial muscles to approximate the bearing of someone else, but his performance will never be anything more than a rough imposture. Now we know that these various physiological, linguistic, and kinetic cues play an important part in the context of human interaction, but we have no idea how to simulate them—and what is probably more to the point, we never will. For one thing, we cannot expect to learn in a matter of hours what others have been practicing throughout a lifetime. For another, to imitate always means to parody, to caricature, to exaggerate certain details of behavior at the expense of others, and to that extent any person who selects a disguise will naturally emphasize those details which *he* assumes are most important to the character he is portraying. In doing so, of course, he is really only portraying a piece of himself. It is interesting to speculate, for example, why the Air Force lieutenant mentioned earlier thought he needed to present himself as a near-delinquent youth with a visible layer of personal problems in order to pose as an enlisted man. Whatever the reasoning behind this particular charade, it would certainly be reasonable for someone to suspect that it tells us more about the investigators' impression of enlisted men than it does about the men themselves—and since we have no way of learning whether this is true or not, we have lost rather than gained an edge of control over the situation we are hoping to understand. What the investigators had introduced into the situation was a creature of their own invention, and it would be hardly surprising if the results of their inquiry corresponded to some image they had in advance of the enlisted man's condition. (It is perhaps worth noting here that impersonation always seems easier for people looking down rather than up the status ladder. We find it reasonable to assume that officers "know how" to portray enlisted men or that sociologists have the technical capacity to pose as drunks or religious mystics, but it is not at all clear that the reverse would be equally true.)

This, then, is the problem. If we provide observers with special masks and coach them in the "ways" of the private world they are hoping to enter, how can we learn what is happening to the people who meet them in this disguise? What information is registered in the unconscious minds of the other people who live in that world? How does the social structure accommodate to this particular invasion?

It is clear, I think, that something happens—something over which we have no control. Let me relate two incidents drawn from the studies mentioned earlier. The first has to do with the Air Force officer who posed as an enlisted man. In their report of the study, the investigators used several pages of a short paper to describe the elaborate masquerade they had fashioned for the observer and the coaching he had received in the ways of the adolescent sub-culture. "So successful was the tutoring," reads the brief report, "that when the time for 'enlistment' arrived, the recruiting sergeant . . . suggested that the observer not be accepted by the Air Force because by all appearances he was a juvenile delinquent."[7] And later, during an interview with a service psychologist, the observer was recommended for re-classification on the grounds that he appeared quite anxious over the death of his father. Now these events may indeed suggest that the pose was successful, for the observer *was* trying to look somewhat delinquent and *did* have a story memorized about the death of his father in an auto accident. But who would care to argue that the diagnosis of the sergeant and the psychologist were inaccurate? Surely something was wrong, and if they perceived an edge of uneasiness which reminded them of anxiety or detected a note of furtiveness which looked to them like delinquency, they may only have been responding to the presence of a real conflict between the observer and his mask. We may leave it to the psychoanalysts to ask whether vague anxieties about "killing" one's father are an unlikely impression for someone to leave behind when he is parading around with a new name, a new background, a new history, and, of course, a new set of parents. The authors of the article tell us that the observer "did have something of a problem to transform himself from a 27-year-old, college trained, commissioned officer into a 19-year-old, near-delinquent high school graduate," and this is certainly easy to believe.[8] What is more difficult to believe is that such a transformation is possible at all—and if it is not, we can have very little confidence in the information gathered by the observer. Since we do not know to what kind of creature the enlisted men were responding, we do not know what sense to make of what they said and did.

The second example comes from the study of the apocalyptic religious group. At one point in the study, two observers arrived at one of the group's meeting places under instructions to tell quite ordinary stories about their experience in spiritualism in order to create as little commotion as possible. A few days afterwards, however, the leader of the group was overheard explaining that the two observers had appeared upset, excited, confused, and unsure of their errand at the time of their original visit, all of which helped confirm her suspicion that they had somehow been "sent" from another planet. In one sense, of course, this incident offered the observers an intriguing view of the belief structure of the cult, but in another sense, the leader's assessment of the situation was very shrewd: after all, the observers *had* been sent from another world, if not another planet, and she may have been quite right to sense that they were a bit confused and unsure of their errand during their early moments in the new job. "In both cases," the report informs us, the visits of the observers "were given as illustrations that 'strange things are happening.'"[9] Indeed, strange things *were* happening; yet we have no idea how strange they really were. It is almost impossible to evaluate the reaction of the group to the appearance of the pair of observers because we do not know whether they were seen as ordinary converts or as extraordinary beings. And it makes a difference, for in the first instance the investigators would be observing a response which fell within the normal range of the group's experience, while in the second instance they would be observing a response which would never have taken place had the life of the group been allowed to run its own course.

My point in raising these two examples, it should be clear, is not to insist on the accuracy of these or any other interpretations, but to point out that a wide variety of such interpretations is possible so long as one has no control over the effects introduced by the observer. A company of recruits with a disguised officer in its midst is simply a different kind of organization than one without the same ingredient; a group of spiritualists which numbers as many as eight observers among its twenty or so members has a wholly different character than one which does not—and so long as we remain unable to account for such differences, we cannot know the meaning of the information we collect.

In one of the most sensible pieces written on the subject, Julius Roth has reminded us that all social research is disguised in one respect or another and that the range of ethical questions which bear on the issue must be visualized as falling on a continuum.[10] Thus, it is all very well for someone to argue that deliberate disguises are improper for sociologists, but it is quite another matter for him to specify what varieties of research activity fall within the range of that principle. Every ethical statement seems to lose its crisp authority the moment it is carried over into marginal situations where the conditions governing research are not so clearly stipulated. For instance, some of the richest material in the social sciences has been gathered by sociologists who were true participants in the group under study but who did not announce to other members that they were employing this opportunity to collect research data. Sociologists live careers in which they occasionally become patients, occasionally take jobs as steel workers or taxi drivers, and frequently find themselves in social settings where their trained eye begins to look for data even though their presence in the situation was not engineered for that purpose. It would be absurd, then, to insist as a point of ethics that sociologists should always introduce themselves as investigators everywhere they go and should inform every person who figures in their thinking exactly what their research is all about.

But I do think we can find a place to begin. If disguised observation sits somewhere on a continuum and is not easily defined, this only suggests that we will have to seek further for a relevant ethic and recognize that any line we draw on the continuum will be a little artificial. What I propose, then, at least as a beginning, is the following: first, that it is unethical for a sociologist to *deliberately misrepresent* his identify for the purpose of entering a private domain *to which he is not otherwise eligible;* and second, that it is unethical for a sociologist to *deliberately misrepresent* the character of the research in which he is engaged. Now these negative sanctions leave us a good deal of leeway—more, perhaps, than we will eventually want. But they have the effect of establishing a stable point of reference in an otherwise hazy territory, and from such an anchored position as this we can move out into more important questions about invasion of privacy as an ethical issue.

In the meantime, the time has probably come for us to assume a general posture on the question of disguised participant observation even if we are not yet ready to state a specific ethic, and a logical first step in this direction would be to assess how most members of the profession feel about the matter. I am not suggesting that we poll one another on the merits of adopting a formal code, but that we take some kind of unofficial reading to learn what we can about the prevailing climate of opinion in the field. If we discover that a substantial number of sociologists are uncomfortable about the practice, then those who continue to employ it will at least know where they stand in respect to the "collective conscience" of their discipline. And if we discover that only a scattering of sociologists are concerned about the matter, we will at least have the satisfaction of knowing that the profession—as a profession—has accepted the responsibility of knowing its own mind.

NOTES

[1] Howard S. Becker and Blanche Geer, "Participant Observation and Interviewing: A Comparison," *Human Organization,* 16 (1957), 28-32.

[2] William C. Caudill *et al.,* "Social Structure and Interaction Processes on a Psychiatric Ward," *American Journal of Orthopsychiatry,* 22 (1952), 314-334.

[3] Leon Festinger, Henry W. Riecken, and Stanley Schacter, *When Prophecy Fails* (Minneapolis: University of Minnesota Press, 1956).

[4] Mortimer A. Sullivan, Stuart A. Queen, and Ralph C. Patrick, Jr., "Participant Observation as Employed in the Study of a Military Training Program," *American Sociological Review,* 23 (1958), 660-667.

[5] John F. Lofland and Robert A. Lejeune, "Initial Interaction of Newcomers in Alcoholics Anonymous: A Field Experiment in Class Symbols and Socialization," *Social Problems,* 8 (1960), 102-111.

[6] To keep the record straight, I might add that I first became interested in these matters when I was a graduate student and applied for one of the observer posts mentioned here.

[7] Sullivan, Queen, and Patrick, *op. cit.,* p. 663.

[8] Stuart A. Queen, "Comment," *American Sociological Review,* 24 (1959), 399-400.

[9] Festinger, Riecken, and Schacter, *op. cit.,* pp. 241-242.

[10] Julius A. Roth, "Comments on 'Secret Observation,'" *Social Problems,* 9 (1962), 283-284.

CHAPTER 23

Ethical Limitations on Sociological Reporting

Joseph H. Fichter and William L. Kolb

In his primary task as the discoverer of new knowledge, the modern scientist is governed by the obligations to search for truth, to be objective, to discern the relevant, to check meticulously his data, and, in some circles, to accept responsibility for the use to which his knowledge is put. This ethical code, however, fails to cover the problems arising from the relations between the scientist and the objects of his observation and experimentation. This may be due in part to the very conceptualization of phenomena as "objects." Only "subjects" have rights which must be respected.

There is evidence, of course, that social scientists are vaguely aware that they incur responsibilities which extend beyond the procedural ethics of science itself: that men are subjects as well as objects, and that even when studied as objects they retain certain of their rights to privacy and respect. Thus the experiments on living human bodies of prisoners, made by Nazi doctors, gained them infamy rather than fame. The theoretical literature of American psychiatry hides the identity of most of its patients. And sociologists and anthropologists frequently attempt to disguise the communities they study.

The lack of consensus in this area of responsibility attests to the fact that the norms underlying such efforts to respect people who are studied have never been systematically formulated as part of the procedure of scientific research and reporting. Indeed individuals and groups receive the greatest protection when scientific research is linked with the doctor-patient relation as in the case of psychiatry. In other areas protection seems to depend upon a diffuse and uncertain feeling of respect for the human "object." This protection is adequate, however, only where it does not interfere seriously with the gathering and reporting of data or where its violation would take such extreme form as to severely shock both the scientist and his society.

Under present conditions, the possibility of disturbance and shock seems greatest where research and reporting directly involve identifiable small groups and individuals. Research workers also seem to be effectively barred from

This chapter was originally published by the American Sociological Association in the *American Sociological Review,* 18: 544-50.

experimentation which threatens the physical wholeness of the individual. Beyond these areas of investigation every research worker seems to be largely on his own in determining what research shall be conducted and what report shall be made so far as the impact of the research and the report of the objects of the study are concerned.

In this state of normlessness even the individual and the small group can be threatened if the possibility of identification is only indirect or if the violation of rights is not obvious and flagrant. Thus men may not be plunged into freezing water involuntarily, but children have been placed in authoritarian situations to discover the effects on their attitudes and behavior. Sexual relations between husband and wife cannot be observed by the family sociologist, but other forms of private behavior have been observed and reported. The psychiatrist will guard the identity of his patient, but the student of a community may report behavior on the part of an individual who can be indirectly identified by other members of the community or by other people in the larger society.

Although the psychologist and the social psychologist face ethical problems in experimenting with human beings, the sociologist seems most vulnerable in his studies of small groups and communities. His problem, since he does not often experiment, seems to be the question of whether there are ethical limitations on the "complete" objectivity of a research report concerning such groups and communities, for it is in this area of research that there are signs that the ethical sense of the sociologist is either dormant or only intermittently and uncertainly active. An explicit code of ethics which will govern the social scientist in reporting such data seems urgently needed.

In attempting to develop a system of relational ethics the sociologist must remember that while the people he studies have rights, these rights cannot be secured by an unqualified assertion of the "subject" status of his objects of investigation. It is an obvious absurdity to assert that these "subjects" are entitled to absolute anonymity, privacy, and protection, for in various circumstances the sociologist may be obligated to describe in full detail the actions of identifiable groups and individuals. Moreover the development of a code of ethics will not relieve the sociologist of moral choice, but can serve only as a guide for the making of decisions for which he must accept responsibility. Having said all this, however, it remains true that sociologists need to formulate a system of ethical norms to protect the objects of sociological reporting. It is as a tentative statement of the conditions relevant to such norms and of a few of the most important norms themselves that the following discussion is offered.

Before presenting our conception of some of the important normative variables in the formulation of such a system of ethics, it is necessary to consider first the matrix of conditions into which the system must be placed. Two aspects of this matrix seem particularly important. The first of these has to do with the various groups of people to whom the reporting sociologist has obligations; the objects of the study are only one such group. The second aspect concerns the fact that even in community and small group studies certain *kinds* of data and certain *modes of data presentation* pose the ethical problem in its most intense form, while other data and modes of presentation offer only minor problems. It is necessary to distinguish these factors, since, as scientists, maximum freedom is desirable and hence no needless restrictions are in order.

In preparing a research report on a small community or group the sociologist has a moral duty toward several different groups. Because his obligations to each of these differ in kind and degree while at the same time they condition and limit one another, it seems necessary to set forth briefly the categories into which they fall.

1. For practical, as well as moral reasons, the sociologist must consider the wishes and needs of those persons who have allowed, invited, sponsored, or cooperated with the study. Management of a factory group, officers of a labor union, ministers, and city officials, are all examples of people who may have some concern for the results of sponsored research. The sociologist's obligations to such persons are truthfulness, the honoring of confidences, scientific objectivity, and honest reporting.

2. The sociologist has obligations to the source from which research funds were obtained. Like anyone who enters a contractual agreement, he has the ordinary obligations to employ these funds honestly and usefully, and to abide by the terms of the agreement concerning publication and ownership of data, and by other explicit provisions which might have been incorporated in the contract.

3. The publisher of the research report has a call upon the moral consideration of the sociologist. Again the obligations are derived from the ordinary desirability of honesty and thoroughness, or from legal rights relating to libel suits and other embarrassments in which the report may involve the publisher.

4. Social scientists in general may be said to have a claim on the findings of the social researcher. The scientist's colleagues have a moral expectation that the findings will be made available to them in a serious, honest, and competent report. In addition to these expectations which do not differ much from expectations of professionals in other areas of work, there are the specifically scientific demands for a free exchange of data and knowledge unhindered by secrecy and suppression.

5. Another kind of group has a similar claim, perhaps not on the individual scientist but certainly on the discipline, to receive the findings of social research. In the long run this group is the society itself, for it is particularly important that social science knowledge ultimately become the possession of

all the people. If there are reasons for the holding back of research findings from the general public for a short time, this group will still contain, at a minimum estimate, the key persons in a community or group who are in a position to utilize the research findings in programs of social improvement. The sociologist himself must bear the responsibility for determining who these persons are, unless they are defined by legal norms of the community of which the social scientist himself is a member.

6. Against the claims of all these groups on the findings of the sociologist, there exist the rights of the community studied, its sub-groups, and its individual members. Their rights to secrecy, privacy, reputation, and respect, will vary according to circumstances and to the demands of the other groups, but they are intrinsically present in a society like our own which in its central tradition accords dignity and worth to the individual. The sociologist has not discharged his duties when he has met his obligations to sponsors, fund sources, publisher, social scientists, and the general public; nor has he completely discharged them when he makes a prefunctory effort at disguise, ambiguity, or anonymity. He is always faced with the moral problem of how much to tell about the lives and habits of the members of the community or small group.

The problem varies in its intensity, however, with the kind of data and with the mode of presentation. It seems obvious that historical material allows more latitude for reporting than contemporary material. Every study of a small group or community seems to require a brief sketch of historical background, and through this research the scientist may discover certain skeletons in the closet. Their revelation may be pertinent to the understanding of the group and will probably not intrude too greatly upon the community's or its individuals' reputations.

Within the area of contemporary material a distinction can be drawn between studies of primitive societies and civilized communities. It is to be supposed that the details of social life among the Samoans were not reported to these people, and if any reputations suffered from such study it was only among non-Samoans. There have been instances, however, of anthropologists' reports getting back to American Indian tribes, causing some dissension and suspicion among the members of the tribe. In either case the sociologist must consider these people as the subjects of human rights, even though the prospect of moral damage may not be great.

In studying contemporary communities the problem of reporting varies according to whether the data concerned are sacred or non-sacred. The analysis of behavior patterns which involve high traditional values (like religion, family and sex, ethnic and group loyalties) should, of course, be as objective as possible, but an effort should be made to avoid needless and callous affront to the people who hold such values and such an effort requires special attention and care. In non-sacred areas (such as economic and political activities, housing and recreational problems) there can be greater freedom of reporting.

A related and equally important distinction must be made between public and private facts. This is something more than the difference between hidden and open knowledge. By definition, the sociologist deals with social and group relations. Hence, in a sense, his data can rarely concern completely private and secret activities. Nevertheless it is obvious that widely-known facts allow a much wider margin of expression in the research report.

The manner of presenting the data may be equally important as the kind of data presented in increasing or lowering the intensity of the moral problem of what to report in a community or small group study. Although the custom of sociologists of providing anonymity to the community, group, or individual is not an adequate safeguard of the rights of these subjects, it does make possible a wider margin of expression than would a complete and open identification. There are, however, other and more important differences of mode of presentation.

The happiest situation for the social scientist is one in which statistical analysis of, and reporting on, the actions and characteristics of people is possible. Where large numbers of people are involved it is obvious that the problem of ethical limitations on the report hardly exists. But even in communities where situations are revealed that may be somewhat distasteful, the sub-groups and the individual may be adequately protected by the use of statistical categories.

As soon as the sociologist leaves the field of quantitative analysis and attempts to describe in conceptual terms the social relations in a small group or community, the problem of what to report becomes much greater. Even when the community is cloaked in anonymity, indirect identification is almost always possible, and there is likely to be a subtle and unintended violation of human rights. The threat becomes even greater when the sociologist adds to his description of the social relations in the group or community an interpretation of the motivation which supports these relations and other social behavior. Thus, where systematic sociological description and interpretation of motivation combine, the sociologist faces the gravest moral challenge, and particularly so where this mode of description and analysis is applied to a leading member of the group. The likelihood that such a person will be identified and his social behavior and personal reputation placed under scrutiny by his follows on the basis of the research report is very great. Here, more than anywhere else, the sociologist must take care not to needlessly injure another human being.

The problem of truth telling thus becomes a circumstantial one. This means that while telling the truth cannot *per se* be wrong or harmful, the ethical question of whether or not to include a certain objective fact always arises in relation to person and circumstances. Thus complete objectivity, or telling all the truth in all circumstances, is not necessarily a morally good act.

This is true for several reasons. The researcher is, of course, bound to secrecy where information has been given in confidence or where he has made promises of secrecy. At the same time, as a scientist, he will discover natural secrets, which by their seriousness demand silence on the part of the reporter. There is also the problem of detraction—the injury of another's reputation by revealing what is detrimental but true about him. If the harmful fact is already widely disseminated or if the subject is mistaken in the belief that the fact will result in the impairment of his reputation, the sociologist may not have any obligation to conceal the fact. Otherwise its revelation is a serious matter.

In summary, it can be said the problem appears in its most intense form when some member of a community or group is singled out for description and analysis and where such description and analysis may result in the revealing of secrets, the violation of privacy, or the detraction of reputation. Placed in this situation the sociologist must evaluate the claims of the individual, or of the sub-group and community, in their relations with the claims of the research sponsors, the donors of funds, the publisher of the report, the expectations of colleagues, and the rights of the larger society. We suggest that if the researcher accepts the values of human dignity and worth and does not want needlessly to injure the objects of his investigation, he will take the following four variables into account in attempting to arrive at a decision.

1. *The sociologist's definition of the nature of science.* Some positivists seem to regard science only as a fascinating game played according to a set of rules.[1] It is doubtful that the sociologist using this conception of science may ever legitimately overrule the rights of the people studied. The simple wish of the people to conceal certain aspects of their behavior must then be considered sufficient to bar the report of that behavior.

If one regards science as a search for truth as an end in itself, the demands of the objectivity of science will carry much weight in the decision to publish all pertinent data. Except in history, however, the truth for which the social scientist searches is nomothetic, not idiographic, truth. It may be necessary to base generalizations on certain idiographic items, but man has the entire span of his career on earth to discover and disclose such items. Certainly a particular item of current behavior turned up in a community study need not be used to support a generalization if such use inflicts injury on the people being investigated.

There is a third conception of pure science. Social scientists may believe that science is both a rigidly ruled game and a search for truth which is valuable for itself, but they usually also believe that science well developed and used by experts or disseminated among the people can make for a better life. There is a sense of urgency about accomplishing this mission of pure science in the modern world. Thus, within this perspective, considerable pressure arises to ignore the rights of people who are scientifically studied. Despite this pressure it remains true that a wilful disregard for the rights of persons and groups to their privacy, reputations, and secrets, will tend to destroy the very values which the scientist hopes his basic research can render more achievable.

Frequently the scientist makes a community or small group study not as a pure scientist but in one sense or another as an applied scientist. He may carry on the research for what he himself considers desirable practical ends; he may be employed by officials of the community or group or by those of the larger society; or he may be employed by some private group with a specific selfish or altruistic interest. In all three of these instances there is pressure to report all the significant findings even though injury may be done to the objects of the study. Nevertheless the sociologist must abide by the rule that he exercise every effort to determine whether or not the values to be implemented by the study, and the probability of being able to achieve them through the use of its findings, justify the harm done to the members of the community or group.

Preoccupation with applied science is frequently accompanied by the temptation to look for and publish data which will further the realization of what the researcher himself regards as the good society or community. He is likely to believe that all of his data must be revealed in all circumstances. It appears to us that a scientist of this persuasion is most in need of the virtues of tolerance, compassion, and love, because he is in danger of placing the considerations of the "good" society above all consideration of individual rights and injuries.

The hired scientist, moreover, cannot avoid responsibility for revealing data injurious to individuals and groups by pleading loyalty to community or nation or by indicating his contractual responsibilities to a private group. Loyalty to community or nation may require injury to individuals and groups, but in such cases the scientist shares whatever guilt is incurred with all other responsible agencies. In instances of purely contractual research the scientist must accept full responsibility, because loyalty to nation or community is not involved. He is free to refuse the job, and if the values of the employing group are wrong or do not justify the amount of injury done the scientist must accept the moral responsibility.

2. *Determination of the extent to which a person or group will be injured by the publication of data concerning their behavior.* Those instances in which the scientist can foretell with certitude that serious injury will be done to the objects of his study seem to be very few in number. It is also likely that the largest proportion of his data will be free of possibly injurious materials. It is the in-between area of probable injury that is most difficult to determine and yet which must be determined.

To know what the effect of exposing a group's secrets will be, to realize how seriously a person's reputation may be damaged, and to visualize the effects of violation of privacy presupposes knowledge on the part of the scientist which he may not have. This knowledge can be approached to the extent to which the scientist saturates himself in the social relations of the group which he studies. It probably cannot be achieved by the aloof scientist who simply culls the reports of those who have done the actual and basic data collecting.

Since there is a great difference between imaginary and objective derogation of reputation, the sociologist may tend to brush off the former as relevant and uncontrollable. Human decency, however, would seem to require that the scientist make an effort to inquire even into this possibility of psychological and subjective injury. The scientist cannot guard against all such contingencies and against the unexpected and unwarranted complaints of people, but he should do his human best to avoid them ahead of time and to be sympathetic to them if they come.

If the sociologist attempts to interpret the social behavior of the people he studies, he must assess the responsibility of the people for their own actions. False sentimentality must not result in the denial of the fact that a person must accept the consequences of the acts for which he is responsible. The scientist cannot erase the responsibilities, duties, and obligations, of the objects of his study. Yet, at the same time, he must recognize that the human being is never completely responsible for his actions, and that in many cases factors over which the person or group has no control may come close to completely determining certain acts. Since the assessment of responsibility will be contained in the research report, injury can be done if the assessment is not carefully made.

3. *The degree to which people or groups are actually members of a moral community of which the scientist is also a member.* At the core of the Western value system is a belief in the basic dignity and worth of the human being. This belief is based on different assumptions according to the particular stream of tradition in which one locates it: the Fatherhood of God, natural law, universal human needs and aspirations, or human reason. Whatever the base, the belief implies that men are bound to one another in a moral community. Membership in this community requires that the individual's rights to privacy, secrecy, and reputation be respected, even though the human beings studied may not be members of the sociologist's own society.

The belief also implies that a man or group can renounce membership in the moral community by choosing modes of action which violate these basic values of dignity and worth. In mid-century it seems probable that men like Hitler and Stalin, organized groups like "Murder Incorporated," and Ku Klux Klan, and some others, have placed themselves outside the moral community and have surrendered the protection of its norms. Thus the social scientist need have no qualms about reporting in full detail the activities of such groups and people. Although this norm has never been explicitly formulated, it has guided a great deal of the research and reporting in social science.

Yet the decision of the sociologist to place particular persons or groups outside the moral community involves great responsibility, and he must be careful that his criteria of judgment permit tolerance, compassion, and wisdom. This is especially the case when he studies "unpopular" racial, religious and political groups, prostitutes, homosexuals, drug addicts, and the psychologically ill, the poor and powerless. It is hardly questionable that these people remain members of the moral community and hence retain their rights of privacy, respect, and secrecy. The needs of the society may require a limitation of their rights by the courts or by the social scientist in his reporting, but basic rights can be limited only to the extent that they *must* be limited. Beyond that point such people must be treated in the same way as other members of the moral community.

The recognition of basic human rights which accompany membership in the moral community is an important means by which social scientists can avoid the dangers of the use of purely subjective criteria. Within the consensus of the Western tradition it is objectively true that there are moral evils and modes of action which place the perpetrator outside this community. We must know as much as possible about such people and the scientist need have little inhibition in the report he provides about them. All other persons and groups, no matter how personally distasteful to the scientist, seem to require the respect of their fellow-members in the moral community.

4. *The degree to which the larger society, the local community, or the group, needs the data of the research.* Real urgency must be defined in terms of the pressing needs of a group, community, or society, or in terms of some impending problem of which the scientist but not the group or community being studied is aware. Rights and duties are never unqualified in society and one of the qualifications seems to be that the society sometimes has a prior right to information which is necessary and useful for itself even though it may be harmful to an individual or sub-group.

The social scientist may find himself in one of several moral situations when he is trying to determine whether or not the social need is greater than the individual or group right. If the duly appointed authorities of a community or of the larger society believe certain information to be vitally needed, there is a *prima facie* case for the scientist to reveal such information. However, these authorities must show to the scientist the ground for the need. If he does not know and cannot find out from the authorities whether there is an urgent need for certain data which will be harmful to individuals and sub-groups, he is free of moral obligation to reveal it. If he is certain that the information is not necessary, he may in good conscience refuse to reveal it even though the authorities demand to know it. It must be recognized that his freedom in such instances is moral and not legal, and he may have to pay a price for his refusal.

In a similar manner the obligations which the scientist has to the group studied may require the revelation of information damaging to individuals or sub-groups. In this instance the scientist himself is likely to be the best judge of the need for his data. If he understands and accepts the basic values of the group and takes his obligation to the group seriously, he may find it imperative to disclose such information. Since he cannot plead ignorance, and since there is no demand from competent higher authority, the responsibility for the assessment of urgency rests squarely on the scientist.

Finally, even though neither the higher authority nor the representatives of the group studied place any demands upon him, he may become aware of facts which are vitally needed by the social group studied or by the society. In such cases he must not only accept the responsibility for violating the rights of individuals and groups, but also must arrive at his decision with very little outside aid. In clear-cut instances where the comparison and balancing of the rights of the various claimants can be easily accomplished, the decision may be easily reached. But it is certainly in this area that the researcher will be forced to consider most thoroughly the importance which he, himself, has placed on the value of the information in its relation to the needs of the group.

The complexities exhibited in the discussion of the four central variables indicate that the problem of ethical limitations on sociological reporting cannot be reduced to a simple either-or proposition of a conflict between the scientific objectivity of a research report and the ethical inhibitions of the person who writes the report. It is apparent that the sociologist must act simultaneously according to a highly developed procedural code for scientific reporting and a code of ethics based on the belief that the objects of his study are also subjects. These codes are not irreconcilable, but the resolution of specific conflicts between them may be a very complex task, involving the claims of many groups and the interrelationships of the four variables. Yet the sociologist must resolve them. If there is a tendency for the sociologist to become more scientific, he must also become increasingly sensitized to the rights, feelings, and needs of the people he studies. Treating them as subjects means that to the best of his ability he will treat them with justice, understanding, compassion, and, in the last analysis, love.

NOTE

[1] "Science after all is only one of the games played by the children of this world, and it may very well be that those who prefer other games are in their generation wiser." Carroll C. Pratt, *The Logic of Modern Psychology* (New York: The Macmillan Co., 1939), p. 57.

CHAPTER 24

Comment on "Initial Interaction of Newcomers in Alcoholics Anonymous"

Fred Davis

In their article "Initial Interaction of Newcomers in Alcoholics Anonymous," (Fall, 1960) John Lofland and Robert Lejeune report on an "experiment [which] consisted in sending six male agents [sic; graduate students in sociology] to A.A. open meetings where they posed as alcoholic newcomers" (p. 103). Several pages further on (pp. 107-08) the authors, demonstrating a keen sense for methodological specification, describe in detail the careful plans and elaborate pains they took to insure the successful perpetration of this ruse upon the membership of several A.A. branches in the New York area. Whereas Lofland and Lejeune appear, judging from the text of their article, blandly indifferent to the professional and ethical implications of their "research design"—indeed, there is nothing to suggest that they were perturbed by anything other than its possible methodological shortcomings—I am certain that many readers of Social Problems will feel impelled, as did I, to take a decidedly different view of the matter.

There is little need to dwell on the more narrowly professional issues occasioned by research strategies of this genre (i.e., those political ones having to do with the power and repute of sociologists to command access to persons and organizations in furtherance of scholarly objectives). Suffice it to say that the leaders and members of no corporate group, especially one imbued with a reformistic spirit of mission, can be reasonably expected to view such acts of premeditated deception with, to understate the case, indifference. To the extent to which A.A. is involved in broad scale, popular undertakings to ameliorate the problem of alcoholism—and its involvement is obviously considerable—Lofland and Lejeune have done a potential disservice to all future investigators who in the course of their investigations may want to enlist the cooperation of this organization. In short, their actions threaten to seriously contract the zone of research accessibility to an important social problem. And, needless to say, the fact that the authors appeared to have been much

This chapter was originally published by the Society for the Study of Social Problems in *Social Problems*, 8: no. 4, 364-65. "Initial Interaction of Newcomers in Alcoholics Anonymous" appears on pp. 107-18 in this volume.

less concerned with alcoholism or A.A. than with questions of social class interaction, in no way absolves them from the responsibilities owed colleagues who are and will be working in this area.

Beyond these practical considerations however, there looms the more cogent issue of the character and extent of the sociologist's license to exempt himself from the expectations, common reciprocities and *modus operandi* of the persons and organizations to which he attaches himself in his role of participant-observer. I can only raise again the same kinds of disturbing, yet ever relevant, questions that many have raised before me. Is such license complete or partial? Enduring on all occasions, or terminal according to time, place and circumstances? Contingent when studying "good" causes and institutions, but uninhibited when studying "bad" ones? Equally applicable in whatever degree to the powerful and powerless alike or, as a matter of expedience, of differential applicability? (A colleague has ventured the disquieting allegation that while sociologists are as a rule scrupulous in setting forth their research auspices and purposes when making first-hand studies of such powerful groups as the military, labor unions and liberal professions, they tend to be a good deal less conscientious on this score when studying such powerless groups and aggregates as isolated religious cults, deviants of various kinds and anonymous respondents at every twenty-third household.) Convincing and unequivocal ethical standards of research conduct for our discipline do not easily follow from the mere posing of these questions. But it is with reference to them that actions of the type engaged in by Lofland and Lejeune must somehow be weighed if sociologists are ever to knowledgeably effect a moral integration between their roles as members of society and participant students of society. Otherwise, the delicate and inescapable intertwining of these roles in field studies can too easily fall victim to accident, ignorance, opportunism and misappropriation by those outside the scholarly community who seek only to further private ends.

More in an inductive spirit therefore, and without presuming to speak in behalf of formalized codes or widely accepted principles of research conduct—neither of which seems yet to exist—let me set forth the counts upon which I find this type of deception repugnant:

1. *The Total Denial of Voluntaristic Rights.* Neither the A.A. branch members nor their leaders appear to have been given any choice in deciding whether they did or did not wish to participate in the experiment. They were simply used. Not only were the concrete purposes of the study kept from them, but no attempt appears to have ever been made to enlist their consent through such doubtfully venial appeals as "helping science" or "helping graduate students get through their assignments."

2. *The Tacit Disrespect Shown for A.A.'s Values, Modes of Operation and Mission.* We know enough about A.A., its ideology and the deep anguish

of many of its members to, I would assume, recognize that "posing as alcoholic newcomers" (e.g., to feign "looking tense and uncomfortable," to jiggle with hidden stop watches when spoken to by a branch member, etc.) constitutes a travesty upon the organization's identity. This is not to say, of course, that the sociologist is compelled to accept as truth the ideology by which the organization represents itself to outsiders. But, it is a far cry from intellectually detaching oneself from an organization's values to engaging in acts which effectively make a mockery of them. And that these were open meetings of A.A. does not, in my estimation, justify treating so lightly the motivational and situational terms upon which A.A. recruits its members.

3. Last, there is what some may treat as only a sentimental objection, but one which despite its elusiveness, I feel, comes closest to the heart of the matter. That is, in field situations in which the sociologist (or anthropologist) openly represents himself to his subjects for what he is (i.e., a person whose interest in them is professional rather than personal) he unavoidably, and properly I would hold, invites unto himself the classic dilemma of compromising involvement in the lives of others. Filling him with gossip, advice, invitations to dinner and solicitations of opinion, they devilishly make it evident that whereas he may regard himself as the *tabula rasa* incarnate upon whom the mysteries of the group are to be writ, they can only see him as someone less detached and less sublime. There then follows for many a fieldworker the unsettling recognition that, within very broad limits, it is precisely when his subjects palpably relate to him in his "out-of-research role" self (or "presentation," depending on one's disassociative bent) that the *raison d'etre* for his "in-role" self is most nearly realized; they are more themselves, they tell and "give away" more, they supply connections and insights which he would otherwise have never grasped. (One is tempted to conceive of this moral paradox as sociologist's original sin, although happily the benign interpositions of area sampling, pre-coded questionnaires and paid interviewers now spare more and more of us from suffering its pangs.)

It is in large measure due to this ineluctable transmutation of role postures in field situations that, when he later reports, the sociologist often experiences a certain guilt, a sense of having betrayed, a stench of disreputability about himself; these, despite the covers, pseudonyms and eletions with which he clothes his subjects. (Or, have I alone heard such "confessions" from fellow sociologists?) In an almost Durkheimian sense, I would hold that it is just and fitting that he be made to squirm so, because in having exploited his non-scientific self (either deliberately or unwittingly) for ends other than those immediately apprehended by his subjects he has in some significant sense violated the collective conscience of the community, if not that of the profession.

Now, the resort to calculated and whole-cloth deception of the type discussed here does not of course escape the final terms of this dilemma which may unalterably be our lot. It does, however, escape the intermediate ones: the discovery that *in vivo* the participant research role becomes something, both more and less than itself; the conscious opening up of self to the possibility of rebuttal, disaffection, divided loyalties, compromising attachments and difficult disclosures; the price of engagement as opposed to that of mere doing. And, it is ultimately in this sense that such actions strike me as less than human, and hence unworthy of a discipline which, whatever else it represents itself as, also call itself by that name.

In closing, may I suggest that it would be wholly fitting for a future issue of Social Problems to devote its pages to an airing of this, the sociologist's, social problem.

CHAPTER 25

Reply to Davis' Comment on "Initial Interaction"

John Lofland

Mr. Davis' letter is written in response to an experiment reported by Mr. Lejeune and myself, but it relates less to our work than to some general moral problems of performing sociological research. I will therefore address my comments to the broader argument in so far as it is possible to separate it from its confusing entanglement with his personal response to our report.

If I may, there is one question specific to the experiment on which I would like to comment first. Mr. Davis writes that A.A. members will possibly be unhappy with our experiment and as a result make it difficult to get their cooperation in future research. This is a conceivable outcome in any field research, and one upon which we always take a chance. Mr. Davis' statement, in this case, assumes two things, both of which are unlikely. First, that A.A. members will read the report and second, that they will be unhappy about what is reported. Concerning the former, the article was not written or reported to facilitate viewing by A.A. members; it is presented in scientific writing and appears in a professional journal, both of which very effectively limit its audience. As to the latter, if some members do read it, it is not evident that the reaction will be "indifferent," or as Mr. Davis means, hostile. In fact, personally, quite contrary to Mr. Davis' personal feelings, I judge the experiment to be favorable to A.A., and do not think that members will necessarily judge it any differently. In his concentration on method, Mr. Davis apparently failed to see the moral and ethical implications of the findings, which I personally regard as gratifying. Of course, my suppositions on this point may be incorrect.

Moving to the more general issues, Mr. Davis is concerned with the character of sociologists' obligations to the science and profession and most

This chapter was originally published by the Society for the Study of Social Problems in *Social Problems*, 8: no. 4, 365-67. *John Lofland no longer subscribes to the argument he presents here. His current position is in essential accord with the views developed by Kai Erikson in "A Comment on Disguised Observation in Sociology," pp. 252-60 of this volume. Professor Lofland's most recent statement on these matters appears in his book, with the assistance of Lyn H. Lofland,* Deviance and Identity *(Prentice-Hall, 1969), pp. 299-301.* — W.F.

prominently with their obligations to others as persons. He states, correctly I believe, that in field research conflicts may arise among one's roles as a scientist, professional and person.[1] His primary claim is that the science and profession should help sociologists achieve a "moral integration between their roles" by establishing for them their personal conceptions of their obligations to others as persons. To facilitate such efforts, he presents some of his own personal standards and moral dilemmas as candidates for translation into professional canons.

It is generally agreed that our obligation to science is the objective, full and unbiased execution and reporting of observation. It is also generally agreed that our obligation to the profession is to conduct research in ways that will not injure the general repute of the profession or thwart subsequent access to research settings and thus hinder the development of the discipline. In his letter, Mr. Davis does not confine himself to his duty of upholding *these* obligations. He almost exclusively devotes his attention to extra-scientific and extra-professional standards because they appear to be different than his own. We all recognize that such statements are not, and cannot, be made as a scientist or professional; they are simply not part of the legitimate criteria for judging research. Therefore, *as* scientists and professionals, we have no reason to be concerned with Mr. Davis' opinions of our personal moral standards; but this is not to say that personal standards are unimportant, quite the reverse as I will indicate below.

Beyond the fact that protestations like this are not relevant, except to one's self, and that they are rather presumptuous, there is, for those who would persist, the important problem of ever generalizing a personal standard and holding it nonviolate for the profession or, indeed, for one's self.

The difficulties involved in asserting immutable professional standards of conduct are clearly illustrated in Mr. Davis' personal standard that one should not study groups unless they know about it and give their permission. A professional rule to this effect would not only make for great past, present and future loss to the discipline, but would be an active violation of many people's moral standards who think that there are some groups, such as professional crime and fascist groups, that should be studied whether they are asked and give permission or not. In other words, in accepting this rule, we could not study "bad" groups, which, as it happens, are also especially likely to be "groups that do not want to be studied." Furthermore, conceivably, it might be important enough to the discipline to justify studying a group even though the particular group refuses. I suspect that Mr. Davis, in taking a second look, would agree.

What actually seems to bother him about unknown observation, is the fact that A.A. is a "good" group and therefore should not be observed unknown. However, if we follow this modified principle we conclude with a kind of double standard of research methodology. In order to apply this as a professional rule we are in the curious position of requiring the profession to determine which are the good and bad groups and to judge the morally appropriate method. I doubt that many of us feel we would be justified in making this pronouncement on the spectrum of groups in the world (aside from the external political repercussions).

I think that the same kind of morass of inconsistencies and embarrassing positions result from attempting to make any personal standard a general professional ethic. Generalizing my own reasons dealing with the particular issue about A.A. above, we come out with the untenable general standards that we should study groups that are not going to read the report and we should always write reports that will make the group happy. Indeed, even concerning the standard on which there is probably the most agreement—that one should not perform research which will lower the repute of sociologists or will close an area—one can think of situations where there are legitimate scientific or moral grounds for performing the research.

None of this should be taken as suggesting there are not real and excruciating moral decisions for the person who is also a field sociologist or that he as a person has no moral obligations. I do suggest that our personal moral obligations and conflict of roles should not, and probably could not, be determined and/or solved by the intervention of the profession at large or other professionals speaking personally. It is probably an inescapable and insoluble part of the attempt to be both a scientist and a person in human groups that one must suffer the pains so eloquently portrayed by Mr. Davis, and that he must make his personal moral decisions alone, based on the situation. In addition, it is also doubtful that any amount of pleading for others to adopt one's own standards or prolonged demands to the profession for an edict of relief alters one's own, or others', personal dilemmas. The most legitimate and workable solution for the profession would appear to be the one we already have: each man works out, as best he can, his own, as Mr. Davis has so aptly captured it, "moral integration."

NOTE

[1] This division was suggested to me by Erving Goffman.

CHAPTER 26

Comments on "Secret Observation"

Julius A. Roth

These comments are not intended so much to take issue with Fred Davis or John Lofland in their exchange of letters printed in the Spring 1961 issue of *Social Problems* (pp. 364-367), but rather to go further into some of the complexities of the issue of "secret research." In most discussions of this issue which I have heard, there is a tendency to over-simplify the issue—to pose "secret research" against "non-secret research" and then put forth the technical or moral advantages and disadvantages of each. Actually, the ends of the continuum from "secret" to "non-secret" probably do not exist and it is the non-dichotomous part of this continuum which is of most interest.

All research is secret in some ways and to some degree—we never tell the subjects "everything." We can escape secrecy more or less completely only by making the subjects participants in the research effort, and this process, if carried far enough, means that there would be no more "subjects." So long as there exists a separation of role between the researchers and those researched upon, the gathering of information will inevitably have some hidden aspects even if one is an openly declared observer. The following are at least some of the reasons for this:

1. The researcher usually does not know everything he is looking for himself when he first starts out and structures his study to some extent as he goes along. Some of the things he finds of interest to study as the research goes on are things which the subjects might have objected to if they had been told about it in the beginning.

2. In many types of study of social behavior, the researcher does not want the subjects' behavior influenced by his knowledge of what the observer is interested in.

3. Even if the subjects of a study are given as precise and detailed an explanation of the purpose and procedure of the study as the investigator is able to give them, the subjects will not understand all the terms of the research in the same way that the investigator does. The terms used have

This chapter was originally published by the Society for the Study of Social Problems in *Social Problems,* 9: no. 3, 283-84.

different connotations to them, their experiential contexts differ, and their conceptions of the goals of the study are likely to be different. Therefore, even in those cases where the researcher has made a deliberate effort to explain to his subjects just what he is going to do, he will frequently find them acting surprised when he actually goes ahead and does it.

When a psychologist gives a subject a TAT and tells the subject that he is simply telling stories, is this "secret research"? Or still further removed, when you give a prospective employee what looks like an application form and then do a personality analysis of his responses, is this, or is this not equivalent to posing as a fake participant?

When we are observing a crowd welcoming a hero, it is obviously absurd to say that we should warn everybody in the crowd that a sociologist is interpreting their behavior. The same can probably be said if we observe the behavior of the passengers we ride on the bus with every day. But suppose we are systematically observing the behavior of fellow workers in a shop or an office? Or the members of one's own family?

Does the manner in which one comes to be a secret observer affect the morality of the situation? Is it moral if one gets a job in a factory to earn tuition and then takes advantage of the opportunity to carry out a sociological study, but immoral to deliberately plant oneself in the factory for the express purpose of observing one's fellow workers? If the outcome is the same—e.g., if the manner in which the observations are used are the same—I, for one, see no moral difference in these two situations, but I find some of my colleagues do not agree with this position.

If the possibility of disrespect for an organization or group is at issue, we are faced with the question of just when a collection of people becomes a self-identifiable group that may have considered itself being researched on. Would this mean that groups which are consciously organized deserve more consideration than those which are not? As observers must we be careful of how we deal with hospital nurses, but be more free in how we deal with patients who are unorganized and are not likely to read our reports? Might it perhaps be considered proper to keep secret notes on the behavior of truck drivers with whom one hitches a ride or with whom one works, but not upon the members of the Teamsters Union as an organization?

Most of us, in fact, never cease observing the social sphere about us and are continually interpreting the behavior of people about us. Some of these observations are systematically organized into a "research project," but most of the observations and interpretations are casual and are never recorded. But there are obviously all levels of observation and interpretation between these extremes and the appropriate place for a boundary line remains a moot point.

Where, then, do we draw the line? How small a group, how intimate a relationship, how much of a commitment of one's own self, how organized or self-conscious a group of subjects, how systematically organized a study is proper before unannounced observation becomes "immoral"?

The point of all these illustrations is that social science research cannot be divided into the "secret" and the "non-secret." The question is rather how much secrecy shall there be with which people in which circumstances? Or, to state the question in a more positive (in more researchable) manner: When we are carrying out a piece of social science research involving the behavior of other people, what do we tell whom under what circumstances? Posing the question in this manner puts us in the same boat with physicians, social workers, prostitutes, policemen, and others who must deal with information which is sometimes delicate, threatening, and highly confidential. We are then in a position to draw upon our own knowledge of these other groups and the way in which they handle information to carry out their work and to draw analogies between those professions and our own.

Secrecy in research is not something to be avoided or that can be avoided. It is rather a problem to be faced as an integral part of one's work. We are more likely to develop a useful and satisfying working ethic by analyzing the research process of the sociologist himself than by drawing up written codes of ethics which merely perpetuate current moral biases and restrict rather than aid further ethical development.

PART SEVEN

Qualitative Methodology and Theory

CHAPTER 27

The New Empiricists: The Participant Observer and Phenomenologist

Severyn T. Bruyn

Researchers in participant observation in the United States and researchers in phenomenology in Europe have been creating new procedures and perspectives in the study of man in society that break fundamentally with those of the older schools of scientific empiricism. The method of participant observation can be observed as developing in the works of American sociologists like Everett Hughes, Maurice Schwartz, Howard S. Becker, Herbert Gans, Anselm Strauss, and William Whyte. The method of phenomenology can be observed as developing in the works of such Europeans as George Gurvitch, Max Scheler, and Alfred Vierkandt. While studies in participant observation have been largely American in origin and studies in phenomenology have been largely European, they both exhibit a number of similarities, especially when they are seen in contrast to traditional empiricism. The similarities are so marked that study of how ideas in these two new developments in research are related could produce the beginning of a rapprochement between the great opposing positions of American and European thought.

My purpose here is to suggest a few of the methodological features which participant observers and phenomenologists have in common when they are jointly compared to traditional scientific empiricism. The phenomenological method as described by Herbert Spiegelberg can serve as a useful model utilizing certain features of this model as a basis for making some comparisons with participant observation and with traditional empiricism.

Spiegelberg describes seven different steps in the phenomenological method which guide the researcher.[1] These steps are as follows:

1. Investigating particular phenomena.
2. Investigating general essences.
3. Apprehending essential relationships among essences.

This chapter was originally published in *Sociology and Social Research*, 51: 317-22. The ideas in this article were adapted from Appendix B in Mr. Bruyn's *The Human Perspective in Sociology* (New York: Prentice-Hall, 1966).

4. Watching modes of appearing.
5. Watching the constitution of phenomena in consciousness.
6. Suspending belief in the existence of the phenomena.
7. Interpreting the meaning of phenomena.

Certain subphases of these steps are especially notable for comparison. The first step contains three: (a) an intuitive grasp of the phenomena, (b) their analytic examination, and (c) their description. In this first subphase, the phenomenologist is required to become highly aware of his subject and its surroundings in order to obtain an accurate intuitive grasp of it. In this sense the phenomenologist is very much like the participant observer in so far as he approaches his subject with every effort to eliminate his preconceptions about it. He has no hypothesis to direct him; he takes special pains to conduct his research with a totally open mind, open in depth to all the stimuli that impinge upon his consciousness during his investigation.

This initial phenomenological rule of openness is reflected in the writings of participant observers who have found that theories or hypotheses can interfere with the accuracy of the findings. In their study of *Boys in White,* Becker, Geer, Hughes, and Strauss, stress this rule as basic to their method.[2]

This meant that we concentrated on *what* students learned as well as on *how* they learned it. Both of those assumptions committed us to working with an open theoretical scheme in which variables were to be discovered rather than with a scheme in which variables decided on in advance would be located and their consequences isolated and measured. . . .

The traditional empiricist sets up many preconceptions of his subject through his study of background materials, his definition of variables, his hypotheses, and the causal order he expects to find among his variables. The phenomenologist and the participant observer, on the other hand, tend to let the variables define themselves in the context of the research. And they examine causal relations between these variables on the basis of the social perception of the subjects themselves. The emphasis of the phenomenologist and the participant observer is upon following those procedures which best allow the subjects to speak for themselves in contrast to the traditional empiricist who emphasizes procedures which help explain the subjects from an independent standpoint.

The fourth step which Spiegelberg calls "watching modes of appearing" stresses the importance of seeing objects as they actually exist rather than as we imagine they exist. For example, if we look at a cube-like object we really see only one side of it with other sides shading off from our perception in a trapezoid-like form. One side, in fact, is totally invisible to us. And yet, when we observe the cube, our imagination normally immediately supplies the whole image. The process is so unconscious that we do not report it as we actually observe it. In field research of community life this experience is paralleled by what participant observers witness when participating only in the activities of one class level. When the observer participating in the upper class, for example, describes the lower classes, these lower classes visibly shade off, so to speak, into general categories. Lower class people are observed as "all wage-earners" or "the people on the other side of the tracks." If the observer were to participate in the life of the lower classes he would find considerable differentiation evident among the people themselves which he did not observe by taking the role of the members of the upper class. Lloyd Warner has already informed us of this experiential phenomenon. Class members of upper and lower extremes of a community cannot "see" the differences existing among the subclasses of those opposite to them. As a sociologist, however, the observer tends to supply the remaining image on the basis of his prior scientific conception of class structure (just as we normally supply the missing side of the cube and do not see the trapezoid-like shape of the sides as they appear to our eyes). The function of the phenomenologist and the participant observer in these cases is to record these dimensions of the object under study as they appear to the consciousness without supplying what the researchers conceive to be the whole object. Only later, are they privileged to supply the modes which complete the image when they finally appear through the total research process.

Edmund Husserl would contend that phenomenology is more fundamental than empiricism as a methodological effort to understand the world.[3] Phenomenology underlies traditional empiricism; it is a kind of foundation to the scientific method. (At one point Husserl called phenomenology the "true empiricism.") Therefore, it cannot be compared with traditional empiricism as though the two methods were polar types. Nevertheless, it is worthwhile summarizing some of the differences which appear evident in both approaches in order to gain insight into their character. The following are three points which both phenomenology and participant observation have in common in opposition to traditional empiricism.

First, the new researchers seek to investigate particular phenomena without preconception of their nature while the traditional empiricist is definitive in his preconceptions and his experimental design prior to his investigation. *Second,* the new researchers observe phenomena that appear symbolically in their consciousness and treat these symbols as data whereas the traditional empiricist observes first what immediately appears to his senses and often restricts his study solely to the realm of sense data. *Third,* the new researchers intuit essences and essential relations existing in the symbolic data they study whereas traditional empiricists operationally define variables which have visible reference and which can then be studied for their correspondence statistically.

The difference between knowing what appears to one's consciousness symbolically and knowing what appears immediately to one's senses by applying experimental controls, is basic here. The phenomenologist, like the participant observer, assumes that reliable knowledge can be gathered apart from sheer reason or sensory observation alone. Even though sense and reason enter the process of understanding at different stages to complement his findings, the observer finds that intuition which surrounds an adequate inter- pretation of symbolic data is also an important part of this process. While it is true that the traditional empiricist has occasionally recognized the useful role of intuition in field work by way of revelations which occur outside his legitimate logical-experimental procedure, he has never sought to explain the intuitive process in terms of a reliable process for gathering knowledge. I would suggest that the emerging methods of phenomenology and participant observation can now serve as an explanation of this intuitive process. What lies behind the sudden revelations in field research—or what Robert Merton has called the "serendipity pattern"[4]—are results of what is embodied in these new research procedures. What Merton calls surprising and unanticipated datum in traditional empirical studies is actually insight produced uninten- tionally through the researcher's unconscious encounter with the symbolic nuances of data—an encounter with a process which has become rationalized in the methods of phenomenology and participant observation. The researcher discovers new meanings in his data as he knowingly participates in the process of social communication which reflect the symbolic life of the people he studies. If he perceives this symbolic life accurately in his role as a participant observer he is rewarded by finding new perspectives cast on his data.

The method of phenomenology and the method of participant observa- tion are not the same in spite of their common differences with traditional empiricism. The phenomenologist studies symbolic meanings as they constitute themselves in human consciousness.[5] The participant observer does this too but he is more concerned with how symbols are constituted in particular cultures and he studies these symbols through the process of taking the role of the people who normally experience these symbols. In the process of taking their role, he becomes personally involved in living with the culture he studies. He then has the problem of balancing his involvement with objective detachment in arriving at an accurate accounting of the culture. Personal involvement with cultural symbols is not a necessary factor entering into the method of phenomenology or the method traditional to empiricism. In fact, the traditional empiricist would condemn any involvement as alien to the values of the scientific process of gaining objective knowledge.

New empiricists, like the participant observer in America and like the phenomenologist in Europe, present a challenge to social scientists today who follow the older traditions of empiricism. A more thorough study of their approaches could provide a basis for resolving some of the problems which have long plagued social scientists without answers. For example, there is schism between what the phenomenologist calls "lived experience" (which is essentially what the participant observer studies) and scientific abstractions and reductionisms. There is also the schism between the moral and the natural worlds of man and the conflicting perspectives they have each engendered in relation to one another. The phenomenologist and the participant observer have been building new ground beneath these schisms. They are both taking man as he is given in his lived experience. They are placing the mechanical, organic, and functional images of man in their proper perspective—not negating their value to the formulation of theory but denying their supremacy in the explanation of society. They are giving supremacy to an inner perspective of man in society which ultimately could lead toward a more comprehensive sociological perspective. They are observing man in his concreteness and subjectiveness as opposed to the abstractness and objectiveness of the traditional empiricist and theorist; they are observing him as a social being with freedom and purpose as opposed to observing him deterministically as the product of external forces. In this process of seeing man from an inner perspective, these new researchers are creating a foundation for a human perspective of man. If this inner perspective were combined with the external perspective of the scientific tradition in the context of social research, the result could have a significant effect upon sociological theory in comprehending man in his wholeness during the latter third of the twentieth century.

NOTES

[1] Herbert Spiegelberg, "The Essentials of the Phenomenological Method," *The Phenomenological Movement: A Historical Introduction* (2nd ed.; The Hague: Martinus Nijhoff, 1965), Vol. 2, pp. 655-70. The method of phenomenology is like participant observation and traditional empiricism in the sense that it is not restricted to the field of sociology by any means but rather exhibits a form which has an interdisciplinary character.

[2] Howard S. Becker, Blanche Geer, Everett C. Hughes, and Anselm L. Strauss, *Boys in White* (Chicago: University of Chicago Press, 1961), p. 18.

[3] Edmund Husserl, *Ideas*, trans. W. R. Boyce Gibson (London: George Allen & Univer., 1931). See also: E. Parl Welch, *The Philosophy of Edmund Husserl* (New York: Columbia University Press, 1941).

[4] Robert K. Merton, *Social Theory and Social Structure* (New York: The Free Press, a Division of the Macmillan Co., 1949), p. 98.

[5] A recent discussion of the nature of phenomenology in relation to sociological theory may be found in Edward A. Tiryakian, "Existential Phenomenology," *American Sociological Review,* 30 (October, 1965), 674-88. Critical appraisals of this article and a reply may be found in *American Sociological Review,* 31 (April, 1966), 258-64.

CHAPTER 28

Discovery of Substantive Theory:
A Basic Strategy Underlying Qualitative Research

Barney G. Glaser and Anselm L. Strauss

In spite of the diversity of problems, approaches and conclusions in the writings of sociologists on qualitative research and analysis, all would seem to support one general position: Qualitative research is a preliminary, exploratory effort to quantitative research since only quantitative research yields rigorously verified findings and hypotheses.[1] The source of this position is that these sociologists appear to take as a guide to being "systematic" the canons of the quantitative analysis on such issues as sampling, coding, reliability, validity, indicators, frequency distributions, conceptual formulization, hypothesis construction and presentation of evidence. Thus these sociologists over-emphasize rigorous testing of hypotheses, and de-emphasize the discovering of what concepts and hypotheses are relevant for the substantive area being researched.

We contend that qualitative research—quite apart from its usefulness as a prelude to quantitative research—should be scrutinized for its usefulness in the discovery of substantive theory.[2] By the discovery of substantive theory we mean the formulation of concepts and their interrelation into a set of hypotheses for a given substantive area—such as patient care, gang behavior, or education—based on research in the area. To view qualitative research as merely preliminary to quantitative research neglects, hence underestimates, several important facts about substantive theory that is based on qualitative research. First, substantive theory is more often than not the end product of research within a substantive area beyond which few, if any, research sociologists are motivated to move.[3] Second, it is the basis upon which grounded

"The Discovery of Substantive Theory: A Basic Strategy Underlying Qualitative Research," by Barney Glaser and Anselm Strauss is reprinted from *The American Behavioral Scientist,* Volume VIII, no. 6 (February, 1965), pages 5-12, by permission of the Publisher, Sage Publications, Inc., Beverly Hills, California. The paper was developed from qualitative research done during a study of terminal care in hospitals, sponsored by NIH grant NU 00047. The authors acknowledge the assistance of Howard S. Becker, Fred Davis, Egon Bittner, Rue Bucher, Virginia Olesen, and Stewart Perry.

formal theory is generated.[4] Third, qualitative research is often the most "adequate" and "efficient" method for obtaining the type of information required and for contending with the difficulties of an empirical research situation.[5] Fourth, sociologists (and informed laymen) manage often to profit quite well in their everyday work life from substantive theory based on qualitative research.[6]

Together these facts raise doubts as to the applicability of the canons of quantitative research as criteria for judging the credibility of substantive theory based on qualitative research. They suggest rather that criteria of judgment be based on generic elements of qualitative methods for collecting, analyzing and presenting data and for the way in which people read qualitative analyses.

The setting out of these generic elements, to be used both in discovering substantive theory based on qualitative research and in judging its credibility, is the task of this paper. In so doing, we shall regard *qualitative research—* whether utilizing observation, intensive interviews, or any type of document—*as a strategy concerned with the discovery of substantive theory,* not with feeding quantitative researchers. We shall take up the following pertinent matters: 1) the collection and analysis of data, 2) the maximization of substantive theory's credibility by using comparative groups in the research design, 3) the researcher's trust in believing what he knows he knows, 4) the researcher's conveying to others in publication what he knows so that others may judge his theory, and 5) the relation of discovery of substantive theory to its further rigorous testing.

JOINT COLLECTION AND ANALYSIS OF DATA

Whether the fieldworker starts out in the confused state of noting everything he sees, because everything may be significant, or whether he starts out with a more defined purpose, observation is quickly accompanied by hypothesizing. When hypothesizing begins, the researcher, even if so disposed, can no longer remain a passive receiver of impressions, but is naturally drawn into actively finding data pertinent to developing and verifying his hypotheses. He looks for that data. He places himself in spaces where his data can be seen "live." He participates in events so that things will pass before his eyes, and so that things will happen to himself which will precipitate further hypothesizing. He may even manipulate events to see what will happen. Although he could manage all these investigatory activities without hypotheses, the hypotheses inevitably arise to guide him.[7]

It is characteristic of fieldwork that multiple hypotheses are pursued simultaneously. Of course, certain events will literally force an important or fascinating hypothesis upon the researcher, so that he spends days or weeks checking out that one hypothesis—especially if its verification is linked with developing social events. Meanwhile other hypotheses are being built into his fieldnotes. Eventually the researcher either actively verifies many of his hypotheses or sufficient verifying events are observed by chance. In either case he no longer packs his notes with evidence pertaining to those particular hypotheses, but goes on to collect data on newer, emerging hypotheses.

The earlier hypotheses may seem unrelated at first, but rather quickly become integrated, to form the basis of a central analytic framework. In fact, fieldworkers have remarked upon the rapid crystallization of that framework, and some have wondered whether later fieldwork does not merely elaborate upon that framework.[8] Whatever the answer, it is certain that experienced researchers quickly develop important concepts, basic categories, and significant hypotheses.[9] Beyond guiding the active search for evidence, these integrated hypotheses immediately provide a central core of theorizing which helps the researcher to develop related hypotheses as well as to prune away those not related. In fact, one hazard of fieldwork is that potentially illuminating perspectives are suppressed in favor of a too rapidly emerging analytic framework.

The analytic framework generally appears on paper in two forms. Analytic comments get written directly into the fieldnotes and are written into occasional memos addressed specifically to matters of analysis. If a research team is involved, the researchers write collective as well as individual memos. Characteristically, researchers withdraw periodically from active field pursuits to reflect upon their observations and write analytic memos. Most field situations force such periods upon the researcher because of the natural lulls in social life. But more important, such respites from active fieldwork are taken by some fieldworkers to avoid collecting huge masses of data without adequate systematic reflection on their research directions and purposes, as guided by their emergent analytic framework.[10]

These reflective periods are immensely important for two additional reasons—other than that the researcher needs occasional relief from observational duty. One reason is, of course, that systematic analysis can better proceed when the researcher thinks uninterruptedly about his observations, interviews and personal field experiences. If a research team is involved, the members can work together better than when scattered about the observational field.

Second, it is necessary to reflect upon what amounts to a process of implicit coding that has been underway since the outset of the research. This reflection by the researcher consists of thinking systematically about the data, in accordance with his basic analytic categories. He need not, however, explicitly, code all—or any—of his notes. Fieldworkers actually run through or reread sections of their notes, in order to verify principal hypotheses. They will also run back "in memory" to verify hypotheses. In either case, they do something akin to what ordinarily is termed coding, but do not necessarily raise coding to prominent independent status. Indeed, even when collecting data, researchers will often have an "ah ha!" experience when they recognize that some observed event belongs in a given category. Moreover, strategic memorable events generate new categories and hypotheses, or cast doubt on the efficacy of certain categories and provide negative evidence against previous hypotheses. Those memorable events are either analyzed immediately after they occur, or keep recurring in memory with nagging persistence until systematically analyzed during memo writing periods.

In short, in qualitative work, just as there is no clear-cut line between data collection and analysis (except during periods of systematic reflection), there is no sharp division between implicit coding and either data collection or data analysis. There tends to be a continual blurring and intertwining of all three operations from the beginning of the investigation until its near end.

This implicit coding goes on even when researchers do not intend to exploit it purposively, but plan to code explicitly all collected material at the close of fieldwork and then to accomplish the major analysis. However, they may soon realize, *if* substantive theory is their goal, that they have implicitly coded enough material to write their theory already. Therefore, the explicit coding operation can become perceived as a stultifying tedium of little worth, for two reasons.

First, the researchers may find that they are not learning anything new enough about their theory—that is, something that will sufficiently modify the *core* concepts and hypotheses of the theory—to make the explicit procedure seem worthwhile. Of course, explicit coding at the study's close can add further elaboration of details to the substantive theory; but the question is always whether or not the additional effort is worthwhile since there is little chance that the core of the theory will change, and details below the level of generality of the theory seldom add to its wider import and applicability.

Second, little more is likely to be learned by explicit coding after data collection because various segments of the analytic framework get firmed up during chronologically different stages of the fieldwork. Once firmed up, neither more data need be gathered nor analysis rethought for the segment, unless further theoretical work necessitates those additional operations. Experienced fieldworkers know that their fieldnotes not only reflect this continuous firming up, but cannot always be read intelligently by outsiders precisely because at later stages of the research a shorthand reporting occurs which is based upon matters long since firmly known.[11]

The continual intermeshing of data collection and analysis has direct bearing upon how the research is brought to a close. The researcher can always try to mine his data further, and he can always collect more data to check hypotheses or to force new ones. And when writing is done within or near the field, the temptation is especially strong to dash back into the field. This last search for data understandably tends to be either of a specifically confirmatory nature (the researcher moving now with considerable sureness and speed) or of an elaborative nature (the researcher wishing to round out his work by exploring some area that was previously untouched or even unconsidered).[12] This last search can be a strong temptation if personal relations formed in the field are satisfying or if exciting new events are developing there. However, collection and analysis of additional data can be a waste of time because the work merely further elaborates details of the substantive theory; again little of core value is learned.[13]

When the researcher is convinced that his analytic framework forms a systematic substantive theory, that it is a reasonably accurate statement of the matters studied, and that it is couched in a form possible for others to use if they were to go the same field—then he can publish his results with confidence. He believes in his own knowledgeability and finds no reason to change that belief. He believes not because of an arbitrary judgment but because he has taken very special pains to verify what he thinks he may know every step of the way, from the beginning of his investigation until its publishable conclusion.

MAXIMIZING CREDIBILITY THROUGH COMPARISON GROUPS

In this section we shall present a strategy whereby fieldworkers can facilitate the discovery of a substantive theory, while simultaneously developing confidence in the credibility of that theory. This strategy involves the systematic choice and study of several comparison groups.

Fieldwork in sociology arose from the ethnological tradition of studying one society or group at a time. The sustaining rationale consisted of what one anthropologist or sociologist by himself might be able to observe, plus the conviction that social structure ought to be captured "as a whole." Consequently fieldwork monographs have tended through the years to take the form of single case studies. Even today most fieldworkers study one group at a time and few focus upon more than two or three groups simultaneously.[14] Such comparisons as exist for single case studies are either brought into the monograph (or paper) by footnoting comparable materials and discussing them or by publishing several comparable studies together in one volume.

However, it is feasible in more field studies than have attempted it to *build into the research design a comparison of at least several—and often many—social systems.*[15] The strategy of choosing multiple *comparison groups* is guided by the *logic* of the researcher's emerging analytic framework. Significant categories and hypotheses are first identified in the emerging analysis, during preliminary fieldwork in one or a few groups and while scrutinizing substantive theories and data from other studies. Comparison groups are then located and chosen in accordance with the purposes of providing new data on categories or combinations of them, suggesting new hypotheses, and verifying initial hypotheses in diverse contexts. It is not too difficult to compare as many as forty groups when one considers that they are compared on the basis of a defined set of categories and hypotheses (not compared on the basis of the "whole" group) and that groups within groups are compared (e.g., different and similar wards within different types of hospitals). These groups can be studied one at a time or a number can be studied simultaneously. They can also be studied in quick succession in order to check out major hypotheses before too much theory is built around them.

Multiple comparison groups function in several ways to improve the research and consequent substantive theory. First and foremost the comparisons maximize the credibility of the final theory in two fundamental ways:

A) By precisely detailing the many similarities and differences of the various comparison groups, the analyst knows better, than if he only studied one or a few social systems, under what sets of structural conditions his hypotheses are minimized and maximized, hence to what kinds of social structures his theory is applicable. In increasing the scope and delimiting the generality of his theory, he saves his colleagues work. Ordinarily, readers of fieldwork must figure out the limitations of a published study by making comparisons with their own experience and knowledge of similar groups. By comparison, they figure that the reported material jibes just so far and no further—for given structural reasons. By using multiple comparison groups, much of this burden of delimiting relevant boundaries for the theory is lifted from the reader's shoulders.[16] In short, replication is built into the research.

B) Another way that multiple comparison groups maximize credibility is by helping the researcher to calculate where a given order of events or incidents is most likely to occur or not to occur. This calculus provides an efficient logical guide to groups, for obtaining more data to fill in theoretical gaps and for verifying his hypotheses. This calculus is especially helpful in his efficient search for negative cases that may necessitate reformulation of a hypothesis. Also, the variety lent his study by multiple comparison groups increases the possibility of his being surprised by unanticipated negative cases.

Multiple comparison groups also permit and generate the speedy development of analysis in two principal ways:

A) The constant comparison of many groups rather quickly draws the observer's attention to many similarities and differences among groups that are important for his theory. From these similarities and differences are generated the theoretical categories to be used, their full range of types or continuum, their dimensions, the conditions under which they exist more or less, and their major consequences. In this way, the full generality and meaning of each category is established.[17] Category development is much slower on a single terrain, and the result is a less generalized category imbued with less meaning.

B) In addition, the differences and similarities among groups speedily generate generalized relations among the categories, which of course become the hypotheses soon integrated into the substantive theory. When a negative case is found in a different group, and since a group is an indicator of a set of structural conditions, while reformulating his hypothesis the analyst compares the set of conditions under which it existed to the set under which it is encountered in order to find the particular structural condition(s) making for the change—which condition(s) can then be taken account of in reformulating the hypothesis. This analytic strategy is far different, more powerful, precise, and informative than comparing positive and negative cases within a single structure.[18] In the latter case, one can only compare the *internal* structure of the negative incident to the positive incidents, since both occur under the same structural conditions. That comparison is likely to sound implausible— even tautological—for one ends up saying that an element of an incident caused itself to be different from all other similar incidents. It is more plausible to point to different sets of *external* structural conditions under which positives and negatives exist and, then, suggest differentiating factors in the cases based on comparison of these sets.

Researchers who work with other types of qualitative data can also utilize this efficient method. Using only interviews, for instance, there is no reason why researchers cannot study comparison groups of interviewees, chosen in accordance with emergent analytic frameworks. And historical documents, or other library materials, lend themselves wonderfully to the comparative method. Their use is perhaps even more efficient, since the researcher is saved much time and trouble in his search for comparison groups which are, after all, found concentrated in the library. As in fieldwork, when his analytic framework is far developed, the researcher who uses library materials can always select additional comparison groups to give himself additional confidence in the credibility of his framework. He will also—like the fieldworker who sometimes stumbles upon comparison groups and then makes proper use of them—occasionally profit from such happy accidents which occur when browsing along library shelves.

TRUST IN ONE'S OWN CREDIBLE KNOWLEDGE

The analytic framework which emerges from the researcher's collection and scrutiny of qualitative data is equivalent to what *he knows systematically about his own data.* Let us discuss why the fieldworker trusts what he knows.

If there is only one fieldworker involved, it is he himself who knows *what* he knows about what he has studied and lived through. They are his perceptions, his personal experiences, and his own hard-won analyses. The fieldworker knows *that* he knows, not only because he's been there in the field and because of his careful verification of hypotheses, but because "in his bones" he feels the worth of his final analysis. He has been living with partial analyses for many months, testing them each step of the way, until he has built his final substantive theory. What is more, if he has participated in the social life of his subjects then he has been living by his analyses, testing them out not only by observation and interview but also in daily livable fact. Hence by the close of his investigation, his conviction about his theory would be hard to shake—as most fieldworkers would attest. This conviction does not mean that his analysis is the only plausible one that might be based on this data, but only that the researcher himself has high confidence in its credibility. What he has confidence in is not a scattered series of analyses, but a systematic ordering of them into an integrated theory.[19] He has, in fact, discovered a substantive theory about delimited arrays of data, through inductive as well as deductive effort, which he is ready to publish.

If a research team is involved, then of course it is their shared knowledge which constitutes the final substantive theory offered to colleagues. Each fieldworker not only knows his own fieldnotes intimately, but has shared his colleagues' observations and experiences by virtue of numerous discussions, "talking out," and memo-writing sessions. The inevitable debates among team members contribute also to the development of a shared analytic framework.

The "real life" character of fieldwork knowledge deserves special underscoring, especially as many critics think of this and other qualitatively oriented methods as merely preliminary to real (scientific) knowing. A firsthand immersion in a sphere of life and action—a social world—different from one's own yields important dividends for the fieldworker. The fieldworker who has observed closely in this social world has had, in a profound sense, to live there. He has not only been sufficiently immersed in the world to know it, but has retained enough detachment to think theoretically about what he has seen and lived through. His informed detachment has allowed him to benefit not only as a sociologist but as a human being who must "make out" in that world. This is true despite the fact that the people there generally do not expect perfect adherence to their ways from the outsider. His detachment has served also to protect him against going more than a little native while yet doing more than a little passing as a native, when the people whom he is studying either have temporarily forgotten his outsider status or have never recognized it. Meanwhile his display of understanding and sympathy for their mode of life permits sufficient trust in him so that he is not cut off from seeing important events, hearing important conversations, and perhaps seeing important documents. If that trust does not develop, his analysis suffers.[20]

The evolving systematic analysis permits the fieldworker quite literally to write prescriptions so that other outsiders might get along in the observed sphere of life and action. That is one benefit of his substantive theory. If he has avoided trouble within the particular social world by following these prescriptions, then presumably they accurately represent the world's prominent features; they are workable guides to action and therefore they can, on this account too, be accorded our confidence in their credibility.[21]

In effect this is how shrewd or thoughtful visitors to any social world feel about their knowledge of these worlds. Not infrequently people successfully stake their money, reputations and even lives as well as the fate of others upon their interpretations. *What the fieldworker does is to make this normal strategy of reflective persons into a successful research strategy.* In doing so, of course, a trained, competent researcher is much more systematic in formulating his ideas than is the ordinary visitor; and if a superior researcher, his knowledge is likely to be generalized and systematically integrated into a theory. In addition, he is much more systematic at verifying his ideas than is the ordinary visitor. Such bias as he brings to the field is more likely to be checked upon, while his hypotheses are more likely to arise within the field of observation than to be imported from the outside. In the latter regard, he also differs from researchers who bring such a working baggage of formal theory into the field that they end not by discovering much substantive theory but manage principally to write footnotes to the imported theory. They are not likely, either, to do very well in the pragmatic test of living by their theory while in the field.

Finally, it is worth special mention that those fieldworkers who do *not* really believe in their own hard-won substantive theory are tempted toward a compulsive scientism. Because they do not trust themselves—their own ability to know or reason—they rely additionally upon questionnaires or other "objective" methods of collecting and analyzing quantified data. Used for this purpose these methods do not necessarily lead to greater credibility, but they do permit the insecure researcher to feel greater security in his "results" without genuine consideration of what queries do or do not need this additional "hard" data. It is also true that the insecure fieldworker may know that he is running away from himself, because of a failure of confidence in his ability to render his knowledge credible, but he cannot stop running!

CONVEYING AND JUDGING CREDIBILITY

When the researcher decides to write for publication, then he faces the problem of conveying to colleagues the credibility of his discovered theory so that they can make some sensible judgment about it. The problem of conveying credibility is dividable into two sub-problems, each of which deserves discussion.

The first sub-problem is that of getting readers to understand the theoretical framework. This is generally done by giving an extensive abstract presentation of the framework and its associated theoretical statements, generally at the beginning and/or end of the publication but usually also in segments throughout the publication. This presentation is not particularly difficult since there exists an abstract social science terminology which is quite as applicable to qualitative as to quantitative data as well as a common sociological perspective which furthers the communication.

The related second sub-problem is how to describe the social world studied so vividly that the reader can almost literally see and hear its people— but see and hear in relation to the theoretical framework. To do this, the researcher ordinarily utilizes several of a considerable armamentarium of standard devices. He can quote directly from interviews or conversations which he has overheard. He can include dramatic segments of his on-the-spot fieldnotes. He can quote telling phrases dropped by informants. He can summarize events or persons by constructing readable case studies. He can try his hand at describing events and acts; and often at least he will give backdrop descriptions of places and spaces. He will even offer accounts of personal experience to show how events impinged upon himself. Sometimes he will unroll a narrative. Chapter headings can also help to convey sights and sounds.[22]

The first and second sub-problems of conveying credibility through plausible reasoning are reflected in the type of concepts that the researcher chooses for writing his substantive theory. With regard to the first problem, his concepts are analytic—sufficiently generalized to designate the properties of concrete entities (not the concrete entities themselves). With regard to the second problem, his concepts also are sensitizing—yield a "meaningful" picture—abetted by apt illustrations which enable one to grasp the reference in terms of one's own experience.[23] Formulating concepts of this nature, hence tapping the best of two possible worlds, takes considerable study of one's data.[24]

Several aspects of the presentation enter into how the reader, in turn, judges the credibility of the theory that the writer is trying to convey. First of all, if a reader becomes sufficiently caught up in the description so that he feels vicariously that he also had been in the field, then he is more likely to be kindly disposed toward the researcher's theory than if the description seemed flat or unconvincing.

Second, a judgment of credibility will also rest upon assessments concerning how the researcher came to his conclusions. The reader will note, for instance, what range of events the researcher saw, whom he interviewed, who talked to him, what kinds of experiences he had, and how he might have appeared to various people whom he studied. That is, the reader will assess the types of data utilized from what is explicitly stated as well as from what can be read between the lines. It is absolutely incumbent upon the reader to make such judgments, partly because the entire publication may be a complete fabrication,[25] but more usually because any analysis may require some qualification.

Such qualification we may term "the discounting process." Readers surely discount aspects of many, if not most, analyses which are published (whether resting upon qualitative or quantitative data).[26] This discounting by the reader takes several forms: the theory is *corrected* because of onesided research designs,[27] *adjusted* to fit the diverse conditions of different social structures, *invalidated* for other structures through the reader's experience or knowledge, and deemed *inapplicable* to yet other kinds of structures. It is important to note that when a theory is deemed inapplicable to a social world or social structure, then it cannot be invalidated by their conditions. It is not correct to say that because a theory "does not fit" a structure, then it is invalid. The invalidation or adjustment of a theory is only legitimate for those social worlds or structures to which it is applicable.

This ongoing discounting process of qualification by the reader allows the researcher to write his theory in general form, because the researcher knows that the reader will make the necessary corrections, adjustments, invalidations and inapplications when thinking about or using the theory. These are qualifications that he could not begin to cover for even a small percentage of one type of reader and, more important, they are qualifications which the researcher must learn to gloss over or to ignore in order to write a substantive theory of some generality.[28] (It is also necessary to leave out qualifications in order to write a theory that is readable, because the rhetoric of qualification is as onerous to read as to write.)

The researcher and his readers thus share a joint responsibility. The researcher ought to provide sufficiently clear statements of theory and description so that readers can carefully assess the credibility of the theoretical framework offered in his publication. A cardinal rule for the researcher is that whenever he himself feels most dubious about an important interpretation—or foresees that readers may well be dubious—then he should specify quite explicitly upon what kinds of data his interpretation rests. The parallel rule for readers is that they should demand explicitness about important interpretations, but if the researcher has not supplied the information then they should assess his interpretations from whatever indirect evidence may be available. These same rules apply to the reading of qualitative materials from libraries and organizational archives, as well as to the writing of those materials.

THE ISSUE OF FURTHER RIGOR

The presentation of substantive theory, developed through analysis of qualitative data, is often done at a sufficient level of plausibility to satisfy most readers. The theory can be applied and adjusted to many situations with sufficient exactitude to guide thinking, understanding and research. Given certain structural conditions under which sociologists work (such as designing specific action programs, or working in a rather well developed substantive area), then more rigorous testing may be required to raise the level of plausibility of some hypotheses.

Under these conditions, it should be a matter of empirical determination as to how the further testing can best be accomplished—whether through more rigorous or extensive fieldwork itself, or through experiments or survey methods. The two essential points in this decision on method are, first, that the testing be more rigorous than previously (not *which* of all methods is the most rigorous); and, second, that the more rigorous approach be compatible with the research situation in order to yield the most reliable findings. What should not enter into the determination of further testing are the researcher's ideological commitments (with associated career contingencies) to only one method; for instance, that a survey is a more rigorous mode of achieving a high degree of plausibility than field observation, and therefore it is the best and only mode to use in all cases. In the actual research situation, a survey may not be feasible nor worth the time or money, nor yield the type of information needed, and indeed it may even distort the information yielded. An approach to an increased, required level of plausibility should be based, therefore, on the use of the method or methods best suited to the socially structured necessities of the sociologist's research situation.

This cardinal rule for determining which method to use for increasing the plausibility of the substantive theory is broken in another way by researchers who are ideologically committed to quantitative methods. They assume out of context that all research requires a rigorously achieved high level of plausibility and that quantitative research, more rigorous than most qualitative methods, is therefore the *best* method to use in *all* research situations. Thus, whatever qualitative research may be done is seen merely as a preliminary provision of categories to use in the ensuing quantitative research. As noted at the beginning of our paper, this position neglects both the importance of discovering substantive theory based on qualitative research and the fact that this substantive theory is more often than not the end product of research within the substantive area beyond which few, if any, research sociologists are motivated to move.

Substantive theory discovered through qualitative analysis is often the end product of research for a variety of reasons. First, those researchers who do try to move beyond substantive theory by testing it with quantitative data are often told by colleagues and editorial boards that they are simply proving what everyone knows sufficiently well already. They are told their work is trivial and a waste of resources.[29] To "save" their work, they are forced to turn their quantitative work of testing the "already known" hypothesis into an effort at discovering, in their data, new substantive fact and theory. Thus, quantitative data is often used not for rigorous demonstration of theory but as another way to discover more theory, and qualitative data results often in a *de facto* conclusive analysis rather than a preliminary analysis.

Second, it is an old story in social science that contemporary interest switches from certain phenomena once that interest is saturated with substantive theory. This switch usually occurs long before satisfactory quantitative research pertaining to the phenomena has taken place. Meanwhile, informed laymen and social scientists manage to profit quite well by the merely plausible work of discovery published by sociologists who carefully analyze their qualitative data. This ability to profit from substantive theory based on qualitative research forestalls the need for future highly rigorous research among most sociologists and laymen.[30] Since the theory works well enough, it is typically only modified, if even that, not by further demonstrative research on a specific hypothesis but by additional related theory. The researcher's primary effort in working with this related theory is to discover new theory, not to correct or test older theory. Once new theory is discovered and developed, any modification of older theory that then occurs will receive post-hoc recognition.

And third—much the most important reason—a great deal of sociological work, unlike physical science research, never gets to the stage of rigorous demonstration because the social structures which sociologists study are undergoing continuous change. Older structures frequently take on new dimensions before highly rigorous research can be accomplished. The changing of social structures means that a prime sociological task is the exploration—and even literal discovery—of emerging structures. Undue emphasis on being "scientific" is simply not reasonable in light of our need for discovery and exploration amidst very considerable structural changes.

CONCLUDING REMARKS

Most writing on sociological method has probably been concerned with how theory can be more rigorously tested. In this paper we have addressed ourselves to the equally important enterprise of how the discovery of substantive theory can be furthered. The formulation of fruitful substantive theory for a substantive area through careful research—as against constructing formal theory for a conceptual area (such as deviance, status congruency, reference groups or hierarchy)—is a major task in sociology. Substantive theory faithful to the empirical situation cannot be formulated, we believe, be merely applying a formal theory to the substantive area. First a substantive theory must be formulated, in order to see which of diverse formal theories are applicable to help further the substantive formulation.[31] And in its turn then substantive theory helps in formulating and reformulating formal theory. Thus substantive theory becomes a strategic link in the formulation and development of formal theory based on data. We have called the latter "grounded" formal theory to contrast it with formal theory based on logical speculation.[32]

Some forty years ago, Thomas and Znaniecki hazarded that one type of qualitative data (autobiographies) might be the most useful kind of data for sociological theory.[33] Anthropologists, however, then and now generally believe that fieldwork data—encompassing observations and interviews as well as case studies and autobiographical accounts—are most useful. And in the recent literature of sociology, there has been some argument on the comparative virtue of various types of qualitative data: for instance, interview *versus* fieldwork data and historical *versus* contemporary data.[34] Regardless of the type of qualitative data preferred, all seem admirably suited for discovery of substantive theory pertaining to the areas and problems with which sociologists are concerned.

NOTES

[1] See A. H. Barton and P. F. Lazarsfeld, "Some Functions of Qualitative Analysis in Social Research," in Lipset and Smelser, *Sociology: The Progress of a Decade* (Englewood Cliffs, N.J.: Prentice-Hall, 1961), pp. 95-122; B. Berelson, *Content Analysis* (Glencoe: Free Press, 1952), pp. 114-34, esp. 133; S. A. Stouffer, *Social Research to Test Ideas* (New York: Free Press, 1962), pp. 1-10, esp. 10; R. K. Merton, *Social Theory and Social Structure* (Glencoe: Free Press, 1957), pp. 15-16 and Chaps. 2 and 3. One author, somewhat ambivalent on this position, seems to agree that discovery in qualitative research is preliminary to rigorous testing, but prefers to establish testing methods applicable to qualitative data using the canons of quantitative work (H. S. Becker, "Problems of Inference and Proof in Participant Observation," *American Sociological Review* [December, 1958], p. 653). For a critique of this general position see H. Blumer, "Sociological Analysis and the 'Variable,'" *American Sociological Review,* 21 (1956), 683-90. Perhaps the latest perspective is the "multiple methodology" approach which sees qualitative analysis as preliminary for some kinds of information (e.g., an enumeration) and the end product for other kinds (e.g., a norm). See M. Zelditch, Jr., "Some Methodological Problems of Field Studies," *American Journal of Sociology* (March, 1962), p. 567; A. Vidich and J. Bensman, "The Validity of Field Data," *Human Organization,* 13 (1954), 20-27; and R. N. Adams and J. J. Preiss, *Human Organization Research* (Homewood, Ill.: Dorsey Press, 1960), pp. 223-24.

[2] The richness of qualitative research for the discovery of substantive theory is well known; for detailed explanations of why this is so see Becker, *op. cit.,* pp. 652-53, 657-58; and H. S. Becker and B. Geer, "The Analysis of Qualitative Field Data," in Adams and Preiss, *op. cit.,* pp. 262-63.

[3] This fact is discussed below in the section, "The Issue of Further Rigor."

[4] This fact is discussed in "Concluding Remarks."

[5] Zelditch, *op. cit.,* p. 575.

[6] This fact is brought out in many ways throughout this paper.

[7] Becker and Geer, *op. cit.,* pp. 270-71.

[8] B. Geer, "First Days in Field Work," in P. E. Hammond, *Chronicles of Social Research* (New York: Basic Books, 1964).

9 Cf., B. Paul, "Interview Techniques and Field Relationships," in A. L. Kroeber, ed., *Anthropology Today* (Chicago: University of Chicago Press, 1953), pp. 430-51.

10Some inexperienced or compulsive researchers, afraid that they are missing important events, fail to create sufficient breathing space for careful analytic memo writing. The same failing is also characteristic of researchers who work with other kinds of qualitative data.

11Again, what is true of fieldwork seems equally true of research using other kinds of qualitative data, such as historical materials, in contrast, say, with researchers who use quantified content-analysis methods upon caches of data.

12Cf., A. Strauss, L. Schatzman, R. Bucher, D. Ehrlich, and M. Sabshin, *Psychiatric Ideologies and Institutions* (New York: Free Press, 1964), Chap. 2. For interviews after field observation see H. Becker, B. Geer, E. Hughes, and A. Strauss, *Boys in White* (Chicago: University of Chicago Press, 1962).

13Though highly unlikely, there is, of course, the small chance that additional data can "explode" an otherwise finished analytic framework and cause the researcher to spend months or years before he is satisfied enough to publish. This hazard is not confined to work with qualitative data, but is especially characteristic of qualitative work.

14Two recent field studies which have compared attributes of a specific type of organization, utilizing many such organizations in many nations, are: W. A. Glaser, "American and Foreign Hospitals: Some Sociological Comparisons," in E. Freidson, ed., *The Hospital in Modern Society* (New York: Free Press, 1963), pp. 37-73; and N. Kaplan, "The Western European Scientific Establishment in Transition," in *American Behavioral Scientist*, 6 (December, 1962), 17-20.

15The logic of our strategy complies with Nagel's directive for "controlled investigation" in any science: "However, every branch of inquiry aiming at reliable general laws concerning empirical subject matter must employ a procedure that, if it is not strictly controlled experimentation, has the essential logical functions of experiment in inquiry" (E. Nagel, *The Structure of Science* [New York: Harcourt, Brace & World, 1961], p. 453). We ourselves used this method in a study reported in a forthcoming volume, *Awareness of Dying*.

16See J. Q. Wilson's strictures on D. C. Thompson's, *The Negro Leadership Class*, in *American Sociological Review*, 28 (December, 1963), 1051-52.

17Consider the full discussion of this point in R. Bendix, "Concepts and Generalizations in Comparative Sociological Studies," *American Sociological Review*, 28 (August, 1963), 532-39.

18The initial advocates in sociology of a search for negative cases have either focused on them within one structure or omitted explicit focus upon structural conditions. They have, rather, focused upon the search for negative incidents within categories of analysis under which they have amassed a series of positive incidents. Becker and Geer, *op. cit.*, pp. 287-88; and A. Lindesmith, *Opiate Addiction* (Bloomingdale: Principia, 1947), Chap. 1.

19This theme is extensively developed throughout H. Zetterberg, *On Theory and Verification in Sociology* (Totowa, N.J.: Bedminster Press, 1963). It is important that one distinguish between the researcher's conviction in the credibility of his theoretical analysis and his conviction that he understands much about the perspectives and meanings of his subjects. Researchers will readily agree that their own theoretical formulations represent credible interpretations of their data—which could be interpreted differently by others—but it would be hard to shake their conviction that they have correctly understood much about the perspectives and meanings of the people whom they have studied.

[20]For a fieldwork account of how tightly closed doors were finally opened after trust was established, see R. Wax, "Twelve Years Later: An Analysis of Field Experience," *American Journal of Sociology,* 63 (1957), 133-42.

[21]The most vigorous of quantitative researchers may write a methodological article from "heart" with no data collection or coding because he simply knows what he knows. He has lived it and he was successful. People will believe him because they know he has been through it. In writing this article, he is merely doing fieldwork on himself.

[22]The researcher's task of conveying credibility is actually much like that of the realistic novelist. The latter generally leaves his analytic framework—his interpretation—much more implicit than does the researcher. Often the novelist's tactics for getting the reader to imagine social reality are more subtle, because he may not only be a more skilled writer but may feel that he can use more license in his presentation. Sometimes too his descriptive task is simpler because his analytic framework is much simpler. Nonetheless, the great novelists have conveyed societal views which readers have long felt to be both complex and real (i.e., credible). We say this not to pit researchers against novelists, but to point out where their respective tasks may be similar and where different.

[23]On sensitizing concepts see H. Blumer, "What Is Wrong with Social Theory," *American Sociological Review,* 19 (February, 1964), 3-10, quote on page 9.

[24]Consider the effort in this direction by H. L. Zetterberg, *Social Theory and Social Practice* (Totowa, N.J.: Bedminster Press, 1962), Chap. 3. The concepts should also be clearly specified so that they can be readily measured by existing techniques, *if* researchers desire to test quantitatively hypotheses based on them.

[25]Note for instance how gullible or unsuspecting readers can believe wholly in purposely fake accounts, such as the papers reprinted in R. Baker, ed., *Psychology in the Wry* (Princeton, N.J.: Nostrand, 1963).

[26]Cf., B. Berger's review of J. Coleman's quantitative study, *The Adolescent Society,* in *Social Problems,* 10 (1963), 394-400; and J. Q. Wilson, *op. cit.* And whether analysis is quantitative or qualitative, later generations of scholars will discount it by placing it within a larger context of public rhetoric; cf., "Appendix: A Note on Imagery in Urban Sociology," in A. Strauss, *Images of the American City* (Glencoe: Free Press, 1961), pp. 255-58.

[27]For instance, when we read that someone has done fieldwork with workers in a factory, we suspect that his interpretive account (as it pertains even to the workers) needs some correction because the administrators have not been similarly studied. What correction is needed may not, of course, be so evident: for instance, some sociologists have studied state mental hospitals from a perspective really borrowed from psychiatry and thus interpreted its structure and functioning from a quasi-psychiatric viewpoint. The needed correction was read in by at least one set of readers, who themselves later studied a mental hospital and came to a rather different conclusion about such institu-

tions (R. Bucher and L. Schatzman, "The Logic of the State Mental Hospital," *Social Problems*, 9 [1962], 337-49). This latter instance suggests that readers are not always merely readers, but can also be or become researchers upon topics about which they have read.

28Consider the discussion of social laws by Nagel, *op. cit.,* pp. 459-66.

29For a few (or many) diverse comments of concern on the trivial results of "precise" quantitative research, see: on their laboring of the obvious, R. K. Merton, "Problem Finding in Sociology," in R. K. Merton, L. Broom, and L. S. Cottrell, Jr., eds., *Sociology Today* (New York: Basic Books, 1959), IV-I; on their uselessness for theory construction, Zetterberg, *On Theory and Verification in Sociology, op. cit.,* Preface, pp. 36, 52, 67; and on their worth in verifying what is already known, A. Etzioni, "Book Review," *American Journal of Sociology*, 67 (January, 1962), 466.

30"While we cannot count on very many research workers being stimulated to conduct crucial tests of middle-range theories, they are likely to be especially stimulated by the concepts that enter into such theories" (H. Hyman, "Reflections on the Relations Between Theory and Research," *The Centennial Review*, 7, no. 4 [Fall, 1963], 449).

31Ignoring the task of discovering substantive theory that is relevant to a given substantive area is the result, in most cases, of believing that formal theories can be directly applied to an area, and that these formal theories supply all the necessary concepts and hypotheses. The consequence is often a forcing of data and neglecting of the relevant concepts and hypotheses that may emerge. Allowing substantive concepts and hypotheses to emerge first on their own, enables the analyst to ascertain which of diverse formal theories may be inclusive of his substantive theories, thus enabling him to be more faithful and less forcing of his data (or more objective and less theoretically biased). This means that one cannot merely apply Parsonian categories right off, but must wait to see whether they are linked to the emergent substantive theory concerning the issue in focus.

32An outstanding example of "grounded" social theory is H. S. Becker, *The Outsiders* (New York: Free Press, 1962).

33W. I. Thomas and F. Znaniecki, *The Polish Peasant in Europe and America* (New York: Knopf, 1918).

34See H. S. Becker and B. Geer, "Participant Observation and Interviewing: A Comparison," *Human Organization*, 16 (1957), 28-34; M. Trow, "Comment," *Human Organization*, 16 (1957), 33-35; and Becker and Geer, "Rejoinder," *Human Organization*, 17 (1958), 39-40.

CHAPTER 29

The Methodology of Participant Observation

Severyn T. Bruyn

In the search for meaning and understanding in human relationships a significant number of sociologists in the classical tradition, as well as in contemporary research, have recognized the importance of participant observation in methodology. The place of this technique in the methodology of social sciences has yet to be thoroughly examined. It still remains a questionable technique for some social scientists largely because it raises some of the most fundamental questions about epistemology and challenges the traditions of science.

This article proposes to confront these questions and challenges in the light of larger perspectives involved in the pursuit of knowledge. To accomplish this purpose we shall review the conclusions of past researchers regarding the social role of the participant observer, then examine questions of epistemology, the challenges the role presents to the scientific perspectives and standards of research, and finally the potential that exists for developing new perspectives for research.

THE SOCIAL ROLE

Certain summary statements can be made regarding the role of the participant observer on the basis of research findings already reported. This should serve to orient our analysis of the methodological foundations of this approach.

1. *The participant observer shares in the life activities and sentiments of people in face-to-face relationships.*

Florence Kluckhohn has thus succinctly described the role as:

... conscious and systematic sharing, in so far as circumstances permit, in the life activities, and on occasion, in the interests and affects of a group of persons.[1]

While the traditional role of the scientist is that of a neutral observer who remains unmoved and unchanged in his examination of phenomena, the

This chapter was originally published by the Society for Applied Anthropology in *Human Organization*, 21: 224-35.

role of the participant observer requires sharing the sentiments of people in social situations, and thus he himself is changed as well as changing to some degree the situation in which he is a participant. However, researchers have found that although he becomes changed through his participation, it is important that part of him remain unchanged and detached. Although "sharing" the experience, he is not entirely of it.

2. *The role of the participant observer requires both detachment and personal involvement.*

In a research report by Morris and Charlotte Schwartz, the involvement of the researcher is recognized and qualified:

The issue is not whether he will become emotionally involved, but rather the nature of the involvement. The involvement, whether it is closer to one end of the continuum (sympathetic identification) or the other end (projective distortion), is very little a function of an observer's role. Rather, it is primarily a function of his experience, awareness, and personality constellation and the way these become integrated with a particular situation . . . Sympathetic identification includes emphatic communication and imaginative participation in the life of the observed through identification and role taking. In this type of involvement the observer is both detached and affectively participating; he feels no need to moralize or judge the interaction; his attitude is one of interested curiosity and matter-of-fact inquiry directed toward understanding the observed.[2]

In seeking to share something of the experience of the observed the researcher must not only become personally involved, he must also acquire the role which can function within the culture of the observed. There is no standard role which he can assume, but the requirements for the selection of the role are evident.

3. *The researcher acquires a social role which is determined by the requirements of the research design and the framework of the culture.*

Some of the types of roles which researchers have considered include: general and specific, active and passive, complementary, and others designated but not fully described. In the Schwartz report on field observation in a mental hospital they note:

The role of the participant observer may be either formal or informal, concealed or revealed; the observer may spend a great deal of time or very little time in the research situation; the participant observer may be an integral part of the social structure or largely peripheral to it.[3]

Active and passive roles are selected for description in their report.

Florence Kluckhohn makes the distinction between general, specific, and complementary roles. In her study of a Mexican village she took the role of a local storekeeper (a role complementary to her customers) and thus came to understand reflectively the lives of the villagers. Her role as a housewife she conceived as a general role similar to that of most women in the village. Other examples of general roles (i.e. identical with a significant portion of persons studied) would be the researcher's role as prisoner in studying prison socialization,[4] or the role of an air force recruit which a researcher undertook in studying a military program.[5]

4. *The scientific interests of the participant observer are interdependent with the cultural framework of the people being studied.*

In his scientific role the participant observer is seeking to apprehend, register, interpret, and conceptualize the social facts and meanings which he finds in a prescribed area of study. He is interested in the people as they are, not as he thinks they ought to be from some standard of his own; he is interested in the uniformities of their culture, in their existent, predictable state of being. To achieve these ends he finds his cultural role an indispensable part of the process.

He finds that only by coming to know people personally can he achieve his scientific aims. In his cultural role he becomes involved, but his procedures, his hypotheses, his experimental design, his social role remain objectively recorded. They are not so rigidly fixed that they cannot be changed. As with all experimental work if he finds that any one of these elements is not broadly enough conceived to encompass the data, he refocuses, reformulates his project in whatever way he finds advisable. He assumes he can do this without ignoring the interests of the people he is observing or the standards of his own research.

The scientific role and the cultural role of the researcher are interdependent and complementary.[6] The personal lives of the people he is studying are of great importance to him in both roles. It may be assumed that without this primary interest in them as persons in his active role as participant observer his study and findings become subject to distortion. His skill in reporting his findings objectively and the means he takes to insure this are also of primary interest to him. He assumes that one dimension makes the other possible. (He also assumes that no wholly "neutral" relation can exist in personal relations; such attempts often result in being impersonal, which is in effect becoming personal in a negative way.) He believes that valuing his subjects as persons increases the likelihood that he will come to understand them in their true state. The two roles not only coexist and complement one another, in some ways they can be seen as two reflections of the same social process as the researcher becomes a natural part of the life of the people he studies.

5. *The social role of the researcher is a natural part of the cultural life of the observed.*

The role of the researcher coincides with the role of the observed in the sense that both reflect the basic social process necessary to live in society. In his description of scientific methodology Cooley has stated:

The human mind participates in social processes in a way that it does not in any other processes. It is itself a sample, a phase, of those processes, and is capable, under favorable circumstances, of so far identifying itself with the general movement of a group as to achieve a remarkably just anticipation of what the group will do. Prediction of this sort is largely intuitive rather than intellectual; . . .[7]

The elements that go into participant observer research are a reflection of the universal process of role-taking in socialization from childhood through adulthood. In his description of a self, G. H. Meade describes the fundamental character of learning as role-taking whose end is the complete self which "reflects the unity and structure of the social process as a whole."[8] Without disregarding the tensions and disharmonies inherent in the social process (which Meade neglected to explore), the aim of the participant observer is to take part in the socialization process just as the other participants do, to the point where his own inner experience can reflect the unity and structure of the whole.

The participant observer has usually been conceived as one who is an outsider and seeks to take part in a culture unlike his own. It is now apparent that the elements that go to comprise the participant observer technique *are fundamental to the social act* (in the Meadean sense) and therefore are to some degree a part of all social research. This explains why a discussion of participant observation must go to the heart of general methodology in the social sciences. The role of the participant observer is in process of refinement, out of the natural social process, just as the role of the physical scientist was refined out of the natural experiments made by ordinary people interested in the world about them.

EPISTEMOLOGICAL BACKGROUNDS

A. Naturalism and Idealism

The technique of any researcher evolves from philosophic traditions and is founded in certain epistemological beliefs about the origin of knowledge. Broadly speaking, two major traditions lying behind the development of the social sciences are naturalism and idealism. Both philosophies have undergone considerable change and development since their modern origin in the seventeenth century.

The formulator of the modern variant of naturalism (having had earlier roots) was Thomas Hobbes, who conceived all of nature as basically materialistic. He believed that all men's actions, thoughts, and feelings could be reduced to their true state as small particles of matter in motion. A later naturalistic interpretation can be illustrated in Jeremy Bentham's official philosophy that all man's actions could be determined and understood on the basis of weighing (literally as would a physicist) the gains and losses people felt existed between pleasureful and painful consequences. A still later development was seen in Karl Marx who raised the particle theory of Hobbes and the physiological theory of Bentham to a broader base in economic determinism. The changing economic forces became the mechanism through which all of culture was determined. Still later, neopositivists broadened the position further to include man's *general behavior* (not simply economic) as the foundation for understanding and predicting man's actions. Throughout this development however, the deterministic-mechanistic image of man was retained and it was assumed that all behavioral phenomena could be quantified.[9] The foundations of modern science have been built from this philosophy.

The modern expression of idealism took form with Berkeley, an English clergyman, who radically held that the external world had no real existence outside of the mental processes themselves. It was clear to him that physical properties could not be known outside the mind, therefore the mind itself was the source of all knowledge. Later developments such as German idealism (as in Kant and Hegel) accepted physical reality but insisted on the supremacy of the mind as a source and creator of knowledge. A still more recent variety, called personal idealism, focuses upon personality as the source of knowledge.

The modern conceptions of idealism base the source of knowledge in experience itself with its many dimensions. Thus, it has broadened to a position which, while emphasizing the importances of certain qualities of the mind to produce knowledge independent of external factors, does not ignore their place in the experience of man. In various ways modern approaches to these early divergent philosophies are interpenetrating as philosophy continues to explore the foundation upon which sciences can build systems of knowledge.[10]

B. The Empirical, Rational, and Intuitive Sources

Empiricism[11] and rationalism are epistemological traditions which have grown to be commonly accepted among social scientists. In various ways they have both been associated with previously described philosophies. Empiricism however, in the narrower usage (associated only with building knowledge from sense data) has largely been associated with naturalism. Rationalism assumes that knowledge may be found or created through the association and dissociation of concepts, that truth may be revealed in the structure of thought. The dispute about which of these sources is more important is no longer serious; it is widely recognized that while different research activities emphasize one or the other, in all experience there is a common interplay, and both are basic to the development of scientific knowledge.

The intuitive capacity of the mind however has been less accepted as a legitimate source of scientific knowledge. Nevertheless the participant observer finds it an important part of his work. Without ignoring the rational process or the importance of his record of sense observations, he must recognize an additional source—the nonrational, nonsensible, affective experience of the observed, as reflected in his own experience. He assumes that there exists in human feelings, a capacity to reveal knowledge which is independent (as well as interdependent with) the rational-empirical sources of knowledge.

The veracity or proof of this position is no more possible outside of itself than is the proof of the rational or empirical traditions outside themselves. These are the initial assumptions that must be made about the nature of knowledge. However the necessity for persuasion or validation remains for social scientists and usually develops through a combination of trusted traditions bearing witness to its own value to the human enterprise. For example one important justifying authority in science today is pragmatism whose major test would be a method's capacity to void knowledge which stands the test of time. Another would be its demonstrated ability to predict or anticipate human action. The participant observer technique has already begun to demonstrate this productiveness, but this should increase still further as the technique becomes increasingly utilized and procedures for its application systematically developed.

In order to clarify and underline the importance of this intuitive epistemological position for the observer, it is necessary to examine in some detail the kinds of data which researchers encounter in their efforts to understand human relationships.

SCIENTIFIC DATA

Social scientific data are symbolic in the sense that all culture is symbolic. A brief review of the basic types of symbols existing in culture should provide a closer look at the subject matter (and the conceptual tools) of the participant observer.

The Sign

George Herbert Meade, Ernst Cassirer, Suzanne Langer, Talcott Parsons, Leslie White and many others have made an important distinction between sign and the symbol which marks the beginning of culture. A sign is any human expression which communicates a message to another in a particularized situation in which the parties are involved. Examples would be the gesture to wave goodbye, or to verbalize "go," or "come here," or to cry for help. The sign is an early development in communication expressed (as Meade illustrates) in the bark of the wolf to the pack or the cluck of a hen to the chickens.[12] The development of language has been traced from the original cry of an organism (sign of need) to a call (a sign expressed to specific individuals) to the word and the differentiation of sentence structures.[13] Anthropologically the graphic expression of this development can be seen from pictographs (illustrations of specific events or things) to ideograms (pictorial symbol of an idea) to phonetic expressions (symbols representing speech sounds). Symbols always stand in place of something or referent. Words may be understood as symbols insofar as they stand for that which is apprehended and are understood by people without making reference to a particular object in their immediate environment. The symbol involves a capacity to abstract and recall; their references become removed from the immediate environment.

Denotative Symbols

The denotative symbol begins where the sign leaves off. These symbols *stand for* observable objects such as chairs or tables. Initially they were in the form of signs directing attention to particular objects, such as the moon, the sun, or Fido the dog. But soon a broader image becomes necessary to communicate not simply the uniqueness of a particular object, but the meaning of objects of a similar nature. The elementary processes of abstraction enter into forming the symbol.

The process is more complex than it would seem to indicate. To know the idea of a table requires considerable previous learning at the tactile or sense reactive level. That is the learner must have had a sense of surface, an impression of solidity, of dimension, etc., before the elements can come together to form something new, a general image, which has a central figure and peripheral possibilities of form which allows judgment as to whether different objects meet primary or secondary requirements.

Denotative symbols are the data with which the strict empiricist is primarily concerned. He is interested in defining operationally the visible world about him. He does this to maintain precision and clarity in his work. However, there is considerably more complexity and indefiniteness than technicians would always admit. A simple reference to a piece of furniture like a sofa has such diverse reflections in our language as davenport, settee, couch, divan, dais, ottoman, daybed, etc., all having their own central images overlapping to some extent. In fact, like the active participant observer, he must make certain inferences that the references he makes are the same among different researchers, *on the basis of verbal agreement.*

Abstract Symbols

As degrees of generality continue to be formulated, the image becomes entirely removed from visibility in the outside world. A symbolic fundament is built out of common experience parts of which (ideas, concepts) begin serving as the source of reference in themselves. For example, the idea of "society" is a highly abstract symbol around which focuses much of sociological theory. Its level of generality is clearly higher than any of its constituent parts, such as "institution," and still more removed from a more denotative component, the "primary group." The theorist assumes, like the operationalist, that there is something common about symbolic development in people which allows agreement in meaning, and if standard procedures are followed, knowledge can be developed at each level of inquiry.

Levy-Bruhl once claimed that primitives could not abstract, that they were prelogical and tended to participate personally in the objects about them without the capacity to differentiate themselves from the inanimate objects. This unconditional description of primitive mentality has since been qualified by recognizing at least an elementary logic in all human culture. The primitive does distinguish between subject and object, but he refuses to believe that

all reality lies in our external perception of it. There is an internal side and there are effects, constraints, from subject to object and from object to subject.[14]

The primitive's failure to develop his logic, to deny the existence of beings in inanimate objects, has been a major basis for the claim to civilized man's superiority. However, in civilized man's efforts to overcome the indistinctiveness and emotional projections of the primitive life, he has become subject to error in denying the other reality, the "sensuous forms" (as Cassirer would describe it aesthetically) of the inner perspective as a source of truth.

Northrop makes the distinction between the theoretic component (highly developed in Western civilization) and the aesthetic component (developed in the East). It is difficult he says, for the Western man to realize or understand Eastern culture because of his irresponsible habit of abstracting everything from experiences. It is difficult for him to appreciate and know a thing for what it is, to know it emotionally, to empathize with it, and consider this an end in itself.[15] As William James would have said, it involves the difference between knowledge about a thing and knowledge of it. The Western scientist is quite capable of developing the former, but quite unprepared to understand the latter.

Emotive Symbols

Like the denotative symbol, "emotive" symbols begin as signs. The origin, however, is to inner needs and feelings rather than indications of external objects. Expressions of pain or surprise, or the child's call for "mommy" are such signs.

In secondary levels of learning these signs, the cry, or call, become emotional conditions which are understood without reference to specific persons. Just as the image of the chair persists through time in the mind of the learner, similarly the emotion of pride or anger takes on a persistence, is talked about, conveyed to others, has a life of its own independent of immediate needs. Thus the tribe develops a feeling of loyalty over a period of time. Ceremonial dancers cultivate religious devotion. The significant feature of the emotive symbol lies in its capacity to persist through time and be shared. It may be evoked by an outside reference; just as the sight of a chair may evoke the idea of one, so the sight of an enemy may evoke the fear or anger; but the inner condition develops an independence which is transmitted among participants and retained over a period of time.

Charles Cooley describes how our language has already given us the data by the mere fact that man has needed to record these states of being:

Under the leading of words we interpret our observation, both external and introspective, according to patterns that have been found helpful by our predecessors. When we have come to use understandingly such words as "kindly," "resolute," "proud," "humble," "angry," "fearful," "lonesome," "sad," and the like, words recalling motions of the mind as well as the body, it shows that we have not only kept a record of our inner life, but have worked up the data into definite conceptions which we can pass on to others by the aid of the common symbol.[16]

Symbols of Sentiment

Emotive symbols move into another stage in which (like abstract symbols) it is not possible to refer to an immediate external cause or reference. Such may be called spiritual symbols or symbols of sentiment representing the spirit of man which has become more deeply set in experience, less moved by outside stimuli, having its own level and pace of development. The expressions of modern man which indicate such conditions, types of anxiety, suffering, joy, are not altogether unknown to primitive man. However, like abstract forms, these symbols are less developed and encountered less frequently.[17]

The primitive's emotional experiences are more particularized in the sense of pain or pleasure, and have some real, if not imaginary, reference to a cause he considers outside himself. Creative suffering perceived as an end in itself, the inner peace in the culture of the mystics, the Buddhistic state of Nirvana, the persistent anxiety of the mobile man in mass society, persist through the daily emotional reactions and changing external stimuli. They vary in their independence from or dependence upon the emotional and physiological needs of the individual and his place in society. Like conceptual development, these symbols (and the conditions they represent) grow more from the association of other like symbols of the inner life than the emotive or denotative symbols to which they are ultimately connected.[18]

Ideological and Substantive Symbols

As these various symbols combine with each other and with the human need for purpose and direction, we can designate other variations on these basic themes. Combinations of emotive and abstract symbols create ideological symbols such as "communism" or "Christianity." Adding denotative references, we find substantive symbols such as the flag or the cross, which represent considerable rational development and deeply felt human interests.

The position of the symbol in the culture of the observed is fundamental to the interpretation made by the participant observer. Robert Redfield describes the various ways an observer may approach this problem by illustrating his efforts to comprehend the inner world of the Mayan villagers of Chan Kom. One approach came to him as several of the villagers traveled with him to the sea coast and expressed amazement at how people could live without maize. Then he began to see the vital position of this symbol in the village life:

So I began to form another way of conceiving parts as related to one another in a system of activity and thought. This third system is neither chainlike or maplike. It is radial: maize is a center and other things are grouped around it, connected to it in different ways, some by a series of useful activities, some by connections of symbolic significance. The mind goes out from maize to agriculture, from maize to social life, from maize to religion. Maize is always the center of things.[19]

The participant observer must comprehend all these basic symbolic forms as he may find them in his area of study. He recognizes that by his acquaintanceship with symbols of sentiment and emotion in a particular setting he is more likely to adequately conceptualize the meaning and significance of events in the lives of those he is observing.

BASIC PERSPECTIVES

Any description of the basic perspectives of men in the pursuit of knowledge necessarily includes only selective abstractions of what in reality merges in varying degrees according to the type of research. Such descriptive statements, in the tradition of the Weberian ideal type, are formulated for the purpose of gaining some further insight into the nature of the participant observer process of research.

Different types of research have indicated two basic perspectives, an inner and outer. The latter assumes that the study of man's *behavior* or conduct is adequate to produce knowledge about social life. The inner perspective assumes that understanding can only be achieved by actively participating in the life of the observed and gaining insight by means of introspection. There is no disjunction between these perspectives in reality because all research involves something of both. However, as one comes to analyze them and the types of research that tend to associate with them, other perspectives reveal themselves as important to understand.

Determinism and Cultural Freedom

As the participant observer enters into the common life of those whom he is studying, he must act within a cultural framework which recognizes a measure of personal freedom, to which responsibility and obligation are attached. The amount and kind of free choice that is recognized varies from culture to culture and such differences become a part of the social role of the researcher.

The frame of reference of freedom which the participant observer assumes would seem to challenge the perspective of scientific determinism which research has inherited from the natural sciences. The dilemma must be resolved at the working level where the participant observer accepts the definition of freedom perceived by his fellow participants, yet also comes to perceive the determining factors in their background.

Social sciences still utilize the perspective of determinism as the basis for interpreting social life; some scientists hold to it as the only correct perspective possible.[20] There should be no need for conflict between the determinism of science and the culture of the observed. There is a rational basis for the researcher to genuinely understand and accept the concept of cultural freedom.

The research design arising from scientific determinism does not generally account for the fact that all factors or variables are to some extent determinants or causes in themselves. Which is cause and which effect depends upon the perspective of the observer. In the cultural framework, the participant observer simply enters into the inner perspective of the determinant, in this case the people themselves, and sees them as determining (causing) the effects about them. From their perspective of personal responsibility and free will, it is legitimately assumed that freedom exists to the extent that knowledge about and power over existential conditions is demonstrable. The two perspectives coexist, have validity, and actually depend upon the position one takes to his subject.

The Causal and Telic Principles

The participant observer seeks to know and become part of the purposes and interests of people. He assumes that all people have aims and that they have some latent or manifest knowledge about means to achieve these aims. The importance of understanding the purposive aspects of social phenomena has been stressed from Durkheim to modern functionalism, but the importance of this perspective to the participant observer requires that it be restated.

Without ignoring causality, in fact being quite aware of causes and effects, he nevertheless comes to act toward people and react toward events within a purposive framework which comes to infuse and pervade his descriptions. The interests and valuations of people become a central pivot around which he guides his conduct and interprets the social setting in which he works.

Analysis and Synthesis

As the participant observer records, interprets, and explains social phenomena, he analyzes it; he takes apart the events and looks at them separately. However, there are two important ways in which contrasting features must be noted by the participant observer. First, he seeks to find some identity with the observed without analyzing them. Analysis at certain stages may prove to be a barrier to his understanding. The researcher seeks a certain kind of communion with the observed and in any efforts to comment descriptively about the situation keeps himself outside it.

There is no place for either rational or emotional comments at the point of intuitive contact. Cooley stresses this point with regard to reflective emotions:

Sympathy in the sense of compassion is a specific emotion or sentiment, and has nothing necessarily in common with sympathy in the sense of communion. It might be thought, perhaps, that compassion was one form of sharing feeling; but this appears not to be the case. The sharing of painful feeling may precede and cause compassion, but is not the same with it. When I feel sorry for a man in disgrace, it is, no doubt, in most cases, because I have imaginatively partaken of his humiliation; but my compassion for him is not the thing that is shared, but is something additional, a comment on the shared feeling. I may imagine how a suffering man feels—sympathize with him in that sense—and be moved not to pity but to disgust, contempt, or perhaps admiration. Our feeling makes all sorts of comments on the imagined feeling of others.[21]

Secondly, the tendency of the participant observer is to seek the essence of the life of the observed, to sum up, to find a central unifying principle. The documents of many anthropologists are evidence of this inclination. Ruth Benedict's descriptions of the two Indian cultures as Apollonian and Dionysian and Opler's culture themes are cases in point.

Of course there are limitations in stressing either mode of interpretation without some reference to the other. The difficulties in synthetic descriptions lay in the tendency to oversimplify (and thereby misunderstand) the nature of the culture. The difficulties of analysis lay in the failure to see the whole, and thereby the significance of the parts. All researchers inescapably apply both modes but the conditions under which they work cause one or the other to be emphasized.

Types of Concepts: Operational and Sensitizing

All scientific research involves the conceptualization of data. The types of concepts employed differ with the kinds of research design. The operational concept is most frequently used in quantitative research. It is defined as a statement of the specific procedures or operations used to identify and measure a phenomenon under study. Another kind of concept more frequently used in research has been described by Herbert Blumer as the "sensitizing concept." Blumer raises the question of how these concepts can be formulated and communicated. He notes that, rather than by formal definitions,

It is accomplished instead by exposition which yields a meaningful picture, abetted by apt illustrations which enable one to grasp the reference in terms of one's own experience.[22]

This statement describes the character of much of participant observer research.

Contrary to the opinion of some operationalists, sensitizing concepts are not all necessarily on the road to becoming definitive, as though they were ideal. Such a position would deny the reality which they represent. By operationalizing a concept, one changes its meaning. Although it is true that all data are subject to measurement, it is also true that when this is done the distinctive character and meaning of the data is lost. Defining an emotion or sentiment, for example, as that which is measured by certain visceral responses, cannot convey the true meaning of that feeling. Sensitizing concepts, therefore, have a right to their own existence without changing their expression by way of enumeration.

Table 1

	Inner Perspective	*Outer Perspective*
Epistemological Background	Idealism Intuitive imagination	Natural materialism Logical empiricism
Explanatory Principle	Teleology	Causality
Acting Framework	Cultural freedom	Scientific determinism
Methods and Techniques	Participant observation Personal documents	Statistics
Aims	Sensitive understanding of human values, institutions; anticipation of new directions	Adequate measurement and prediction of human behavior
Mode of Study	Synthetic emphasis	Analytic emphasis
Concepts	Sensitizing	Operational

Merging Reality

Anyone accustomed to the discipline of research knows that the types listed in Table 1 are only abstractions of what in reality tends to merge together in various ways. The ways in which this dichotomy of perspectives (illustrated in Table 1) does not fit reality is as important to understand as the abstraction itself.

A complete statement of how these divergent perspectives have crossed in history and in the configuration of actual research projects would involve a lengthy dissertation. However, a few basic points will illustrate the crossings: 1. The participant observer is sometimes a part of a larger quantitative study and may enumerate his data to contribute solely to the larger quantitative study. 2. A functional (telic) analysis of social phenomena may very well also be quantitative in nature. 3. The history of idealism as an epistemological theory has also included theories of determinism. 4. Sociological analysis need not be cast in a deterministic framework.[23] 5. The participant observer (as has been noted) is aided by his senses and reason as well as by intuition; the logical empiricist is aided by intuition.[24] 6. Max Weber's concept of bureaucracy involved a process of synthesis (putting together of significant elements) as well as analysis, as does most of theoretical work.

With these and other exceptions which could be noted, the ideal type still stands on the basis of the emphasis which is given to each perspective. That is, the use of the participant observer to simply quantify data, while useful in some cases, is not the general role he assumes; while quantitative methods are used in functional analysis, the functional interpretations must be made on the basis of participant observation which characterizes the work of researchers who study their own culture;[25] while at times idealism has included deterministic perspectives, its emphasis in history has been on freedom; while the rational-empirical-intuitive capacities are interdependent, one or another is more evident in different research designs; much of highly abstract theoretical formulation involves intuitive observation.[26]

SCIENTIFIC STANDARDS

The standards of objectivity, control, reliability and validity are still important concerns for the participant observer. These guides to research require reexamination in the light of what they mean today.

Objectivity

Objectivity is an ideal, a state which is always in process of becoming. It is never fully achieved by any investigator in any final sense. It is a condition of reporting without prejudice, but it need not be a report without feeling or sentiment. There are two ways in which the participant observer assumes that feeling and objectivity may coexist.

First, it is possible for the investigator to have a feeling of respect for his subjects and remain open and unprejudiced in apprehending and reporting about their way of life. Second, it is possible for the sentiments of people being studied to be conveyed in the report without prejudicing the accuracy of correctness of the report itself.

Maurice Stein describes a "dramatic theory" developing among some sociological circles which focuses the problem of the participant observer.

From a dramatic standpoint, the central problem of the community sociologist is to achieve an objective perspective that encompasses the partial perspectives held by various groups in the community in such a fashion as to call attention to hidden processes without losing sight of the meanings of the various partial perspectives. The playwright seeks to present his characters sympathetically without going so far as to allow the sympathy they evoke to swallow the larger meanings that emerge when they are viewed within the context of the entire plot and action of the play. The play suffers as much when the context is allowed to override full presentation of diverse characters. The playwright seeks a profound balance and it is similar to the balance sought by the community sociologist.

Dramatic sensibility then consists of the capacity to encompass multiple interpretations of a social world within a larger context which distinguishes objective structures without obliterating subjective meanings.[27]

Participant observer methodology broadens the limits of the scientific framework to permit ideas for social and cultural studies which would not ordinarily be entertained.

Reliability and Validity

The participant observer does not need to defend the reliability or validity of his data (in the traditional sense) in certain stages of his work. This point has been sufficiently discussed in the research on personal documents.[28] As research proceeds, however, the accuracy of the denotative references of the subject's statements adds to the objectivity of the research. A description of the connection between the inner and the outer world of the subject is fundamental to a complete report.

The participant observer technique in some ways has already proven itself to be more reliable than other methods available. In the article previously quoted, Florence Kluckhohn describes how the direct interview and the questionnaire create special or unnatural situations. The subject may not know how to respond to formal methods, may unconsciously or purposely err, or may have a faulty memory. In contrast, the participant observer is there in the social setting which the interviewer may be seeking to learn about, and has the opportunity to record what actually happens. He is in a position to evaluate any rationalizations which the subject may make to a questionnaire or a formal interview.

Guides to Adequate Research

Rules which are appropriate for the participant observer to follow in his research are generally applicable to all research. Nevertheless, through practical experience, there is developing a know-how, and a set of principles which guide the observer around the pitfalls which are peculiar to his kind of work. A few of these guides can be summarized in the following directives.

1. *Examine all significant rules existing in counter-position in a circumscribed social setting*

The inclination of observers is to so identify with a particular segment of the population being studied that their work is hindered or their reporting is obstructed. Two pitfalls are in evidence here. First, the tendency of "over-rapport" in which too close a contact with the observed does not allow an investigation into certain questions without serious breech of the relationship.[29]

Second, the tendency to report sympathetically the plight of the subject under study. For example, studies of the juvenile delinquent in his natural setting have tended in some cases to romanticize his role. Examining only the symbolic meaning of "cop" in the life of the young slum dweller may shut out or overshadow the meaning of "brat" or "cop-killer" for the police officer. The participant observer should include both subject and object in contra-position to convey objectively the social context.

2. *Relate the research problem to a larger social context*

In the field of industrial relations the role of the laborer needs not only to be examined with reference to the counter-position of manager, but ideally the two powers need relating to the community and the economic system in the context of the whole society. There are limits to any research problem to be sure, but accurate references to the nature of the larger context adds to the objectivity of the report.

3. *Examine and describe the participant observer's own status in the social system*

A participant observer can very well make use of the findings and guides developed in the sociology of knowledge as a bridge from the biases inherent in his social position to a point of objectivity. Merton's paradigm is a good beginning guide.[30]

The stages of his acceptance into the community are vital to the kind of data he will receive.[31] The kind of image which those around him have of him provides a basis for their response to him. By examining and reporting these facts carefully, the research may avoid this easy pitfall.

4. *Observe the subjects under contrasting social and isolated settings*

Misconceptions have been avoided and insight added when this directive is followed. Howard Becker reports an experience in studying medical students:

> Thus, students in their clinical years may express deeply "idealistic" sentiments about medicine when alone with the observer, but behave and talk in a very "cynical" way when surrounded by fellow students. An alternative to judging one or the other of these situations as more reliable is to view each datum as valuable in itself, but with respect to different conclusions. In the example above, we might conclude that group norms may not sanction their expression.[32]

5. *Evaluate the information as any personal document*[33]

6. *Indicate the proportion or segment of the group which expresses the norms or conduct being recorded*

7. *Carefully specify the procedures used so that other investigators may follow and check the findings from the same (and from different) social positions in the setting under study*

8. *Examine indexes of distortion in reporting and evaluate the data with reference to them*[34]

NEW PERSPECTIVES

The study of participant observation stimulates new perspectives. Just as the social scientist has consciously transposed and developed his techniques and methodology from the physical and organic sciences, so he may become conscious of the possibilities in other disciplines, including the humanities and the arts. He is far from alone in his pursuit of the meaning and objective character of culture and social conduct. He has a special opportunity to produce new blends, new research which will cast the social scene into a more human (and therefore a more realistic) form.[35]

Given the separate academic disciplines existing in their own right, there is still room for considerable fruitful exchange among them. For example, the fact that the subject matter of the social sciences and literature is so similar, makes it unusual that so little attention has been given to studying and comparing the approaches of each. The social scientific descriptions of latent and manifest functions, of social incongruities and dysfunctions in institutional settings, have long been a part of the devices of literary expression.

In the rhetorical allusion, in satire and irony, in the metaphor, the analogy and allegory, in the parable, and many other age-old artistic and literary modes, may be found important instruments of inquiry and analysis, yet unexamined in the methods of sociological studies. The employment of such literary devices need not distort or misrepresent the essential purpose of sociological reporting. As techniques to convey social meaning (derived from empirical studies), they can be as useful and vital as have been the modes of logic or statistical analysis to scientific research.

Such literary devices need not be conceived as masked instruments of ideological or moral doctrine. They should rather be seen as tools of the intellectual craftsman to be used well or badly according to his training and experience. In a rather thorough analysis of the use of allegory in modern literature, Edwin Honig summarizes its instrumental character:

In one of its aspects allegory is a rhetorical instrument used by strategists of all sorts in their struggle to gain power or to maintain a system of beliefs. (Such usage and the motives lurking behind it have recently had the close study of critics as part of the semantic problem of symbolic action.) In addition to serving the expression of ideological aims, allegory is a fundamental device of hypothetical construction. In this broad way allegory is part of the creative process, observable in all literature generally, where the formulation of vital beliefs seems essential to maximum expressiveness.

The literary allegory does not oppose a realistic account of the universe. Its very power lies in its giving proof to the physical and ethical realities of life objectively conceived.[36]

Some of these literary mechanisms, have been built into the structure of language from its very beginnings.[37] With language so basic to social life, sociologists are coming to see their fundamental place in their work. Anthropologists have already recognized their importance in the study of primitive society. Robert Redfield describes the necessity of the ethnographer and the sociologist to make use of such devices in making their descriptions of community life.

In the portraitures accomplished by art, exaggerations, distortions and substitutions of one sort or another play important parts. Caricature and satire are special forms of portraiture. Each describes the whole by overemphasizing something felt to be significantly true of the whole. Metaphor and analogy offer different and parallel images for understanding the whole, as does the parable: a narrative standing for a human something other than itself. And in the more nearly scientific portraiture of communities, metaphors and analogies play a useful part. No one expects Professor Fortes to produce the tangible warp and woof of Tallensi social structure; the words bring forward a metaphor which helps us to understand Tallensi life, and, indeed, the concept of social structure itself.[38]

There is no longer a necessity to justify the use of these rhetorical figures. The need now is for their study, and more critical use as part of the methodology of the social sciences.

The parable has its own place in the record of man's search for knowledge. It has often been employed by charismatic founders of religious movements in an effort to convey meanings which they believe have not yet been grasped by their followers. The function of the parable is to set a moral or spiritual truth aside from the usual affections of the self so that it can be grasped more objectively or at least on another level of experience. It is usually a short fictitious narrative which is intentionally obscured so that it requires some reflective thought before it is grasped. It is not a device for hidden persuasion; it requires voluntary effort to see the meaning. It functions to establish or verify a new experience, a new understanding of an old principle, or a new state of mind. Students of theology have much to contribute to the sociologist in their studies of this medium of communication. Sociologists can utilize such knowledge in their analysis of the diffusion of the religious movement throughout the society.

Such studies have various applications to the field of sociology. They can increase our understanding of the social character of language; they can cast light on the field of communication and studies of socialization; they can act as an enhancement (as well as a self-corrective)[39] of professional descriptions of social life.

The field of art has its own contributions to make. A study of the state of the aesthetic observer viewing an art object cannot help but add insight into the role of the participant observer as he observes the actors in his social setting. In a provocative discussion of aesthetic experience, Cassirer comes to Aristotle's theory of catharsis and interprets how, through tragic poetry, a person takes on new attitudes toward his emotions.

The soul experiences the emotions of pity and fear, but instead of being disturbed and disquieted by them it is brought to a state of rest and peace. At first sight this would seem to be a contradiction. For what Aristotle looks upon as the effect of tragedy is a synthesis of two moments which in real life, in our practical existence, exclude each other. The highest intensification of our emotional life is thought of as at the same time giving us a sense of repose. We live through all our passions feeling their full ravages and highest intensity. But what we leave behind when passing the threshold of art is the hard pressure, the compulsion of our emotions; and he is able to transfer this mastery to the spectators. In his work we are not swayed and carried away by our emotions. Aesthetic freedom is not the absence of passions, not stoic apathy, but just the contrary. It means that our emotional life acquires its greatest strength, and that in this very strength it changes its form. For here we no longer live in the immediate reality of things but in a world of pure sensuous forms. In this world all our feelings undergo a sort of transubstantiation with respect to their essence and their character. The passions themselves are relieved of their material burden. We feel their form and their life but not their encumbrance. The calmness of the work of art is, paradoxically, a dynamic, not a static calmness.[40]

Cassirer quotes Hamlet in speaking of the function of dramatic art which might as well be interpreted as the function of the participant observer in recording and interpreting his observations of a particular culture.

The purpose of playing, [as Hamlet explains] both at the first and now, was and is, to hold, as 'twere, the mirror up to nature; to show virtues her own feature, scorn her own image, and the very age and body of the time his form and pressure.

But the image of a passion is not the passion itself. The poet represents a passion but does not infect us with this passion. At a Shakespeare play we are not infected with the ambition of Macbeth, with the cruelty of Richard III, or with the jealousy of Othello. We are not at the mercy of these emotions; we look through them; we seem to penetrate into their very nature of essence. . . . It is not the degree of intensification and illumination which is the measure of the excellence of art.[41]

The cultural organization of people may be viewed in many ways other than its symbolic character, which has been of principle use in this article. It can be viewed as an aesthetic creation and described from the models of art criticism. For example, culture, like any art object, has many dimensions: its material product, its expression, its form, its function in the social order. If the sociologist were to begin by analyzing the *form* which culture assumes, by using a model in art criticism, he would guide his study through the principles of harmony, balance, centrality, and development, and pursue his analysis by way of their derivatives—recurrence, similarity, gradation, variation, hierarchy, and progression, all of which can be aesthetically perceived and reported in an empirical study of a cultural system.[42]

The technique of participant observation is basic to the methodology of the social sciences. It presents real dilemmas for the researcher who identifies his field solely with the physical sciences. In this article the congruities and incongruities of these dilemmas have been sketched and judged in the light of the scholarly pursuit of knowledge. This pursuit is conceived as a creative one in which new techniques, new perspectives are continually being formulated. The methods of the social sciences cannot remain static; in full regard of the standards of research which are its heritage, it must move on in its probe of the character, the drama, and the meaning of human enterprise.

NOTES

[1] Florence Kluckhohn, "The Participant-Observer Technique in Small Communities," *American Journal of Sociology,* 46 (November, 1940), 331.

[2] Morris S. Schwartz and Charlotte G. Schwartz, "Problems in Participant Observation," *American Journal of Sociology,* 60 (January, 1955), 350.

[3] *Ibid.,* 344.

[4] Hans Reimer, "Socialization in the Prison Community," *American Prison Association Proceedings* (1937), 151-155.

[5] Mortimer A. Sullivan, Jr., Stuart A. Queen, and Ralph C. Patrick, Jr., "Participant Observation in a Military Program," *American Sociological Review,* 23 (December, 1958), 660-667.

[6] The problems and conflicts which can arise between these roles (not the subject of discussion here) are reported elsewhere. See: William Foote Whyte, *Street Corner Society* (University of Chicago Press, 1955), pp. 279-358; Arthur J. Vidich, "Freedom and Responsibility in Research," *Human Organization,* 19 (Spring, 1960, No. 1), 3-4.

[7] Charles Cooley, *Sociological Theory and Social Research* (Henry Holt & Co., 1930), p. 308.

[8] Anselm Strauss (ed.), *The Social Psychology of George Herbert Meade* (University of Chicago Press, 1956), p. 221.

[9] Recent conceptions of naturalism broaden its form to cut across the stream of Western thought, including some modern strains of idealism. See: Vergilus Ferme, "Varieties of Naturalism," in *A History of Philosophical Systems* (The Philosophy Library, 1950), pp. 429-440.

[10] For a modern system of metaphysics which links the traditions of idealism and naturalism see: D. W. Gotshalk, *Metaphysics in Modern Times* (University of Chicago Press, 1940).

[11] The term empiricism has developed varied meanings which can be described on a continuum from rigidly defined procedures for obtaining sense data with no inferences of a "subjective" kind, to the acquisition of knowledge on the basis of experience, which stands in contrast to the normative or ethical field of knowledge. The usage in this article refers to the former end of the continuum.

[12] Strauss (ed.), *op. cit.,* p. 213.

[13] G. Revesz, *The Origins and Prehistory of Language* (Longmans Green and Co., 1956).

[14] Paul Radin, *The World of Primitive Man* (Henry Schaman, Inc., 1953), p. 49.

[15] Filmer Stuart Cuckow Northrop, *Meeting of East and the West* (Macmillan, 1946).

[16] Cooley, *op. cit.,* p. 299.

[17] An example of primitive suffering which appears from the report to exist at this level of symbolization may be found in: Knud Rasmussen, *Observations on the Intellectual Culture of the Caribou Eskimo* (Copenhagen, 1930), pp. 52-55. Quoted in Radin, *op. cit.,* pp. 76-78.

[18] This rough classification of symbols could obviously bear further analysis, but remains in this form only to indicate the kinds of cultural data the participant observer must learn to apprehend and interpret.

[19] Robert Redfield, *The Little Community* (University of Chicago Press, 1955), p. 22.

[20]Donald R. Taft, *Criminology* (Macmillan, 1956), pp. 343-346.

[21]Cooley, *op. cit.,* p. 102 n.

[22]Herbert Blumer, "What Is Wrong with Social Theory?" *American Sociological Review,* 19 (February, 1954, No. 1), 9.

[23]McIver's concept of "dynamic assessment" illustrates an effort to overcome the deterministic perspective. Robert M. McIver, *Social Causation* (Ginn and Co., 1942), pp. 292-293.

[24]From his logical perspective, any discovery not evident in operational procedure would be defined as "rational processes" operating at the subliminal level of consciousness.

[25]Arthur J. Vidich, "Participant Observation and the Collection and Interpretation of Data," *American Journal of Sociology,* 60 (January, 1955), 385.

[26]Contrariwise, participant observation has contributed to the breakdown of Weber's concept into more predictable parts. Alvin W. Gouldner, *Patterns of Industrial Bureaucracy* (The Free Press, 1954).

[27]Maurice R. Stein, *The Eclipse of Community* (Princeton University Press, 1960), p. 325.

[28]"It should be pointed out, also, that the validity and value of the personal document are not dependent upon its objectivity and veracity. It is not expected that the delinquent will necessarily describe his life situations objectively. On the contrary, it is desired that his story will reflect his own personal attitudes and interpretations, for it is just these personal factors which are so important in the study and treatment of the case. Thus, rationalizations, fabrications, prejudices, exaggerations, are quite as valuable as objective descriptions, provided of course, that these reactions be properly identified and classified." Clifford Shaw, *The Jack-Roller* (Albert Saifer Publications, 1930), pp. 2-3.

[29]S. M. Miller, "The Participant Observer and Over-Rapport," *American Sociological Review,* 17 (February, 1952), 97-99.

[30]Robert Merton, *Social Theory and Social Structure* (The Free Press, 1949), pp. 217-245.

[31]Robert W. James, "A Note on Phases of the Community Role of the Participant-Observer," *American Sociological Review,* 26 (June, 1961), 446-450.

[32]Howard S. Becker, "Problems of Inference and Proof in Participant Observation," *American Sociological Review,* 23 (December, 1958), 655.

[33]Louis Gottschalk, Clyde Kluckhohn, and Robert Angell, *The Use of Personal Documents in History, Anthropology and Sociology* (New York Social Science Research Council, 1945), pp. 15-27, 38-47. Reference in Howard S. Becker, *op. cit.,* p. 654.

[34]Schwartz and Schwartz, *op. cit.,* p. 347.

[35]This does not call for a super-discipline or new eclecticism among the social sciences. Like other disciplines they are circumscribed in their search for knowledge. The physical sciences do not wrestle with purpose in their data; the biological sciences do not reckon with sentiment; art, literature and drama do not characteristically pursue knowledge systematically, building propositions into a coherent theory of life. The social scientists in their turn do not search out the uniqueness of an event as an end in itself as does the poet or the artist. The social scientists cannot derive moral truths out of their studies as would the theologian or a playwright.

36Edwin Honig, *Dark Conceit* (Walker-dePerry, Inc., 1959), pp. 179-180.

37Susanne K. Langer, *Philosophy in a New Key* (Mentor Books, 1942), pp. 111-115.

38Redfield, *op. cit.,* p. 162.

39It is worthwhile to examine the use of metaphors, similes, a set of images, in any sociological analysis as they affect the total meaning conveyed to the reader. Caroline Spurgeon sets an example by her study of the substructure of Shakespeare's tragedies. By the use of various literary figures the reader is unwittingly led to conclusions by way of various literary devices. For example, in Hamlet the various images of disease (ulcer, cancer), a motif which suggests that the Prince is not to blame, but the whole state of Denmark is diseased. Caroline Spurgeon, *Shakespeare's Imagery and What It Tells Us* (Cambridge, 1935).

40Ernst Cassirer, *An Essay on Man* (Doubleday, 1956), p. 190.

41*Ibid.*

42D. W. Gotshalk, *Art and The Social Order* (University of Chicago Press, 1947), p. 114. This text presents a most unusual model for art criticism.

CHAPTER 30

Social Theory in Field Research

Joseph Bensman and Arthur Vidich

In the last fifteen years a central concern of both sociology and anthropology has been the relationship between theory and research. One of the turning points in this discussion was Merton's comment on the position of sociological theory,[1] in which he calls for more attention to "theories of the middle range"—"theories intermediate to the minor working hypotheses evolved in abundance during the day-by-day routines of research, and the all-inclusive speculations comprising a master conceptual scheme from which it is hoped to derive a very large number of empirically observed uniformities of social behavior."[2] Other studies addressed to issues in the relationship between theory and research are represented in the work of Mills, Blumer, Becker, Abel, A. K. Davis, Becker and Boskoff, Znaniecki, Borgatta and Meyer, Coser and Rosenberg, and Goode and Hatt, to mention only a few. All these authors have criticized the hiatus between low-level theory dealing with factually exact minutiae and the world-sweeping generalizations of theorists who appear to fail to appreciate the time-consuming task of systematically gathering and interpreting data. In addition, the older classical theorists have been explicitly criticized for being more interested in probing specific problems than in developing theoretical systems, independent of specific cases. This has led to a movement to construct a general theory that can be independent of specific data, but for the most part the authors mentioned have joined the issue on the disparity between generalized theory and low-level theory.

Two methods have been developed to provide a link between empirical observations and higher theory:

1. Closed logical-deductive models which presuppose that *co-ordinates* can be established which will make possible linkages between the models and the open systems of the empirical world.[3] When the general dimensions of elements or units of systems have been specified, the investigator can develop complex models of systems based on the various combinations and relation-

This chapter was originally published by the University of Chicago Press in the *American Journal of Sociology,* 65: 577-84.

ships of the elements in them. It may be a personality system, a terminologi-
cal system, a social system, a cultural system, a kinship system, a motivational
system, etc. A fundamental method in the construction of such systems is the
comparison of specific empirically open systems with the abstract, common
elements necessary to any social system.

2. The "codification of theoretical perspectives,"[4] in which the researcher-theorist attempts to state systematically the relationship of existing
theories to each other. Specific and discrete theories which have been used in
the past on specific problems are examined, and the investigator attempts to
discover the fundamental dimensions, implicit and explicit, of each, after
which he compares them.[5] In making comparisons, the codifier discovers overlapping areas, convergences, different levels of generality and generalization,
and different vectors of observation and perspective. He constructs paradigms
and models of the various theories so as to offer a complete theoretical point
of view which points to the data necessary to answer theoretical problems.
The net product is a heuristic model which serves as a basis for future
research.

Both these approaches to theory have been offered as corrections of the
unsystematic uses to which theory has been put in the past. It is useful,
however, to inquire what the older "unsystematic" and "specific" theory
purports to do and how it focuses on the relationship between theory and
research. Blumer has indicated that adherence to unsystematic theories
sensitizes the theorist and the researcher who is familiar with a wide range of
theories to a plurality of possibilities—to wide ranges of data.[6] Shils has
specifically shown how the older, unsystematic theorists have helped him to
locate and define one of the major problem areas in modern society, and he
provides a vivid description of their part in the evolution of his own research
and his perspective on society.[7] Blumer and Shils both show that the researcher-theorist can probe and check his data against a number of perspectives in theory and then discern the theoretical possibilities of them.[8] The
researcher discovers novel and previously unspecified relationships in his data.
Unsystematic theory, in this way, can lead to creative work.

To explore systematically one way in which unsystematic theories have
been used, we will confine ourselves to specific research problems in which we
have recently been engaged:[9] How is a small rural community related to the
large-scale mass society? How does the mass society affect the public and
inner life of the individuals of the community? How does the mass society
affect the social structure of the town, particularly its class structure and the
character of its institutional arrangements? What is the response of the small
town institutionally and individually, to the institutions and agencies of the
mass society that affect it?

EVOCATION OF THEORY FROM OBSERVATION

In response to the research organization's inquiry into possible sources of creativity among members of the community,[10] the observer's attention was directed to the locally owned and operated telephone company, whose management was considering a program of expansion. A newspaper's announcement of a proposed plan to install a new telephone system, with underground cables, dial phones, and an automatic central switchboard, offered an example of creative activity in community life which seemed ideal for investigation.

It was discovered that the force behind the drive for expansion was not the local operator but the state telephone company. In fact, the elderly local owner and policy-maker would have preferred to keep the installation as it was, since he had neither the stamina nor the capital to undertake the expansion. However, he could not resist the expansion program because he was dependent on the state company.

The local system was linked to the state system, through connecting trunks and long-distance lines, to all neighboring towns and the state and the nation at large. In addition, the local company's installations and finances bound it closely to the state company, which provided it with an auditing service, engineering consultants, advertising layouts, etc. The responsibilities of the local company were for maintenance, collections, and ownership. The state company was interested in promoting the expansion program because it found the local installation cumbersome and awkward; incoming calls could not be handled easily or automatically, and much attention from outside specialists was required. All these irritants could be removed, and service could be improved, by modernization.

The state company did not want to buy the local company. It appeared that it wanted to retain this and other independents as "competing independent companies." The local owner could not close down, though he might have liked to, because the state Public Service Commission would not permit termination of a public service. Since the company existed and since some improvements had to be made, the local community announced and undertook the expansion program. Almost nothing about the expansion, however, could be attributed to local action.

When the various external influences in the local "spontaneous" action were noticed, the attention of the authors was directed to an entirely different range of problems from those which led to the original inquiry. Not only were state agencies, other bureaucracies, and a whole range of experts decisive in the case of the telephone company but similar connections and influences were at work in politics, education, religion, and the cultural life of the community. Local educational policy, religious affairs, public policy and politics—all were intimately related to policy-determining groups far removed from the town. The question then was: How is it possible to comprehend and interpret the relationships between local and external action in a way that is true to the basic facts and elements observed? We turned our attention to various unsystematic and unsystematized theories developed in the past to handle similar data and problems: those of Redfield, Weber, Tönnies, Veblen, Merton, Lynd, Warner, Mills, Sapir, and Tumin. In each case we applied their perspectives to our data. In effect, we asked: "What in their theories would permit us to comprehend our data?"

In the case of each theory which our initial finding made salient, we had a directive for data which could be elicited by further field research. Thus, for example, Veblen's study of the country town makes the point that the political conservatism of rural life rests in the rural village because economically it dominates the surrounding agricultural area. We did not find this to correspond with our observations and could only account for the difference by noting that Veblen wrote in a day when rural banks were strong and apparently autonomous agencies. While many things in Veblen's study of the country town rang true, it did not provide us with a basis for further investigation of our particular problem. On the other hand, Sapir's analysis of spurious culture, which emphasizes the role of cultural imports, directed us to view all phases of the cultural life of the community as a successive series of imports made at different times since 1890. In short, existing theory gave our field work a focus, and we could conduct it along the lines thereby suggested.

Theories were helpful in opening our eyes to specific facts about our problem. For example, Sapir called our attention to the agencies of cultural penetration; Mills and Selznick, to the agencies of institutional penetration and organizational co-optation. In some instances a theorist's minor point became a central point to us, while his central point seemed irrelevant. In no case did we view any theory as offering us a solution to our problem, nor did we use any one theory exclusively to direct our observations. Research, for us, did not demonstrate, document, or annotate theory, but rather it exhausted the theories that came to our attention. Sapir's theory of the genuine culture was exhausted when nothing was found in the cultural life of the community that was indigenous to it—when everything cultural could be traced to an external source. In our procedure a theory was exhausted if and when it either yielded little follow-up data or if the data suggested by the theory were not forthcoming.

THE EXHAUSTING AND "DESTRUCTION" OF THEORIES

If a theoretical perspective does not yield the expected data, the question to be raised is: What facts and what theories are necessary to account for the gaps left by the specific theory? When one set of theories does not exhaust the potentialities of the data, other sets can be employed to point to and to explain the facts which remain unexplained. Thus, for any initial statement of the field problem a whole series of theories may be successively applied, each yielding different orders of data and each perhaps being limited by the special perspectives and dimensions on which it is predicted.[11]

The relationships between theories and levels, orders and vectors of analysis, are not resolved a priori but rather on the basis of the contribution of each perspective to the solution of the research problem. The order achieved (if the research is successful) is not the logical order of concepts, but the order of uniformities in the social structure of the community. The value of these unsystematic theories is not in their formal order but in their heuristic usefulness.

Each of the theories provides a set of questions asked of the data, and the data lead to the continuous destruction of unproductive theories whenever the theories no longer yield new data or fail to solve the original problem. The reverse is also true: the theory may lead to the evocation of new data by focusing observation and its assessment.

THE SUBSTITUTION OF THEORIES

However, it has been our experience that, when new data are evoked by a theory, they lead quite frequently to the reformulation of the research problem, sometimes in a way that leaves the original theories (in this case dealing with penetration, external influences, etc.) inadequate. This is the case in which the data evoked by the observation forces such a radical shift in perspective that new theories must be called forth. For example, in tracing both the impact of the mass society on the community and the response of the community to agencies of the mass society, it was relatively easy to discover that different social and economic classes responded in different ways. Farmers as a class, for example, were the only group directly protected and aided by federal legislation, but not all farmers responded similarly to the benefits it brought them. A farmer's reaction to federal legislation had an important effect on his local class position. Small businessmen had lost their monopoly of the local market to the large urban chains, and they responded to the loss in a psychologically and economically defensive manner. The connections of the professional class to the outside world were almost exclusively cultural, but these enhanced their prestige in the local community, etc. In examining the problem of penetration, we could not look at the town as a unified whole but had to examine how each class was related to the outside world.

As a result of these observations it was necessary to recast our problem as a consideration of class. Class had to be considered, however, in terms not only of the specific problem of mass society but also of the general theories of class. In posing our problem as a class problem, again a whole range of new theories was evoked, including those of Warner, Lynd, Kaufman, Hollingshead,

Weber, and Marx. However, again, theories of class were not considered *sui generis* but rather as pragmatic devices which would bring us to a solution to the original problem; that is, the alternative data which would be selected by different theories were considered initially only in terms necessary to solve the problem of the relationship of the local class structure to the mass society, using as many dimensions as theory would allow. The new focus meant making an examination of all relevant class data.

When the data had been re-examined and additional research had been conducted on class, theory was used in an additional way. The conception of the class structure of the community which we had developed in our research was criticized in the light of the class theories with which we were working.

THEORIES IN THE CRITICISM OF FIELD WORK

The procedure we followed was to take various theories of class and to postulate them as hypothetically fruitful and, then, to ask what would the hypothetical yield of each be toward exhausting the data then locally available. Some data that should have been elicited by certain of the theories were not present in the initial field work. The question was then raised: Is this a deficiency of the theory or of the field work? It was necessary to reanalyze the data already gathered and to make additional observations in order to make sure the fault was not the researcher's in these theoretical respects. This does not mean that all theories were equally productive or, in fact, productive at all.

We found that the prestige associations reported in Warner's work were not to be found in the initial analysis of our data. We postulated Warner as a critic of our analysis and then found that we had to ask ourselves why our analysis had not revealed socially exclusive local groups based on prestige. However, while Warner's system forced us to find groups of the type he describes, the class system we had discovered and described did not appear in most other respects to fit his model.[12] This does not prove or disprove the validity of Warner's work, which might in other communities be more meaningful; however, it did not cover the whole range of our data. In the same way, the theories of Hollingshead yielded valuable data, but again the phenomena were not entirely the same.

Theories of class led to another refocusing of the problem, this time in the area of politics.[13] It became apparent that members of different classes played different roles in local political life. Accordingly, we considered the political theories of Weber, Centers, Marx, V. O. Key, Mosca, Neumann, Michel, and Mills.

Each successive application of theory, derived in each instance from stimulation given by the immediately preceding investigation, caused us to take into account new orders of data which in turn forced us to select different types of theory. Thus the method compelled us to consider not only politics but the relationship between political and non-political leadership, between the public ideology of the town and the private lives of its members, the role of religion in local life, and modes of personal adjustment to the social system. Our original starting point turned out to be merely a starting point for an examination of the major intitutional and psychological problems of the community.

The successive modifications of our problem followed from the interplay of new data and new points of view. Only a portion of this process took place during the field phase; some was a result of the re-examination of field records, and some occurred during the writing-up of the data.

Let us summarize the functions that unsystematic theory can serve and the conditions under which it can be employed in research:

1. The specification of possible areas of field work as the researcher leans upon the educated perspective of his predecessors to guide him to important and significant areas of investigation.

2. The criticism of field work while doing it. Alternative perspectives in theory yield alternative perspectives in field observation.

3. The discovery of the limitations of one's original statement of the problem; the continuous discovery of new data compels new formulations of the problem.

4. The discovery of the limitations of one's own theory by its continuous confrontation with empirical observation.

5. The discovery of new dimensions of the problem.

6. The reconstruction of one's problem, field work, and past theory into a further limited and discrete theory to handle the problem. Such a theory is not final or general but adequate only to the specific problem in the specific field. However, this type of theoretical solution, in turn, provides raw materials for other research posing new problems, and these new problems as they are studied by other investigators in other settings contribute to the continuous cultivation of new theories.

THE RELATIONSHIP BETWEEN HEURISTIC AND SYSTEMATIC THEORY

Heuristic theory as outlined above is operative at every level of research: the statement of the problem, the gathering of the field data, the analysis and evaluation of the findings, and the analyzing and reporting of the results. However, heuristic theory is highly limited in that it does not produce generalized findings valid beyond the statement of the specific original problem. The generalization of the findings after observation, analysis, and interpretation must depend on other types of theory. Theorists of systematic theory have assumed the function of generalization.

As an enterprise, systematic theory can integrate new research findings with established theory and findings, thus accomplishing a continuous evaluation and assessment of research and heuristic theory. However, this can be accomplished only if general systematic theory pays attention to the differences in the problems, in the levels of heuristic theories, and in the field situations in which the problem and the theory are specified. The attempt to seek the common features of all social systems or of a hypothetical "the social system" overlooks the specific validity and the specific character of most heuristic theory and all research. If systematic theory is at all possible as an aid to scientific research, it must reach out and establish its empirical co-ordinates to the empirical world. It can do this only if it takes into account the limited and specific character of heuristic theory.

THE CODIFICATION OF THEORY AND THE HEURISTIC APPROACH TO THEORY

There is relatively little difference between the theoretical enterprise that codifies theoretical perspectives and heuristic theory as described above. The major difference—and it is very important—is in the timing of the integration of the theoretical perspectives brought up for consideration. Codification of theory attempts to bring together and relate the various theoretical dimensions that can be brought to bear on a problem by the rigorous logical analysis of received theory in terms of the theories themselves. All these theories are considered in one analytical operation; ideally, the composite perspective derived from them is applied as a unit to a field situation.

Contrary to codified theory, heuristic theory allows past theory to remain as a residue of latent possibilities which the research worker can bring to bear on his specific field problem. He cannot know in advance exactly what orders of theory are relevant to his problem until he discovers its nature in the field and what resistances to his preconceptions emerge as his field work progresses. Totally new perspectives emerge as he discovers these resistances. New perspectives, new levels, new orders, and new dimensions of data become salient, regardless of what level of codification he has considered in the past; in the field, in the encounter with the world, the press of the data is manifold, continuous, and not easily amenable to preconceived selection. Moreover, the level of detail of data, the precision of analysis, and the concepts employed are functions of the merging perspectives of the field worker in the field. It can thus happen that whole areas, codified in the past, may prove worthless for coping with a specific problem, though the past codifications may be valuable for other problems. However, there is no level of codification sufficiently precise to be applicable when empirical data become the focus of attention.

To exhibit all possible dimensions of a problem in advance, codification would have to be extremely complex, cumbersome, and unworkable (e.g., in one problem the authors reached 256 formal logical possibilities of the data without ever reaching its substantive level, and, because of the complexity, one is, in effect, forced to work with heuristic concepts rather than with the full range of logically deducible possibilities. One deals with five or six major cells in a logical matrix and ignores a host of others which, for purposes of social science, are conceived of as logical but irrelevant. As a result, the researcher-theorist must continuously refine his theoretical analysis in terms of his problem and data.

LIMITATIONS OF HEURISTIC THEORY

Heuristic theory, as subjected to the rigors of specific substantive problems, has a number of limitations:

1. It cannot work if the research worker on a priori grounds is unwilling to entertain the possibility of using or seriously considering all or a variety of the available theories. Commitment to one school or theory means, in most instances, commitment to selected levels of data. These forms of commitment prevent the research worker from criticizing his findings from alternative points of view and may blind him to the exhausting of his own favored theoretical approach. In the heuristic approach there is no guaranty that such standards of open-mindedness will prevail or that self-criticism can and will be made. Science, then—particularly social science—must depend not only on self-criticism but on the criticism made by others, willingness to accept which then becomes the basis of social science.

2. The *ad hoc* rotation of theoretical perspectives does not in itself guarantee the exhaustion of the empirical data if it is only ritual eclecticism. The only purpose in considering many perspectives is to solve or to redefine the problem. The listing of the alternative possibilities of different theories is not a solution, since listings are not a structural relationship of data. The end objective of the procedure is not only to find what data are relevant to the problem but also to determine how they are functionally related. The only point that needs emphasis is that the functional relationships are products of the research and not of a priori theorizing.

3. These procedures of exhaustion and rotation of perspectives are dependent on the contingencies of field work, the investigator's background, and his sensitivity to his data; hence there is no guaranty that their use will assure success. There is no immutable deductive procedure which automatically guarantees the production of new concepts, theories, or findings. The research worker must face the possibility of failure in the knowledge that it

may be due to the way in which he handled the problem.[14] Scientific inquiry means living an intellectually dangerous existence.

4. The method outlined here is amenable to not all types of research. Experimental studies assume that causes can be postulated in advance and that the problem in research is simply one of determining their conditions and efficiency. Large-scale surveys frequently telescope all the procedures of research described above into a single operation which does not and cannot allow for the continuous modification, substitution, and refinement of hypotheses and problems on the basis of field experience. The survey worker, in the absence of these intermediate checks on his thinking, may be forced to pose all at the same time a wide range of theoretically possible alternatives resulting from a priori formulations and hunches, hoping that one or more of his theoretical dimensions will be productive after the field work is done and analysis is completed. He frequently finds that a limited number of areas are highly productive, but, since in the beginning he had to consider on a priori grounds a variety of alternative areas, time and funds limit the depth to which he can analyze those variables which finally proved productive. This is the familiar phenomenon of knowing better how to make a survey after it is done than at the beginning.

It is apparent from this discussion that in no case can the research worker feel that he has fully solved his problem. He must recognize that new levels of theory and new theories of which he may not have been aware at the time might have required new levels of data and further exhaustion of theory. At best, he can feel that he has advanced his problem along an infinite path so that his work need not be repeated. One must recognize that there is no final accumulation of knowledge and no final solution, in the usual meaning of these terms.[15]

NOTES

[1] Robert K. Merton, "The Position of Sociological Theory—Discussion," *American Sociological Review,* 13 (1949), 164-68, republished in substantially the same form in Robert K. Merton, *Social Theory and Social Structure* (rev. ed.; Glencoe, Ill.: Free Press, 1958), pp. 4-10.

[2] Merton, *Social Theory and Social Structure,* pp. 5-6.

[3] Edward Shils has described this process in a similar way as follows: "The role of general theory consists of a general systematic scrutiny of particular facts: then the theory is either disconfirmed by the facts and is replaced by one more adequate to them, or the hypothesis and corresponding theory are confirmed and the problem is settled." "Primordial, Personal,

Sacred, and Civil Ties: Some Particular Observations on the Relationships of Sociological Research and Theory," *British Journal of Sociology*, 8, No. 2 (June, 1957), 130–45.

[4]Merton, *Social Theory and Social Structure*, p. 12. Also see James Olds, *The Growth and Structure of Motives* (Glencoe, Ill.: Free Press, 1956), pp. 21-22, on "the limited theory viewpoint" in which the position of H. G. Birch and M. E. Bitterman (in "Sensory Integration and Cognitive Theory," *Psychological Review*, 58 [1951], 355-61) is used as an illustration.

[5]Best exemplified by Robin M. Williams, Jr., *The Reduction of Intergroup Tensions: A Survey of Research Problems of Ethnic, Racial, and Religious Group Relations*, Social Science Research Council Bull. 57 (New York: Social Science Research Council, 1947), esp. Chap. 3. Similar studies are Merton, "The Sociology of Knowledge," in *Social Theory and Social Structure*, pp. 217-45; R. Sarbin, "Role Theory," in Gardner Lindzey (ed.), *Handbook of Social Psychology* (Cambridge, Mass.: Addison-Wesley Press, 1954), pp. 223-58.

[6]Herbert Blumer, "What Is Wrong with Social Theory?" *American Sociological Review*, 19 (1954), 3-10.

[7]Shils, "Primordial Ties."

[8]Shils's article, "Primordial Ties," is a case history of this procedure. He has shown how the interplay between his research experience and received theory has led him to discard, revamp, and reinterpret the different theorists with whom he has been concerned, accordingly as his experience with different sets of data has called forth and brought into perspective different elements and segments of the theorists with whom he has been concerned— mainly Tönnies, Cooley, Mayo, Schmalenback, Lenin, Weber, Parsons and Sorel.

[9]The analysis of these problems is reported in the authors' *Small Town in Mass Society: Class, Power and Religion in a Rural Community* (Princeton, N.J.: Princeton University Press, 1958).

[10]Cornell Studies in Social Growth, sponsored by the Department of Child Development and Family Relationships, New York State College of Home Economics, Cornell University, with the aid of funds from the National Institute of Mental Health, the United States Public Health Service, and the Social Science Research Council. The present study, as well as the original one upon which this one draws, is an independent by-product of Cornell studies and does not represent the authorized viewpoint of the project.

[11]Similarly Robert Redfield, in *The Little Community* (Chicago: University of Chicago Press, 1955), takes five different societies, each studied from a different perspective, and demonstrates how the perspective limits the data.

[12]The ladies' book clubs, card-playing groups, men's clubs and associations, and "Old American" families resemble groups found by Warner, but other classes in our study did not; e.g., "Old American" families, or what we called the "Old Aristocracy," occupied symbolically important positions but could not be called an "upper-upper" class.

[13]In our first work politics received only scant attention; only the role of the lawyer as an intermediary between local government and state agencies had been examined by us (Bensman and Vidich, *Small Town in Mass Society*, Chap. 4).

[14]John Dewey, *The Quest for Certainty: A Study of the Relation of Knowledge and Action* (New York: Minton, Balch & Co., 1929).

15The following studies point to a similar conclusion: Max Weber, "Science as a Vocation," in *Essays from Max Weber,* trans. and ed. H. H. Gerth and C. Wright Mills (New York: Oxford University Press, 1946), pp. 129-56; Homer G. Barnett, "Comment to Acculturation: An Exploratory Formulation," *American Anthropologist,* 58, No. 6 (December, 1954), 1000-1002; Robert Redfield, "The Art of Social Science," *American Journal of Sociology,* 59, No. 3 (November, 1948), 181-90; Herbert Blumer, *An Appraisal of Thomas and Znaniecki's "The Polish Peasant in Europe and America"* (New York: Social Science Research Council, 1939); Dewey, *The Quest for Certainty*; Allen H. Barton and Paul F. Lazarsfeld, "Some Functions of Qualitative Analysis in Social Research," *Sociologica,* 1 (1955), 321-61; Maurice R. Stein, *The Eclipse of Community: An Interpretation of American Community Studies* (Princeton, N.J.: Princeton University Press, 1960); Barrington Moore, Jr., "The Strategy of Social Science," in his *Political Power and Social Theory* (Cambridge, Mass.: Harvard University Press, 1958), pp. 111-59; and C. Wright Mills, *The Sociological Imagination* (New York: Oxford University Press, 1959).

CHAPTER 31

Participant Observation As Role and Method
in Behavioral Research

Marion Pearsall

As the behavioral sciences and the professions using their findings have moved steadily toward greater integration at theoretical and substantive levels, there has also been more integration at the methodological level. One such general method is that of participant observation, which has become increasingly popular in recent years in settings ranging from communities and organizations to small groups, and from the field to the laboratory. Numerous, though widely scattered, articles in journals, books, and research monographs attest to increasing sophistication in its use.

Much of the literature, however, makes no clear distinction between participant observation as a role, participant observation as a body of techniques, and participant observation as a methodology. The parts are analytically separate and have actually been used in varying combinations and proportions which many investigators fail to make explicit when reporting their use of participant observation in a study. Do they mean a special, definable role; and if so, how does such a role affect their data? Are they implying some particular set of techniques? Or should the reader infer a certain kind of theoretical orientation?

In the belief that clarification is necessary for further development of this approach in nursing research, I propose to examine these three elements as they have been developed by the original users of the method in anthropological, sociological, and social psychological fieldwork, with some reference to derivatives in other professions.

Of course, any research in which a human scientist faces an equally human subject necessitates both observation and participation. To some degree, therefore, most human behavioral research involves participant observation whether the scientist is aware of and in self-conscious control of the method or not. As used here, however, participant observation refers to some deliberate expansion of either or both "participation" with, or "observation" of human research subjects.

Reprinted, with permission, from *Nursing Research,* Winter, 1965, Vol. 14, no. 1.

At one extreme, the term "participant observer" refers to a master role assumed for purposes of getting data from live subjects by whatever methods and techniques appropriate to a particular research design: visual observation in any or all of its special forms, interviewing in one or more of its many varieties, and so on through the long list of human and technical means now available. Many, if not most, anthropologists would favor this broad definition. After all, they were the original participant observers, using whatever means come to hand to get their data.

At the other extreme, the term is limited to informally conducted but systematically recorded observations. There may be supplemental data from conversational interviews, but formal interviewing is excluded. This definition seems to be applied primarily in rather controlled environments such as hospital wards and is used by some social psychologists and, especially in recent years, by research nurses.

Between the extremes, and incorporating some of each, participant observation perhaps most commonly refers to research aimed at maximal knowledge of the beliefs and behavior of human beings in their natural settings interpreted in terms of some general theory or combination of theories from one or more of the behavioral sciences. Such sociologists as use the method would probably feel most comfortable with this definition. The present paper will try to stay fairly close to this middle ground but will veer in the direction of the anthropologist's even broader meaning.

THE ROLE

Using the last definition, participant observation is a device for getting information and also a set of behaviors in which the observer is himself involved (1,2). The goal is valid, verified data analyzed in a manner which is scientifically and philosophically sound, but without harm to the human subjects. To achieve the objective, the investigator chooses from the several versions of the master role: 1. complete observer; 2. observer-as-participant; 3. participant-as-observer; or 4. complete participant.

Complete Observer

Short of concealed one-way-viewing mirrors (which would of course eliminate "participation" completely) or situations involving large crowds, opportunities for implementing the complete observer role are rare. Modern urban society does, however, offer the potential complete observer a number of relatively invisible roles such as janitor, cleaning woman, elevator operator, and other ubiquitous but unnoticed occupational types. And personnel in large, busy organizations such as modern hospitals are often so intent on their work that undetected observation of their activities is possible for brief and even quite extended periods. Elsewhere also, the observer may reduce participation to a nonverbal level and detach himself psychologically from his subjects, refusing to interact meaningfully with them. But he does so at the risk of losing verbally communicated information beyond the fruits of eavesdropping and the perhaps more serious risk of ethnocentric or egocentric rejection of information through failure to grasp its significance to the people themselves. He also treads on ethically shaky ground.

Complete Participant

With the complete participant also, true identity and purpose are hidden in a way difficult to defend morally and only dubiously defensible scientifically. In addition, the task of recording data secretly after long hours of playing some cover-up role (nurse or patient perhaps, to name two that have been used in studying hospitals) demands more physical, intellectual, and emotional stamina than most scientists possess. There is, moreover, the constant threat of exposure and the still greater possibility that the hoped-for anonymity of a later report will be unmasked, releasing all the righteous indignation reserved for spies and traitors and reducing chances for further research in other groups as well as the one immediately affected. Or the investigator may indeed become a complete participant psychologically, "going native" to the point of accepting his subjects' view of their world uncritically in a manner detrimental to objective analysis.

Observer-as-Participant and Participant-as-Observer

In other versions of the role, both the observer and the observed are aware of the special nature of their relationship. Their formulation and understanding of the situation will differ, but both are seeking acceptable answers to the questions: "Who am I?" "Who is he?" "Who are we in this relation?" In fact, observer-as-participant and participant-as-observer differ primarily in the handling of these questions, though they tend to vary also in terms of the length of the relationship and the number of individuals involved.

For the observer-as-participant, observation (of verbal responses as well as more literally observable behavior) is dominant by choice or from the necessity of engaging in numerous brief contacts with many persons. There is little chance for involvement with the affairs of any single person or group. There are distinct advantages to this "outsider" role since people are often willing to express private views and feelings to an attentive stranger that they would not report to their boss or wife, or if they are inmates of a prison or hospital, to their custodians (3,4). There is little temptation either for the observer to go native or for the natives to try to include him permanently in their lives. At the same time, the role limits opportunities for gaining knowledge of total situations.

By comparison, the participant-as-observer can penetrate farther beneath the surface of public behavior and superficial expression. In the course of extended contact, respondents who react initially only to the stimulus of direct questions become informants who instruct the investigator in the intricacies of their personal and social worlds. And informants become friends, or sometimes enemies. In this version of the role it is possible to collect minutely detailed data on a wide range of topics and verify them by careful cross-checking from multiple sources.

Constant participation plus the use of specialized skills and techniques place the observer in the midst of social and cultural activity, though he must inevitably remain to some degree a perpetual and unassimilable stranger. Participation, however, which tends to increase and be more sociable, takes time and energy, often at the expense of observation and systematic recording. It also so immerses the observer in the local scene that he may cease to notice significant items. He moves toward complete participation as his subjects, who never understand or accept their position as fully as the observer does his, seek to place him in the more congenial roles of neighbor, fellow worker, fellow inmate, and the like.

At the same time, there seems to be a general tendency for both the observer and the observed to vacillate between the observer-as-participant and participant-as-observer positions. People tend to handle the vaguely, and often more than vaguely, disturbing presence of a difficult-to-place stranger by alternately pulling him into their ranks where he would be subject to group sanctions, and pushing him out again when his behavior becomes too unpredictable or suspicious. Similarly, the participant observer, in his struggle between maximizing his data and protecting his role, edges toward greater participation and richer information and then retreats to more detached observation as he senses the threat of overinvolvement.

The Nurse in the Participant Observer Role

Nurses assuming the participant observer role in any of its versions face special dilemmas, as several have indicated (5,6). A nurse in a study of nursing obviously has advantages in regard to background knowledge that anyone else would take months or years to acquire. There may be a further personal advantage since a person already accustomed to modern medical settings with their Space Age technology, busily impersonal ways, and seriously ill patients, should suffer less "culture shock" than less-inured observers. By the same token, a nurse is more likely to overlook much that is relevant because she no longer perceives it.

Whatever the initial advantage, tensions may be expected between some of the norms associated with research and their almost opposite counterparts in nursing practice—between disinterested observation and interested action, for example. In the face of such conflicts, the pull toward complete participation in the already familiar capacity of nurse is likely to be strong, the more so because others also find the nurse role clearer than that of scientific observer. Movement in the opposite direction is probably less attractive, though overcompensation may lead to an artificially rigid complete observer stance. In either case, nurses using the role need unusual clarity of objectives if they are to use nursing experience to further rather than obstruct research and, under other conditions, use research experience in the service of nursing.

IMPLEMENTING THE ROLE

Initially the observer selects the desired master role, but he must play it collaboratively with his subjects in their home territory and largely on their terms. On the basis of past experience, advance information about the study site, and a rapid assessment of the local situation, he must decide where and how to enter the chosen organization, community, or other social entity. He must establish the legitimacy of his project with official and unofficial leaders first, but this is no guarantee of acceptance by others. On the contrary, identification with upper echelons often increases the difficulty of establishing profitable relations with other segments of the population.

Success depends ultimately on the extent to which the research role is accepted as legitimate by people who of course are trying to place the observer by the more customary criteria of ascription (age, sex, race, physical characteristics) and achievement (education, occupation, income, social class, manners, and the like). The observer has no recourse from his ascribed traits; but he can to some extent modify behavior associated with his achieved status to conform to local expectations and thus minimize differences that threaten rapport. Altering behavior to the point of disguise, however, is ordinarily neither necessary nor desirable.

What seems more necessary is a brief getting-acquainted period in which the observer is himself observed. He makes himself accessible to all while engaging in highly visible and, hopefully, non-threatening activities such as familiarizing himself with the physical setting, making maps or charts on which to locate later actions and events, visiting casually with everyone, and learning the language—which may be the "language" of an occupation or profession rather than a strange dialect. Whatever the activity during this phase, it has the dual purpose of yielding information and accustoming people to the observer's presence. In fact, local reactions to the observer are important as data since one of the assumptions of participant observation is that people cannot long maintain a special kind of behavior for the benefit of a stranger. Once used to his presence, they lapse again into usual routines, although they may still occasionally react to the peculiar status of the outsider in their midst.

THE METHODS

Participant observation is a role, or set of behaviors. It is also a device for getting and analyzing information. For the anthropologists who first developed the method, participant observation as a set of techniques includes any or all appropriate means for gathering, recording, verifying, and analyzing data on humans in their natural settings (7,8). In this section the anthropological position will be taken as the model in order to include the whole range of techniques associated with the method. It is precisely because there are such wide variations in usage that it is essential for investigators to specify the techniques as well as the role when referring to the use of participant observation in research proposals and reports.

With the broadest as with the narrowest definitions of the technical attributes of the role, the particilar means chosen will depend on the theoretical requirements of the research design, on characteristics of the place and population to be studied, and in no small measure on the personal and professional qualifications of the investigator. In all cases, the method stresses detailed description that preserves as much of the total context of behavior as possible. To this end, participant observation as used in anthropology and some branches of sociology frankly combines techniques of observation with those of interviewing, beginning with relatively unstructured operations in a new setting and ending with more systematic testing of hypotheses as the outlines of the organization or culture become clearer. The process is much the same with social psychologists using the method except that they tend to think of formal interviewing, the use of questionnaires, and the like as being supplemental to rather than an integral part of the method.

Observations

As the label implies, observation is what the method begins with, ends with, and uses throughout to verify and integrate information from all sources. In contrast to casual observation, participant observation is carefully planned to serve some formulated research purpose, is recorded in some permanent form, and is subjected to checks and controls for validity, reliability, and accuracy. In the process, the observer notes the where, when, what, how, and with whom of all action in a way that clearly identifies every individual, place, time, and type of activity. Events are recorded by word description, notational symbols, graphs, flow charts, movies, sound tapes, or other devices according to the degree of detail and precision needed. The records are the necessary evidence for generalizations about who and how many behave in stated ways under specified conditions. Based as they are on many observations of spontaneously developed natural situations, the data are relatively independent of the subjects' willingness or ability to report their own behavior accurately.

Interviewing

Observation has obvious limitations as a research tool, however. It is generally impractical to observe large populations, nor is it feasible to observe events of very long duration where years or months rather than days or hours are the important time units. Moreover, some activities invariably prove inaccessible for social or merely physical reasons while others occur too infrequently for adequate coverage. Finally, observation is at best only an indirect path to beliefs, values, attitudes, and other intangibles. Interviewing is therefore the second major ingredient of participant observation for anthropologists and a necessary supplemental method for those who would restrict the definition to observation. Interviewing is both a direct source of information on belief and knowledge systems and a form of vicarious observation to increase case examples of various types of overt behavior.

Since the method's ultimate goal is usually an abstract model of the society and/or its culture, the universe to be sampled is information rather than people (9,10). Consequently, unlike most survey research, it is not assumed that all answers are equally valid and valuable or that it is best to select respondents randomly. Instead, the selection favors persons who are especially knowledgeable with regard to various activities and bodies of knowledge. As informants, or "expert witnesses," (in contrast to "respondents") they provide evidence for statements about the major organizational structures and cultural foci of the group. Questions of pervasiveness, range of variation, and typicality of the various beliefs and practices are then answered by observations and further interviews with more randomly selected respondents.

Selection of Informants

The selection of actual informants of course depends on the research purpose and on the location of individuals in the society. Thus, the director of a nursing service is a more likely source on over-all policy and organizational goals than a nursing aide; but the aide may well know more about "what really goes on" at the ward level. On the other hand, having gathered information from the experts on a subject, it is equally important to sample the knowledge and opinion of others of the same subject to ascertain differences and discrepancies within the society.

The principal criteria for choosing and evaluating informants (whether information is sought by means of observations primarily or through the use of formal interviews) are effective exposure to the knowledge plus the ability and willingness to communicate it clearly and accurately. These are really complex criteria, and their application is a continuing process. Some of the observer's methods are essentially those of the historian in establishing the credibility of historical documents (11). That is, the observer asks certain questions about each research subject: How reliable is he? How competent is he to know and tell the truth? How does his position in the society limit or color his views? More specifically, was he an eyewitness or participant in the events he reports? If not, what were his sources of information? Was he an interested party? And why is he confiding in the observer? Finally, are his statements and other actions plausible and internally consistent through a series of observational contacts? Paradoxically, the participant observer must believe everything he sees and hears at the same time that he doubts the truth of everything. In the final analysis, his judgments are based on a total impression of persons, roles, and institutions gained from a combination of participation, observation, interviewing, and the use of any other sources available to him.

THE METHODOLOGY

Roles and research techniques are not science. It is only at the methodological level that participant observation can serve science. Here role and technique serve the interests of organizing, classifying, and analyzing data in terms of some theoretical problem. At this level, participant observation is especially suited to idiographic studies which seek to preserve as much of the uniqueness and complexity of particular social systems as is compatible with the requirements of general theory. In its broadest form participant observation has special value for exploratory studies designed to identify research problems and generate hypotheses for future testing.

Put somewhat differently, more structured studies of the relationships between a few pre-selected and controlled variables are unlikely to discover facts or suggest interpretations which have not been previously known or postulated. In contrast, the broadly cast net of observations and interviews of participant observation maximizes the possibility of finding unexpected facts which in turn suggest new interpretations of human behavior. Or the method may be used to test the limits in natural settings of propositions derived from experimental studies or from "ideal type" theoretical models.

Such use of the method requires detailed coding of thousands of separate items of information. The major categories may be set by the initial statement of the research problem; but they are subdivided, modified, refined, and revised as the observer learns the specifics of the system he is investigating. The study may then be redesigned or refocused in the light of accumulating evidence that variables not originally considered are actually necessary to the analysis.

The revisions are made in reponse to the interplay between fact and theory as the research progresses through three somewhat overlapping phases. The first phase begins before any data are collected and continues through the observational period. It includes the selection of problems and concepts and the search for behavioral indicators. The second phase extends through most of the period of active participant observation. Its main activity is gathering data on the form, frequency, and distribution of the relevant phenomena. The third phase also covers most of the observational period and then continues through the writing of a final report. Its goal is incorporation of the research findings in an explanatory model of the society or culture in terms of the original, but now modified, theoretical framework (12,13,14).

A Case Example

The phases can be illustrated with a study of the types of behavior associated with the position of nursing supervisor in a large general hospital (15,16). Lacking any prior knowledge of the position, the investigator chose a conceptual framework from role and organizational theory that was broad and flexible. The hospital was simply viewed as a social structure with a set of interrelated and coordinated statuses, or positions, and associated roles. The research problem was to locate and explain the position structurally, to delineate both ideal and actual dimensions of the role, and especially to identify points of stress in the organizational structure or in discrepancies between the ideal and the actual as perceived by the supervisors.

The research method selected was to observe 14 of the 30 supervisors for one shift each, interviewing each formally with six open-ended questions that took about 30 minutes to answer, and engaging in conversations about the position with the supervisors and other hospital personnel. The primary concern in selecting the particular supervisors for the study was to cover all three shifts in each of four units of the hospital, but a secondary concern was to include as wide a range as possible in terms of specialties and differences in length and type of professional experience.

In *the first phase* of the study, several unanticipated problems of theoretical and practical import came to light. For example, the difficulty of transferring roles across shift lines, expecially when one person on the incoming shift receives several roles from as many different persons on the outgoing shift, became apparent. Similarly, concepts not included in the original statement of the research proposal were introduced when the phenomena suggested their utility. The notion of cultural pattern, for instance, became the organizing principle for handling the succession of discrete acts in the supervisors' sets of behaviors. Finally, actions and attitudes that could not have been predicted turned out to be key indicators of the role. Identifying these led to simple statements about the occurrence of this or that phenomenon and their probable relevance.

Checking and testing the observations and provisional hypotheses of the first phase is the business of *the second phase*. It is possible to introduce schedules and other data-gathering devices at this stage that meet the assumptions of various statistical tests. However, where the goal is the understanding of social systems, cultural patterns, or organizational processes, statistical procedures are not as yet very helpful. In determining the frequency and distribution of many beliefs and practices the participant observer must settle for a kind of quasi-statistics of rough frequencies with numerous case examples. Thus, in the nursing supervisor study, time and activity tables based on observation provided a simple quantitative base which, with more qualitative case history material, supported the final model of the role.

Still, the participant observer wants many rather than few examples for each generalization, and he wants supporting evidence from a variety of sources. The study cited here concluded that there are two central, or basic, themes to the role of nursing supervisor. Without exception, these were manifested in the behavior of every supervisor; and they were manifested in several ways.

First, for example, it was observed that all of the supervisors displayed interest in two, but only two, of the many report forms they handled. These two pieces of paper (the "daily ward report" and the "daily time sheet") symbolized quite dramatically the almost equal concern over, first, the number and condition of their patients and, second, the number and quality of nursing personnel on their floors. It was also observed in reports between nursing shifts that the supervisors spent most of their first half hour and again most of their last hour in discussing these two topics. The centrality of patients and staffing problems was further confirmed by observations of the number, kind, and duration of actions on early and late supervisory rounds to the floors. These twin themes were clearly observed to dominate the role of the nursing supervisor. Indeed, to the outside observer, other activities seemed only partially and imperfectly assimilated to this central core.

Analysis goes on in all phases, but only in *the third and final phase* does it become the major activity of the participant observer. All findings are then incorporated into an abstract representation of the observed society as seen through the conceptual framework of the study. Conclusions are drawn about the nature of the system and the relations between and among the parts of the system; and the whole is related to relevant general theories.

Applying the method, the report on the study of nursing supervisors preserved much of the factual detail of the role as played by fourteen different persons in a single hospital. But by abstracting regularities and common denominators the findings were presented in a theoretical model of social structure seen as a system of interrelated roles. From that perspective, some of the implications of the position's location in the social structure became clear. For example, the position commands a broader view of the total organization than that of head nurse on one ward but a considerably more restricted view than the position of a director of nursing services. This has many implications for the way the supervisors play their role in situations involving the general goals of the hospital as distinct from the objectives of their own particular floors.

Abstraction from observations of a multitude of separate acts also led in this instance to delineation of a basic pattern common to all supervisors regardless of shift or specialty—a symmetrical succession of activities beginning and ending with reports across shift lines, with early and late rounds sandwiched between. Observed activities that differed from one shift or specialty to another were seen as variations on a shared basic role. Some of the variations tended to compete and even conflict with the expectations of the basic pattern to which the supervisors were observed to be most deeply committed. The theoretical model obtained by this research method served to highlight the structural stresses and recurrent role strains in this particular hospital. At the same time, they were general enough to serve as a hypothetical model of the same role in other hospitals, subject to further testing.

SUMMARY AND CONCLUSION

To summarize, participant observation is at once a role, a means of getting data, and a methodology for understanding human behavior in natural contexts. It is essential to separate and specify these several aspects when reporting research studies because only in this way is it possible to assess the influence of role, techniques, and methodological orientation on research results.

As a role, participant observation implies other and reciprocal roles such as subject, respondent, informant, or perhaps semi-collaborator. To date, we do not understand the influence of any of these reciprocal roles very well. On the observer's side also, the role is temporary and to a degree "unnatural." He may choose from a limited number of forms along a continuum from that of complete observer to that of complete participant, but we have little systematic knowledge of the effect of the role on either the quantity or quality of the data he obtains.

Theoretically, the complete observer and the complete participant are least disruptive of a group's activities; but the former sacrifices completeness for objectivity while the latter sacrifices objectivity and systematic recording to gain a more complete experience of the subjects' world. In the other forms of the role, observer-as-participant and participant-as-observer, the observer acknowledges his research purpose but does not avoid entering into mutually meaningful relations. But how best to maintain the proper balance between disinterested observation and emphatic participation is still a major problem.

As a device for amassing detailed information on complex events and situations, participant observation ranges from the eclecticism of the anthropologist to the parsimonious elegance of the experimental social psychologist. Perhaps the most distinctive characteristic of the method in its broadest definition is the use of key informants as extra eyes and ears of the observer. The observer of course must still verify and evaluate the information in terms of his growing familiarity with the total picture, but he is dependent on informants within the system and acknowledges this dependence.

As a methodology, participant observation is as concerned with the sociocultural and psychosocial background of human behavior as with the behavior itself. The goal therefore is maximal knowledge and understanding of human behaviors in context. The methodology is guided by, but not slavishly bound to, the theoretical assumptions of a preconceived research design. Starting with broad conceptual frameworks, the methodology emphasizes an ongoing interplay between fact and theory, and phenomena and interpretation that becomes more abstract and narrow as it seeks fewer but more controlled variables as a study progresses. The final product is a model that retains much of the identity and character of the original phenomena but in sufficiently abstract form to permit comparison with other entities of the same general type.

REFERENCES

1. Gold, R. L. "Roles in sociological field observations." *Soc. Forces* 36:217-223, Mar. 1958.

2. Junker, B. H. *Field Work: An Introduction to the Social Sciences.* Chicago: University of Chicago Press, 1960.

3. Trice, H. M. "The outsider's role in the field study." *Sociol. Soc. Res.* 41: 27-32, Sept. 1956.

4. Nash, D. J. "The ethnologist as stranger: an essay in the sociology of knowledge." *SW J. Anthrop.* 19: 149-167, Summer 1963.

5. Poulos, Evangeline S., and McCabe, Gracia S. "The nurse in the role of research observer." *Nurs. Res.* 9: 137-140, Summer 1960.

6. Malone, Mary. "The research nurse and social science research." In *The Role of the Nurse in the Outpatient Department,* by W. C. Bennis and others. New York: American Nurses' Foundation, 1961, pp. 86-88.

7. Herskovits, M. J. "Some problems of method in ethnography." In *Method and Perspective in Anthropology,* ed. by R. F. Spencer. Minneapolis: University of Minnesota Press, 1954.

8. Adams, R. N., and Preiss, J. J., eds. *Human Organization Research.* Homewood, Ill.: Dorsey Press, 1960.

9. Back, K. W. "The well-informed informant." *Hum. Org.* 14: 30-33, Winter 1956.

10. Vidich, Arthur, and Bensman, Joseph. "The validity of field data." *Hum. Org.* 13: 20-27, Spring 1954.

11. Gottschalk, Louis. "The historian and the historical document." In *The Use of Personal Documents in History, Anthropology and Sociology,* by Louis Gottschalk and others (Bulletin No. 53). New York: Social Science Research Council, 1945, pp. 3-75.

12. Becker, H. S., and Geer, Blanche. "Participant observation; the analysis of qualitative data." In *Human Organization Research,* ed. by R. N. Adams and J. J. Preiss. Homewood, Ill.: Dorsey Press, 1960, pp. 267-289.

13. Zelditch, Morris, Jr. "Some methodological problems of field studies." *Amer. J. Sociol.* 67: 566-576, Mar. 1962; 68: 250, Sept. 1960.

14. Bruyn, Severyn. "The methodology of participant observation." *Hum. Org.* 22: 224-235, Fall 1963.

15. Pearsall, Marion. *Nursing Supervisors: A Social Profile,* Boston: Massachusetts General Hospital, 1957. (Mimeographed)

16. ————. "Supervision—a nursing dilemma." *Nurs. Outlook* 9:91-92, Feb. 1961.